SUPPLEMENT TO THE HANDBOOK OF MIDDLE AMERICAN INDIANS

Volume 4 Ethnohistory

SUPPLEMENT TO THE HANDBOOK OF MIDDLE AMERICAN INDIANS

 VICTORIA REIFLER BRICKER, General Editor

VOLUME FOUR

ETHNOHISTORY

RONALD SPORES, Volume Editor

With the Assistance of Patricia A. Andrews

UNIVERSITY OF TEXAS PRESS, AUSTIN

First edition, 1986

Requests for permission to reproduce material
from this work should be sent to:
  Permissions
  University of Texas Press
  Box 7819
  Austin, Texas 78713

LIBRARY OF CONGRESS CATALOGING
IN PUBLICATION DATA
Main entry under title:
Ethnohistory.
  (Supplement to the Handbook of Middle Ameri-
can Indians; v. 4)
  Bibliography: p.
  Includes index.
  1. Indians of Central America—Collected
works. 2. Indians of Mexico—Collected works.
I. Spores, Ronald. II. Andrews, Patricia A. III.
Series.
F1434.E88 1986   972'.00497   85-20361
ISBN 0-292-77604-7

CONTENTS

General Editor's Preface
Victoria Reifler Bricker   vii

1. Introduction
    Ronald Spores   3

2. Classic Maya Dynastic Alliance and Succession
    James A. Fox and John S. Justeson   7

3. Prehispanic Background of Colonial Political and Economic
    Organization in Central Mexico
    Frederic Hicks   35

4. Ethnohistory of the Guatemalan Colonial Indian
    Robert M. Carmack   55

5. The Southern Maya Lowlands during Spanish Colonial Times
    Grant D. Jones   71

6. Indians in Colonial Northern Yucatan
    Nancy M. Farriss   88

7. Kinship and Social Organization in Early Colonial Tenochtitlan
    Susan M. Kellogg   103

8. Socioeconomic Dimensions of Urban-Rural Relations in
    the Colonial Period Basin of Mexico
    Thomas H. Charlton   122

9. One Hundred Years of Servitude: *Tlamemes* in Early New Spain
    Ross Hassig   134

10. Techialoyan Codices: Seventeenth-Century Indian
    Land Titles in Central Mexico
    H. R. Harvey   153

11. Colonial Ethnohistory of Oaxaca
    John K. Chance   165

Reference Abbreviations   191

Bibliography   193

Index   223

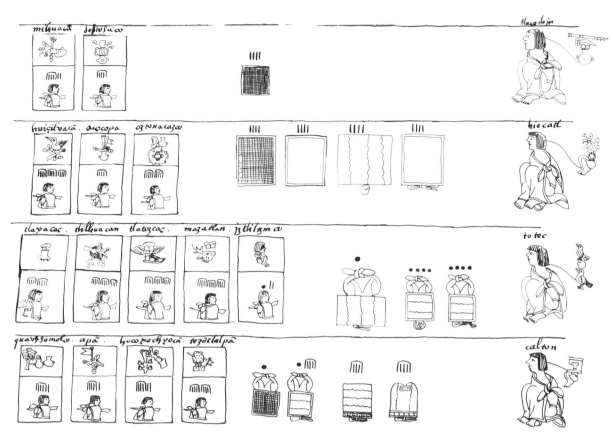

FIGURE 3-2. The lands, *macehualtin*, and tribute of four nobles of Tepetlaoztoc. From *Códice Kingsborough*, fol. 4v.

under the command of the *teuctli*. The lands of a noble house were not necessarily in the immediate vicinity of the house itself. They usually consisted of a number of separate fields widely scattered throughout the kingdom (*Códice Kingsborough* 1912; H. F. Cline 1972c; Hicks 1982; Prem 1978).

A lineage often included more than one noble house, and this was particularly so in the case of a royal lineage. There was also a hierarchy of noble houses. The sources from Tlaxcallan and Huexotzinco, for example, refer to houses called *huehuehcalli*, *pilcalli*, and *yaotequihuahcacalli*, all in some way dependent on *teccalli* (Carrasco 1976a; Anguiano and Chapa 1976:151–152; *Matrícula de Huexotzinco* 1974:fols. 744v–747r, 855r,

858r). The functions of *huehuehcalli* ('old house') are obscure, but the *pilcalli* were clearly houses headed by *pipiltin* of a *teccalli* who had been granted lands and subjects by the *teuctli*. The *yaotequihuah* was a military status, and Anguiano and Chapa think the *yaotequihuahcacalli* may have been the houses of ennobled commoners.[3]

A nobleman was elevated to the rank of *teuctli* on the initiative of his king (*tlahtoani*), and there was a lengthy and elaborate ceremony of investiture (described in Toribio Motolinía 1971:339–344; Muñoz Camargo 1892:45–46; Carrasco 1966a:134–138). Directed by priests, it involved fasting, piercing the nasal septum (to receive the proper jewelry), and a lavish expenditure of wealth.

39

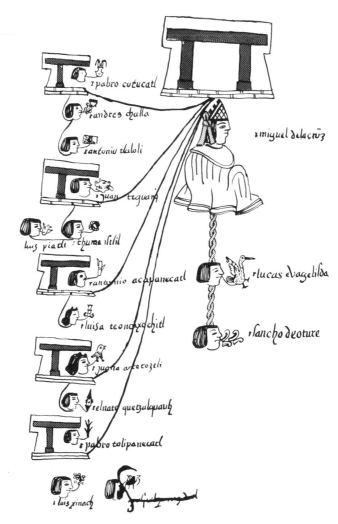

FIGURE 3-3. The head of a noble house and others of his lineage (*tlacamecayotl*, lit. 'rope of people'), and other houses dependent on his. From *Matrícula de Huexotzinco*, fol. 744v.

When a nobleman was made a *teuctli*, he was given a grant of land which he could distribute to his own dependents, and the authority to build a palace.

A *teuctli* was in turn dependent on a *tlahtoani*. A *tlahtoani* was a ruler, but the word also designated a grade of nobility. The ceremony of investiture that elevated a *teuctli* to *tlahtoani* status was even more elaborate than that of a *teuctli* (see, e.g., Durán 1967: 2:399ff.), and in the case of a dependent *tlah-toani* (see below), it was held in the city of his supreme *tlahtoani*. A *tlahtoani* was the head of an extensive royal lineage (*tlahtohcatlaca-mecayotl*), with numerous branches headed by *teteuctin*. He was head of the political, religious, and economic structure of his domain, or *tlahtohcayotl*,[4] and his palace, which was also called a *tecpan* or *teccalli*, formed the nucleus of what might become an urban settlement. A temple precinct would be nearby, and many of his dependent nobles built their *tecpan* near his (Anguiano and Chapa 1976:142; Muñoz Camargo 1585:fols. 6v–7r, 8v; Calnek 1974a).

Ordinarily, only nobles of recognized lineage could attain *teuctli* status. One account (Carrasco 1966a:135) states that merchants could be made *teteuctin* in Cholollan, but only in that city, and not in Tlaxcallan or Mexico. The rank of *teuctli* was hereditary. A *teuctli* designated one of his sons (by a noble woman) as his heir, or if he had not done so before he died, the nobles of the house met and selected one among them for the post. The successor inherited his predecessor's title and official duties and was subject to confirmation by the *tlahtoani*. The lands of the house were passed on intact.

In the powerful states of the Triple Alliance—Tenochtitlan, Tetzcoco, and presumably also Tlacopan (Tacuba)—the royal lineages controlled immense quantities of land and *macehualtin*, gained through the appropriation of lands of Azcapotzalco, Chalco, Xochimilco, and other subjugated regions in the Valley of Mexico, and through land reclamation (e.g., Alvarado Tezozomoc 1975: 268–271, 395; Durán 1967:2:83, 101–102, 113–114, 151). The kings there had the means to elevate a great many of their sons to *teuctli* status, and royal polygyny assured an adequate number of them. King Nezahualpilli of Tetzcoco had forty wives (not counting concubines) by whom he had 144 children (Alva Ixtlilxóchitl 1975–1977:2:152), and a document of the 1570's states that there were some three hundred members of the royal lineage ("descendants of Nezahualpilli") living at that time (Hicks 1978:139). Moteuczomah II of Tenochtitlan is said to have had over 150 children (Soustelle 1961:178). Not all noble houses in these states were branches of the royal lineages (Hicks 1982), but they did comprise an extraordinarily large percentage of the nobility, as compared, for example, with Huexotzinco (Prem 1978 and personal communication). We actually have no figures on the number of noble houses in the Valley of Mexico, but Nezahualcoyotl of Tetzcoco is

said to have ordered the construction of "over four hundred" (i.e., a great many) houses and palaces for those who attended his court (Alva Ixtlilxóchitl 1975–1977:2: 101). In Tlaxcallan, Ocotelolco, one of the four *tlahtoani* seats ("*cabeceras*") of that kingdom, had either thirty-six or forty-eight *teccalli*, with three *pilcalli*, twenty-three *huehuehcalli*, and eleven *yaotequihuahcacalli* dependent on them. The other three *tlahtoani* seats had between fourteen and fifty-two *teccalli* each (Anguiano and Chapa 1976:143–147, 151–152). In Huexotzinco in 1560, there were seventy nobles of *teuctli* status (Dyckerhoff and Prem 1976:172).

TLAHTOHQUEH AND THE STATE

A *tlahtoani* (pl. *tlahtohqueh*) was a king. He was the head of an extensive noble lineage, actually a royal lineage, and his dependent *teteuctin* headed branches of it. The *tecpan* or palace of a *tlahtoani* was the administrative headquarters of the state or of that part of it which he headed. It included not only the residences of the king, his wives, and his dependent kin, but most of the state's administrative facilities as well: courts and council chambers, storehouses, armories, guest accommodations, ritual structures, gardens, possibly a market plaza and a ballcourt, and often much more. Temples and associated structures were in the immediate vicinity. It was the heart of the city from which the *tlahtoani* ruled, and around it were built the palaces of many of his dependent nobles (Sahagún 1954:41–45; Alva Ixtlilxóchitl 1975–77, 2:92–100, 150; Muñoz Camargo 1585, fol. 8v).

Each *tlahtoani* bore a title, which was passed on to his successors. For example, the ruler of Tetzcoco bore the title of *Chichimeca teuctli*, and the ruler of Tenochtitlan was the *Colhuah teuctli*. In Chalco, the various *tlahtohqueh* bore such titles as *Teohuah teuctli*, *Tlaillotlac teuctli*, and again *Chichimeca teuctli*. The names of rulers, and other nobles as well, are frequently followed by their

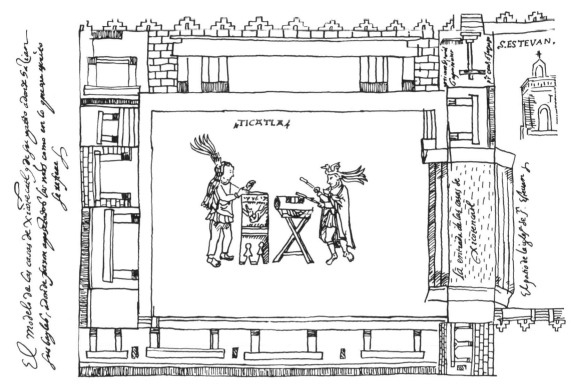

FIGURE 3-4. The palace of Xicotencatl, *tlahtoani* of Tizatlan, Tlaxcallan. From Muñoz Camargo 1585.

titles. *Tlahtoani* actually designates a grade of nobility; it was the title that indicated the extent of his authority.

While a *tlahtoani* was a king, he was not necessarily a monarch. A curious feature of Mesoamerican political organization, and one that has not received the attention one might expect, is that there was normally more than one *tlahtoani* in a state. Each had his own headquarters palace, his own dependent *te-teuctin*, his own lands, and his own *mace-hualtin*; and thus his own military force. Important decisions that affected all of them were usually made in concert, however, and they normally united in war when necessary, and supported each other in construction projects, the suppression of revolts, and in other ways.

There are at least two major variants on this pattern of multiple *tlahtohqueh*. In one, the several *tlahtohqueh* rule jointly and are structurally and juridically equal. In the other, one *tlahtoani* is clearly the supreme ruler, structurally and juridically dominant over the others. There are also intermediate cases, which I suspect come about most often when one of several theoretically equal *tlah-tohqueh* becomes de facto more powerful than the others. There can also be a hierarchy of *tlatohqueh* in a state, with multiple *tlahtohqueh* ruling jointly at one or more levels.

The first variant—joint rule—is the most common, but the second—centralized rule—is characteristic of the most tightly controlled and powerful states. Joint rule is exemplified by Tlaxcallan with four *tlahtohqueh*, Xochimilco with three, Huexotzinco with four, Tepeyacac with three, and varying numbers at different times in the history of the several states of Chalco (Muñoz Camargo 1892; Caci-ques de Xochimilco 1870; Carrasco 1977; Ca-

42

rrasco in *Matrícula de Huexotzinco* 1974:4–5, Cerón Carvajal 1905:28; Chimalpahin 1889; 1965; Durand-Forest 1981:160–167; Zimmermann 1960). Mexico also had two co-equal *tlahtohqueh* (of Tenochtitlan and Tlatelolco) during the time they were dominated by the Tepanec of Azcapotzalco.

Centralized rule is exemplified by Tetzcoco, whose supreme *tlahtoani* ruled over fourteen dependent *tlahtohqueh*; by Tenochtitlan after the overthrow of Azcapotzalco, when its *tlahtoani* had dependent *tlahtohqueh* in Ecatepec, Itztapalapan (Ixtapalapa), Xillotepec, and Apan; and by Azcapotzalco during its peak of power in the early fifteenth century, when its *tlahtoani* replaced the *tlahtohqueh* of eight subject towns with his own sons (Alva Ixtlilxóchitl 1975–1977; Hicks 1984; Chimalpahin 1889:107–108 [7ᵐᵉ rel., yr. 1440]; *Anales de Tlatelolco* 1948: pars. 77–79; *Anales de Cuauhtitlan* 38:192–194). Cholollan is somewhat deviant. It had two supreme rulers, the *tlalchiyach* and the *aquiyach*, who are referred to as *tlatohqueh* (e.g., *Historia tolteca-chichimeca* 1976:153), but they had some exceptional priestly functions, and there were other *tlahtohqueh* subordinate to them (Rojas 1927; Olivera and C. Reyes García 1969; Carrasco 1971a).

There are basically two processes by which multiple *tlahtohqueh* come into existence: the fission of a royal lineage and the alliance of two or more royal houses. Both processes can result in either joint rule or centralized rule, but they work differently depending on which it is to be.

Fission resulting in joint rule can be illustrated by the formation of three of the four *tlahtohcayotl* of Tlaxcallan. Colhuahteuctli Cuanez, *tlahtoani* of Tepeticpac, the first Tlaxcaltec "*cabecera*," shared his realm with his younger brother Teyohualminqui, who established himself as *tlahtoani* in Ocotelolco, the second "*cabecera*." The reasons for Colhuahteuctli's decision to elevate his brother to this status are not given, but it may have been because he had built a power base of his own, since Ocotelolco later became more powerful than Tepeticpac. The third *tlahtoh-*

cayotl, that of Tizatlan, can be traced back to a prince of Ocotelolco who separated and founded his own *tecpan*, and one of whose successors was elevated to *tlahtoani* status (Muñoz Camargo 1892). Fission also accounts for the existence of two *tlahtohqueh* in Chalco-Tlalmanalco. In 1303, Yacahuetzcatzin Teohuah teuctli, *tlahtoani* of the Nonohualcah, Teotlixcah, and Tlacochcalcah, divided his realm with his son, the *tlamacazqui* (priest) Chalchiuhtlatonac. The latter was installed in Itzcahuahcan with the title of Tlatquic teuctli, and ruled over the Xicocalcah, Calmimilolcah, and Tzacualcah. Yacahuetzcatzin continued to rule in the section called Opochhuahcan, and kept as his own subjects the Colilicah, Cuacuilcah, and Itzcotecah (Chimalpahin 1889:25–26, 46).

Alliance resulting in joint rule was a frequent process in the early history of Chalco. In 1267, for example, the Chichimec *tlahtoani* Cuahuitzatzin Tlaillotlac teuctli, together with Itzcauhtzin Atlauhtecatl teuctli, arrived in the region of Amaquemehcan (Amecameca), where they established themselves in Tzacualtitlan Tenanco. There they encountered other Chichimec lords of the Totollimpaneca, namely Tliltecatzin Chichimeca yaotequihuah (whose son had earlier married Cuahuitzatzin's daughter) and his younger brother Atonaltzin Chichimeca teuctli. They divided the territory among themselves and founded the city of Amaquemehcan (Chimalpahin, in Zimmermann 1960:59; cf. Chimalpahin 1958:107–108; Durand-Forest 1981:180–181). Later, in 1295, the Tecuanipa people arrived, led by Yaopol Tziuhtlacauhqui Tzompahuaca teuctli, and they were invited to settle, as allies, in Tecuanipan Amaquemehcan (Chimalpahin 1963:48–49; 1965:139–141; Zimmermann 1960:52). It was also evidently an alliance that led to the establishment of the fourth *tlahtohcayotl* of Tlaxcallan, that of Quiyahuiztlan. It was derived from a noble lineage that entered Tlaxcallan in the time of Colhuahteuctli Cuanez and was given lands on which to settle (Muñoz Camargo 1892:90, 96). One can also see the Triple Alliance of

Tenochtitlan, Tetzcoco, and Tlacopan as resulting in something that was at least very close to joint rule, even though the *tlahtoani* of Tenochtitlan was de facto more powerful than the others.

When fission is involved in the formation of centralized rule, it is usually a matter of a powerful *tlahtoani* creating new *tlahtohcayotl* for his dependent kin, as a way of tightening his control over a large region. During the second quarter of the fifteenth century, Itzcohuatl, *tlahtoani* of Tenochtitlan, created a new *tlahtohcayotl* in Ecatepec, and he later established his sons as *tlahtohqueh* in Itztapalapan, Xillotepec, and Apan (Chimalpahin 1889:98, 107–108 [7ᵐᵉ rel., yrs. 1428, 1440]). Nezahualcoyotl of Tetzcoco created a new *tlahtoani* seat in Chiauhtla for his infant son (Alva Ixtlilxóchitl 1975–1977:2:89). Earlier, Tezozomoc of Azcapotzalco had installed eight of his sons as *tlahtohqueh* in conquered cities, but he did this in most cases simply by ordering the assassination of the legitimate *tlahtohqueh* of those cities (*Anales de Cuauhtitlan* 1938:193–194).

Alliances which result in centralized rule tend to occur when an immigrant group under noble leadership is given lands by an established *tlahtoani*, and its lord, although raised to *tlahtoani* status, remains dependent on the established ruler. In the twelfth century, the rulers of Cholollan enlisted the support of seven Tolteca-Chichimeca groups from the Valley of Mexico as allies against rebellious subjects. They raised at least some of the Tolteca-Chichimeca lords to *tlahtoani* status, and indicated to them the lands over which they would rule once the rebellion was crushed. Even then, they still had to subdue the native inhabitants of the lands assigned to them. When finally established, they remained dependent on Cholollan, and their successors received their investitures there (*Historia tolteca-chichimeca* 1976:171ff; L. Reyes García 1977a:76ff). In Acolhuahcan in the Valley of Mexico, the *tlahtohcayotl* of Otompan (Otumba) apparently derives from the grant of lands by the *tlahtoani* Techotla-latzin of Tetzcoco to Otomi refugees from Xaltocan (Alva Ixtlilxóchitl 1975–1977:2:36).

Mexico is a little deviant. After settling on the island in the lake, the Mexicah split into two groups, the Tenochcah and Tlatelolcah, but they did not have a nobility then. Later, each of the two groups received *tlahtohqueh*, but from two different royal houses: Tlatelolco from Azcapotzalco and Tenochtitlan from Colhuahcan (*Anales de Tlatelolco* 1948:pars. 212, 217–299; Torquemada 1975: Bk. 2, Ch. 12).

Joint rule of course implies equality only in a structural and juridical sense. One *tlahtoani* may come to have more lands and *macehualtin* than another, and so have more de facto power. For example, in Xochimilco under Triple Alliance domination, the *tlahtoani* of Tepetenchi had more lands and subjects than the other two had (Carrasco 1977). Sometimes this may be converted into structural and juridical inequality. During most of the fourteenth century, the seven or more *tlahtohqueh* of Cuauhtinchan acknowledged one of their group, from the dynasty of Teuctlecozauhqui, as their supreme ruler (*centlahtoani*), but he, in turn, was dependent on the two supreme *tlahtohqueh* of Cholollan (L. Reyes García 1977a). The two *tlahtohqueh* of Mexico were equal so long as they were under Tepanec domination, but when the Tepanec were overthrown, only one of them, the *tlahtoani* of Tenochtitlan, made the alliance with Tetzcoco and Tlacopan that gave him the power to carry out conquests and eventually, in 1473, to conquer Tlatelolco and bring its royal dynasty to an end (Alvarado Tezozómoc 1975:387ff). Finally, the de facto dominance of Tenochtitlan eventually was such that when Moteuczomah II was installed as *tlahtoani* in 1503, he could formally declare himself the supreme *tlahtoani* (Alva Ixtlilxóchitl 1975–1977:2:188).

The centralized state would appear to be a structure that can potentially provide all of the *tlahtohqueh* involved, at whatever level, with greater coercive power over their people, because it provides an automatic

FIGURE 3-5. Acolhuahcan placed under Tepanec domination. On a day 4 Rabbit, a Tepanec captain, atop an ancient Toltec temple, addresses the people of the twelve *tlatocayotl* of Acolhuahcan, assembled in a field near Cuauhyacac. In the first row are figures representing Tetzcoco, Huexotla, Cohuatlichan, and Cohuatepec; in the second row Chiauhtla, Tezonyocan, Tepechpan, and Acolman; and in the third row Tepetlaoztoc, Chiucnautlan, Teotihuacan, and Otompan. The men placed as governors are seated on mats; one is a Chichimec of Tetzcoco, the other a man named Tlotzin (Falcon), of Toltec lineage. Behind the Tepanec captain are figures representing the Tepanec, Tlatelolco, and Tenochtitlan, and a military captain. Hidden on the hill of Cuauhyacac is the weeping Nezahualcoyotl, who watches the proceedings, and his companion Huitziltetzin. From *Codex Xolotl*, Plate VIII; cf. Alva Ixtlilxóchitl 1975–1977: 1:344–345.

chain of command through which the coercive power of the entire state can quickly be mobilized. Joint rule, on the other hand, represents a balance of power which, in the absence of a supreme overlord, must have been difficult to upset. If one of the *tlahtohqueh* were to seek to increase his power by expanding his control over land and *'macehualtin*, the others would either do likewise or unite to halt his expansion. The picture changes, however, if the joint-rule state is under the overlordship of another. It was under the protection of Cholollan that Teuctlecozauhqui of the Cuauhtinchantlacah was able to establish himself as *centlahtoani*, and it was after the Mexica conquest and *pax mexicana* that two of the *tlahtohqueh* of Tepeyacac were able to amass lands and *macehualtin* at the expense of other noble houses and of unsubjugated commoner groups (L. Reyes García 1977a:88ff.). One would also

expect a centralized state to be able to mobilize labor more effectively for construction projects, and thus one would expect the palaces, temples, and other buildings in the headquarters city of a supreme *tlahtoani* to be more grandiose than those associated with joint-rule states.[5] However, a joint-rule state can be quite effective at defending its common territory, as the survival of Tlaxcallan attests.

THE COMMONERS

An extensive lineage organization integrated the nobility, so it has been possible to make use of kinship terms to describe the upper strata of ancient Mexican society. Only nobles had this extensive lineage organization, however. There is no evidence for anything comparable among the commoners, and, as a general rule, there were no recognized kin-

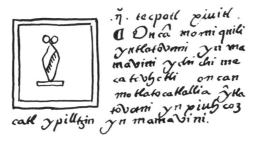

FIGURE 3-6. Royal succession in Cuauhtinchan. Death of Mamahuini Chichimeca teuctli, and succession by his son Xiuhcozcatl, in the year 2 Flint. From *Historia tolteca-chichimeca*, fol. 41v.

ship ties linking nobles and commoners. These were all state-level societies, and relations between nobles and commoners were political, not kinship, relations (Carrasco 1961; 1971b; 1976a).

Commoners generally lived in local groups called *tlaxilacalli* or *calpolli* (sometimes *tlaxilacalpan* or *calpolpan*) or, at least in Morelos, *chinamitl*.[6] These local groups were most often rural hamlets, but in a large and tightly nucleated city like Tenochtitlan, they might be sections of the city (Caso 1956; Calnek 1974a). We know little about the internal structure of these entities, which in any case probably varied, both regionally and by the nature of their inhabitants' duties. Most of them probably contained a youths' house (*telpochcalli*) and a shrine or community house (probably called a *calpolco* or possibly sometimes *calpolli*).

The word *macehualli* usually denotes 'commoner' but actually means 'subject' (the Spanish generally glossed it as *vasallo*), and Nahuatl texts virtually always use it in that

sense. But commoners varied in the degree of their subjection. In some cases, it amounted to little more than an obligation to serve their *tlahtoani* in war, to offer gifts on the appropriate occasions in acknowledgment of his authority, and to respond to occasional calls for draft labor (*cohuatequitl*). More often it involved, in addition to that, a rigorously enforced requirement to give periodic labor service and a specified tribute. It is possible that the word *macehualli* applied only to commoners who were in this more intense form of subjugation (L. Reyes García 1977a:106ff), but by the time of the Spanish conquest, this included the vast majority of commoners. Only from parts of the Valley of Puebla do we have accounts of commoner groups in the more limited form of subjugation, and these were not called *macehualli*.

In the Valley of Mexico virtually all commoners were subject to a lord of a noble house or a state institution, or to the ruler. Even the land on which they resided and the plots they cultivated for their own subsistence were considered to belong to their lords, and the commoners' use rights to them were contingent upon their performance of their duties (*tequitl*). *Macehualtin* subject to a particular noble were obligated to cultivate his fields and to provide domestic service in his house, and if there were craft or service specialists among them, they gave the products of their craft or specialized service. Commoners not subject to a particular noble or noble house were subject to the *tlahtoani* directly. Some were obliged to give regular labor service on a rotational basis to the palace, to one or another of the state institutions, or otherwise as the ruler or other appropriate official directed. Others were obliged to cultivate fields to provide food for the extensive royal palace, for the personnel of state institutions, and for commoners performing labor service in the palace or elsewhere away from their homes. All commoners were subject to the *cohuatequitl*, extraordinary labor service for special projects. Specialists gave service in work at their craft or other specialty (Hicks 1982; 1984;

46

Calnek 1975:46–48; Carrasco 1978: 29–32; Dyckerhoff and Prem 1978; Rojas Rabiela 1979). The local official whose duty was to oversee the fulfillment of these *tequitl* obligations was generally called a *calpixqui* or *tequitlahtoh* in the Valley of Mexico, but *calpoleh* ('one who has a *calpolli*', pl. *calpolehqueh*)[7] is recorded from Morelos and one locality in Puebla (L. Reyes García 1979). He could be a commoner himself if he did not supervise nobles.

Much the same system is described in accounts from the Valley of Puebla (e.g., Anguiano and Chapa 1976; Dyckerhoff and Prem 1976; Carrasco 1963; 1969; L. Reyes García 1977a; Olivera 1978; Prem 1978) and the Valley of Morelos (Carrasco 1964; 1972; 1976b); indeed, wherever there were noble houses there were lands and *macehualtin* to serve them, and this service followed essentially the same pattern everywhere.

Some commoners, however, appear not to have been subject to nobles in quite this same way. In the Valley of Puebla, particularly in the Cuauhtinchan region, there were communities of land-holding commoners who acknowledged the political authority of a *tlahtoani* but were not required to give labor service or tribute on a regular basis and were not called *macehualli*. Luis Reyes García (1977a) includes among them the twenty-five Tolteca-Chichimeca *calpolli* that came to Cuauhtinchan from Chollollan in the thirteenth century. These entities had leaders, but in referring to one of them, the *Manuscrito de 1553* (a recently discovered Cuauhtinchan chronicle published by L. Reyes García 1978:80–100) states that he was not a lord, but "only our father" (*zan totah*), and that they did not give him tribute. After the conquest of Tepeyacac and Cuauhtinchan by the Triple Alliance in 1471, these *calpolli* began to be subjugated by those *tlahtohqueh* of Tepeyacac that had the support of the Triple Alliance; the people were reduced to *macehualli* status and were required to give tribute and rotational labor service (Olivera 1978:98; L. Reyes García 1978:87). Zorita's (1941:87ff) account of the *calpolli*, which is

based on information provided by Fray Francisco de las Navas and hence probably comes from Cuauhtinchan (Baudot 1976:433–461; L. Reyes García 1979; Hicks 1982:244), apparently refers to units of this kind. After the Spanish conquest, some of them brought suit in Spanish courts to regain their lands, and others may have been able to retain their holdings up to the time of the conquest.

By the time of the Spanish conquest, the powerful centralized states of the Valley of Mexico had reduced virtually all of their commoners to *macehualli* status. With the possible exception of some urban artisans in Tenochtitlan (see below), we know of no commoners who were not subject to regular tribute or service obligations to nobles. However, accounts of the early history of the Valley of Mexico mention immigrant groups who lacked a nobility of their own, yet who were apparently not in a subjugated status. Among these were the Tlaltecahuaqueh, one of the first groups to settle in Chalco-Tlalmanalco (Chimalpahin 1889:27), and the Mexica when they first arrived on the Tepanec island in the lake (*Anales de Tlatelolco* 1948:pars. 203–217). The *tlahtohqueh* of the Valley of Puebla, at least before the Mexica conquests, may have lacked the coercive power to reduce all commoners to this status.

Zorita (1941:143–154) used the word "*mayeques*" to refer to commoners subject to an individual noble, but this word was never in general use (Hicks 1976:67–68). It appears only in Zorita's account, in a letter by Martín Cortés (1865), and in the Spanish (but not in the Nahuatl) heading of a sixteenth-century roster from Morelos, part of a proceeding which involved both Zorita and Martín Cortés (*Nuevos documentos . . . Cortés* 1946:185). L. Reyes García (1977a: 106, 122) suggests that the word "*mayeque*" as used by Zorita corresponds to *macehualli*, a word which does not appear in Zorita's account.

Another category of commoner consisted of purchased slaves, pawns, or others lacking access to subsistence resources of their own.

These people are rarely mentioned in the Early Colonial sources, and their role in the economy remains poorly understood. As far as we can tell from the few specific cases known (e.g., Carrasco 1964:205; 1972:232–233, 236–237), they seem to have been used primarily as household servants, and the women sometimes as concubines. If the householder had sufficient land, however, he might provide such a servant with a small plot to work.

LAND TENURE

The land tenure of central Mexico has continued to attract the attention of scholars because it is so central to the political and economic system of this agrarian society. Traditionally, studies of land tenure have focused on the Nahuatl terms used to designate different civil categories of land, terms such as *altepetlalli*, *calpollalli*, *pillalli*, *teuctlalli*, *tecpantlalli*, and *tlahtohcatlalli*, and less commonly, *yaotlalli*, *teotlalli*, *milchimalli*, and others (see, e.g., Torquemada 1975:Bk. 14, Ch. 7; Alva Ixtlilxóchitl 1975–1977:2: 90–91; Zorita 1941:90, 142–144; Dyckerhoff and Prem [1978] extract the appropriate sections of all the major published sources on land tenure). These terms are all made up of *tlalli* 'land' (sometimes *milli* 'field' and, in Cuauhtinchan, *cuemitl* 'cultivated field'), prefixed by a word designating the entity to which the land pertains. Their etymologies are thus clear, but their role in the land tenure system has been the subject of some debate. Recent research in early Colonial records provides some additional terms, such as *huehuehtlalli* 'old land', *cihuatlalli* 'woman's land', *teuccihuatlalli* 'noble woman's land', and *tlalcohualli* 'purchased land' (S. L. Cline 1984; L. Reyes García 1977a.98, 105).

The main variables considered in most discussions of land tenure are the use to which the harvest was put, the source of the work force, and whether or not the land could be alienated. Friedrich Katz (1966) and Alfonso Caso (1963) were particularly concerned with

property rights. Both singled out certain lands as being "privately" held, while others were "public" or "communal." Víctor Castillo Farreras (1972:81–82), however, questioned the existence of private property in land and proposed a basic twofold division between lands worked for the worker's own benefit (*calpollalli*) and lands of the city. Alfredo López Austin (1974) presented a more complex scheme, but as for property rights, he too distinguished between *calpollalli* and all other lands, which he calls lands of the *tlahtohcayotl*. Carrasco (1978:26), on the other hand, believes that the basic distinction was between lands held for life and linked to the status of nobility and lands linked to a specific political post. In either case, allocation was determined by the rulers. Dyckerhoff and Prem (1978) distinguish between (1) land linked to individuals (*pillalli*), (2) land linked to corporate bodies (*calpollalli*), and (3) land from which the state derived revenue (all remaining categories).

The distinction between *tlahtohcatlalli* and *tecpantlalli* has long been a puzzle, but at least for the Tetzcoco region, Dyckerhoff and Prem (1978:203–209) make a good case for considering *tlahtohcatlalli* to have been large fields worked collectively to provide food for the state granaries, while *tecpantlalli* were subsistence plots for those *macehualtin* who owed labor service to the palace, and who were also called *tecpanpouhqueh* (cf. Hicks 1984). As for *cihuatlalli*, Carrasco (1974) finds that these were dowry lands, at least in the Tetzcoco area. In 1435, King Nezahualcoyotl of Tetzcoco re-established Quetzalmamalitzin as a dependent *tlahtoani* in Teotihuacan and gave him his daughter as a wife. With her went dowry lands referred to as *cihuatlalli*. These lands passed to her son Cotzatzin, who succeeded Quetzalmamalitzin, but then they were called *tetzcohco tlahtohcatlalli*, apparently because, although they were in Teotihuacan, they continued to belong to the royal lineage of Tetzcoco.

The principal factors of production and sources of wealth and power in ancient Mexico were land and labor.[8] Power and a life of comfort came not so much from control over land per se as from control over manpower. A noble of course needed the food and other agricultural products the land provided, but he also desired land for the labor it would support. The general pattern, at least in the Valley of Mexico, was that land was assigned by the ruler to the royal palace, a noble house, or one or another state institution (including the temples) and was inherited thereafter. The recipients used some lands to provide food for the noble personnel and for commoners while they were performing nonagricultural service for them, and used others to provide subsistence plots to commoners attached to them, theoretically as compensation for their work.

It appears that in the Valley of Mexico, at least by the sixteenth century, commoners could not possess land in any kind of freehold tenure. They were settled in communities which were often called *calpolli*, and at least some of the land they cultivated for their subsistence was called *calpollalli*. However, Fernando de Alva Ixtlilxóchitl (1975–1977:2:91) includes *calpollalli* among the lands which "belonged only to the heirs of the kingdoms and lordships [*señoríos*] and to no one else." Testimony in a sixteenth-century document from Xochimilco (cited in Hicks 1982:243) explains that a commoner has no right to own land, and when a noble gives him land, it is only in order to serve that noble.

In the Valley of Puebla, however, we have seen that there were at least some *calpolli* that did not give regular tribute and service to nobles, and whose members were not called *macehualli*. The lands of these entities were administered through *calpolli* headmen, apparently independently of the *tlahtoani* or any other noble. We are not told what these lands were called, but since they belonged to a *calpolli*, it is reasonable to suppose they were called *calpollalli*. They did not, however, belong only to kings and lords.

The question of the alienability of land has received considerable attention. Some mod-

ern scholars have concluded that *pillalli* could be sold (e.g., Caso 1963:872; Calnek 1975:53–54), while others are doubtful at best (e.g., Carrasco 1978:28; Castillo Farreras 1972:72–83). Several of the early sources do contain statements which indicate that at least some categories of land could be sold. Juan de Torquemada (1975:Bk. 14, Ch. 7) tells us that that owners of *pillalli* "could in some manner sell or dispose of them if they were not in some way entailed," and Alva Ixtlilxóchitl (1975–1977:1:386) mentions a law of Nezahualcoyotl that prohibited a person from selling the same piece of land twice. *Tlahtohqueh* of course had near-absolute power, and they could and did dispose of the land under their direct control, sometimes in ways suggesting sale. Alva Ixtlilxóchitl (1975–1977:2:172) tells us that Nezahualpilli, *tlahtoani* of Tetzcoco, coveted a fine *teponaztli* (drum) that a prince had taken as conquest booty, and offered him "certain places and other gifts" for it (the prince refused, so the *tlahtoani* ordered the drum seized). Bernardino de Sahagún indicates that rulers could also wager lands (1954:29; cf. Durán 1967:1:200). But these and other instances only tell us what was or was not possible; they do not tell us how the system worked.

A *tlahtoani* who ruled with the support of nobles of his and allied houses, who were given specific duties and responsibilities in the administration and defense of the kingdom, made grants of land and *macehualtin* to these nobles to enable them to carry out their duties. They supported their *tlahtoani* in his pursuit of power in the expectation that they would receive such grants, and the grants were made in the expectation that the receiver would continue his support and carry out the duties of his office. The head of a noble house in turn gave lands to his dependent *pipiltin* for similar political reasons, and also to his *macehualtin*, so that they could serve him. For the *tlahtoani*, the whole system would be weakened or destroyed if the *teuctli* who had received lands under these conditions were to transfer them to a person the ruler had not selected for the post, and whose loyalty and capabilities had not been demonstrated. Carrasco (1978: 27–28) thus doubts that lands, including *pillalli*, could be freely sold.

Of course the system did not always work as it should. Some royal princes, for example, did not live up to expectations (e.g., Alva Ixtlilxóchitl 1975–1977:2:169). Sahagún (1969:71) quotes a ruler expounding to his subjects on the evils of *pulque* and negatively exemplifying an official of Cuauhtitlan as a "great noble" who "drank up all his land; he sold it all" (to whom, he does not say). But such cases are extremely rare. In many Early Colonial documents, the histories of land-holdings are traced back to Prehispanic times, and one can find numerous instances of administrative transfers of land or of the tribute and services of the *macehualtin* on the land. I know of no instance, however, where the land was transferred by means of an outright sale in Prehispanic times. After the Spanish conquest, of course, the sale of land became an integral part of the new system. Sue Louise Cline (1984) notes the emergence after the conquest of a new civil category of land, *tlalcohualli* 'purchased land', and infers that once lands were so designated, they could be freely bought and sold. The evidence seems to indicate that, regardless of occasional exceptions, the way the system worked was that the basic means of production, land and labor, were distributed through the political system and not through the market.

TRADE, TRIBUTE, AND MARKET

We have seen that tribute, in goods and in labor, was an important part of the domestic political economy in most central Mexican states. *Macehualtin* gave tribute to their lords, and rulers gave these lords the means to obtain tribute. Tribute was the principal mechanism through which nobles or certain commoners holding official positions obtained goods produced on lands they controlled. Through redistribution, nobles and com-

moners received goods from their *tlahtoani*, which they could in turn distribute to their dependents, kin, or others of their choosing. By this mechanism also, commoners were provided with food and perhaps other necessities while they were on duty in the service of their lords.

This was the state sector of the economy; it worked primarily through redistribution, and has been characterized by Calnek (1978: 102) for Tenochtitlan as an extension of the patrimonial domestic economy of the royal palace. But central Mexico was also a region of great markets and of long-distance professional merchants, the *pochtecah*. The relationship between redistribution and market exchange has concerned various scholars (e.g., Berdan 1977; 1978b; Calnek 1978; Carrasco 1978). Carrasco (1978) has concluded that while land and labor were distributed through the state sector, the market served primarily for the distribution of consumer goods. Here we must understand "labor" to refer to that which was treated as "unskilled": agricultural work, domestic work (including the production of cloth), and other kinds of manual labor. With that qualification, Carrasco's conclusion holds true, at least for most parts of central Mexico.

Market and tribute were in no sense competing institutions. As the Aztec empire expanded and tribute flowed into Tenochtitlan from conquered regions, the market plaza at Tlatelolco—the principal market of the imperial capital—also grew. By the time of the Spanish conquest, it appears to have been the largest marketplace in central Mexico, if not in all of Mesoamerica (II. Cortés 1963: 72–73).

The major market plazas (*tiyanquiztli*), as a rule located in *tlahtoani* seats, belonged to *tlahtohqueh*. They were usually built adjacent to, or even as part of, the royal palace, although over time, as new rulers built new palaces, such proximity might be lost. In a state with several *tlahtohqueh*, moreover, the *tiyanquiztli* might belong to only one of them. Thus the principal market plaza of Mexico was in Tlatelolco, not Tenochtitlan,

tyanquizco ytemachtiaya fraymartin.

La prim²ᵃ predicacion del sancto Euang en Tlaxcala en medio de la plaça por los frayles de la orden delS⁰r S.⁺ frand, y el modo de enseñar q tuvieron.

FIGURE 3-7. The market plaza of Ocotelolco, Tlaxcallan, during the first preaching of the Christian gospel there. Vendors offer collared slaves, poultry, foodstuffs, pottery, and other goods. Note ballcourt. From Muñoz Camargo 1585.

and the market of Tlaxcallan belonged to the ruler of Ocotelolco and was next to his palace (Alva Ixtlilxóchitl 1975–1977:2:93; Alvarado Tezozómoc 1975:320, Ch. 30; Muñoz Camargo 1585:fols. 4r, 7v). The *tlahtoani* received as tribute a portion of the goods brought by sellers, and a major market plaza would also have a ballcourt, where games were played on market days, apparently to attract people (H. Cortés 1963:76; Anderson, Berdan, and Lockhart 1976:138–139; Torquemada 1975:Bk. 14, Ch. 14; Motolinía 1971:381; Alva Ixtlilxóchitl 1975–1977:2:96; Muñoz Camargo 1585:fol. 4v; this document also contains an illustration of the Ocotelolco market plaza, showing a ballcourt; see Fig. 3–7). All exchanges were supposed to take place in the *tiyanquiztli* (Durán 1967:1:179).

In the major cities—and most sources follow Motolinía (1971:375) in listing Mexico, Tetzcoco, and Tlaxcallan as examples—markets were in operation every day, but in smaller cities they were usually held every five or twenty days. Rulers appear to have regarded their *tiyanquiztli* primarily as places where the city's long-distance merchants brought their exotic goods for sale after giving the *tlahtoani* his due, and where these same merchants obtained the goods they took to trade. Except for certain cities whose markets served as entrepots or "ports of trade" (Chapman 1957; Berdan 1978a), they did not function as interlocking nodes in an interregional system of market exchange. Hassig (1982a) indicates that the periodic markets in *tlahtoani* seats were not staggered. Twenty-day markets were everywhere held on the first (or last)[9] day of the solar-year month, and five-day markets (which were the most numerous) were held on the year-bearer days of the 260-day cycle, every fourth one coinciding with a twenty-day market. Only if there were minor markets within a *tlahtohcayotl* might their market days be somewhat staggered. This arrangement, while having no adverse effect on the operations of long-distance merchants, would surely have hindered the development of a class of small-scale merchants making a living by operating from market to market within central Mexico.

All this would suggest that markets were "peripheral," patronized largely by target-marketers using the market only to satisfy occasional needs for special consumer items (cf. Kurtz 1974). Yet if that were all they were, it is doubtful that they would have been as well supplied and as well attended as at least some of them clearly were. Moreover, it would not have been possible to rely on them as dependable sources of supply for goods needed on a regular basis. In some smaller states, perhaps, markets were indeed "peripheral,"

and it was not necessary to rely on them for daily needs on a regular basis. Most needs would have been met through the tribute and redistributional system.

This was not the case in Tenochtitlan, however. Calnek (1978:100) believes that not more than a quarter to a third of the population of that city could have been supported by the foodstuffs entering the city as tribute, and Berdan (1976:189–190) believes the bulk of this was used for administrative expenses, the royal household, military campaigns, and storage against emergencies. The small *chinampa* gardens that adjoined many of the houses in the city were too small to provide more than an occasional supplement of fresh produce for the householders (Calnek 1974a: 48–50). Calnek also presents evidence that the great growth of the city in the century preceding the Spanish conquest was due not only to the expansion of the administrative bureaucracy, but also to the expansion of new occupations in specialized craft or service activities. The city became a center of craftsmanship, and while some of the craftsmen did work for the ruler to supply the royal palace, many of them made products for the market, where they could be obtained by merchants who carried them to distant regions to exchange for exotic raw materials (Calnek 1975:48; 1978:103–105; Scholes and Adams 1958; Sahagún 1959:83–92). This development occurred, moreover, at the same time that Tenochtitlan was expanding its empire and receiving increasing quantities of goods as tribute.

Elizabeth M. Brumfiel (1976:222; 1980: 466) has suggested that if some of the goods obtained as imperial tribute were systematically placed on the market, it would be assured that an adequate supply of these goods would always be available for purchase, since they would have been produced and delivered on schedule in response to political demand, rather than in response to the irregular economic demand of target-marketers. Such assurance would have made possible the rise of a class of full-time craft specialists who relied entirely on the market both to dispose of their products and to acquire the raw materials they needed, and also to obtain their food and other daily necessities. If this gave Mexica craftsmen who produced for the market a cost advantage over those in other parts of the Valley, it may have encouraged the other communities to specialize in producing food, rather than craft items, for market exchange (Hassig 1982b:42–43). This would help assure an adequate supply of food in the Tenochtitlan-Tlatelolco markets.

The craftsmen of Tenochtitlan were commoners, but their obligations to the nobility of the city are still unclear. They of course acknowledged the authority of their *tlahtoani*, and apparently they were all subject to *cohuatequitl* as well as military service (Scholes and Adams 1958:31; cf. Durán 1967:2:313). Yet it is also stated (e.g., Scholes and Adams 1958:29, 51) that they did not give regular tribute. This may simply mean that they worked at their crafts rather than at manual labor in fulfilling their *tequitl* obligations (Hicks 1982), but it may also mean that they were not the direct subjects—*macehualtin* or *"terrazgueros"*—of either the *tlahtoani* or any specific noble, and that they worked at their crafts full-time through a market system.

THE SPANISH CONQUEST

Spanish rule brought far-reaching changes in the Mesoamerican political and economic system. The native states were abolished, and with them the military and religious organizations that supported them. The Spanish recognized the native nobility, but only as a means for effecting a sort of "indirect rule" over the native population. Native rulers were still termed *tlahtohqueh* in Colonial Nahuatl documents, but they were no longer kings, merely *"caciques,"* vassals of the king of Spain. The domains of once-powerful rulers were reduced to a single *"cabecera,"* or head-town, with its *"sujetos,"* or dependent communities. Many rulers became little more than foremen, responsible for the delivery of tribute to Spanish *encomenderos*.

The Spanish also introduced a distinction between polity and economy, a distinction that was hard to make in the Prehispanic system. Many of the Indian nobles, having lost control of the state, sought to convert the vestiges of their political power into economic power. To that end, the descendants of former rulers often attempted to claim former state lands as their "patrimonial" lands, their subjects as their tenants (*"terrazgueros"*), and their tribute as "rent." They made use of Spanish courts to establish these claims, which they presented within a Spanish legal framework so as to have the support of Spanish law. Today the proceedings of these legal cases are often a good source of ethnographic information on the Prehispanic period, and an even better source on the processes by which traditional power-holders tried to adapt to a new political, economic, and legal system.

The many changes that took place in the Early Colonial period are beyond the scope of this article, but they are relevant to the study of Prehispanic society as well as for understanding processes of culture change. Most of our sources were written during this period of readjustment and readaptation, and our ability to interpret them requires a knowledge of that period and of the system imposed by the new power-holders, to which the native Mexicans were forced to adapt. Fortunately, there have been many advances in our knowledge of Colonial ethnohistory, as other chapters in this volume show.

NOTES

1. A copy of the Glasgow manuscript was kindly lent to me by Wayne Ruwet. After this paper was completed, a facsimile edition of the manuscript was published in Mexico by the Instituto de Investigaciones Filológicas, Universidad Nacional Autónoma de México, under the editorship of René Acuña (Muñoz Camargo 1981).

2. When the stem *-pil-* is used with the literal meaning of 'child', it almost always occurs in possessed form, e.g., *nopil* 'my child'

or *topil* 'someone's child'. The absolute form *pilli* always means 'noble'. When *pilli* 'noble' is possessed, its stem becomes *pillo*, and the words also have different plural forms; thus *nopipillohuan* means 'my noble persons', while *nopilhuan* means 'my children'. I thank Frances Karttunen for this clarification.

3. *Yaotl* means 'enemy' and *tequi-huah* would be literally 'one who has the duty (or tribute)', hence *yaotequihuah* is literally 'one who receives the tribute of enemies'. In Chalco, *yaotequihuah* was the title of a high politico-military official. In the Valley of Mexico generally, a *tequihuah* was a skilled warrior, and in Tenochtitlan and Tetzcoco, the *tequihuacacalli* was a council of war associated with the royal palace (Sahagún 1954:43; Pomar 1941:34). Except where otherwise stated, my linguistic analyses are based primarily on J. Richard Andrews (1975).

4. The suffix *-yotl* means 'pertaining to'; hence *tlahtohcayotl* literally means 'kingship', but it seems to connote that over which a *tlahtoani* ruled. The Spanish word *cabecera* is frequently used for a town that was *tlahtoani* seat, but it implies a kind of localization that does not correspond to any Nahuatl concept.

5. The great land reclamation projects undertaken by the Triple Alliance (Parsons 1976) probably reflect the large numbers of people under its control, plus its special needs, more than the centralized rule of its component states.

6. The basic meaning of *chinamitl* is 'enclosure'. In the southern Valley of Mexico it usually refers to a *chinampa* (raised field); *chinampan* is the place where raised fields are located. For the use of *chinamitl* as a local group, see Carrasco (1976b:104).

7. The *-eh* suffix (pl. *-ehqueh*) is an agentive, thus 'one who has a *calpolli*'. Apparently it could mean either a person who belongs to one or a person who has charge of one.

8. I exclude tools and other capital goods because in this preindustrial economy they were obtained in the same way, and at essentially the same cost, as consumer goods. Power came from control over land and *macehualtin*, not tools.

9. Caso (1971:345) believes the day in ancient Mexico was considered to begin at noon. If so, it is understandable that Spanish writers would be confused as to whether the market began on the last or the first day of the month. It was probably the first, since some sources tell us that the market began at noon.

4. Ethnohistory of the Guatemalan Colonial Indian

ROBERT M. CARMACK

THE ORIGINAL four volumes of the *Handbook of Middle American Indians* devoted to ethnohistory (vols. 12–15) by design heavily emphasized sources rather than content. Very little was said about historically studied Indian institutions, especially for the Colonial period. In part that was a reflection of the "state of the art" for, as Henry B. Nicholson (1975:501) says, "far more attention has been directed toward the 'pure' pre-Cortesian culture than toward the 'contaminated' ones of post-Conquest times." That situation has begun to change, if the Guatemalan case is representative of Middle America as a whole, and we are beginning to reconstruct substantive aspects of native colonial culture. Thus, in the following summary of colonial Indian ethnohistory of Guatemala, content will be stressed over sources.

Ethnohistory is not viewed here as a discipline but rather as an orienting methodology: "a special set of techniques and methods for studying culture through the use of written and oral traditions" (Carmack 1972:232). Its major forms have consisted of special social or culture histories of non-Western societies, historical ethnographies of those societies,

and their historiographies ("folk" views of the past). To date, there has been little attempt to reconstruct colonial Indian culture (historical ethnography), though Francisco de Solano (1974) is an exception. Similarly, studies of the Guatemalan Indians' view of their past, especially as this might relate to the Colonial period, are lacking. Most of our studies then, represent attempts to reconstruct Indian social history, and that will be the focus of the summary to follow.

One of the main problems in summarizing the recent results from studies on the colonial Guatemalan Indian is to integrate the more general histories with limited studies of specific areas and communities. I have chosen to extract the major issues raised by the general studies, with their suggested interpretations, and to examine them ("test" them) in the light of the more specific studies. This means that I have allowed the issues to be defined by others. I do not claim that they necessarily represent the most important issues that could be raised, or that I would personally raise, but I do think that few scholars would deny their relevance for ethnohistory. This "empirical" mode of problem selection

55

also means that some studies, otherwise valuable, are less relevant to this summary than others. Hence, it should be clear that no attempt is made to exhaust all the studies available. Finally, the summary is based on scholarly works rather than primary or even secondary (e.g., the chroniclers) sources themselves.[1]

General Studies of Colonial Guatemalan Indians

The general works on colonial Guatemala that I consider to be the most important in terms of the ethnohistoric criteria outlined above are as follows: (1) Ralph Beals' (1967) summary of Posthispanic Mesoamerican acculturation processes. His sequence is said to apply to Guatemala, following closely a previous sequence worked out for the Maya by Oliver LaFarge (1940). (2) Severo Martínez Pelaez' brilliant, polemical book (1970) on the colonial creoles of Guatemala. He devotes considerable attention to the Indians, primarily in terms of their economic relationships with the creoles and Spaniards. (3) Murdo MacLeod's (1973) detailed account of economic history in Guatemala and the other Central American countries. The Indians are not the primary focus of his study, but they are extensively dealt with, even if in a general way. (4) Francisco de Solano's (1974) reconstruction of Indian life in the Guatemalan colony during the eighteenth century. The study contains much detail on Indian life during the sixteenth and seventeenth centuries and presents what might be considered an intellectual Spaniard's view of the conquest.

Other more general works worthy of mention are Silvio Zavala's (1967) brief summary of colonial Guatemalan institutions, especially during the sixteenth century; Jesús M. García Añoveros' (1980) reconstruction of the Guatemalan diocese late in the eighteenth century; William Sherman's (1979) study of sixteenth-century slavery in Central America; Magnus Mörner's (1964) reconstruction of *mestizaje* in the Audiencia of Guatemala; and

Salvador Rodríguez Becerra's (1977) account of the initial colonization of Guatemala. These works tend to be limited either in topic or time, but must enter into any discussion of colonial Guatemalan ethnohistory.

The authors of the general works cited above have raised a number of central issues relative to colonial Guatemalan Indians. These will be briefly summarized first, in order to "test" them later within the context of a number of "case studies" that in recent times have been researched within Guatemalan ethnohistory. The cases deemed sufficiently detailed to provide a fair test are the following: (1) my own attempt (Carmack 1983) to reconstruct colonial social life and process in Tecpanaco, a highland Guatemalan Indian community; (2) Douglas G. Madigan's (1976) and Sandra L. Orellana's (1976) studies of Santiago Atitlan through time; (3) Christopher H. Lutz' (1976) reconstruction of colonial demographics and social change in Santiago de Guatemala; (4) W. George Lovell's (1980) historical geography of the Cuchumatanes.

Almost everyone agrees that a valid macrocosmic view of the colonial Indian of Guatemala can only be gained through a series of empirical regional or microcosmic studies. We are still far from having such detailed accounts for even the major regions of Guatemala, much less for particular communities or institutions. Nevertheless, we do have some studies of this type, and they shed important new light on the more general picture of colonial Indian Guatemala.

Some Central Issues Derived from the General Studies

The Conquest

A central issue relative to the conquest itself is raised by Beals (1967) and Solano (1974), who argue that throughout much of Mesoamerica the Spanish conquistadores were seen more as liberators than conquerors. In many cases, the Spaniards were joined by opponents to the major native powers under Spanish attack, and for them the conquest was seen as political insurrection. The idea that the natives experienced drastic culture shock with the conquest is rejected, and the claim is made that Spanish rule at first brought general "peace and prosperity." This has been specifically argued for Alvarado and Guatemala (Sherman 1980), though the initial violence of the Guatemalan conquest is universally recognized. Despite the destruction of native peoples and replacement of indigenous rule by Spanish hegemony, the overall picture is seen to be one of remarkable Spanish success due to "mutual accommodation of the European and native social systems" (Beals 1967:453; also Solano 1974:465).

Demographic Trends

MacLeod (1973; 1980) has argued that demographic trends were highly variable from one region to another in colonial Guatemala. A drastic population decline occurred with the Spanish conquest, starting even before contact when as many as one-third of the natives are said to have been killed off by diseases introduced into the area. Overall declines ranged from 50 to 95 percent, with the greatest losses in lowland areas. The lowland areas became heavily non-Indian during the Colonial period, and their demographic revival was delayed until late in the eighteenth century. Highland Indian areas generally experienced less of a decline, and a revival of population growth began there in the midseventeenth century or earlier. Absolute population figures for Guatemala at conquest and during the sixteenth and seventeenth centuries remain only rough guesses at this stage of our investigations. Solano (1974) claims that such drastic declines are exaggerated, the result of inflated estimates for Prehispanic populations. His studies also lead him to conclude that native populations were already growing by the beginning of the seventeenth century, and had surpassed Prehispanic levels by Independence.

Indirect Rule

Most authorities agree that the primary Spanish objectives were to control the Indians as a labor source, and to block separatist movements by the Spaniards in America (Rodríguez Becerra 1977; Beals 1967). These objectives were carried out initially through indirect rule, it is claimed. A stratified caste-like social structure was promoted, separating Spaniards from Indians, while assimilating the native aristocracy. The peasants were left largely intact by organizing Indian towns with syncretized native-Spanish social institutions. Cultural indoctrination was left to the missionaries, who used native languages, simplified Catholic ritual, and syncretized forms—especially dance-dramas and *cofradía* rites—for that purpose.

Historical Phasing

Beals (1967) and Solano (1974) argue for what Beals calls the "First Colonial Indian Period," from about 1550 to 1720, when early Indian receptivity resulted in cultural accommodations. He notes that the particular accommodation reached in any area depended upon which religious order officiated there (the Dominicans were the most *laissez faire*), the extent to which the natives had been "congregated," the degree of *mestizaje* (racial mixing) taking place, and the relative losses from disease. Indian uprisings were relatively small and infrequent during this period of colonial history. Beals' "Second Colonial Indian Period," from about 1720 to 1820, is said to have been a time when Indians and Spaniards became more isolated from one another. The Indian communities closed, became more nativistic, and differentiated into the "infinite variety of the contemporaneous Mesoamerican Indian communities."

MacLeod (1973; 1980), in contrast with Beals, finds the seventeenth century to have been a time of isolation for the natives, as the Spaniards moved into the countryside to survive economic depression. The Indians were able to "reconstitute fairly autonomous cultures," though the native aristocracy began to disappear. Institutions like the *cofradía* and *caja de comunidad* ("community fund") helped integrate these communities, and served as "screen[s] behind which ceremonies and fiestas could be conducted without too much Spanish interference." The eighteenth century, on the other hand, was a time of increasing contacts between Spaniards and Indians as the economic pace quickened in the Guatemalan colony. Production for exporting, especially sugar, indigo, cochineal, and cattle, placed heavy labor demands on the Indians. In the fertile areas around Santiago de Guatemala, along the coast, and in the east, the Indians were heavily acculturated by such labor and became largely ladinoized during this period. Even in the highland Indian areas, there were increased acculturative pressures from oppressive taxes, forced buying and selling (*derramas*), and labor recruitment (e.g., *repartimientos* lasted very late in Guatemala). Traditional native cultural patterns were disrupted, and the Indians increasingly came into conflict with non-Indian peoples (creoles, mestizos).

Spurious Nature of Native Culture

A central issue raised most emphatically by Martínez Peláez (1970) has to do with the extent to which native community and culture were created by Spanish exploitation of the Indians. The argument is made that native cultural and language diversity was not aboriginal, and that traditional patterns of dance, dress, music, crafts—usually thought to be Prehispanic in origin—were actually inferior, inaccurate patterns resulting from colonial alienation. According to this view, the Indians were workers rather than peasants, and their cultures class- rather than ethnic-based. While Solano (1974) also thinks the Indians were proletarians, he stresses the

ethnic (and linguistic) nature of their structures. Indian cultures, especially as they developed in the eighteenth century, were an amalgam of native patterns that had been outwardly clothed with Christian forms.

Dynamic Nature of Class Stratification

Related to the same issue is Martínez Peláez' (1970) claim that class divisions *within* the colonial caste structure (Indians and Spaniards) provided the most important exploitative relationships. Thus, whereas *peninsulares* sought relatively limited tribute and labor of the Indians, creoles were much more oppressive because they depended on Indian land, labor, fees, and services for their very survival. They employed terror to maintain this exploitative relationship. Mestizos, born outside caste structure, were unable to form class structures, and so became outcasts, "*castas*." But as mestizos increased in numbers, they came to compete with the Indians for land, free labor, community office, and petty trade.

Mercantile Capitalism

The variable influence of colonial mercantile capitalism on Indian culture emerges as a related but additional issue. As noted above, MacLeod (1973) finds the history of Guatemala (and Central America) to have been dominated by the search for a key export crop, and the cyclic booms and busts were created by each successive one. The issue for the Indian may be seen in the dichotomy made by some authors between hacienda and plantation enterprises. The hacienda (*estancia, rancho*) was a limited capital investment, a conservative form that allowed the Spaniards to retract in time of economic depression. Indian cultures could flourish, even nativize, within a hacienda setting. The plantation (*ingenio, trapiche*) was capital intensive, geared to the export market. Indian cultures were rapidly transformed and natives ladinoized in the plantation environment.

58

This difference between haciendas and plantations has been used to explain the retention of Indian culture in the western highlands and its disappearance around Santiago de Guatemala, on the Pacific and Atlantic coasts, and in the East.

Indian Rebellions

A final issue to which Martinez Peláez (1973) and MacLeod (1980) have called attention is the role Indian rebellions played in colonial Guatemalan social life. Martinez finds them to have been endemic to all phases of the Colonial period and ascribes their cause to the abuses that went beyond the limits the Indians were able to bear. The argument is made that such rebellions did not alter colonial structure, but only functioned to warn the Spaniards that they had gone beyond practical limits. Adjustments were made all the way up the line—from native aristocrats to *corregidores* to the *audiencia* president, and on up to the Crown officials. Solano (1974) thinks the rebellions were primarily directed against the abuses of the Indians' own native leaders.

Let us now examine these issues in the light of the case studies.

TECPANACO CASE

Tecpanaco is a pseudonym for a large Quiche-speaking community typical of Indian communities in the western highlands of Guatemala. I have analyzed the documentary sources available in order to reconstruct the dynamic processes of colonial life there (Carmack 1979; 1982).

The idea that the Spanish conquest was partially seen by the natives as a liberation finds support in the Tecpanaco case. Natives from there fought under their provincial lord against the Spaniards, but rather quickly capitulated. They appear to have almost immediately switched to the Spanish side, and aided the conquistadores in the defeat of the ruling Quiche from Utatlan. Later, they continued their support of the Spaniards in the conquest of the Mams at Zaculeu and in quelling the rebellion of Quiche rulers at Totonicapan. The fact that a few slaves were taken from Tecpanaco suggests, perhaps, that there was some resistance to the Spaniards among the natives, but details are lacking. We have no evidence of any major revolt, however, indicating that the first contact with the Spaniards did not result in dramatic culture shock.

The population size of Tecpanaco at contact has been reconstructed at approximately 7,000–9,000, though these figures are highly speculative. Information on whether there were significant losses due to diseases prior to the conquest itself is totally lacking. Losses during the sixteenth century are estimated at 60–75 percent, as by 1587 there were 2,000 inhabitants in Tecpanaco. The decline was probably due to diseases, for the most part, and seems typical of highland losses in general. Also typical was a seventeenth-century revival, though it appears to have been very slow at first; by the end of the century the population still consisted of only about 2,500 persons. The eighteenth century was a time of rapid growth, with an increase of almost 100 percent, in fact. Tecpanaco had about 5,000 inhabitants by the beginning of the nineteenth century, and was closing in on the Prehispanic level. The pattern, then, is squarely within the general highland trends worked out by MacLeod.

Evidence from Tecpanaco indicates that Spanish rule might well be described as "indirect" until late in the Colonial period. The local native aristocracy (the "*caciques*") was allowed to continue, and we have a recorded instance of an extraordinary accession ceremony in which the first native lord was initiated as the Spanish-backed ruler (Recinos 1957:95–115). But the number of "royal" lineages was reduced to four (Vicos, Hidalgos, Calel, and Gómez), and their privileges diluted. It is also possible to document the step-by-step process by which the *caciques* were replaced as important rulers by the Spaniards and commoner Indians.

The Indian "*pueblo*" established at Tecpanaco was at first based largely on Prehispanic provincial divisions, but soon became reduced to a single center located in a formerly unoccupied zone. The old ward divisions (the twenty-two *amak'*) were also retained at first, but were later officially replaced by larger territorial divisions (four "*parcialidades*"). Franciscan missionaries indoctrinated the natives of Tecpanaco in the Quiche language and apparently allowed some religious syncretism to occur: e.g., there is evidence that the patron god of the Quiche state (Tojil) was syncretized with the town patron saint, Santiago, and the native goddess (Awilix) with Saint Isabel. Certainly much of the traditional religious structure remained in place, and even the most powerful collaborators with the Spaniards were basically "pagan."

The "First Colonial Indian Period" at Tecpanaco fits better with MacLeod than with the Beals and Solano model. There was accommodation with the Spaniards, and the Franciscan missionaries were well received. But *congregación* was very limited in its effects, and the Spaniards were largely kept out of Tecpanaco. The native elders were cooperative as long as community affairs were not much interfered with. Rebellions were small scaled and uncommon. Most conflict seems to have revolved around the *caciques*, who were opposed on numerous occasions by both the commoner Indians and Spaniards.

The "Second Colonial Indian Period" was definitely *not* one of increased separation between the Indians and Spaniards. Instead, the picture that emerges is one of increasing encroachment into native affairs by both Spaniards and creoles. The Spaniards tried to bring reform into government and religion, while the creole haciendas led to meddling in Indian land and labor affairs. Nativistic processes can be detected, but they were violent reactions to outside encroachments. And

they overlapped town boundaries, expanding to widespread regional movements (e.g., Tecpanacans participated in the Atanasio Tzul nativistic movement) (Contreras R. 1951). Thus, community cultural differences probably decreased rather than increased during this phase.

Martínez Peláez' argument that colonial Indian cultures were largely creatures of exploitation would seem to be exaggerated if judged by the Tecpanaco case. Much aboriginal structure persisted, largely through the valiant and continuous struggle by the Indians against Spanish attempts to destroy it. Native stratification, with the advantaged *caciques* at the top, was never completely destroyed; patrilineal clan structure remained the dominant rural social form; and customary ritual, including the traditional marriage rites, continued to be practiced in elaborate detail. As late as 1750, the "secular" priests at Tecpanaco observed that the Indians there were still "pagan" in both belief and practice. This view is consistent with an important social fact: the Indians were primarily peasants rather than laborers. The vast majority of them were subsistence farmers, and their labor obligations were relatively sporadic and light.

Martínez Peláez' emphasis on importance of "class" rather than "caste" divisions is appropriate for the Tecpanaco case. The creoles, not the Spaniards, became the landlord class relative to the Tecpanaco Indians and were their chief exploiters. They extorted their lands, misused them in labor, and controlled local political offices, although, as noted above, this exploitation was mild compared to that in other areas of Guatemala. The *caciques* also took on landlord class characteristics, which accounts for the continued conflict between them and the Indian masses. The mestizos, called "*ladinos*" at Tecpanaco, steadily increased in numbers and by the end of the Colonial period totaled about five hundred. They worked as artisans in town and as laborers on haciendas, thus forming small "petty bourgeoisie" and "rural proletariat" sectors. They were deeply resented by the Indians, who identified them with the creoles.

Class stratification within the Indian caste was significant too, even though it was only incipiently formed. Besides the landlord *caciques* mentioned above, a small quasi-bourgeois "class" emerged, consisting of artisans and merchants engaged in the production and trading of woolen goods. They opposed the Indian peasants on all the major issues, such as how to deal with Spanish encroachments. As discussed below, they constituted a radical element in Tecpanaco Indian society.

Mercantile capitalism of the hacienda form clearly defined the macrocosmic economic environment to which Tecpanacans were most closely tied. Haciendas rather than plantations dominated the region, as creoles surrounded the town with cattle and maize ranches beginning in the early part of the seventeenth century. They were rather humble enterprises, and, while causing the Indians some problems, they were far from devastating in their cultural influence. In fact, later the Indians were able to regain most of the lands lost to haciendas, native practices flourished, the community remained strong, and *mestizaje* was minimal. Even Church lands were relatively minor holdings, and mostly controlled by the Indian *cofradías*.

Indian rebellion was continual in Tecpanaco, but greatly intensified in the latter part of the Colonial period as the Spaniards strengthened their control over community life. Economic matters, such as tributes and land, were important, but the intensity of violence was most closely linked to the degree to which the Indians' cultural integrity was threatened. The issues were always quite local, and opposition was directed primarily against the creoles rather than officials of the Crown. The Indians never seem to have understood the wider issues. Leadership came from a small socioeconomic "class" broken off from the caste structure.

These "petty bourgeois" Indians used nativistic symbols to recruit large numbers of peasant Indians. They called for the elimination of all non-Indians from the community, a return to local political autonomy, and the establishment of a regional Quiche "king."

Perhaps Martínez Peláez is correct in saying that such movements did not alter the colonial structure, but they did improve conditions for the Indians locally by allowing more self-regulation. They never led to liberation in the modern sense, though they played a role in the gaining of independence from Spain.

CUCHUMATAN CASE

The mountainous northwestern region of highland Guatemala has long been culturally and historically distinct from the rest of Guatemala, and information on the colonial Indians from there provides interesting contrasts with other regions. For the summary to follow, I rely primarily on Lovell's (1980; also 1982) recent geographically oriented study of the region.

The conquistadores were certainly not seen as liberators by the Cuchumatan Indians. They aided the Quiche at first in offering resistance to the Spaniards and later fought at least seven bloody battles against the European invaders. There was also considerable joining together of "armies" to combat the Spaniards, as forces with as many as five to ten thousand warriors were reportedly organized. The Indians' unified opposition to the Spaniards was, perhaps, partly the result of the area's geographic isolation and the lateness of the conquest there. By the 1525–1530 period when the Cuchumatanes finally came under Spanish attack, the Spaniards' motives must have been quite clear. Little is known about the first years of Spanish control over the Cuchumatan Indians, or whether they experienced strong culture shock. The fact that there was an active *congregación* program in the area suggests the existence of widespread disruption of their highly dispersed settlements. *Parcialidades* of Indians speaking different languages were placed together in the same communities, and this must have created a difficult situation. Our evidence suggests that widespread "*decongregación*" took place in the centuries subsequent to *congregación* itself (carried out in the decade of th 1540's).

Lovell accepts the idea that there was substantial population decline among the Cuchumatanes, due to disease, even before the arrival of the Spaniards, though there is no direct evidence for this. His reconstruction of 150,000 total inhabitants for the conquest period (1525–1530), based on the size of native armies, seems more reasonable than the 260,000 figure estimated for the pre-disease year of 1520. Whichever figure is accepted, population declined precipitously during the next 150 years and numbered only about 16,000 in 1670. This represented a decline of almost 90 percent, a high figure for highland zones. Population began to grow slowly but steadily thereafter, reaching a total of about 30,000 by Independence. Thus, the Cuchumatan pattern corresponds to the highland one. The drastic decline is explained as resulting mainly from disease, especially the *gucumatz* and *matlazahuatl* plagues of the second half of the sixteenth century. But epidemic outbreaks continued all the way into the nineteenth century.

The extent to which the Spaniards applied indirect techniques to rule over the Cuchumatanes is not well documented. The first missionary work in the area was carried out by Dominicans, who were responsible for the ambitious *congregación* activity. By the end of the sixteenth century, however, religious jurisdiction for most of the forty Cuchumatan communities had been turned over to the Mercedarians, who were less missionary oriented. There is some evidence that town centers were laid out over Prehispanic temples and shrines, and that the ethnic *parcialidades* making up the new communities were allowed to retain cultural differences: they held land jointly, provided ritual services, collected tribute, etc.

Lovell's reconstruction of change in colonial Cuchumatan conforms to MacLeod's rather than Beals' model. Very early on, but especially during the seventeenth century, Spanish control over the Indians became weak. *Encomienda* rights and tribute and labor obligations were all relatively weakly developed. In their isolation, the Indians were able to create a "conquest peasant culture," synthesizing native and Spanish elements. There were reports of "wild and uncivilized" Indians living in the area, and of native shrines being used for "acts of barbarism." This situation is said to have prevailed without much change through the eighteenth century and up to Independence.

Lovell finds the Cuchumatan Indians to have been sociologically peasants during the Colonial period. Later obligations were never onerous, even less so than in other areas, presumably because of the area's remoteness and lack of major resources of interest to the Spaniards.

The issue of class and caste is not much discussed, though there is evidence of a small *cacique* class that survived at least into the seventeenth century and took on some Spanish ways. The question of mestizo encroachment into the Indian communities is also little discussed. There were few mestizos anyway, except around the only important urban center, Huehuetenango.

Mercantile capitalism in the Cuchumatan area primarily took the form of hacienda ranching. Plantations of size were apparently absent, and the small-scale production of tropical crops in lowland zones was carried out by Indians (e.g., in the Ixcan zone by Indians from Santa Eulalia). Mining of silver at Chiantla developed early and continued in limited scale throughout the Colonial period. Indian labor for the mines was obtained through debt peonage from the beginning, rather than through *repartimiento*. It may be significant that Chiantla was also the site of the most important annual fairs and markets of the Cuchumatanes during the Colonial period. Possibly the emergence of a substantial *ladino* sector in Huehuetenango was related to those developments. In general, however, the major Spanish economic institutions with which the Indians had to contend were agricultural and sheep haciendas. These became important during the eighteenth century, especially in the *altos* zone above Huehuetenango. The Indians labored as peons on the haciendas in small numbers, but more importantly they competed with creoles for land during the seventeenth century. Lovell's observation that the Indians were able to retain many of their lands and much of their community integrity despite the haciendas should be understood in terms of the capital-extensive nature of the hacienda institution.

The Cuchumatan Indians are said to have opposed Spanish control, but indirectly, through constant resistance to taking on European ways. Open rebellion appears to have been absent and, paradoxically, the only significant violence reported took place between different Indian groups. Land disputes in the late eighteenth and early nineteenth century between Indian communities, or between *parcialidades* within the same community, sometimes resulted in the burning of fields and houses and the taking up of small arms by one faction against another. The Spaniards found it difficult to mediate these disputes, but were able to control the violence.

Atitlan Case

The community of Santiago Atitlan, with its town center along the lake shore and rural holdings in the southern piedmont zone, provides the next case study. It is an especially useful case because the community territory included a lowland zone and a transitional highland zone. The summary to follow is taken from studies by Madigan (1976) and Orellana (1976).

The conquest of the Tzutujil Indians of Atitlan was relatively easy, and partly self-inflicted: they appear to have sent emissaries to Cortés to elicit his aid in the settlement of a serious internal land dispute they were having on the piedmont. The Atitecos pro-

vided at least moral support to the Spaniards in the war with their enemies, the Quiche, but later had to be forced into submission as the Spaniards threatened to burn their precious cacao fields. They appear to have remained loyal after that, and served the Spaniards in several important ways. Early contact between the Atiteco and Spanish cultures is described by Madigan generally as "a complex series of intricate exchanges accompanied with a filtering process."

Madigan's reconstruction of colonial Atitlan demographic trends corresponds with the lowland pattern outlined by MacLeod. From a Prehispanic population of about 50,000, the conquest brought a drastic 90 percent decline to about 5,000 in 1545. It is argued that the decline started before actual contact with the conquistadores. Disease is given as the primary cause of the decline, though forced migrations and other social dislocations were factors. Population continued to drop until late in the Colonial period (about 1780), from about 5,000 to 1,200. Epidemic cycles, as well as low birthrates due to "voluntary restraint" brought on by poor socioeconomic conditions, are given as the principal reasons for the continued demographic decline. Finally, population began to grow shortly before Independence (reaching 2,100 in 1821), as the plagues ran their natural course and the first vaccinating was introduced (as early as 1804 in Atitlan).

There appears to be some disagreement, or at least difference in emphasis, between Orellana and Madigan on the issue of indirect rule. Orellana suggests that much native political and social organization was allowed to continue. The native *caciques* continued to maintain the Prehispanic *señorío*, and the clans and many religious beliefs and practices persisted, largely through the syncretistic *cofradías*. The *señorío* lasted only into mid-sixteenth century, however, and the *caciques* and clans were gone by the end of the eighteenth century. Nevertheless, under the direction of the Franciscan priests, local-level town organization and religion retained much native structure. Madigan claims that

"Within the realm of political and societal organization, the Indian society underwent major transition. . . . The Spanish crown and the Church granted little quarter to these native institutions." Nevertheless, his detailed analysis of the colonial situation reveals that native institutions remained strong, as did the somewhat modified corporate community.

There were no distinctive "first" and "second" Indian phases in Atitlan, unless the sixteenth century is contrasted with the subsequent two centuries. Considerable Spanish interference in native affairs took place during the sixteenth century, primarily in the form of *encomienda* services and labor for the Crown and Church. With the decline of the cacao market in the seventeenth century, the Spaniards pulled back, and the Indians enjoyed much greater social space. This sociocultural isolation was only slightly interrupted by subsequent economic developments, such as in indigo or sugar production, partly because Atitlan lost its piedmont lands early (sixteenth and seventeenth centuries). Nor were the eighteenth-century political and ecclesiastical reforms of much consequence in the area, according to our sources. Orellana claims that the last two centuries of relative isolation led to fragmentation into small, discrete Indian communities, and to increased Spanish-native syncretism, especially through the *cofradías*. Belief in the native deities continued, as did clan sponsorship of processions embued with the Prehispanic patterns (Orellana 1975). So Atitlan remained strongly Indian, while its former lowland holdings became largely mestizo in culture and racial type.

Our sources, then, do not deny that native institutions were modified, but they clearly suggest that considerable native structure was retained within Atitlan colonial Indian culture. The Tzutujil Indians struggled to retain their ethnic identity as Atitecos, and this is described more in peasant than in class terms. The Indians of Atitlan were strongly affected by labor obligations in the sixteenth century, but after the decline of the *enco-*

miendas in the early seventeenth century the demands diminished. *Repartimiento* was weak, and labor on the lowland plantations took the form of seasonal work, partly to avoid tribute payments.

Our sources provide little information on either caste or class divisions affecting the Atitecos. The usual *corregidores*, priests, and *hacendados*, presumably creoles, were present, and after the sixteenth century they somewhat mildly exploited the Indians. But the forced selling (*derramas*), land *composiciones*, *repartimientos*, and various taxes and tributes were not excessive, partly, we are told, because Atitlan was not economically strategic to the colonial powers. The *caciques* hung on until at least the mid-seventeenth century, but we read little of them or of possible conflicts between them and commoner Indians. Nor do we learn of possible "middle classes" emerging within the Indian caste, except for a reference to certain Indians who dressed like *ladinos* migrating to the coast. Our sources are also silent on what role the mestizos may have played in colonial Atitlan social life.

Mercantile capitalism in the Atitlan area at first (about 1524–1630) took the form of cacao production, which the Spaniards exploited through the *encomienda* system. But cacao production itself remained largely in the hands of Indians, and other export crops such as sugar and indigo were locally too unsuccessful to generate large plantation enterprises. Nevertheless, coastal lands were quickly lost by the Indians, and native populations there rapidly disappeared (mostly through disease) and were replaced by mestizos. For the Atitecos around the lake the hacienda was the main external economic institution confronting them. They worked on wheat haciendas in neighboring highland zones, and provided some "free labor" on hacienda-like plantations in the piedmont zone. This activity did little to disrupt their community or cultural forms, and colonial Atitlan was basically a place of cultural traditionalism.

Unfortunately, our sources have nothing to

say about possible Indian rebellions at Atitlan. Presumably, organized violence was relatively infrequent and weak, though one also suspects that the topic has been neglected by these researchers.

SANTIAGO DE GUATEMALA CASE

Santiago de Guatemala is a special case, since the area was apparently not heavily populated Prehispanically. Many of the Indians resident there were brought in to provide labor for the ruling Spaniards, who made it their colonial center. The summary of events to follow and their relation to the issues outlined above is taken largely from studies by Lutz (1976; 1982).

The Prehispanic natives residing in the Panchoy Valley, where Santiago de Guatemala was later to be constructed, were subject to the Cakchiquel of Iximche. We know nothing of their reaction to the Spanish invasion, which was carried out at the invitation of the Iximche rulers. By 1527, when the Spaniards chose Panchoy as the site for their capital, the Cakchiquel were in revolt and the area was generally unpopulated. From that point on, Santiago was clearly a center of Indian exploitation rather than liberation. Indians were forcibly brought into the center, at first as slaves to labor on the *milpas*, and after 1549 as tenants to farm the wards of the new town. The only exceptions would be the Mexican Indians who aided the Spaniards in the conquest, who were settled in the Almolonga district, and a small number of Indians who fled to the city to carry out commerce and escape local tributes and other obligations.

As might be expected, Colonial period Indian demographic trends in the Santiago de Guatemala area are complex. The Indian population of the valley in 1549 consisted largely of some 3,000–5,000 freed slaves. There appears to have been some overall population decline during the remainder of the sixteenth century, but there were periods of both rises and declines as a result of

disease and abandonment of the area. For example, between 1574 and 1581 the number of Indian tributaries dropped from 2,663 to 2,300. In the wards closest to the city, the overall trend was one of substantial decline. The Indian population then stabilized and began to grow until the mid-seventeenth century. The increase was due to natural rather than migratory causes. The Indian population began to decline again after 1650 and continued to do so until Santiago was moved from the Panchoy Valley in the mid-1770's. Most of the decline occurred in the wards near the city, where losses averaged about 35 percent for the last century of occupation. Miscegenation with mestizos and other groups, combined with recurring diseases, caused the decline.

The Indian population of Santiago de Guatemala was brought there in order to serve the Spaniards, and an attempt was made to keep the Indians segregated from the Spanish and mestizo segments. Nevertheless, some indirect rule existed at the lower (ward) levels, and possibly there was even some political continuity from the indigenous past in the form of elite native *"principales."* The Mexican *caciques* who aided the Spaniards in the conquest were given special privileges with respect to self-rule. In general, Indian landholdings were newly granted by the Spaniards, with certain conditions attached to them, and interference in local rule was typical. Priests from the many monasteries interfered in native affairs even more than did secular officials. Native culture was relatively quickly lost, especially when compared with the case of the rural communities beyond the city's reach.

Lutz finds no support for the idea of a break between early Spanish-Indian "accommodation" and later "separation" phases. The Spanish attempted to establish separate "republics" in the mid-sixteenth century, but this failed from the beginning. Poor Spaniards and mestizos invaded the Indian wards where, through processes of miscegenation and culture contact, the Indians were progressively acculturated to Spanish ways. The process was exacerbated by decline of the Indian population and by absenteeism in order to avoid tribute and labor obligations.

The Santiago de Guatemala case would appear to conform closely to Martínez Peláez' view that the Indians' culture was created out of their exploited condition. Indeed, the Indians became workers for the Spaniards—slaves, tenants, servants, and laborers—but the palpable effect was not a spurious native culture. It was, rather, "*ladino*" culture. This was, then, a true case of "proletarianization," but one obviously different from the process occurring in the rural communities of colonial Guatemala.

As noted, the Spaniards attempted to maintain caste relations with the Indians, and the Indians felt the full force of legal discrimination; e.g., Indian crimes were dealt with swiftly by the judicial apparatus, while Spanish crimes were largely ignored. But the crucial social dynamic was the interplay between the mestizos and the Indians. Both groups tended to form laboring "classes" which inevitably coalesced, despite Spanish attempts to separate the "*castas*" from the Indians. There is some indication that the Indians recognized the advantages of merging with the mestizos (to avoid tribute and other obligations), and that this was an important factor in the class formation process.

Santiago was the directing center of colonial mercantile capitalism. The area itself, however, received only limited development of plantation agriculture, while haciendas specializing in wheat production were widespread. The effects of hacienda labor may have been small compared to the labor demands of the Spanish capital itself. Indian labor was needed for work in mines and on plantations elsewhere, to build and repair the city (which was damaged several times by earthquakes), to provide the domestic needs of the city elite, etc. Even in the relatively dispersed settlement system of the Guatemalan mercantile capitalist economy, labor demands from the urban center were consid-erable. Urban centers appear to have been roughly equivalent to the plantations in their cultural destructiveness, and this explains the radical acculturation of the Indians attached to the city.

Indian rebellion does not appear to have been an important factor at Santiago de Guatemala. The Indians were tightly controlled through the Spanish patronage system, the formation of a mestizo militia, and a strong native authority structure (with local police). In addition, the Indians were deeply fragmented, their wards having been thoroughly encroached upon by mestizos and poor Spaniards from the sixteenth century on.

OTHER CASES

Coverage of colonial Guatemala can be expanded by examining cases with more limited findings about Indians from other areas. While these cases do not permit discussion of all the major issues outlined above, they shed light on particular issues.

Totonicapan

Thomas T. Veblen's (1975) study of forest preservation in the Department of Totonicapan contains much useful information about Indian affairs there during the Colonial period. His study overlaps with my reconstruction of colonial Tecpanaco culture (see the case study above).

Veblen's (1977) reconstruction of demographic trends in Totonicapan parallels the highland model described by MacLeod. He hypothesizes a 50 percent decline in native population due to diseases even before the arrival of the Spaniards in Guatemala. Another 50 percent decline took place during the years of conquest, from disease, death in battle, and losses from harsh labor obligations. Still another 50 percent decline occurred between 1541 and 1570, for similar reasons. This represented an overall 80–90 percent loss in total population (from about

66

100,000 to 13,000). Population continued to drop until the mid-seventeenth century, as a result of cyclic disease epidemics, but thereafter slowly began to grow again (in fits and starts). By the second half of the eighteenth century, the demographic trend was one of rapid growth, total population reaching 30,000–40,000 by Independence.

Veblen documents some influence from Spanish mercantile capitalism on Indian culture of Totonicapan. Considerable European productive technology was adopted during the sixteenth century by the Indians, especially the growing of wheat and raising of sheep. The seventeenth-century depression brought increased numbers of Spaniards and *ladinos* into the area, and their presence, along with increased pressure on the land resources (since sheep herding and even wheat agriculture were less efficient than the traditional *milpa* horticulture), stimulated the development of crafts (especially carpentry and weaving) and trade. The Indians experienced economic growth and even some prosperity during the seventeenth and eighteenth centuries as a result of these "mercantile" developments. The Indians were also generally able to retain their forests and lands, though increasing demographic pressures led to land disputes between Indian groups. Native communities, on both the municipal and *parcialidad* levels, were able to protect their lands through collective ownership.

Central Quiche

My brief reconstruction of colonial Indian life in the central Quiche area (Carmack 1981:305–341) treats some questions relevant to the general issues being discussed here. In particular, evidence is found to support Beals' and Solano's claim that mutual accommodation was reached between the Spaniards and Indians during the sixteenth century. This is true despite the fact that the conquest period itself was devastatingly disruptive of Quiche social life at first.

I have documented the process by which the second generation of *caciques* at Quiche were able to obtain many of the old privileges of the native aristocracy. They retained the services of a goodly number of their traditional serfs, presided over political successions and judicial proceedings, collected tributes (albeit for the Spaniards), and continued to direct the writing of "books" (composed now in Latin characters). This form of indirect rule went quite far, and for a while during the sixteenth century the Quiche "king" actually presided in a room next to the president of the colony. There was also accommodation in religious matters, the missionaries allowing the Indians to retain much of their native religious structure in return for acceptance of external Christian forms. The *Popol Vuh* might be seen in this light as an example of how profoundly native beliefs were retained, with only minor syncretic additions.

This picture of developing Indian culture in colonial Quiche corresponds more closely with Solano's model than with Martínez Peláez', though admittedly my study was oriented to tracing cultural persistence. Haciendas were established in the area during the eighteenth century, but the Indians remained overwhelmingly peasants rather than laborers. The ancient ethnic lines—Quiche, Tamub, Ilocab—continued to have some effect, especially in the collective struggles to protect territorial boundaries. The old native aristocracy eventually lost out to more egalitarian rule, though they waged a concerted battle to retain their privileges all the way into the nineteenth century. Ancient rural structures, clans and cantons, were promoted to primary status within the emerging atomized, peasant-village organization. Simultaneously, religious beliefs lost their more general, "theological" features, though their populist forms were fundamentally native in origin. Peasantized transformations of native religion they may have been, but they were not proletarianized spurious alienations. The nativization of culture in the Quiche area was

67

already well established by the beginning of the eighteenth century.

Verapaz

Verapaz is a region that clearly experienced a different colonial history from other parts of Guatemala. The following summary is taken largely from Arden R. King (1974) and André Saint-Lu (1968).

The "peaceful" conquest of Verapaz would appear to approximate closely to Beals' ideas about "mutual accommodation" between Indians and Spaniards. After initial failures of military conquest, Las Casas and the Dominicans were allowed to pacify the Verapaz without secular Spanish interference. Beginning in earnest in 1544, the Dominicans were able during the next twenty years to convert most of the Kekchi and Pokomchi Indians to Christianity, to settle them in towns, and to control their social life. They were notably unsuccessful in the lowlands to the north, where the Chol, Manche, Mopan, and Lacandon Indians resisted Spanish contact until they were militarily bludgeoned into submission at the end of the seventeenth century.

Much more so than in other areas, the Indians of Verapaz became literate, conformed to the Christian sacraments (e.g., marriage), learned Spanish crafts, and became successful traders. At least for the sixteenth and seventeenth centuries, Dominican pacification seems to have worked. The Indians accommodated to Spanish institutions and became a relatively prosperous peasant-artisan class tied to the Church.

A few Spaniards had illegally entered Verapaz from the beginning, and by the eighteenth century they became an important social factor especially in the southern zone (around Salama). A prosperous sugar plantation flourished there, and though the Indians were not heavily involved in peonage, some were trapped into slavery on the plantation. During that century too, the Indians' zeal for the Church faded, partly because the missionary spirit had been lost and ecclesiastical affairs were poorly run. The Indians are said

to have abandoned the towns in large numbers for the countryside. Presumably, though we are not informed specifically on this point, strong nativistic tendencies were at work during this last century.

Central and Eastern Guatemala

The closest thing we have to an ethnohistoric study of the Valley of Guatemala area is Lawrence H. Feldman's (1971) dissertation on the "symbiotic" region of central and eastern Guatemala. In general, the study is ahistorical, for little attempt is made to study cultural forms in their temporal context, and most effort is devoted to reconstructing the hypothetical Prehispanic states of the region. Nevertheless, considerable colonial data are reviewed, and glimpses of colonial Indian life appear.

One of the issues for which Feldman's study is relevant is the question of whether or not colonial native culture was primarily a spurious creation of Spanish exploitation. Using dictionary sources for the most part, Feldman argues that much native economic production continued into the Colonial period. Some of the continuing "industries" were indigenous food cultivation, fur collecting, hunting, salt-making, honey production, cacao arboriculture, resin-making, gourd- and pottery-making, weaving, featherwork, mining of precious stones and metals, and ground stonework. District markets continued too, with ancient product specialization by community (eight districts are reconstructed), along with long distance trading in "exotics" (e.g., copal, salt, metates).

Feldman also takes up the issue of the capitalization of the Indian economy, a focus absent in most of the studies from other areas. He notes (all too briefly) the introduction into the native economy of "general purpose money," which, along with improved means of transportation and freer trade, transformed district markets into regional systems. This was part of a larger process of centralization by which Indians were tied to the political "commonwealth" of the colony. In this, Feld-

68

man's view seems to parallel Beals' claim that Spanish rule brought a certain degree of "prosperity" to and "accommodation" with the native culture.

CONCLUSIONS

Having "tested" with data from specific cases some of the general propositions about Guatemalan Indian colonial life proposed by historical scholars, I shall now attempt to draw some conclusions from the exercise. Since the experiment has been far from rigorously designed, and the data are all too incomplete, one cannot expect the "empirical generalizations" to have very high scientific status. But if they help give an idea of the progress to date in this field and cast some light on colonial Indian culture in Guatemala then, perhaps, the exercise is worthwhile.

It is clear from the case studies that little research has been devoted to the conquest period itself (ca. 1520–1541) (but see Sherman 1979 and MacLeod 1973). While it is true that some native groups sided at first with the Spaniards, others did not (e.g., central Quiches, Cuchumatan Indians). Some resistance from all the groups appears to have taken place subsequent to initial contact, and there can be little doubt that social disruption and cultural dissonance were profound during those first two decades. "Peace," "prosperity," and "mutual accommodation," if they came at all to any of the Indians of Guatemala, were largely relegated to the seventeenth rather than the sixteenth century (central Quiche may have been an exception). We may never know much about the first years of colonial life in Guatemala, because much documentation for that period of time appears to have been irretrievably lost.

MacLeod's rather than Solano's model for demographic trends in colonial Guatemala is generally confirmed by the case studies. We are left with the impression that lowland Indian populations may have actually disappeared *in toto* in many places. Highland Indian population declines also appear to

have been shockingly drastic, although I personally believe that Prehispanic figures have been reconstructed too high, making the declines appear higher than they actually were. Especially has there been too much speculation about large losses throughout the highlands because of the introduction of disease prior to the coming of the Spaniards. There is no firm evidence for this claim as yet.

The degree to which indirect rule was applied by the Spaniards with respect to the Indians appears to be more a function of Spanish strategic interest in an area than of general policy. This may be seen in the contrast between Spanish control of the Indians of the isolated Cuchumatan area and those living adjacent to Santiago de Guatemala. Our cases also suggest that active native opposition to Spanish intrusion in their affairs was a crucial factor in the development of a degree of native autonomy. Even the Indians of Santiago de Guatemala struggled for more self-rule, though without much success.

MacLeod's social phases are supported by these cases over those of Beals and Solano. Speaking generally, if there was a phase of isolation between Spaniards and Indians it would be primarily the seventeenth century. The sixteenth century presents a scene of widespread contact and dislocation until late in the century, while the eighteenth century saw a return to this condition on a greater scale. Thus, colonial nativistic institutions were laid down earlier than Beals and Solano had thought, and the struggles of the eighteenth century partly resulted from the Indians' attempts to preserve traditional cultural patterns. Of course, as MacLeod points out, where Spanish intrusion—especially economic—was too great (as around Santiago de Guatemala), such nativistic patterns were destroyed and the Indians acculturated.

The case studies lend little support to Martínez Peláez' claim that colonial Indian cultures were spurious creations out of their proletarian condition. The persistence of Prehispanic patterns is traced for such cases as Tecpanaco, Atitlan, Quiche, and central Guatemala, areas where also the Indians are shown to have been largely peasants rather than workers. In the two cases where there is a suggestion that much native culture was lost, Totonicapan and Verapaz, the social conditioning took the forms of craft specialization and commercialization rather than stringent labor obligations. Santiago de Guatemala is the one case where the Indians were definitely proletarianized, but their culture became *ladino* rather than "spurious Indian."

The case studies are disappointing with respect to what they reveal about the Indians' involvement in changing caste and class structures. Surprisingly little attention has been given to internal Indian stratification or the relationship of the mestizos to Indian social life (Martínez Peláez, of course, is the main exception to this). The Tecpanaco case suggests that commercialized Indian sectors may have formed a dynamic element in colonial life, especially during the eighteenth and early nineteenth centuries. It is perhaps implicit in all the case studies that the creoles and mestizos were in more direct relationships with the Indians than were the Spaniards, but the specific characteristics of these relationships are little investigated.

The claim that haciendas were less destructive of Indian cultures than plantations finds strong confirmation in our case studies. The Indians of Cuchumatan, Tecpanaco, Totonicapan, Atitlan, and Quiche were all primarily exposed to the hacienda structure and yet were able to function as nativistic communities. Urban centers emerge as a third major type of socioeconomic force affecting the Indians and, as suggested by Santiago de Guatemala and Huehuetenango, appear to have been as destructive of native culture as plantation enterprises. Our cases further suggest that the Indian economic system itself may have been capitalized far more than we had realized. This is indicated for the Indians of central Guatemala, Verapaz, and Totonicapan (for more on this issue with respect to Totonicapan, see Carol A. Smith 1972). In general, however, and with the possible exception of Madigan's study of the Atitlan Indians, specific cultural responses within the Indian communities and regions have not been studied in the context of the colony's cyclic economic patterns.

The case studies reveal relatively little about Indian rebellions. Nevertheless, they suggest that revolts were not as common during the seventeenth and first half of the eighteenth century as they were later on, and that questions of land tenure were often fundamental to the process. The Tecpanaco case suggests further that the native rebellions were not mere cyclic expressions of the need for relief from economic repression, as claimed by Martínez Peláez, or revolts against *cacique* rule, as suggested by Solano. They had their own complex internal political and social dynamics, and they were as much concerned with cultural as with economic preservation.

Indian revolts in Totonicapan associated with the Independence movement in Guatemala (Contreras 1951) hint that such events may have had a greater impact on general colonial politics than we have realized. The possibility that this may have been the case, and that it continues to be so today in Guatemala, gives an urgency to ethnohistoric studies of the colonial Guatemalan Indian not to be taken lightly.

NOTE

1. A number of general histories of colonial Guatemala and Central America have recently been prepared (e.g., Chinchilla Aguilar 1975; Woodward 1976; Sánchiz Ochoa 1976); along with most of the previous histories of colonial Guatemala (Milla 1937; Villacorta 1938; Bancroft 1866–1887; Batres Jáuregui 1920), they tend either to be narrowly narrative or to pay little attention to the Indians.

5. The Southern Maya Lowlands during Spanish Colonial Times

THE ETHNOHISTORY of the southern Maya Lowlands is at a crossroads. Older views of the region now appear unsatisfactory in light of important new information. However, this information is but a tip of the empirical iceberg that, once thoroughly explored, will certainly challenge the details of any synthesis that is attempted at this time. It is therefore less useful now to summarize a constantly shifting data base than to review the recent development of ideas in the region, to draw attention to important research developments, and to suggest future research directions.

The southern Maya Lowlands long appeared to have faded into obscurity during Postclassic times, while the northern Lowlands seemed to have increased in importance during the same period. It was therefore reasonable to assume that the focus of Spanish colonial activity in the northern Lowlands reflected these unbalanced circumstances. The Spanish system, that is, exploited the region that was richer in human resources and ignored a southern area of little importance since the "collapse" of the ninth century. However, recent Postclas-

sic period research indicates that some areas of the southern Lowlands remained active throughout that period. In addition, ethnohistorical studies demonstrate that parts of the southern Lowlands were heavily populated during the Colonial period and retained an essentially Postclassic way of life for nearly two centuries following the Spanish conquest of northern Yucatan. The Spanish found this region to be intractable and rebellious, a threat to the pursuit of colonial policies beyond its boundaries.

This chapter suggests that earlier perspectives on this region often distorted or ignored what is now obvious reality. Earlier research designs, it is argued, skewed our perceptions of the Colonial period Maya Lowlands taken as a whole. This brief critique hopefully provides a revised perspective from which new, more productive research may emerge.

While the emphasis of this discussion is upon Colonial period ethnohistory, knowledge of Preconquest circumstances is of such importance to an understanding of the impact of colonialism and the continuity of Preconquest tradition that the general state of research on the Postclassic southern Maya

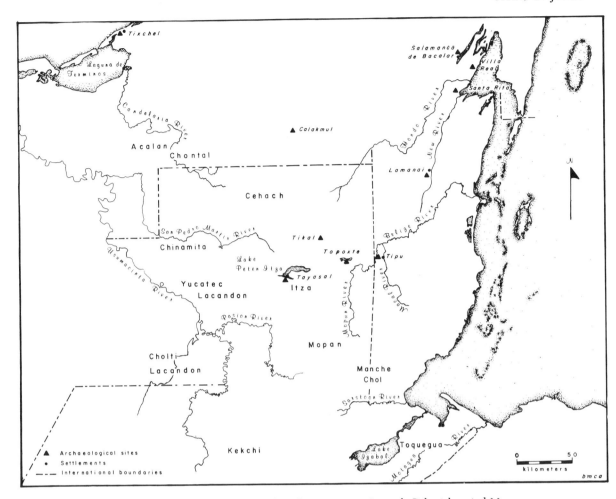

FIGURE 5-1. The southern Maya Lowlands indicating major Spanish Colonial period Maya groups.

Lowlands must be raised, however briefly. Recent archaeological and historical perspectives force us to recognize that activity was intense in the southern Lowlands on the eve of the Spanish conquest of northern Yucatan. Furthermore, the region's subsequent strong anti-Spanish posture through at least the close of the seventeenth century was itself an important factor in the operation of the larger colonial society, particularly that of northern Yucatan. Although the precise nature of Postclassic-Colonial period continuities and discontinuities is still poorly understood in the southern Maya Lowlands, such processes emerge as central to a larger, pan-Yucatecan,

historical and regional perspective. Earlier research designs have, unfortunately, seldom led to a productive exploration of the factors underlying these processes.

Although the southern Maya Lowlands have long been a stepchild of Maya research for all but Classic times, there is a limited tradition of research and speculation about the region in later times. Until recently, however, most of this research had been primarily a by-product of Classic-oriented research. For the Colonial period there is a growing recognition of the value of historical archaeology as a key to understanding the Postclassic-Colonial transition; but, like co-

72

lonial documentary research, such research strategies are still in their infancy. This situation is in stark contrast to the more advanced state of historical knowledge in the northern Lowlands, where serious efforts to combine archaeological and historical methodologies have prevailed ever since the initiation of the Carnegie Institution interdisciplinary research program in 1930. Even in northern Yucatan, however, little historical archaeology has been carried out that might bridge the Postclassic-Colonial gap; for this region the processes of early colonial impact remain known to us almost entirely through historical documentation. However, historical archaeology offers, when used in conjunction with documentary evidence, significant potential for a better understanding of the Colonial—as well as the Postclassic—period (cf. A. P. Andrews 1983).

This chapter, then, reviews the major traditions of research in the southern Maya Lowlands, attempting to account for the still nascent state of Colonial period research. Although the precontact question is addressed in general terms, the period of central focus begins with Hernán Cortés' 1525–1526 *entrada* through the Peten on his way from Coatzacoalcos to Honduras. That event marked the beginning of an extended period during which Postclassic traditions continued to thrive in certain areas, while colonial efforts to extend political, economic, and ecclesiastical controls were fragmentary and localized in both time and space.' The elusiveness of the region to direct colonial control did not end with the Spanish conquest of the Itza and their neighbors around Lake Peten Itza in 1697; nor was there a sharp break in the gradual eighteenth-century replacement of Spanish control of the eastern regions by British logging interests. The Maya remained a viable but poorly known force throughout the eighteenth century, fading into obscurity only shortly before the massive migrations of northern Yucatec Maya escaping the Caste War beginning in 1848 (Bricker 1981; Dumond 1977; G. D. Jones 1977; Reed 1964).

The region under consideration may be compared with that delineated for the Classic period southern Maya Lowlands. T. Patrick Culbert tentatively identified five archaeological zones within the Classic southern Lowlands, whose northern boundary he drew, roughly speaking, from the Laguna de Terminos up the Candelaria River to the northern boundary of the Peten, arching northward to include Calakmul and finally following the Hondo River northward to Chetumal bay (Culbert 1973:4–10). South of this line he distinguished the Central Zone, at the heart of which was Tikal; the Belize Zone, corresponding with the present boundaries of that country; the partially more upland riverine Southeastern Zone, including the sites of Copan and Quirigua; the Pasion Zone south of Lake Peten Itza and Belize; the Usumacinta Zone to the west of the Central Zone; the Southwestern Zone, environmentally external to the lowland context; and the Northwestern Zone, "northwest of the Maya Lowlands near the juncture of the Central Chiapas Highlands and the Tabasco coastal plain" (Culbert 1973:10). The southern and western boundaries of the region thus defined lie beyond the Maya Lowlands proper but were included in order to examine questions of trade and cultural contact with adjacent regions.

Such delineations are valuable for earlier periods (cf. Freidel 1979; Rathje 1971) but there is still insufficient archaeological and historical information to justify their extension in the Postclassic and Colonial periods. The only comprehensive attempt to redraw boundaries for the Colonial period has been that of J. Eric S. Thompson, who proposed a southern region of Yucatec-speakers to whom he gave the name Chan Maya (Thompson 1977:Fig. 1-1). Roughly speaking, the Chan Maya region included Culbert's Belize Zone, Central Zone, Usumacinta Zone, and northern Pasion Zone, along with a small area of the southern East Coast Zone. While the northern boundary of Thompson's Chan Maya region was linguistically vague, merging into similar but more northern Yucatec groups, much of the western and southern boundaries of the region was surrounded by speakers of variants of Chol and Maya.

COLONIAL PERIOD RESEARCH IN THE SOUTHERN MAYA LOWLANDS

Three recent research traditions may be delineated for the study of the Colonial period southern Maya Lowlands. The first of these emphasizes the ethnographic value of the Colonial period evidence for understanding various aspects of Classic period Lowland Maya society. This tradition, although hardly unified in terms of particular interpretations and methodology, seeks empirical continuities or analogies between the Classic and Colonial periods, while demonstrating relatively little concern for the historical processes that might have provided the substance of continuities or the structural basis for analogies. The second tradition focuses upon the problem of the transition from protohistorical conditions to those of early colonialism. Such an approach must, of course, rely on archaeological as well as historical documentation. Finally, there are studies which concern themselves with the effects of colonialism upon native society and—less frequently—with the active role of the native society in shaping the colonial society itself. These latter two approaches are complementary, of course, differing epistemologically from the ahistorical and analogical tradition in important ways.

The Classic-Colonial Connection

The bulk of earlier writings on the southern Maya Lowlands during Colonial times had as their primary concern the reconstruction of Classic Maya society and culture. There was little appreciation in these writings of the specific nature of the historical processes that bridged Classic and Colonial times. In fact, the Postclassic period—so apparently elusive in the archaeological record—was all but ignored in ethnohistorical studies in favor of the analogical potential of Colonial period

ethnographic data for a better understanding of the Classic Maya.

Most prominent among advocates for the Classic-Colonial "leap of faith" was J. Eric S. Thompson, whose interest in the ethnohistory of the region spanned nearly his entire career (1938; 1951; 1977). Thompson's work was often complex and always characterized by an interdisciplinary zeal seldom matched by others. Although this work is therefore difficult to characterize fairly in terms of simple thematic underpinnings, certain consistencies in his later writings suggest that the purpose of his ethnohistorical preoccupation was largely to clarify questions about the Maya Classic period. These aims are particularly apparent in three of his important later articles (1970:3–47, 48–83; 1977), although they may be discerned in earlier writings as well.

Thompson's most ambitious effort to bring ethnohistorical evidence to bear on archaeological questions was his influential and controversial "Putun (Chontal Maya) Expansion in Yucatan and the Pasión Drainage" (1970: 3–47). This article may well have done more to confuse than to clarify a series of empirical issues, including above all the actual identity of the "Putun," whose collective reality is often unquestioned in archaeological circles. I must skirt this controversy here in favor of a more general methodological observation concerning Thompson's ethnohistorical *tour de force*: That is, Thompson used a variety of Colonial period documentary sources, including native texts, to shed light on Late Classic activities in the southwestern Maya Lowlands and the eventual "abandonment of the ceremonial centers and the overthrow of the Maya nobility" (ibid.:4); the later establishment of Chichen Itza and related centers in northern Yucatan; the late migrations from northern Yucatan that established an "Itza" presence in the central Peten; and the survival of Chol speakers along the lower Lacantun River through the late seventeenth century. The Chontal Putun serve in Thompson's remarkable analysis to make sense of the principal population movements, political de-

74

signs and conflicts, and interregional systems of trade for the entire Maya Lowlands from the closing years of the Classic until the beginning of the Colonial era. Remarkably, however, only two lines of evidence hold together this vast undertaking—that is, bits of Late Classic evidence pertaining to the Pasion and Usumacinta river sites and Postclassic evidence from Chichen Itza, on the one hand, and a wide range of Colonial period documentation, on the other. It was a brilliant and plausible model, perhaps, but one formed with late documentary evidence stretched to the breaking point across vast territories (almost the entire southern Lowlands!) that were virtually unknown for the half-millennium comprising the Postclassic.

Thompson noted modestly that the ultimate correctness of his conclusions was of less importance than the fact that he had "drawn to a small extent on archaeology, but to a far larger extent on the rich and very extensive literature of the Colonial period. Students of the Maya past are extraordinarily lucky to have at hand such a wealth of ethnohistory; the archaeologist neglects it at his peril" (1970: 47). However, the use to which he put such evidence could provide but the weakest threads of language and custom to bridge poorly known times and spaces. For Thompson documentation was the key to understanding the remote past and its relationships with the ethnography written in those documents, but frequently he used this Spanish period evidence to cast illustrations upon the remote past rather than to unravel the complex, troublesome puzzles of historical process.

In his Huxley Memorial Lecture for 1966, written four years earlier than the Putun article, Thompson (1970: 48–83) utilized Colonial period data for a far less methodologically controversial purpose. Examining the entire southern Lowlands, he concluded that indigenous population loss due to European diseases amounted to about 90 percent in some areas by the beginning of the seventeenth century (ibid.:71). He thus challenged "the belief that the Central area was largely

deserted at the arrival of the white man" (ibid.), citing the origins of that belief in the mistaken impressions created in modern times by low contemporary population densities. In pursuing the lines of demographic evidence, Thompson also provided the first serious attempt to delineate ethnic and linguistic boundaries for the entire southern Lowlands.

As straightforward as his demographic conclusions appeared to be, they were actually to be used as support for his model of the expansionist Putun. Thompson argued that at the time of Spanish contact the southern Maya Lowlands (his "Central area") fell into "two sharply contrasting" types of polity:

On the one hand there are well-populated areas or provinces, each with a central and authoritarian political organization, and generally wealthy in terms of pre-Columbian values; in contrast to these are those areas in which each town or village is independent with no evidence of any supravillage organization. Towns are smaller than in the first category, normally not exceeding one hundred houses (probably spread over a wide area), and generally a hut of regular house type, although somewhat larger, serves as the temple. Population is considerably less dense and there is little evidence of wealth.

(J. E. S. Thompson 1970: 73–74)

Those in the first category (Potonchan and neighboring Tabasco; Naco, Nito, and the "coast from the Chamelecon River to the Rio Dulce" [Honduras], Chetumal; the Copan province; the inhabitants of Acalan-Tixchel along the upper Candelaria River; and the Itza province of Tayasal in Central Peten) were, Thompson maintained, Putun or Putun-influenced peoples. Those in the residual category ("the Manche Chol, the Mopan Maya, the Cehach, the Tipu and Belize River settlements, and the Lacandon-Prospero peoples") were, on the other hand, descendants of those Classic period peoples who had been overcome by the Putun expansionists (ibid.:76–79). The small number of such survivors of the Great Classic popula-

75

tions was due in large part to "a lack of will to live after the old cultural pattern of life based on the ceremonial center ended" (ibid.:81).

Thompson's preoccupation with the use of ethnohistoric evidence as a key to understanding the Classic-Postclassic discontinuity led to misleading conclusions. Most serious was his failure to distinguish between ethnicity and political economy: as, for example, at Chetumal, where a possibly Putun-affiliated elite ruling group probably controlled a wider economic system in which the bulk of producers were non-Putun Yucatec. Similar situations may have also characterized the central Peten, where so-called Itza rulers controlled trade relations and some production in a region that was certainly non-Putun in ethnic composition. Thompson's claims for ethnic identity among the ruling elites of the southern Maya Lowlands at the time of Spanish contact were based on the thinnest of evidence, while he chose to ignore the much stronger evidence for the dynamic political and economic relations between dominant, expansionist groups and the subject groups that they dominated. Ethnic continuity is an elusive goal to seek—and a far less interesting one, it might be argued, than the history of human relations as an aspect of processes of political and economic change. The Putun may have played a role in such processes; however, Thompson's definition of them as an ad hoc collection of diverse peoples may well have obscured the complexities of ethnic and political economic change that must have characterized the southern Maya Lowlands during Postclassic times.

In his last major ethnohistorical synthesis, Thompson (1977) revised his earlier thinking and produced a new synthesis of the colonial documentation for the "Chan Maya" region (see above):

It is here advocated that in vocabulary, pronunciation, personal names, religion, and religious practices the Maya speakers of variant forms of Yucatec in the Petén and adjacent Belize, including the so-called Itza,

as known to us from colonial sources and present-day observation, are closer to the Mopan Maya than to the Maya of Yucatán. Consequently, it is proposed that those Petén Maya, the Mopan Maya, the Cehach, the Chinamita, and the Yucatec-speaking Lacandon should be constituted a subgroup, related rather closely to the Yucatec Maya but attached with considerably looser bonds to the Putun and Chol-speaking groups to their west, south, and southeast.

(J. E. S. Thompson 1977:3)

This article remains today the best general synthesis of the distribution of languages and ethnic groups in the southern Maya Lowlands, although some specialists will continue to argue over specific points (see ibid.: Fig. 1-1). Furthermore, Thompson's virtuosic display of the then available Colonial period documentation was not marred, as it had been earlier, by a preoccupation with "Putun" invasions and expansion. The Putun, in fact, deserved only two brief references; even the "so-called Itza" of Lake Peten were no longer associated with the Putun, as they clearly spoke a dialect of Yucatec (ibid.:22).

Yet Thompson, in apparently casting aside the Putun argument, became even more fully committed to direct historical and ethnographic continuities between the Classic and Colonial periods. The Chan Maya, he argued, were indeed more like the northern Yucatec Maya than the Chontal-Chol in language, political organization, and other cultural aspects; their modern ethnographic counterparts, however (the modern Yucatec Lacandon and the Mopan), were not northern Yucatec Maya but rather direct descendants of the Chan Maya of Colonial times. The Chan Maya, in turn, were direct descendants of the Classic Maya of the same geographic region, preserving even some of the original political boundaries of the Classic period!

I would go so far as to suggest that those provinces of Uaymil and Chetumal reflected political groupings of the Classic Period, the former recognizable by the Río Bec and probably Chenes architecture (we do not know Uaymil's western boundaries); Chetumal, by Petén affiliations. Indeed, I had that in mind in drawing the central portion of the Chan northern border, for colonial sources tell nothing on that matter.

(J. E. S. Thompson 1977:37)

Because few Maya scholars could accept such speculation on Classic-Colonial continuities, there is danger that Thompson's otherwise significant contribution to southern Lowlands colonial ethnohistory might be unjustly lost.

In several recent papers and an extensive and useful bibliography, Nicholas M. Hellmuth (n.d.; 1970; 1971; 1972; 1977) attempted to provide evidence for the contention that the study of Colonial period documents is of value primarily for their use in reconstructing Classic period Maya society. Writing of materials on sixteenth- and seventeenth-century Peten that he had located in the Archivo General de Indias, he noted that

Eyewitness observers described in vivid detail population, settlement pattern, architecture of residential and ceremonial buildings, religious rites, political organization, trade, and other aspects of contact period Maya life. Numerous newly found censuses contain birth, marriage, family and death facts plus other information needed for thorough comparative demographic studies. This information will necessitate revisions of current models for supposed lowland Maya behavior and will provide factual data with which archaeologists can propose more reliable reconstructions of the Classic Maya way of life through ethnographic analogy.

(Hellmuth n.d.:1)

Hellmuth's intention in organizing and presenting the data was to correct any misapprehensions, which were all too current in the 1960's, that Landa's *Relación* (Tozzer 1941) was a reliable source as an ethnographic analogy for the southern Lowlands (Hellmuth 1970; 1972:222). Like Thompson, he believed that "the 16th century populations of the Southern Maya Lowlands were direct descendants of Maya of the Classic Period" (1970:n.p.), and that ethnographic analogies for archaeological reconstruction should be based upon the ethnohistoric analysis of records pertaining directly to the region. Whether or not this assumption was correct, Hellmuth's insistence that the source materials for the region should be studied in depth can hardly be faulted. However, one might well question whether the production of a series of detailed purely descriptive ethnographies based on these sources, as suggested by Hellmuth, was either possible or desirable (Hellmuth n.d.:12; 1970). The value of most Colonial period documentation lies less in its ethnographic data than in the information provided on the relationships among colonial people and forces. To extract descriptive ethnography from its political economic context in the hope of providing pure analogy for an earlier period is to deprive the documentation of its greatest value.

In a paper delivered in 1976 (G. D. Jones 1979), I considered the Classic-Colonial analogy from yet another perspective. Rejecting various attempts to utilize ethnographic analogies from contemporary Tzotzil Maya in highland Chiapas in reconstructing Classic Maya society, I also rejected—as I do now—static applications of ethnohistoric analogies to earlier social forms. Arguing, with Barbara J. Price (1974), that any ethnographic analogy must be tied with its archaeological counterpart by demonstrated direct historical continuity, I wrote that

One of the principal failings of most previous attempts to develop models from Maya ethnohistory and ethnography has been the static nature of the analogies drawn. Until structural forms that are discerned at any one point in time can be analyzed as particular adaptations to conditions of the moment, and until a sequence of such structural adaptations can be reconstructed for a given area over a significant period of time, the results of applying such analogies to the archaeological framework will be deficient in the realms of direct historical application and explanation. I therefore suggest to lowland Mayanists that while ethnohistorical and ethnographic analogies for the southern lowlands may eventually add major insights into archaeological studies of processes of social organization, archaeologists should demand of ethnohistorians and ethnographers nothing less than full scale longitudinal studies of postconquest structural adaptations in their own territory.

(G. D. Jones 1979:84)

In this context I explored the gradual decline of the political and economic power of the Itza polity between 1525 and 1697—from Cortés' *entrada* to the Spanish conquest of Tayasal. This decline, an outcome of indirect Spanish policies beyond Itza borders, resulted in the gradual collapse of centralized political institutions before the 1697 conquest, and in their total collapse in the years immediately following. That level of sociopolitical integration that survived may have been equivalent to nineteenth-century Yucatec Maya "major settlement clusters" described elsewhere (G. D. Jones 1977).

Ethnographic analogy, I maintained, must be based upon the comparison of such processes of centralization and decentralization at different points of Maya history (G. D. Jones 1979:92). Such comparisons would be similar to John C. Harsanyi's use of "comparative dynamics" as a form of explanation in the social sciences (Harsanyi 1960). The similarities between the Colonial and earlier periods would lie, that is, in the transformation processes that led to centralization and decentralization of political and economic institutions. Today I would approach such a contention with considerably more caution, for unless the conditions characterizing the two periods are truly comparable (the judgment of which is problematical), any analogical conclusions would be misleading. At least until both the Postclassic and the Colonial southern Lowlands are understood much more fully, such comparisons can be attempted only with considerable peril. I would

still maintain, however, that colonial ethnohistory in the region must have as its primary objective the study of *colonial processes* of social, political, economic, and ideological change—not the study of trait distributions either as ends in themselves or as models for the study of cultural survivals. Such descriptive work will remain essential to the larger effort but should not overshadow the wider historiographic problems of Colonial period ethnohistory.

The Postclassic-Colonial Transition

In contrast to those who have treated Colonial evidence largely as a key to questions of Classic period archaeology, a handful of researchers have considered the historical problem of the transition of the southern Maya Lowlands from Postclassic to Colonial times. The transition problem is a methodologically troublesome one, for even though it substitutes the direct historical approach for the analogical one, it requires the analytical and empirical synthesis of both archaeology and ethnohistory. The methodology has recently been referred to as the "conjunctive approach" of archaeology and ethnohistory by Robert M. Carmack and John M. Weeks (1981), who discuss the benefits and problems of the approach as applied to the study of the Quiche capital of Utatlan in the Guatemalan highlands (cf. Carmack 1981).

George L. Cowgill's important dissertation, "Postclassic Period Culture in the Vicinity of Flores, Peten, Guatemala" (1963), remains the only study to date that makes a major effort to correlate Postclassic archaeological evidence with the readily available ethnohistorical data for the Lake Peten region. As one of a handful of such studies for the entire southern Lowlands, this study stands out as a pioneering effort of major proportions.

The effectiveness of Cowgill's approach was limited by the fact that his archaeological evidence for Postclassic occupations came primarily from surface collections. Nevertheless, he was able to demonstrate the presence of significant deposits of Postclassic ceramics at the Itza capital of Tayasal itself (the island of Flores), at San Miguel opposite Flores along the shore of the so-called Tayasal peninsula, at Santa Elena and San Benito, and on Lake Sacpuy west of Lake Peten (Cowgill 1963:11–71). The identification of the Postclassic ceramics with the ethnohistorically known Lake Peten Maya posed a major problem for Cowgill and remains something of a puzzlement even today. While Cowgill's attempt to resolve this problem and his efforts to assess the possible nature of Itza migrations from northern Yucatan as reported in native documents are by no means the last word on the subject, his analysis was well informed and provocative (ibid.:128, 444–471). Cowgill's study was cogently reviewed in an excellent unpublished paper by Michael G. Hotchkin (1978), who also reviewed more recent archaeological investigations of the Peten Postclassic.

The principal stumbling block to the application of a "conjunctive approach" to the southern Lowlands has been the paucity of archaeological data for either the Postclassic or the Colonial period. Much of the Postclassic research, scant as it is, is summarized by William R. Bullard, Jr. (1973), Grant D. Jones, Don S. Rice, and Prudence M. Rice (1981), and Arlen F. Chase (1976; 1985a; 1985b). Although Bullard, who carried out archaeological studies at Topoxte on Lake Yaxha and at Macanche, was certainly interested in the Peten Postclassic as a tradition distinct from that of the Classic, he explicitly accepted Thompson's earlier views on the non-Putun Maya:

My impression is that the Postclassic people of Peten existed mainly in peasant-level groups without strong social class differences or strong political controls. They seem to have been relatively isolated from the major cultural events which occurred elsewhere in the Yucatan Peninsula; there are no indications that they had appreciable influence on other Maya groups. In Thompson's (1967) characterization of Protohistoric Maya

groups, they would rate as "static" rather than as "expansionist."

(Bullard 1973:241)

Bullard regarded such "static" populations as ethnically distinct from the "small expansionist 'elite' groups" from northern Yucatan who may have founded Topoxte and the Itza presence at Tayasal in Late Postclassic times (ibid.:241). Such conclusions, however, were based on the thinnest of archaeological grounds and with little convincing continuity between historical and archaeological sources of data. At worst, the negative connotations of the terminology employed were likely a factor in the continuing lack of interest in the archaeology and ethnohistory of areas beyond the Itza-dominated central lakes region.

Arlen F. Chase's recent proposal (1976) that the Itza capital of Tayasal was located on Topoxte in Lake Yaxha and not at the generally assumed location of Flores in Lake Peten Itza raised again the Postclassic-Colonial transition as a subject for serious study in that region. Although his interpretation of the locational question was countered with a battery of detailed ethnohistorical evidence (Jones, Rice, and Rice 1981), the authors of that critique could offer little to clarify the archaeological side of the question. The critique, however, raised questions about the uses of ethnohistorical methodology and the promise for improvements in the dovetailing of archaeological and ethnohistorical research designs. The Rices' recent archaeological work at Topoxte, Macanche, and Lake Salpeten (P. M. Rice and D. S. Rice 1985; D. S. Rice and P. M. Rice 1980; 1984) has done much to clarify the Late Postclassic temporal sequence (c.f. A. F. Chase 1979; P. M. Rice 1979a; 1979b), although that research has not yet been able to demonstrate evidence of the Postclassic-Colonial transition itself. Positive demonstration of that transition in the central Peten is now but a matter of time, for the locations of several historically occupied sites have in all probability been identified.

Archaeological study of the Late Postclassic site of Santa Rita, believed by some to

79

be the site of Chetumal, may also ultimately clarify the Postclassic-Colonial transition (D. Z. Chase 1981; 1985). Occupational continuity into Colonial times at Santa Rita, however, might be difficult to demonstrate even if that site were the ancient Chetumal; Chetumal itself was very likely abandoned by its indigenous inhabitants even before the devastations wrought by the Pachecos in their violent conquest of the region in 1544 (Chamberlain 1948:234). It has been suggested that the Spanish town of Villa Real, inhabited briefly at the site of Chetumal twelve years before the Pacheco conquest, might have been at the site of that name located along the coast north of present-day Ciudad Chetumal (Bautista Pérez 1980; Escalona Ramos 1943; 1946). However, Villa Real was almost certainly the mission settlement of Tamalcab, while Chetumal was in all probability on or near Corozal Bay (Jones 1984a).

The Royal Ontario Museum's current excavations at Lamanai (Indian Church) on New River Lagoon in Belize have demonstrated a remarkable continuity of Maya occupation from Preclassic through historic times (Pendergast 1975; 1977; 1981; 1985). Lamanai was a center of major proportions throughout the Postclassic and was under Spanish colonial control from the mid-sixteenth century until the outbreak of rebellion throughout the region in 1637. The recently discovered site of Tipu on the Macal or Eastern Branch of the Belize River in western Belize indicates continuous occupation from at least the Middle Postclassic through the eighteenth century and perhaps even later. Both Lamanai and Tipu were *visita* missions, first mentioned in 1582 in a list of *visitas* under the secular *curato* of Bacalar (Scholes et al. 1938:63). Both sites are documented in a variety of presently available Colonial period sources (reviewed in G. D. Jones 1982; 1983; 1984a). Postclassic-Colonial period sites such as these, neither of which suffered the degree of later occupational destruction present at Flores, the site of Tayasal, offer significant promise for the

application of a combined archaeological-ethnohistorical approach to the study of the Postclassic-Colonial transition. I return at the close of this section to the question of model-building and research design that might make the study of these historic sites most fruitful in the years to come.

Colonial Transformations in the Southern Maya Lowlands

Although efforts to assess the Postclassic-Colonial period transition are barely under way, there is an older tradition of ethnohistorical writing that documents the impact of Spanish colonialism on indigenous society. However, these studies have been few in number, and they have tended to concentrate on areas closer to centers of Spanish control, along the fringes of what has continued to be regarded by many as a vast, unknown frontier. The core area of that frontier, with few exceptions, has eluded intensive examination and remains as poorly understood for later periods as for protohistoric times.

One such work stands out, over forty years after its publication, as seminal to our understanding of the Colonial period. France V. Scholes and Ralph L. Roys' monumental *The Maya Chontal Indians of Acalan-Tixchel: A Contribution to the History and Ethnography of the Yucatan Peninsula* (1948) was one of the truly distinguished products of the Carnegie Institution of Washington's programs of archaeological and historical research that dominated Maya studies for nearly thirty years (Carnegie Institution of Washington 1930–1950; 1950–1958). As an examination of the interaction of European and native society along the northwestern fringes of the southern Maya Lowlands, it is of central importance for all subsequent writing on the area, past and future. No ethnohistorical study of the area has approached the depth of scholarship and knowledge displayed in this remarkable work. The authors' use of previously unknown Colonial documents, including native sources, was virtuosic and

80

encyclopaedic, and their historiographic caution was impeccable.

Most of *The Maya Chontal* comprised a detailed historical analysis of the Chontal-speaking Acalan settlements along the Candelaria River under Spanish rule and their ultimate removal in the late 1550's to Tixchel on the Gulf Coast near Laguna de Terminos. They provided much rich ethnographic documentation, including data on the long-distance riverine trade networks of the Acalan merchants, the influence of Mexican cultural features, details of political inheritance and internal political organization, and the size and precise location of the Acalan towns. There can be little doubt that much of this material directly influenced Thompson's writing on the so-called Putun Maya (J. E. S. Thompson 1970).

Embedded in Scholes and Roys' detailed historical documentation was a perceptive account of the effects of Spanish colonization, especially in the areas of missionization, *encomienda* organization, and population loss. In addition, the authors extended their net beyond the Chontal-speaking region to examine the Paxbolon-Maldonado papers, which document the Missions of Las Montañas, a set of early-sixteenth-century missions in the interior Yucatec-speaking Cehach region. Their description of these missions provides the best documentation to date of the complex interplay of indigenous and migrant Yucatec Maya activity in the face of frontier zone colonial missionization.

The *Maya Chontal* was a pioneering work of great importance, for it established both a high level of scholarship and a full commitment to the study of the impact of colonial activity on indigenous Lowland Maya groups. The coverage was exhaustive in scope for much of the northern half of the Peten and adjacent areas of Mexico. As analysis, however, the study was less satisfactory than as thorough description. Historical events, ethnographic details, and insights on the effects of Spanish activities on the indigenous society were often intermixed in hodgepodge

fashion, and the reader emerges with little sense of the role of this region in a larger view of the structure and process of the total colonial society.

Just as Scholes and Roys' study focused upon the northwestern fringes of the southern Maya Lowlands (the Candelaria River zone Chontal and the Yucatec-speaking Cehach [cf. Villa Rojas 1962]), Jan de Vos' recent chronicle of the Spanish conquest of the *selva lacandona* concentrates upon the western fringes of that larger region (de Vos 1980). Far more than a study of conquest, de Vos' work provides a meticulously documented description of the sixteenth- and seventeenth-century struggle of the Chol-speaking Lacandon of the upper Usumacinta River area to maintain their independence from secular and ecclesiastical forms of colonialism (cf. the brief but most useful review of these events in Bricker 1981:46–52). The study is a model of major importance for those who sense that rich primary source documentation might be available for other regions on the frontiers of colonial control. That the *selva lacandona* was itself a central aspect of the wider Guatemalan colonial system—a "dangerous" frontier of indigenous as well as highland fugitive migrant apostates—emerges clearly as a central theme in the conquest process.

On this frontier there was ultimately no refuge for independent Maya, whatever their origins. The final 1695 conquest of Sac Bahlan (or Sac Balam, Nuestra Señora de los Dolores), the last major Chol Lacandon settlement in the region, represented the virtual annihilation of the western Chol frontier of the southern Maya Lowlands and the initiation of pacification activities that would lead to extermination of the frontier population by the end of the eighteenth century.

De Vos, in addition to providing a thorough account of the Chol Lacandon frontier during the Colonial period, also provides a useful but brief ethnographic synthesis (1980:169–204). In addition, he presents a valuable synthesis of the "Lacandon problem," that is, the issues of origin concerning the contemporary Yucatec-speaking Lacandon population and the seventeenth-century Yucatec-speaking inhabitants of Nohha or Prospero (ibid.:227–246; cf. Nations 1979).

Several recent contributions also explore the Colonial period ethnohistory of the southeastern boundaries of the southern Maya Lowlands, particularly in the lowlands of Alta Verapaz, Izabal, southeastern Peten, and southern Belize (Bricker 1981:36–38; Feldman 1975; 1978; King 1974:21–27; Saint-Lu 1968; J. E. S. Thompson 1974). Spanish conquest of this region began in earnest during the 1570's, and missionary, reduction, and relocation activities were intense throughout the next century and a half. Lawrence H. Feldman (1981:5), who has recently consulted Spanish primary sources on the region, has pointed out the importance of the surviving Manche Chol settlements north of Lake Izabal and in southernmost Belize well into the seventeenth century. Documentation of the colonial experience of the Mopan, Cahabon region Kekchi, Motagua River Toquegua, and Mache Chol is well under way, but there is still no thorough examination of this area in print.

To these studies of the boundary regions of the southern Maya Lowlands may be added my own recent attempts to reconsider the broader questions concerning the protracted nature of the conquest of the Central Lakes region of the Peten, the heartland of Itza resistance that remained unconquered until 1697 (G. D. Jones 1982; 1983). Central to this reconsideration is a recognition that Spanish failure to conquer the central Peten, despite early conquest "successes" in the Acalan Chontal and Cehach regions to the north and northwest, in the Chol Lacandon *selva*, and in the Verapaz lowlands and neighboring regions, was due in part to a reliance on the northern Belize riverine Yucatec Maya communities as the strategic route through which the Itza conquest would ultimately be pursued. The Belize Missions subregion (G. D. Jones 1982) was the most crucial boundary or fringe area of the southern Maya Lowlands insofar as the final conquest of the "last fron-

tier" of the central Peten was concerned. The following paragraphs explore briefly the evidence that may tentatively support this perspective.

At the time of Cortés' spectacular march across the central Peten in 1525–1526, the Itza Maya and their closest neighboring allies were without doubt the politically and economically dominant peoples of the southern Maya Lowlands. The Itza rulers themselves, known by the title Can Ek, claimed to be direct descendants of northern Yucatec Maya who had migrated to the region, perhaps at the time of the collapse of Mayapan in the mid-fifteenth century (López de Cogolludo 1688:Bk. 9, Ch. 4). At the time of Cortés' *entrada* these rulers engaged in and perhaps even controlled trade relations over a vast area from Acalan and the Cehach region to the north to at least as far south as the Sarstoon River (H. Cortés 1976:243–245). The content of this trade is still not entirely clear, although cacao was probably the principal product imported from the southern allies of the Itza and other Lake Peten Maya. Over the next century this trade network gradually collapsed as Spanish conquest activities in the northwestern and northern frontier zones as well as the southeastern frontier areas weakened the external political and economic alliances of the central Peten core region.

However, these early Spanish conquest activities, which simultaneously destroyed what appears to have been an extensive Chontal and Chol-dominated overland trade route along the western and southern fringes of Itza-dominated territory and perhaps along the Caribbean Coast to the east as well, may have created an increased dependence of the Itza upon the riverine trade routes between Belize and Chetumal Bay. The Spanish soon recognized the significance of this region as a strong potential front for external Itza economic and political alliance. Although at present we understand little about the content of these alliances in protohistoric and Early Colonial times, it is clear that by the early seventeenth century northern and western Belize provided a "natural" trade route to the central Peten from Chetumal Bay along the Hondo River and the New River and a short distance overland to the upper branches of the Belize River (the Mopan River and the Macal River). The successful Maya struggle for control over this region in the seventeenth century was a critical factor in the protracted conquest of the Itza.

The roots of Spanish conquest in this important riverine zone may be traced to Alonso Dávila's unsuccessful efforts to subdue the Chetumal region and the neighboring Uaymil province in 1531 and to the subsequent brutal conquest of the same area in 1544 (Chamberlain 1948:99–127, 232–236). Recent research suggests that the 1544 conquest under Melchor Pacheco reached at least as far as Tipu, which was the most important town of the province of Dzuluinizob (G. D. Jones 1984a). To the Dzuluinizob towns along the upper Belize River fled Maya refugees from the new *encomiendas* around Bacalar and from northern Yucatan. A massive rebellion in 1546, affecting Spanish-controlled Maya communities from Bacalar north to the Sotuta-Cupul region of eastern Yucatan, further stimulated the formation of a vast network of Maya refugee settlements isolated from Spanish control in the riverine areas of northern Belize (G. D. Jones 1983). Such north-south migration continued over the next century, creating a constant influx of Yucatec-speakers, nobility and commoners alike, into Belize and adjacent areas of present-day Mexico and Peten.

It was on the basis of Colonial period information concerning the northern half of Belize that Roys constructed the extensive boundaries of the "Chetumal province," an area that he considered to be of protohistoric significance (Roys 1957:157–165). Recent analysis suggests that the southern boundary of Chetumal was at the southern end of New River Lagoon and that south of this was the province called Dzuluinizob (G. D. Jones 1984a). It is not known whether in 1531 the Chetumal area was under the control of the Chontal Acalan–affiliated elite at Chetumal

or of the Itza of the central Peten, or whether it was independently allied to either one or both of these seats of power. In any case, the effect of the conquest events of the 1530's and 1540's was to create a hostile region of Yucatec-speaking Maya of both local and northern origins. Our knowledge of this region as a zone of colonial activity begins in 1582 with the appearance of a list of nine or more secular *visita* missions south of the mouth of the Hondo River. I have suggested that this area, controlled by the *cura* of Bacalar, be designated the Belize Missions subregion (G. D. Jones 1982:282).

The indigenous non-Christians of the Belize Missions subregion and their apostate brethren from the north found themselves in a classic frontier situation, bordered on their flanks (with the Itza to their west and the Spanish to their north) by powerful, expansion-oriented neighbors. Over the next century, events indicate that this frontier population, apparently dominated by elite northern Yucatecan cacao planters and traders, took advantage of this situation in an equally classic fashion, attempting to maintain political and economic independence against a set of ever-increasing odds. Spanish interests in the region were twofold: On the one hand, the *encomenderos* of Bacalar (see Gerhard 1979:69) viewed the extensive production of high-quality cacao throughout the area as a potential source of tribute collection. On the other hand, the establishment of permanent missions and other forms of colonial control was seen as a means for pursuing, along the riverine routes to the Peten interior, the eventual conquest of the Itza.

Events, however, eventually turned to favor the interests of the Maya population. Following unsuccessful Franciscan efforts in 1618 to evangelize the Itza with the support of the leading inhabitants of Tipu—the most important of the cacao-producing *visita* towns of the Belize Missions subregion—the area grew increasingly hostile to all forms of Spanish activity. In about 1636, following outbreaks of underground anti-Christian religious cults at Tipu and a subsequent auto-dafo in 1619, the entire region broke out in rebellion (López de Cogolludo 1688:Bk. 11, Ch. 12). From that year until 1695 the Belize missions were sealed off from virtually all Spanish control, ultimately forcing the Spanish to pursue the final conquest of the Itza heartland along a road constructed southward to Lake Peten Itza through the long-conquered territory of the Cehach. Although the details of Spanish strategies in this failure to conquer the last Maya frontier until 1697 are yet to be fully documented, there can be little doubt that Maya resistance activities in the Belize Missions subregion played a central role in the failure of plans for an earlier, more felicitous conquest through a pacified zone along the major eastern riverine arteries to the central Peten.

The considerable wealth of the Belize Missions subregion played a major role in the region's continued independence. Tipu and probably the other Maya towns of the upper Belize and New rivers were major exporters of high-grade cacao as well as vanilla and annatto. The Itza, with their southern sources of cacao disrupted due to early conquest of the Manche Chol and Mopan areas, came to depend increasingly upon their close neighbors to the east. From the Itza the Belize settlements received woven clothing made from Peten cotton and dyes. Tipuans and their neighbors also supplied the Itza with axes and machetes, procured from northern Yucatan in exchange for cacao and other agricultural products and perhaps for trans-shipped Peten cloth as well (see documentation in G. D. Jones 1982:283–285; for a much more detailed discussion see G. D. Jones 1983).

A further aspect of the Itza-Belize Missions subregion alliance, which took the form of Itza military assistance and the intermarriage of the Tayasal and Tipu nobilities, appears to have been rooted in ideology. The Tipu region rebellion of the mid-1630's was clearly inspired by religious revitalization activities that were stimulated by the Itza. Similar activities appeared among the Man-

che Chol at about the same time (Bricker 1981:37), suggesting a major effort by the Itza to stimulate anti-Christian, anti-Spanish activity all along their eastern and southern frontiers.

Details of such processes of frontier persistence depend upon intensive documentary exploration. There is no doubt that any model that purports to account for the protraction of Spanish conquest activities and the simultaneous maintenance of independent Maya political economy and ideology will be subject to revision with the acquisition of more satisfactory data. Such documentary exploration is currently under way. However, equally important is the documentation of such processes by means of the archaeological record. David M. Pendergast's investigations of the *visita* mission site of Lamanai on New River Lagoon have already begun to generate a body of data concerning sixteenth- and seventeenth-century life (Pendergast 1975; 1977; 1981; 1985). Given the conquest model outlined above, the recent discovery of Tipu itself and the initiation of archaeological research at that site in 1980 promise an important additional body of evidence that can provide the working basis for interdisciplinary cooperation in understanding processes of change and continuity in this frontier Maya situation (G. D. Jones and Kautz 1981a; 1981b; E. Graham, Jones, and Kautz 1985). The first several seasons of research at Tipu (located at Negroman on the Macal River) have tended to confirm both active Spanish colonial influence and the continuity of Maya ceremonial activity for some years following initial Spanish contact about 1544 (G. D. Jones 1984a; 1984b). We are beginning to realize that the southern Maya Lowlands were in some areas active bastions of a Postclassic way of life long after other regions had been conquered and subdued. When we understand that such a way of life was integrally related to demographic, political, and economic factors even in the colonial centers of northern Yucatan, we can begin to perceive the necessity of understanding the

Postclassic-Colonial transition and the processes of colonial expansion and indigenous resistance as thoroughly integrated subjects of investigation.

To recapitulate an earlier point, the interaction of historical archaeological and ethnohistorical research strategies brings together under a single integrated methodology the investigation of the Postclassic-Colonial transition and the study of long-term trends of adaptation to colonial conditions. With such strategies at hand, we need no longer rely upon ethnohistorical data as temporally isolated points of departure for the reconstruction of more ancient societies by means of analogical procedures. While there may well be lessons for the Classic period to be learned from the Colonial record, such lessons cannot be applied until we appreciate fully the complexities of the dynamic integrations which that record documents. Only a broadly applied direct historical methodology will reveal such complexities; nearly all of the work is yet to be done.

FUTURE RESEARCH DIRECTIONS

The directions that future research might take in the study of the Colonial period southern Maya Lowlands fall clearly into two major categories. First, there are obvious, troublesome gaps of strictly empirical nature. Certain regions are all but unknown, as are certain time periods. Second, there are less obvious but no less important problems of a topical nature that should be approached as issues and hypotheses that might guide strategies of research. These two are, of course, related and overlapping, and the following comments must in their brevity overlook the great complexity of these interrelationships.

Empirical Gaps

The regions most poorly represented in the available literature remain the central Peten,

Belize, and the southeastern frontier comprising northern Verapaz and adjacent lowland regions. It is encouraging to know that work in these areas is under way, although much basic documentary research remains to be done. Perhaps the most serious ethnohistorical gap remains the central Peten, despite the existence of extensive documentation pertaining especially to the closing years of the seventeenth century. Thorough study of the Itza and their neighbors during the first two centuries of colonialism should, as argued above, be a first-order priority in Maya ethnohistory.

It goes without saying that historical archaeological research in all areas is poorly developed. As ethnohistorical study pinpoints locations for an increasing number of Colonial period sites, such research becomes increasingly feasible. Historical archaeology must, however, dovetail its strategies not only with ethnohistorical research but also with a broader archaeological program designed to explore Postclassic and Postclassic-Colonial period transitional problems. In fact, it might be argued that historical archaeology, ethnohistorically informed, will be a principal key to the clarification of the Late Postclassic situation in many areas of the southern Maya Lowlands.

The eighteenth century, ignored in this chapter, is virtually unknown for most of the southern Maya Lowlands. De Vos treats this period in the Chol Lacandon region (1980: 205–226), and Feldman has indicated that rich documentation for the eighteenth century exists for Belize (1981). Peter Gerhard (1979:67–75) provides a useful but brief review of materials pertaining to areas under the control of Salamanca de Bacalar. There is excellent documentation for the Peten following the Itza conquest through the entire eighteenth century. This poorly understood period, as well as the nineteenth century, is crucial for understanding the aftermath of the Itza conquest.

Topical Issues

Demographic studies of the region, first introduced by J. E. S. Thompson (1970:48–83), offer an important challenge, particularly in the analysis of the large-scale north-south migrations of the sixteenth century. Sherburne F. Cook and Woodrow Borah (1974:1–170) were able to treat the *partido* of Bacalar only cursorily. However, Nancy M. Farriss' observation that "flight" from centers of colonial control in Yucatan was central to the demographic study of that region can now be related to the pattern of increasing northern Yucatec Maya control in areas such as the Belize Missions subregion (Farriss 1978; 1984:199–223). Recognition of the immense scale of north-south migrations during the Colonial period as well as the Caste War period of the nineteenth century may well force Maya scholars to reconsider the possible role of large-scale migration during earlier periods of political dislocation in the Maya Lowlands.

The study of systems of indigenous production and exchange during colonial periods of complex interregional articulation is obviously crucial. Programmatic statements pertaining to earlier eras in the Maya Lowlands (Rathje 1971) as well as more detailed pan-regional studies of particular trade goods (A. P. Andrews 1983) may provide conceptual inspiration for intensive Colonial period studies of production and exchange in the southern Lowlands. This is an area of study that is especially conducive to integrated archaeological and ethnohistorical research designs.

In more general terms we are now reaching the point at which studies of local and interregional political economies—studies that integrate "indigenous" systems with the wider colonial system—are both possible and necessary. Such a study underlies the model presented above for the impact of the Belize Missions subregion upon the protracted maintenance of Itza autonomy, but the necessary empirical research is still at an early stage. We still understand very little, for instance, about the precise nature of the political economy of the central Peten region itself during the Colonial period. Since the maintenance of this core region was critical to the pursuit of general colonial policy, to wider systems of production and exchange, to the survival of neighboring zones of refuge, and to the stimulation of religious revitalization as an expression of political independence movements, the political, economic, and ideological underpinnings of the central Peten populations should be a first priority for all future research in the southern Maya Lowlands.

Although this chapter has emphasized a "Maya perspective" for understanding the historical processes of this region, it is no less important to clarify the Spanish colonial perspective as well. This is a particularly difficult undertaking, for the conquest of the southern Maya Lowlands was pursued from both northern and southern fronts, from both Guatemala and Yucatan. While there are hints of a grand design in the gradual conquest of the region, the details of formulation and execution of a broad policy, albeit one riddled with conflict and troubled by a long series of setbacks, are not well understood. Perhaps a task best suited for the colonial historian, this issue must, of course, be undertaken in full awareness of the complexities of indigenous response to colonial policy and action.

It should now be clear that the colonial experience of the southern Maya Lowlands must be examined anew in the broadest sense possible. We must recognize that the region is to be understood as a whole, each subregion or local ethnic group playing a role in a wider process of conquest and resistance. Just as conquerors developed and implemented strategies, often misguided and unsuccessful, to whittle away the fringes of this vast territory in order ultimately to claim the great Itza prize, the Maya inhabitants also variously pursued regional and pan-regional strategies to frustrate efforts at conquest. The picture that emerges is far larger, more complex, and more integrated, from both Maya and Spanish perspectives, than we might have imagined on the basis of reading sub-regional studies. Future studies must, while not sacrificing the depth that regional and local perspectives provide, keep sight of these pan-regional processes. The subject matter of the Colonial period ethnohistory of the southern Maya Lowlands should refer wherever possible to the question "How can we understand what happened?" Anything less will not do justice to the heritage of evidence before us.

6. Indians in Colonial Northern Yucatan

NANCY M. FARRISS

IKE THE SIXTEENTH-CENTURY Spanish colonists, modern scholars have found the Maya Indians to be Yucatan's chief exploitable resource. Attracted primarily by the region's archaeological remains, the Carnegie Institution of Washington earlier in this century supported a blitzkrieg of ancillary research in linguistics, botany, ethnography, geography, meteorology, history, and ethnohistory. This massive program and the further efforts it stimulated have produced an abundance of information on the colonial Indian that had no rival in Mesoamerica until the appearance of Charles Gibson's single-handed contribution to the colonial history of the Valley of Mexico (1964). The quantity of data that the Carnegie program made accessible to scholars, especially in the form of edited documents, remains unequaled in southern Mesoamerica.

Our understanding of colonial Maya history has not kept pace with this harvest of information. The lag is due in large measure to the predominance of a special subgenre of ethnohistory that has flourished in Mesoamerican studies, and particularly in Yucatan. I take ethnohistory to be anthropology

with a time dimension or history informed by anthropological concepts. Ethnohistory in Yucatan has most often, with important exceptions that I shall note, functioned as a handmaiden to archaeology, defining its task as culling from historical documents information that will help illuminate the area's Precolumbian past. In other words, the colonial Indian has been viewed as a vestige.

This emphasis is understandable. Scholars were first lured to Yucatan by its magnificent Precolumbian ruins, products of a civilization that remains Yucatan's chief claim to uniqueness. Without the ancient Maya, Yucatan would be simply another ex-colonial backwater, valuable as a source of case studies for comparison in connection with this or that topic of broader concern but without intrinsic interest of its own. It is for this reason no doubt that archaeology has been the prima donna of regional disciplines. It has set the framework of scholarly enquiry, posing the questions that ethnohistory, linguistics, botany, and others have sought answers to. These questions have been increasingly sophisticated of late, but they are not historical ones, or at least not colonial historical ones.

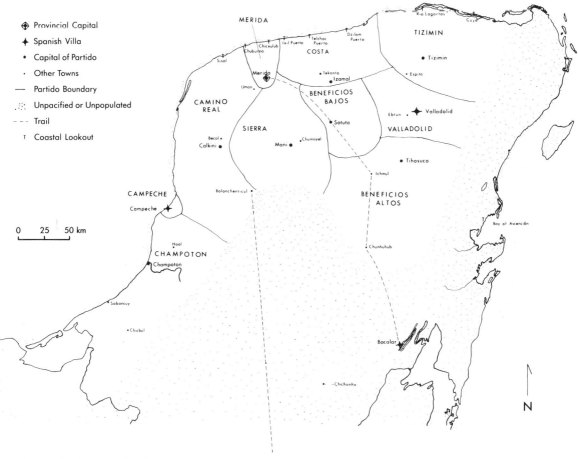

Provincial Capital
Spanish Villa
• Capital of Partido
• Other Towns
— Partido Boundary
.∴ Unpacified or Unpopulated
- - - Trail
τ Coastal Lookout

0   25   50 km

FIGURE 6-1. Yucatan, 1780.

Ralph L. Roys is the preeminent practitioner of this genre. Colonial historiography in all its subfields is so indebted to Roys' monumental *oeuvre* that it seems niggardly to point out any limitations. His *Political Geography of the Yucatan Maya* (1957), an encyclopedia of information painstakingly assembled from a wide variety of primary sources, is an indispensable tool for any study of colonial Maya demography, settlement patterns, and indeed almost any aspect of geopolitical organization. His translations and interpretations of documents written in Yucatec Maya have given other scholars direct glimpses into the colonial Maya world,[1] which they would otherwise have to view solely through Spanish eyes. Those who seek to read untranslated documents on their own, especially the more esoteric texts, must inevitably draw on Roys' vast knowledge of Maya philology.

In most of Roys' own work, as distinct from his collaborative efforts with historians, the colonial Maya serve as a source for the Preconquest history of the region rather than as subjects in themselves. The quantity of colonial material assembled is vast, but it must often be subjected to further sifting and re-

89

organizing within a different analytical framework before it will yield insights into the colonial Indian experience. A case in point is the *Indian Background to Colonial Yucatan* (Roys 1943), in which the mention of, say, Early Colonial trade in beeswax is embedded in a discussion of Precolumbian apiculture. Another example, less known to colonialists, is Roys' *Conquest Sites and the Subsequent Destruction of Maya Architecture* (1952). The title betrays its archaeological emphasis and has doubtless obscured the fact that the data primarily concern colonial church construction, with much tangential but useful material on evangelization, labor demands, and parish administration.

The retrospective focus of much Yucatecan ethnohistory helps to account for its emphasis on regions ordinarily regarded as peripheral if not wholly irrelevant to colonial history. The frontier zones along the Caribbean Coast and the base of the peninsula, which were either conquered late or abandoned early, have served archaeologists' and ethnohistorians' purposes precisely because they have remained relatively "uncontaminated."[2] Yet the assumption of marginality carries risks. No sharp break separates Preconquest from Colonial in either time or space. Anyone seeking clues to Precolumbian mysteries among the Peten Itza and other unpacified groups must consider the impact, both direct and indirect, of the nearby Spanish presence. Similarly, no study of the pacified Maya to the north can safely ignore the impact on them of a highly permeable colonial frontier, across which goods, people, and ideas flowed freely in both directions.

Here I would cite several studies whose chief value lies precisely in their focus on temporal and spatial flux in this border zone. The well-known monograph by France V. Scholes and Roys (1948) and several recent articles by Grant D. Jones (1979; 1982) all enhance our understanding of Precolumbian as well as Colonial Maya society. But they do so by emphasizing change rather than static structures and by taking into account the larger context in which Postconquest processes of change unfolded rather than by searching for fossil remnants.

THE COLONIAL REGIME

If the colonial Maya on both sides of the frontier have often been studied in isolation from the larger colonial context, this is in part because that context until recently has been very nebulous. In an unusual reversal of priorities, the literature on colorful Yucatan has emphasized Indians at the expense of Spaniards and the interaction between the two. In most regions of Latin America, where historians and their traditional concerns with elite groups have predominated, Indians, when they have figured at all, are viewed largely from a Spanish perspective, as so many units of labor or souls to be saved.

Obviously both perspectives are necessary. Although much of Indian life may have gone on beyond the notice or ken of the colonial masters, colonial rule impinged upon almost every facet of that life in one way or another. Even where indigenous social patterns and the systems of meaning that informed them were not radically transformed, colonial rule provided the sets of constraints within which changes occurred and continuities were preserved.

The Maya of Yucatan seem to have weathered colonial domination with uncommon success. While many groups in central Mexico, and especially in other coastal lowlands, merged genetically and culturally into what was to become the dominant mestizo society, the Yucatec Maya retained their overwhelming numerical preponderance and much of their way of life. Their mode of subsistence, many of their social forms, and, above all, the basic principles around which they ordered their lives and their interpretations of reality remained essentially unaltered after three centuries of colonial rule. Linguistically the Maya had colonized the Spanish, for it was the creoles and the mixed bloods who learned Yucatec Maya and even spoke it among themselves.[3]

I doubt that the Maya were inherently

more impervious to Spanish influence than other comparably advanced groups in Mesoamerica. Perhaps they were more accustomed to foreign conquest. During the peninsula's long history of Precolumbian intrusions, they may have developed a certain capacity to absorb foreign influences without being overwhelmed by them. A more important difference was in the nature of the colonial regime. Whether or not Yucatec Maya culture was inherently more resistant to change, or more resilient, the external forces for change were considerably weaker there than in the more economically advanced regions of the viceroyalty. The Spanish brought with them to the New World a common blueprint for colonial society. The results, however, were far from uniform. The local environment, both physical and human, in each case modified the blueprint, shaping the particular type of colonial regime that was established and with it the particular colonial experience of the Indians.

Central Mexico has long dominated the historiography of Mesoamerica, and understandably so, given the region's importance as both the economic and the administrative center of the viceroyalty. But suspicions, hardening into certainties, have arisen about the applicability of central Mexican models to the viceroyalty's poorer sisters.

Yucatan presents some notable contrasts with the Central Highlands. A climate inhospitable to Europeans and their crops and, above all, a lack of exploitable resources condemned the region in Colonial times to commercial isolation and poverty. But geography will not account entirely for the particular variety of colonial regime that developed in Yucatan. The Spanish empire contained many poor, peripheral regions; indeed the majority fall into that category. What distinguished Yucatan within Mesoamerica was the combination of a dearth of natural resources with a relative abundance of human resources. And this explains Yucatan's peculiar type of backwardness: the long reliance on Indian tribute as the region's economic base.

By tribute I mean not merely or even

mainly the *encomienda* system, which persisted in Yucatan into the last quarter of the eighteenth century. I refer to all the various methods the Spanish had devised for extracting goods from a basically unmodified Indian economy. These largely unauthorized supplements, which came to represent a far larger share of Spanish income than the strictly regulated *encomienda* tribute, included a whole host of unsanctioned fees, fines, and "gratuities" to support the local bureaucracy; the *limosnas* or *ovenciones*, a form of ecclesiastical tribute; requisitions of grain well below market price when paid for at all; and, most especially, the widespread system of *repartimiento*, the major source of exportable goods and therefore the major source of wealth in the colony. The *repartimiento* had a certain commercial air to it, in that the Indians received cash advances for future repayment, primarily in the main export products of cotton cloth and beeswax. But the Indians were unwilling parties to the exchange, and the element of coercion, along with the grossly unfavorable terms, places these transactions clearly in the category of tribute rather than trade.[4]

Recent studies of Yucatan's colonial economy (Farriss 1980; García Bernal 1972a; 1978; M. E. P. Hunt 1974; 1976; Patch 1976; 1979) all agree, explicitly or implicitly, that the area lagged far behind central Mexico in the transition from a tribute to a market economy. The implications of this lag for the Maya are considerable. As long as the Spanish merely extracted from the Maya their accustomed goods, such as maize and cotton cloth, which they produced in their accustomed way while retaining ownership of the means of production, the Maya would have to make far less drastic adjustments in their own social arrangements, or even in their symbolic systems, than as peones or wage-earners in Spanish-owned and -directed enterprises.

Exactly how far Yucatan lagged behind the viceroyalty's dynamic center is a key issue, and the development of the hacienda is a key indicator. For the absence of mining and the other entrepreneurial activities stimulated by the mining industry made the hacienda virtually the sole vehicle both for transforming the local economy and for integrating the Indians more fully into it. I would date the emergence of the hacienda as the region's principal economic base in the late eighteenth century. Stimulated by a rapidly growing local population and especially by a sudden expansion in export opportunities, the small cattle *estancias* that had been increasing slowly in size and numbers since shortly after the conquest began to expand dramatically. More significant than the increase in the size of herds was the concurrent introduction of commercial agriculture on a large scale. Spanish estates replaced the independent (if not always willing) Indian producer as the major supplier of maize and eventually turned to the even more lucrative and labor-intensive export crops of sugar and henequen.

The delayed shift to commercial agriculture meant that the struggle for land between the Spanish estates and the Indian communities came late to Yucatan. For much of the Colonial period, land was so abundant as to constitute a free good. Property boundaries were vague, and the conflicts that arose were conflicts over land use, between the owners of free-ranging, semi-feral cattle and the cultivators of unfenced, shifting *milpas*. The destruction of *milpa* crops, although undoubtedly a great nuisance, did not figure very prominently in the litany of grievances that the Indians and their local champions entoned against the Spanish colonists. By the time the cattle and Indian populations had increased sufficiently in the late eighteenth century to make coexistence difficult, the Indians were facing a much more serious threat. For as the *estancias* became transformed into haciendas they began to claim exclusive rights to vast tracts of land that they had once been content to share with the Indian communities.[5]

Labor was always a scarcer and therefore more valuable resource than land. But so long as the Spanish chose to rely mainly on the Indian economy to supply local needs and

the export trade, their direct demand for labor remained low. Their heaviest demand was for domestic servants, and for these they continued to rely on the grossly inefficient, intensely resented, but relatively undisruptive system of rotating labor drafts.

Draft labor was also used for transport and construction, for salt extraction, and for some commercial *milpa* production on land that was either rented or more often requisitioned from the Indian communities. The communities' most serious competition for labor came from the *estancias*, although their labor needs for stockraising and small-scale maize production were also relatively low. The *estancias* were able to attract Indian tenant farmers far in excess of their needs by offering the Indians protection from the incomparably more burdensome obligations of *pueblo* life. Estate residents still had to pay tribute and *ovenciones*, but they could usually count on escaping the most onerous of these obligations, the *repartimiento* and the labor drafts. In so doing they of course increased the burden on the Indians who remained behind (Farriss 1984:Ch. 7).

The luxury of employing such a substantial amount of labor in domestic service rather than in productive occupations is an indication of the undeveloped state of Yucatan's colonial economy. That and the continued reliance on the cumbersome labor drafts long after other colonies had shifted to more efficient methods of labor recruitment also suggest one reason for the long persistence of the primitive tribute system in general: that the crisis in the labor supply which afflicted all the colonies in the sixteenth and seventeenth centuries was relatively mild in Yucatan.

The question of labor is as much a demographic as an economic one. Yucatan has been well served by studies in demographic history.[6] What we can conclude from the two major studies is that, in biological terms at least, colonial rule was considerably less devastating in Yucatan than in central Mexico (Cook and Borah 1974; García Bernal 1978). Yucatan unquestionably suffered its own "demographic catastrophe" during and after the conquest. But the decline was also unquestionably less severe and proceeded at a much slower and more uneven pace, with substantial recovery in the early seventeenth century interrupting the general downward trend. Where the two studies differ is in the shadowy period between this recovery and the clear upward curve of the latter part of the eighteenth century. Manuela Cristina García Bernal's revisions (1978:79–143), which are based on much new and less equivocal evidence, also conform more closely with the general body of seventeenth-century sources I am familiar with. All suggest a very sharp and sudden drop around the middle of the century (perhaps double the first Postconquest loss of 25 percent), rather than a steady, gentle decline, with a nadir being reached shortly before the mid-1700's, as postulated by Sherburne F. Cook and Woodrow Borah (1974:112–114).

Disease alone will not account for the population decline or for the contrast between central Mexico and Yucatan. The effects of various kinds of stress on both mortality and recovery should be considered, although they are much harder to calculate. Demography may be symptomatic of the colonial regime, reflecting the contrast between central Mexico and Yucatan, where conquest was less devastating in its immediate effects, though more protracted. More than symptomatic, I would say that it is both a cause and an effect. The relative abundance of labor (that is, the slower rate of population loss) and the primitive tribute economy helped to sustain each other. Spaniards had less stimulus to take charge of production directly. With less drastic disruptions in the traditional way of life, Indian society could reorganize after the trauma of conquest and resettlement (*congregación*) and begin to replenish itself.

Why, then, the precipitous decline in the middle of the seventeenth century which was not reversed for at least another fifty years? This crucial period remains shadowy, but the evidence suggests a disequilibrium in the tribute (in the broadest sense) system, reaching a crisis in the 1660's, when an increasingly heavy burden of *repartimientos* and other exactions came on top of a series of epidemics and famines. The increase in burdens may have been in part fortuitous in the shape of a particularly rapacious governor, whose *juicio de residencia* fills several *legajos* in the Archivo General de Indias (Escribanía de Cámara 315-A to 317-C; García Bernal 1972b; Farriss 1984:Ch. 2). Perhaps the static tribute system simply reached a point where an ascending curve of Spanish demands (because of a gradual increase in Spanish population), without any basic technological or organizational innovations, bisected a descending curve of Indian resources. Disruptions in food production, lowered resistance to disease and famine, mass flight to zones of refuge, social disarray at community and family levels: all reinforced each other to sustain a prolonged deficit in the balance of births and deaths.

As for the processes of stabilization and recovery, we need more precise information on their timing to supplement the usual biological explanations. No doubt increased immunity through natural selection played a major role, but both Spaniards and Indians also pursued conscious policies of self-preservation. The former eased their demands of *repartimiento* and other assessments; and the latter developed a new institution, the *cofradía*, to help cope with the twin evils of Spanish demands and crop shortages (Farriss 1984: Ch. 9).

COLONIAL MAYA SOCIETY

The colonial Indians as subjects in their own right, rather than as sources of information about the Precolumbian past or as objects of colonial rule, have primarily been the province of ethnohistory in the broad sense that I defined earlier of combining questions and methods from both anthropology and history. There is no reason why history on its own, without an anthropological bent, should not deal with the effects of colonial rule on Indian sociocultural systems; it is simply that for the most part historians have found other topics to be of more compelling interest.

The literature on the Postconquest Indian in Mesoamerica has tended to focus on the Indian community as the unit of study. Kinship systems are elusive in the colonial documentation and simple to the point of nullity in modern times. And whatever larger polities existed at the time of conquest, from empire to mini-state, quickly disintegrated into smaller components. In Mesoamerica at least, though not apparently in the Andes, the territorially based community of *pueblo* and dependencies seems to have been an enduring feature of Indian social organization from Precolumbian times to the present, with or without extended kinship ties that may have originally coexisted as a basis for social integration.

Microanalysis of the community as an isolated unit carries the risk of obscuring wider ties, not only with the dominant colonial or national society, but also with the rest of Indian society. In colonial Yucatan such ties existed and could on occasion support concerted action, but they were otherwise highly tenuous and unsystematic and increasingly unrelated to former political links. Yet, in other regions, especially highland Guatemala and Chiapas, distinctive ethnolinguistic boundaries have survived the Postconquest breakdown of formal structures. These boundaries are also supported by internal networks of economic exchange, and it would be worth exploring further the correlation in Mesoamerica between the degree of ecological diversity, fostering regional integration, and the persistence of strong, if largely informal, supracommunity organization.

The community remains nonetheless the most obvious unit of analysis and has often been too the principal subject of analysis, as the key to Indian social organization both before and after the conquest. The standard model for the entire Postconquest period has long been Eric R. Wolf's "closed corporate community," which he sees as a response to conquest: the besieged Indians' withdrawal into tightly knit communities to defend their culture and land from Spanish encroachment (Wolf 1957). Recent studies of colonial Indians in Yucatan have questioned the model's applicability to that region. There the principal effect of colonial rule seems to have been the loosening of community ties; and if a corporate social structure (of Precolumbian origin, by all accounts) survived, it did so despite considerable movement away from and between communities.

Population Movements

Three types of population movement, which I have called flight, drift, and dispersal (Farriss 1978), seem to have been unusually prevalent in colonial Yucatan, especially the first of these. The characteristic Maya response to famine, epidemic, or any other crisis was to take off into the unpopulated bush. Many returned once the crisis had passed, but others made their way to the unpacified regions to the east and south.

Scholars have long been aware, as were the colonial authorities, that a substantial portion of the population losses recorded in colonial Yucatan were due to flight rather than mortality (Molina Solís 1904–1913: vols 1–2; Cook and Borah 1974: 114–120, 178). The existence of zones of refuge, with organized groups of unconquered and apostate Maya sharing the same language and most of the same customs, affected social and political realities as well as demographic profiles on the other side of the frontier. We do not know how many Maya became permanent refugees or how far they had to be pushed before making this choice. But there were limits of tolerance, defined in part by the frontier's accessibility. And if the ease of escape subverted the colonial regime in Yucatan, challenging the absoluteness of Spanish rule, it also undermined the strength of social ties among the Maya themselves. Flight was no doubt primarily a form of protest against Spanish domination. But the Maya were also moving around in large numbers within the pacified areas. This movement, a seemingly aimless drift from one community to another, is easier to trace in the colonial records than it is to explain. It directly challenges the picture of "closed" Indian communities that needed to restrict access to limited resources, and might therefore encourage outmigration to new areas or cities. The colonial Maya were moving into, as well as out of, long-established communities and during times of population increase as well as decrease.

The colonial Indians' refusal to stay put will come as no surprise to scholars familiar with the Andean area or other parts of Mesoamerica. The degree of restlessness in Yucatan seems to have been uniquely high within Mesoamerica (Robinson and McGovern 1979:5–7), and it has only become apparent through a recent series of studies based on parish registers. Kevin Gosner (1979) was the first to note the large proportion of outsiders listed in the registers of Uman parish near Merida in the late eighteenth century; up to two-thirds of the marriage partners and their parents and sponsors were noted as *naturales* of other communities. That these findings were not peculiar to the time and place is evident from a number of reports and censuses and from an expanded study by David J. Robinson (1979) covering four parishes from the late seventeenth to the early nineteenth century.

We may yet find some basis for questioning the magnitude of the internal migrations the records seem to reveal for colonial Yucatan. Until then we are faced with an exceedingly high rate which varied over time and from place to place but might reach the level of one-third of the adult Indian population. These movements do not necessarily signify the disintegration of the corporate community. Community boundaries can be preserved even when permeable in both directions. But we need to know considerably more about the spatial and temporal patterns of migration before we can conclude with certainty how they reflected and affected colonial Maya social organization.

Such patterns are difficult to detect in the maze of crisscrossing tracks that cover the peninsula. A few regularities have been discovered, and I offer here a tentative model of internal migrations from my own expanded study of population movements, a model that seeks to account both for the regularities and for the apparent lack of any overall coherence (Farriss 1984:Ch. 7).

To understand these movements it is useful to break the process down into three separate choices: leaving home, not returning, and resettling elsewhere. Migrations were not always or even usually a steady trickle of people. They correlate with and were immediately caused by particular crises, in which many people scattered from their home communities. The decision not to return had various motives, but land hunger can be eliminated from them, since people were as likely to move to densely populated parishes with many Spanish estates as to areas where land was much more abundant. Escape from accumulated tax debts is a much more likely motive, supported by the finding that when people moved at all they usually moved to another district altogether (Robinson 1979:11).

The reasons for choosing a specific new location are still the most elusive. David Robinson has opened a promising line of enquiry that should be pursued: the reconstruction of family ties among migrants. It may be that people followed family members, friends, or neighbors, as they have done the world over in migrating from their hometowns, although the slight degree of regularity noted in the records could as well be explained by the movement in one stage of one or two entire families. Either way, one seeks some larger pattern transcending particular towns, and some general attraction in the new locations besides distance from debt collectors or the presence of kin.

The most we can discern at the moment is certain tendencies. One of them is a movement toward Merida, the provincial capital, which Marta Espejo-Ponce Hunt (1974: 225–227, 237) sees as luring Indians to nearby *pueblos* and then to the suburban *barrios*. Hunt was unaware of the considerable exodus out of the *barrios* and also movements that "leapfrogged" the city (Robinson 1979:18–20). Still, there was clearly a gradual buildup of population in the Merida vicinity at the expense of other regions. The attraction was economic but not so much in the sense of opportunity as of security that association with Spaniards could provide from the vicissitudes of village life (some of the vicissitudes of course having been created by the Spaniards themselves). In the eighteenth century and possibly earlier, Spaniards were looked to for immediate and concrete relief. During famines, Indians flocked to Merida and the surrounding area, where grain supplies—requisitioned from the countryside as well as imported—were concentrated, to beg from private and public stores. The authorities sought to return the survivors to their villages, but many remained.

The search for security, temporary and long-term, could send people in the opposite direction too, away from population centers and in particular away from the Spanish. Outsiders were also evident in the remoter parishes, and if their populations nevertheless failed to increase, it was because they suffered a further drain across the nearby frontiers and out of the colonial censuses. Thus, a very general two-way flow can be seen, the choice between them dictated by individual calculation of whether survival would be enhanced by greater proximity to or removal from the colonial masters, who came increasingly to control the region's resources. Either choice, and indeed all the migrations, reflected a less than compelling attachment to particular communities.

The third type of population movement, dispersal from congregated or nuclear towns to dependent hamlets, I have discussed at length, mainly in terms of the centrifugal force exerted by the system of shifting agriculture prevalent in the region (Farriss 1978). I have since added to the physical convenience of dispersed settlement the social advantages of physical distance from the *pueblo*, which brought greater freedom from

social constraints and the burdens of community membership (Farriss 1984:Ch. 6).

The Fate of the Nobility

Discussions of movement away from and between communities touch only obliquely on what was happening within the communities, which after all remained the focal point of colonial Maya life. Migration and dispersal may have weakened the communities, but they did not destroy them. Migrants were incorporated into similar structures elsewhere; ties with dispersed population were not totally severed until the haciendas were turned into quasi-communities themselves, acquiring in the hacienda churches the emblem of full social autonomy.

Without looking at Postconquest Indian society from the inside, we can only guess at the impact of Spanish domination and its variations over time and space. I shall concentrate here on one topic that is particularly amenable to comparisons, the changing role and status of the native nobility. This topic has received much attention in the literature, partly because it is relatively well documented, but also because the fate of the nobility is such an important yardstick for the changes in indigenous social organization as a whole.

Precolumbian Mesoamerica shared certain basic similarities in sociopolitical organization which were common to and in fact serve to define the areas of advanced civilization throughout Latin America—the areas sometimes referred to as "Nuclear America." Whether incorporated into the Aztec and Inca empires or still autonomous, all the polities were some form of territorial state ruled by hereditary lords, with a stratified social structure consisting of a nobility of various ranks, a mass of subordinate but more or less free commoners, and a group of slaves/serfs who were directly dependent on the nobility.

These same areas also now share the basic characteristics of a peasant society. And, although the transformation was more gradual and complex than originally thought, the new social order appears to have been well established by the end of the Colonial period.

My question is whether the changes in native society outlined for central Mexico, including Oaxaca, and Peru hold true for Yucatan. The initial stages seem common enough. The larger hierarchical political structures were broken up into constituent units and the power of territorial rulers confined to their own local areas, a conscious Spanish policy that was also aided, as I have suggested earlier, by an erosion of economic ties. In Yucatan this meant that, regardless of the degree of centralized control that had existed in a particular province, and that varied greatly, all the native lords were reduced to the level of *batab*, a local ruler with sovereignty over a single town, who in some cases had ruled independently and in others had been subordinate to provincial or subprovincial lords (Roys 1943: Ch. 9; 1957).

A concurrent program of *congregación* drew scattered subordinate villages into the principal towns, so that territorial stratification was compressed from both directions into a uniform level. Subordinate *batabs* continued to defer for a time to their former lords, the provincial *halach uinic*; some remnant of the old hierarchy persisted longer in the *cabecera-visita* relationship within the parishes. But each incorporated community, the colonial *república de indios*, had total autonomy in theory and increasingly in practice (Farriss 1984: Ch. 5).

Where Yucatan seems to depart from the standard Mesoamerican—and Andean—model is in the fortunes of the ruler and lesser nobility within the circumscribed limits of the single community. The model offers two diverging destinies, both of which entail the disappearance of the indigenous nobility *within* indigenous society. One segment of the nobility, the fortunate few, managed to preserve high status and wealth, transferring their traditional sources of wealth within native society into landed estates and commerce in the Spanish style. They not only competed successfully with Spanish entrepreneurs; they emulated the Spanish in lan-

guage, dress, and way of life, including absentee residence in the cities. Only their native titles distinguished them, titles that they succeeded in preserving by operating through the Spanish system.

These acknowledged hereditary *caciques* succeeded in retaining and developing their wealth but at the expense of local political power. They withdrew from Indian society while continuing to claim some of the material rewards of sovereignty. The understandable disaffection of their *macehual* "subjects," combined with their increasing identification with Spanish society, eventually completed the process of separation (Gibson 1964:156, 163–164; Taylor 1972: 35–36).

The majority of the nobility remained within native society either by choice or by necessity and became gradually depressed into the mass of *macehuales*. They lost their wealth, based as it was on a rapidly dwindling labor supply that the Spanish were competing for. They also lost their political power to the rival structures of the elected municipal *cabildo*, created by the Spanish and used by *macehuales* with Spanish encouragement to challenge and replace the hereditary leaders (Gibson 1964:156–163, 167–169; Spalding 1970; MacLeod 1973:135–142). In either case, by assimilation into Spanish society or into the common mass of Indians, the native nobility *qua* native nobility ceased to exist.

A somewhat different picture emerges from the records on Yucatan as presented in two recent studies of colonial Maya social organization, the one a detailed study of the community Tekanto in the eighteenth century by Philip C. Thompson (1978), and the other my own more comprehensive but inevitably more superficial regional survey from conquest to independence. The deviations are not startling but significant enough to require some explanation. It is possible, of course, that much of the divergence is in interpretation, arising from different perspectives and different sources. Both studies take a more emic approach to the colonial Indian than has been common, relying more on the admittedly fragmentary native sources and seeking to discover what meaning the Indians gave to what the Spanish sources reveal. There is also the anthropologist's (and crypto-anthropologist's) predilection for continuity that comes from an emphasis on structural-functional analysis, as opposed to the historian's emphasis on change. Let me examine briefly some of the deviations that emerge from the two studies.

The first is that the *cacique* class, the descendants of the old territorial rulers, remained within native society. More accurately, they retreated back into it after an initial flirtation with assimilation. Scholes and Roys have given a detailed account of one protagonist's progress through this early, experimental stage in their Acalan-Tixchel monograph (1948:175–291). But Don Pablo Paxbolon was one among many Hispanized *caciques* who were able to use their local authority and their positions of confidence serving the Spanish to reinforce each other and to secure a high-ranking position for themselves in the new order.

Why their successors were unable to consolidate this position is not certain. I suspect that the obstacles were mainly economic, due to the area's retarded transition to the market economy. The primitive tribute system could not support two rival elites in the same style, and the Maya elite lost out to the Spanish in their traditional economic bases of long-distance trade and control over native labor, itself a shrinking resource. Unlike central Mexico and Peru, Yucatan offered little opportunity, and that too late, to parlay traditional sources of wealth into a new base of commercial agriculture and local trade. The native nobility was left to squeeze what they could from the native economy in unequal competition with the Spanish.

Within fifty years or so after conquest, the *cacique* class in Yucatan had disappeared from view. There is strong evidence, however, that they disappeared only from Spanish view. They had retreated back into Maya society (some had never left) and there continued to enjoy privileged access to both wealth and political power, although on a greatly reduced scale.

There is one known exception, the Xiu family of Mani province, whose papers Roys has used, supplemented with material from central Mexico, for his earlier account of the *cacique* system in Yucatan (1943:129–171), an account that not surprisingly closely resembles the central Mexican model. The Xius were, I think, an unusual and not wholly successful imitation of this model: removed from the local power structure, but without assimilating into Spanish society; gaining confirmation of hereditary titles, but titles that had no wealth attached to or supporting them. If other noble families did not bother to seek official acknowledgment of their rank, it was because their position within Maya society depended on recognition from their fellow Maya and not from the Spanish.

What are the criteria for establishing the preservation or disappearance of a native nobility, or any nobility for that matter? First, there must be some structural and functional continuity. This may have been more pronounced throughout Mesoamerica than commonly realized. In Yucatan, at any rate, social stratification persisted throughout the Colonial period despite compression from above and below. This compression failed to erase the line dividing the masses from a privileged minority. The first group hovered around the line of bare subsistence and had no say in the conduct of community affairs; the second, while far from rich by the standards of the Precolumbian lords or the new rulers (though not necessarily poorer than all Spaniards), monopolized what wealth was available within the colonial Indian economy and controlled through public office the lives and labor of the majority—subject of course ultimately to the authority of the Spanish overlords (P. C. Thompson 1978:183–192, 332–345, 366–369; Farriss 1984:Chs. 6, 8).

The municipal *cabildo* and the rest of the local administrative apparatus introduced by the Spanish may have been designed to supplant the traditional system of government, but the replication of function, structure, and sometimes nomenclature within the new system suggests that they did not succeed. Even the religious establishment, which would seem to have been appropriated *in toto* by the Christian clergy, contained strong links with the past: through the *cofradía* system by which the Maya leaders reconstituted their mediatory role between the community and the supernatural—in the guise of the corporate deity-saints; and more obviously through the figure of the *maestro cantor*. This powerful personage, who served as the *cura*'s deputy and alter ego in all but the major sacraments, has been traced to the Precolumbian *canbeçah* or teacher, an alternate title he retained in colonial Maya and Spanish documents (Collins 1977). My own reading is that the *maestros* also incorporated many of the attributes of the *ah kines* or chief priests, as these were gradually suppressed (Farriss 1984:Ch. 11).

A Colonial period native elite with similar functions to the Precolumbian ruling group could perhaps be found all over Mesoamerica and is not necessarily the same as a native nobility. To qualify as nobility, there must be some formal distinction in rank correlating with the socioeconomic divisions and differential access to political office, and that distinction must be hereditary.

Ideally one would trace the descendants of the Precolumbian nobility and their political and economic fortunes down through the Colonial period. Predictably, the records are too spotty for this. However, many scattered bits and pieces that I have assembled, plus the large chunk that has survived from the town of Tekanto from the late seventeenth century to the nineteenth century, point to the group's survival. For a start, there is evidence that the Maya continued to distinguish between *macehualob* (commoners) and *almehenob* (nobles) until at least the end of the Colonial period (P. C. Thompson 1978:222–233; Roys 1939). There is also evidence for a correlation between the status of *almehen* on the one

hand and wealth and political office on the other. Moreover, the title of *almehen*, which translates literally as one whose ancestry can be traced through both the male and the female lines, continued to be hereditary in fact as well as theory. In other words, public office was linked in some way to lineage.

Yet public offices were supposed to be either appointive or elective under the administrative system created by the Spanish. The key to the discrepancy lies in the dynamics of local political power and the indigenous rules of succession that governed them. According to the rule of primogeniture which the Spanish applied to the *cacicazgos*, Colonial Maya politics appears to be a bit of a free-for-all. But then Precolumbian politics might seem equally disorderly by the same narrow criterion, especially in the Late Postclassic. Leaving aside the many illegitimate seizures of power by force and concentrating solely on the accepted rules of succession, we find that leaders were chosen from among eligible lineages. The evidence for Colonial times is consonant with the same principle. Only eligibility for office was hereditary, and actual accession to political power was determined by some consensus among the entire pool of eligibles. Thus, a territorial lordship might fall to a brother or younger son, presumably chosen by agreement among the senior members of the patrilineage, but possibly also in consultation with the lesser nobles who filled the lower slots in the hierarchy.

In Colonial times the formal procedure was election by the *cabildo*, which drew its members from the larger pool of eligibles, with a pro-forma confirmation from the provincial governor. This apparently hereditary elite continued to be divided into two tiers. The first was a restricted group of what could be called *batab* lineages, which provided candidates for the higher, life-time (or at least long-term) offices of *batab*, patron of the *cofradía*, *maestro cantor*, and *escribano*. The *maestro* had control over succession to the last two offices, which depended upon the qualification of literacy imparted by the *maestro*. The second, larger group filled the lower ranks of the civil-religious hierarchy in a system of ascending rotation that Philip Thompson has linked to the ritual calendar of the Maya (1978:299–323).

The pattern is discernable, but what the fragmentary evidence will not tell is the extent of deviation from it. There are some well-documented shifts in family fortunes, a few cryptic allusions to "upstarts", and no doubt some proportion of the many officials listed whose antecedents cannot be traced had none to boast of. Aristocracies have commonly experienced attrition and allowed a certain amount of replenishment from below to survive, and I do not know at exactly what point the boundary separating nobility from commoners can be said to disappear.

Whatever the degree of mobility within colonial Maya society—and all the movement should be viewed against the background of factional struggles and dynastic reshufflings that characterized the Postclassic period—I find no evidence that the Spanish encouraged any attacks on the nobility's exclusive claims. The major ruling dynasties were merged into a larger category of *batab* lineages, and no doubt the local gentry experienced some shifts in personnel, if not some expansion. Nevertheless, the principle of hereditary access to political power was still preserved, with wealth—itself partly dependent on inheritance—probity, and adroitness at political manuevering all playing their part in the dynamic. Nor do I see why the Spanish authorities, if they did exercise more control over the choice of leaders than the records suggest, would try to impose candidates with dubious credentials or support populist challenges, in violation of their own hierarchical principles and their own interests.

Nevertheless, the Indian nobility did eventually disappear as a distinct social group in Yucatan as in the rest of Mesoamerica. If the when and the how have yet to be established, this may be because the denouement was prolonged into the somewhat hazy post-Independence period, where scholars have not pursued it. There one might find that noble descent lingered on as a mark of distinction within Maya society for some time. But a more useful way to chart Postconquest social change would be to look at the substance or meaning of rank. Seen as a vessel containing power and wealth, hereditary nobility would cease to exist when emptied of its contents, even if the vessel itself remained unshattered by parvenu challengers.

This occurred late in Yucatan by the established central Mexican chronology. The sixteenth-century conquest greatly reduced the nobility's power in Yucatan but left much for a second, less heralded assault beginning in the late eighteenth century. The modernizing policies of the Bourbon reformers—pursued in more extreme form by republican Liberal regimes—though more subtle, were in their way as destructive as the original conquest.

I have mentioned some of the main features of this assault, which was a combined attack on the economic base of Indian communities and on the political power of their leaders (Farriss 1984:Ch. 12). The last shreds of that power were removed with the post-Independence abolition of the *repúblicas de indios*, after a trial run under the short-lived 1812 Constitution of Cadiz.

That loss might seem a welcome relief, since public office is supposed to have been a main vehicle for the impoverishment of the colonial Indian nobility. This was not, however, necessarily or even usually the case in Yucatan so long as the Indian officials had control over the public resources of the community—that is, as long as they possessed political power. The divorce between leadership and political power marks the chief distinction between Indian politics in colonial Yucatan and the modern civil-religious hierarchies, including the cargo system described for the Maya highlands, which is also supposed to impoverish its participants.

Like participants in the cargo system, the Indian elites in colonial Yucatan, whether or not they can be defined as a nobility, performed elaborate and expensive ritual roles on behalf of their communities. In addition, they were held liable for the collective burden of tribute in its various forms. They sometimes suffered personal losses because of these sacred and secular responsibilities, especially in times of acute population decline. But they were not endemic losses. Until they lost political power, the elites were able to mobilize *macehual* labor and other community resources, such as *cofradía* property, to support public ritual, meet Spanish demands, and maintain or replenish their own wealth. Some were simply more successful than others in corporate and private finance. The systematic impoverishment of the elites would more likely take place when expectations for their support of the religious cult continued, while their capacity to draw on public resources was diminished: in other words, when they lost political power.

CONCLUSION

The work that has been done on colonial Yucatan underlines the need for caution in generalizing about all of Mesoamerica from central Mexican evidence. Yucatan was different by a variety of measures. Some of them may be revised from either side—or both sides—in the direction of convergence; the majority will stand.

Similar caution is needed in interpreting the differences. It is easy to see Yucatan as a simple case of arrested or delayed development, with quibbles confined to the extent of the lag behind central Mexico. The temptation is still to rely on a central Mexican model, merely transposing to a later date changes that were evident there in the sixteenth century. This is only one step removed from assuming that all of Mesoamerica was homogeneous.

The idea of identical but delayed processes is certainly risky in the economic sphere. The one aspect of dependency theory that all economists seem to agree on, however they may view the prospects for development, is that time lag produces structural differences.

If Latin America was (is) one of the peripheral regions in terms of the world economy, Yucatan was (is) a periphery of a periphery, or of a secondary metropolis. It is no more likely to replicate the exact processes of change in central Mexico, than central Mexico is likely to follow the same path as western Europe. Even now Yucatan has yet to reproduce the economic and social complexity of colonial Mexico. When the hacienda emerged, it was never tied to a strong local market, and the hacienda was a relatively brief episode in Yucatan's transition from semi-autarchy to export monoculture.

The same might apply to the reshaping of Indian society under Spanish rule. We may be dealing with somewhat different processes instead of a simple time lag. A less abrupt and drastic break with the past would allow the Indians time to develop their own adaptations to Spanish pressures, somewhat analogous to what has been called "strategic acculturation": making some changes in order to preserve essentials. We would, thus, expect culture change to occur everywhere, even among those groups that seem most conservative, most "untouched." Change would be a universal, but one that, according to the speed and thoroughness of colonization, would proceed to a greater or lesser degree along Indian lines.

NOTES

1. Among the major documents Roys translated and edited are the Chumayel version of the *Book of Chilam Balam* (1933), a set of land titles from the village of Ebtun (1939), and a Late Colonial collection of Maya incantations (1965).

2. See Chapter 5 of this volume.

3. Detailed treatment of most of the topics raised in this chapter, along with references to the relevant documentary sources, can be found in my recently completed study of colonial Maya society (Farriss 1984). On Maya-Spanish cultural exchanges, see especially Chapter 3.

4. See García Bernal (1972a:126–133) on the *repartimiento* and Farriss (1984:Ch. 1)

for an extensive discussion of the economic base of the colonial regime.

5. On the Late Colonial shift to commercial agriculture, see Patch (1976; 1979: 196–224) and Farriss (1980; 1984:Ch. 12). On Maya concepts of land tenure and Early Colonial land use, see Farriss (1984:Ch. 9).

6. Among the more important studies, Cook and Borah (1974:1–179) cover the entire Postconquest period to 1960, García Bernal (1978·7–166) deals with the period 1550–1700, and Patch (1979:225–264) and Farriss (1984:Appendix I) add new material on the late eighteenth and early nineteenth centuries. See also Robinson and McGovern (1979) for a detailed study of one parish, based on parish registers.

7. Kinship and Social Organization in Early Colonial Tenochtitlan

SUSAN M. KELLOGG

THE PURPOSE of this chapter is to describe and analyze kinship patterns and household organization of the Mexica of Tenochtitlan and Tlatelolco during the mid- to late sixteenth century. Primary evidence, derived from legal documents contained mainly in the *Archivo General de la Nación*, Mexico City (AGN), will be emphasized. While the main focus will be on analysis of archival documentation pertaining to Mexica social organization in the Early Colonial period, several theoretical issues and one methodological issue will also be considered.[1]

The first theoretical issue concerns variation in patterns of Indian social organization. Although it cannot be disputed that indigenous state- and class-organized society in the Basin of Mexico underwent pronounced transformations caused by the Spanish conquest, one of the chief tasks faced by Mesoamerican ethnohistorians is to distinguish variations in the ways different geographical areas, ethnic groups, and urban-rural settlements responded to social change. The conquest was not a uniform force working on an undifferentiated mass of Indian customs, and ethnohistorians must give careful attention

to the social and material resources that Indians were able to invoke in adapting to foreign pressures.

A second issue is the place of the *calpulli* (*calpolli*) as a unit in Aztec social organization. The history and content of discussions of Aztec kinship and social organization is well known to Mesoamericanists. Pedro Carrasco (1971b) has ably summarized much of this literature, so discussion here will be brief. Until the 1960's, descriptions of Aztec society tended to focus on a narrow question: whether social organization was kin-based, with the *calpulli* as a clan or clan-like unit, or complex and urban—that is, not kin-based, with the *calpulli* seen simply as a territorial division. (See Morgan 1877; Bandelier 1877; 1878; 1879; Radin 1926; Moreno 1931; White 1940; Monzón 1949; Vaillant 1944; Kirchhoff 1959; and Soustelle 1961.)

Since the 1960's, anthropologists have moved beyond this unproductive dichotomy. Eric R. Wolf (1959), Robert McC. Adams (1966) and Carrasco (1971b) view Tenochtitlan as an urban, class society characterized by ranked, ambilateral kin-based groups, *calpulli*, though their analysis of such units is

103

primarily based upon a source (Zorita 1963) which refers to areas outside of Tenochtitlan itself. (See also Rounds 1979 and Bray 1978.) Carrasco (1976a) refines these ideas. He cautions that social organization throughout central Mexico should not be viewed uniformly and states that, while in some cases the *calpulli* might be thought of as based on kinship or common ethnic affiliation, "fundamentally it was a matter of an economic and political relation between the *macehuales* of a *calpul* and the *teccalli* on which they depended" (1976a:33; my translation). He argues that the *calpulli* is best thought of as a political and administrative subdivision and that the members of noble houses (*teccalli*) formed lineages. But even this concept of the *calpulli* must be viewed as varying regionally and is perhaps more appropriate to the Puebla-Tlaxcala region upon which Carrasco concentrates than to Tenochtitlan.

The nature of the *calpulli* in Tenochtitlan has been examined by Luis Reyes García (1975) through linguistic analysis. His sources were materials written in Mexico City during the sixteenth century, including archival documents also used in this chapter. He concludes that, at least in Tenochtitlan, "*Tlaxilacalli* must be understood as a place of residence in which a *calpulli* or temple existed with its *calpolleque* in charge of the cult and with its *calpullalli* or lands assigned to the gods" (ibid.:25; my translation).

Thus, there is reason to believe that the *calpulli* as a unit in Aztec social organization may have been overemphasized in earlier anthropological accounts. Archival information pertaining to Tenochtitlan rarely mentions the *calpulli* (and never in contexts we might expect if it did represent some type of localized ambilateral/cognatic descent group); its conspicuous absence from the documentary record calls into question the notion that it was central to social organization in Tenochtitlan. While the *calpulli*—as temple— may have been central to Tenochtitlan's religious organization (and may even have organized people into social units based on

common religious affiliation), it is not viewed here as related to kinship and descent.[2]

Another theoretical issue pertains to anthropological interpretations of modern Indian kinship patterns. Hugo G. Nutini has perceptively commented on the longstanding assumption that

the structure of kinship and the family in Indian and Mestizo communities throughout Mesoamerica is basically Spanish, or at least that kinship and family forms represent an acculturative transformation in which Spanish elements predominate at the expense of traditional Indian elements. (1976:5)

Ethnohistorical studies of Indian kinship based on primary evidence are necessary in order to examine more fully the diversity of Indian kinship and family life and how they became transformed over time. While the Mexica of Tenochtitlan lost their cultural distinctiveness, other Nahuatl-speaking groups did not, and ethnohistorical studies will aid in analysis of how kinship patterns changed or were maintained over time.

A final issue, methodological rather than theoretical, follows from the preceding discussion: the importance of paying close attention to the terms the Aztecs themselves used to describe their kinship system. (See also Nicholson 1963.) Language can be used as an index of indigenous conceptions of kinship and social organization, allowing anthropologists and ethnohistorians to adopt a more "emic" perspective regarding Mexica social organization in Early Colonial Tenochtitlan. In order to examine this kinship system, a model will first be set forth; then evidence supporting the model will be elaborated. The last part of the chapter will detail Mexica household organization and the ways that this organization was tied into and related to the kinship system.

A MODEL OF THE MEXICA KINSHIP SYSTEM

While the Mexica kinship system is usually described as either patrilineal (Bandelier

1878; Vaillant 1966) or ambilateral (Monzón 1949; Sanders and Price 1968; Carrasco 1971b), it will be characterized here as "cognatic."[3] The concept of cognatic descent is consistent with the idea that descent-based entitlement and descent-based corporate groups can be formed by tracing descent from male or female links (Keesing 1976:260). Thus, in cognatic descent systems there is a *structural* equivalence of men and women.[4]

The Mexica cognatic descent system appears to have been based on two underlying principles: that the children of a married couple had equal rights from and claims on the mother and the father; and that all siblings were equivalent. While there was a certain bias toward men in specific contexts—especially land inheritance[5]—it is hypothesized that this pattern reflects males' overall higher status in the society and their tendency to manage property, especially landed estates (of course the latter is particularly true of males of the upper/noble class).

Both Bernd Lambert (1977) and Roger M. Keesing (1976) have indicated that patrilineal or patrifilial lines of descent can exist in certain contexts within or alongside cognatic descent systems or bilateral kinship systems. More striking than any evidence of the higher status of males (and the way this status might have influenced the Mexica kinship system), is the evidence, in many kinship contexts, of the structural equivalence of males and females. Nowhere is this seen more clearly than in the ideology or cultural beliefs surrounding the Mexica kinship system.

Evidence from the *Florentine Codex* suggests that the child was thought of as connected bodily to both the mother and the father; that is, a child was seen as sharing the substance of both of them (Sahagún 1969: 175, 216). This bilateral biological connection was then made use of metaphorically in other realms of social organization, so that a certain structural equivalence between men and women was expressed.

Perhaps the best example of such a metaphor is that leadership was often characterized as being like motherhood and fatherhood. A noble, addressing the inhabitants of Tenochtitlan upon the installation of a new ruler, said, ". . . it is assuredly true that he is thy real mother, thy real father" (Sahagún 1969:79). Parents addressed the leaders of the *telpochcalli* and referred to their children as *amoconetzin* and *amopiltzin*. *Conetl* means 'child' and was used by a woman; *pilli* in this context also means 'child', but was used by men as well as women; and *amo-* is a possessor prefix meaning 'your'. Thus, the parents were implying that the leaders were to be both mothers and fathers to the children.

The structural equivalence of men and women is further exemplified by the belief that women who died in childbirth were like men who died in war. They went to the same afterworld, and young warriors were said to want a finger, or some hair, from the body of such a woman so that they might place such relics on their shields and be brave in battle. Continuing the metaphor, after a woman had a child, whether a boy or girl, "the midwife shouted; she gave war cries, which meant that the little woman had fought a good battle, had become a brave warrior, had taken a captive, had captured a baby" (Sahagún 1969: 167).

Thus, in setting up an equivalence, or at least a parallelism, between war and birth, an equivalence between men and women was implied. The same equivalence was implied in metaphors about leadership.

This cognatic ideology penetrated beyond the realm of ideas and beliefs into the realm of social action. Early Colonial archival evidence shows this to be the case in two contexts: inheritance and residence rights. Several Mexica wills from the Early Colonial period demonstrate that male and female children had equivalent rights in the estates of antecedents (parents, grandparents, or great-grandparents).[6] Men and women received equal rights to urban houses and house sites and often to land, though women's abilities to activate their rights to land were limited. In addition, in tracing claims of inheritance to house sites, the number of male and female links used to trace a claim back to an earlier owner (sometimes the founder of a site), used as a kind of reference point, was the same. However, males were claimed as the focal antecedent three times as often as females. In land claims, males were used as links twice as often as females, and were the focal antecedent four times as often. Thus, there was a definite patrifiliative bias, especially in land claims, which might make women's claims appear exceptional. But there is evidence against such a hypothesis.

These claims and inheritances did not occur only when there were no male heirs. Both mothers and fathers left property to daughters and sons. Few genealogies given in these suits were composed of all males; those taking this form were special because they were genealogies of males asserting relationships to high-ranking nobles. Inheritance data demonstrate that, although male dominance in political and economic action influenced inheritance, one principle of the kinship system was the structural equivalence of male and female siblings.

In addition, analysis of Early Colonial residence patterns fits into the suggested cognatic nature of the Mexica kinship system. Use rights and rights of alienation of house sites in Tenochtitlan were based on patrifilial and matrifilial ties. Residence patterns of complex families (defined below), those which probably most closely resembled Prehispanic family and household patterns, show that residence rights could be based on matrifiliative or patrifiliative ties. Of forty-one such units, ten were based on inheritance from a woman, most often through a mother or grandmother. Thus, links flowing from and through women were utilized in the formation of residential units. While this residential evidence alone would not suggest a cognatic system, the use of female antecedents and links in the transmission of residence rights is consistent with such a system.[7]

Perhaps the most interesting aspect of the Early Colonial Mexica kinship system is that relatively shallow corporate descent units seem to have existed. These units were referred to in Early Colonial legal documents. One was called *tlacamecayotl*, which means literally 'rope of people' (*tlacatl* 'man, person'; *mecatl* 'rope' or 'tie'; *yotl*, a suffix that turns a noun into an abstract, expressing a "quality or attribute independent of the subject" (Sullivan 1976:35; my translation). The verb *mecauia*, in its reflexive form, means 'to fall while tied' (Molina 1970:55r; my translation), which metaphorically might tie together the ideas of falling and birth or descent. *Mecayotl* means 'ancestry, or consanguineal relationship' (ibid.). Pictures of ropes were often used as a pictorial symbol of genealogy by Mexica witnesses in Early Colonial court cases and seem to have symbolized kinship, birth, and the umbilical cord.[8] The term *tlacamecayotl* is viewed, therefore, as expressing a cognatic descent concept, similar to that of "descent line" (Periano 1961:97). It expresses the relationship between an ancestor and his or her descendants, traced through one or more connecting links. Such descent lines seem to have been the basis for shallow descent groups.

The term *teixhuihuan*, on the other hand, was a descendant- rather than ancestor-focused concept, and literally meant 'someone's grandchildren'. The literal meaning is an important clue to the kin unit and the descent implication of the term. It referred to a "group of cousins" (Carrasco 1966b:155) and thus had a group referent. This descent unit meaning is further supported by Spanish translations of this or related terms (*noxhuihuan* or *iixhuihuan*, literally 'my' or 'his/her grandchildren') in several Early Colonial documents as *un deudo descendiente* 'a descendant', *parientes* 'kin', or *todo sus descendientes* 'all their descendants'. As in *tlacamecayotl*, the principle of the equivalence of all siblings underlay the concept of *teixhuihuan*. Both of these terms denote structurally significant groupings and boundings within any individual's kin universe. While it is difficult to examine in detail the functions of these units, the meaning of each

106

concept and its structure can be illuminated as the evidence bearing on the nature of these units and the Mexica kinship system is examined.

ETHNOHISTORICAL EVIDENCE ON KINSHIP

That the term *tlacamecayotl* was in some way connected to Classical Nahuatl concepts of kinship and descent is not unfamiliar to Aztec scholars (Calnek 1974b; n.d.; Carrasco 1976a). In fact, Calnek (1974b) defined *tlacamecayotl* as a cognatic descent group or stock and described it in detail. His description is logically derived from a description of Aztec kinship given by one of Bernardino de Sahagún's informants included in Book 10 of the *Florentine Codex*. A similar strategy, of examining Sahagún's description and using it as a basis for a logical description of certain features of *tlacamecayotl*, will be followed here. This section of Book 10 is quite interesting because it represents "the only known text which takes the concept of *tlacamecayotl . . .* as its major theme" (Calnek 1974b:196). In discussing *tlacamecayotl* (*sucesión de parentesco* 'succession of relationship' as Sahagún [1905–1907:6:199] himself translates it), certain kin were listed, and the attributes of the good and bad kinsman and kinswoman of

each type were enumerated. It is revealing to ask which kin were listed, and which were not.

Figure 7-1 (based on Calnek 1974b:199) shows those kin terms listed arranged according to whether they have a male/female referent or not. It is observed, first, that few collaterals were included, only uncle, aunt, and nephew or niece.[9] The glosses make clear that they were included only as substitutes for lineal kin. *Tlati* 'uncle', for example, is described as "Provider for those who are orphaned, the entrusted one, the tutor, the manager" (Sahagún 1961:3).

Second, if we focus on the Ego/*mintontli* 'great-great-grandparent' relationship, we see that an individual could have used any combination of male or female antecedents to show lineal descent from a specific *mintontli*, and could use either a male or female antecedent each generation up when tracing this relationship. And a *mintontli* could also have been male or female. Finally, theoretically, if each *mintontli* began a cognatic descent line, then any Ego could belong to up to sixteen such lines.[10]

From Sahagún's description of *tlacamecayotl*, we might then envision a cognatic descent line structure with the following features logically derived from it:

mintontli

(PPPP)

achtontli (PPF)		*ueltiuhtli* (PPM)
culli (PF)		*citli* (PM)
tatli/tlatli (F/FB, MB)		*nantli/auitl* (M/MZ, FZ)

(Ego)

pilli/conetl (C) // *machtli* (♂ Ego SbC)/*pilotl* (♀ Ego SbC)

ixiuhtli

(CC)

FIGURE 7-1. Kin terms included in *tlacamecayotl*. Abbreviations: P, parent; F, father; M, mother; Sb, sibling; B, brother; Z, sister; C, child. (See Offner 1983:179, where he mentions a possible new interpretation for the kin terms determined by sex of speaker.)

1. Such lines emphasized the connection of relatives lineally, from descendant to ancestor.

2. Either male or female links could be used to legitimize a person's membership in a specific descent line; and the focal ancestor—to whom membership or rights claimed was traced—could be male or female.

3. There were several means by which an individual might have come to choose that or those lines in which he or she had primary rights and those in which he or she held secondary or even tertiary rights.

4. These lines may have served as the basis for shallow corporate descent groups.

Before discussing these structural features further, it will be useful to describe in more detail three examples of the use of the term *tlacamecayotl* in Early Colonial documents from Tenochtitlan.[11] In the first example, a witness simply stated that he did not know the *tlacamecayotl* of the defendant: ". . . *amo no nicmati yn itlacamecayo . . .*"/'. . . I also do not know his *tlacamecayotl* . . .' (AGN-T 55-5:fol. 3v; my translation). The second example comes from the same suit, in which the plaintiff later testified about how she had come to inherit the land under contention, saying:

yn ica in totlacamecayo in tocol ytoca tocuil-
tecatl mopilhuati matlactin ĝnchiuh auh ça
ce in mopilhuati ytoca tlacachin auh totatzin
in nehuatl anna xoco yhuâ ceĝntin teyxhui-
hua ôcate . . .

. . . concerning our *tlacamecayotl*, our grandfather named Tocuiltecatl had children, he engendered ten, but only one had children, named Tlacochin, and he was the father of me, Anna Xoco, and other grandchildren who are there. (AGN-T 55-5:fol. 7r; my translation)

In the Spanish translation of this particular document, included in the suit, the term *totlacamecayo* was translated as *linaje* (lineage) which, in Spanish, signifies offspring, progeny, or kin.

The final example of the use of the term

tlacamecayotl comes from a lawsuit dated 1593, the record of which is housed today in the Bibliothèque Nationale de Paris, concerning the sale of a house site. Diego de Francisco accused his half-brother, Felipe de Santiago, of selling a house site which was really Diego's property. Felipe, of course, claimed the property as his own. Felipe traced his claim back to his great-grandfather and great-grandmother, Yxtlilteohua Tecpanecatl and Hueyticitl. This couple had six children, one of whom gave birth to Felipe's mother, Ynes (who married Gaspar López, Felipe's father, but also the father of Diego by Gaspar's second wife; see Fig. 7-2). One of Felipe's witnesses described Felipe's kin relationships in the following way:

ŷ fellipe yn itatzin felipe ytoca gaspar ca zan
môtli auh ynes ca huel chane ôcan ŷ tecpan-
caltitlan: yn felipe ca huel ôcâ teyxuiuh yn
itic calli auh yn icolhuan y moch ehuaya: yn
inâtzin felipe quinomomimiquillique ypanpa
huel itech pouhticca: ŷ fellipe yn teixhuiuh
Ca ynâtzin quiquetztia yn calli mixiuhqui
zan ce xiuhuitl y motlaneuhque: ŷ gaspar
ynamic catca yn ines: ypanpa cêcan ytech
moyollallitiua yn felipe yn icolhuâ catca p°
poliuhtoc pedro Cochpin miguel lazaro
juana xoco yehuantzin yn itlacamecayohua
y felipe de stiago . . .

. . . Felipe's father was called Gaspar, who was only the son-in-law, but Ines was truly a *vezino* of Tecpancaltitlan. Felipe is truly a grandchild in the house and his grandparents all went away, and then Felipe's mother [and others] died, when it truly belongs to him. His mother built the house, Ines, who gave birth, and her spouse Gaspar left after only one year. So that everyone will understand, Felipe's grandparents were Pedro Poliuhtoc, Pedro Cochpin, Miguel Lazaro, Juana Xoco, they were his *tlacame cayohua* . . . (BNP 112:fol. 28v; my translation)

The term *itlacamecayohua* has a possessor prefix, perhaps indicating the group or unit aspect of the term, and is pluralized. In the

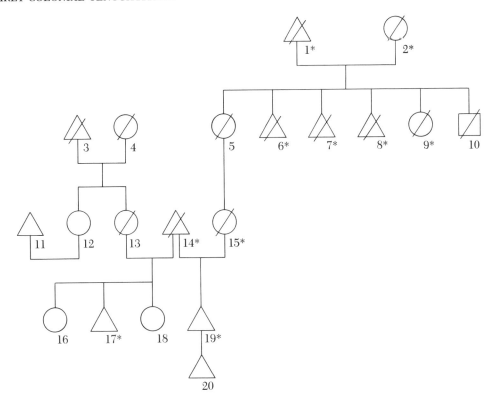

1. Yxtlilteohua Tecpanecatl
2. Hueyticitl
3. Juan Tepuso
4. Catalina Xoco
5. Ana Tiacapan
6. Pedro Poliuhtoc
7. Pedro Cochpin
8. Miguel Lázaro
9. Juana Xoco
10. (unnamed)

11. Pedro de las Casas
12. Francisca de Riberol
13. Beatriz Papan (d. ca. 1570)
14. Gaspar López (d. ca. 1588)
15. Ynes
16. María
17. Diego de Francisco
18. Juana
19. Felipe de Santiago
20. Juan Martín

FIGURE 7-2. Genealogy, BNP 112 (1593). Asterisks indicate people mentioned in the text; others are individuals cited in genealogical information in the suit.

plural possessive form, Carrasco defines it simply as 'relatives' or 'members of the lineage' (1976a:21; my translation). The Spanish translation of the term was *deudos muy cercanos* 'very close relatives' (BNP 112: fol. 26r).

In describing the structural features of *tlacamecayotl*, defined as a cognatic descent line, it was stated first that these lines emphasized the connection of kin lineally. Only full siblings would belong to all the same *tlacamecayotl*, but they would not necessarily all elect primary identification with the same one(s). Tremendous fluidity in identification and membership is envisioned here. The fluidity was perhaps related to other aspects of Aztec social organization, particularly household structure and residence patterns, which will be discussed further below.

Since tracing a lineal connection between

descendant and ancestor is thought to have been important, it would be useful to show an indigenous concept through which such descent was traced. A clue to the existence of such a concept is found in Early Colonial documents discussing the inheritance of rights to houses or land. This inheritance was often said to be from *"tiempo ynmemorial"* (time immemorial) through *"linea recta"* (straight line).

The concept of tracing descent through "straight line" was a Spanish phrase to describe inheritance, but it may also indicate an indigenous way of thinking about tracing descent for inheritance, resembling the Nahuatl concept, *tlamampan*, used to count back generations. Each link, plus the descendant and ancestor, was counted to arrive at a calculation of degrees of kinship (Carrasco 1966b: 159–160). The point to emphasize here is that a connection would be traced by "straight line" from an individual to an ancestor. And that line would be a cognatic descent line, traced through male or female links to a male or female ancestor.

That males or females could be used as links or ancestors in genealogical reckoning is very clear from the case material in AGN-Tierras. That they were not used as links or ancestors in equal numbers has been mentioned above.

The third structural feature of *tlacamecayotl*, as logically derived from Sahagún's description in Book 10, is that there would have been several means by which an individual might have chosen that or those lines in which he or she had primary rights and those in which he or she held secondary rights. It is important to remember that each individual was theoretically a member of sixteen cognatic descent lines, one traced from each of his or her great-great-grandparents. Literature on cognatic descent suggests that there are two ways in which these choices might have been made:

One is to specify that a couple can live with either the husband's or the wife's group; but whichever they choose, their child belongs

to that group. Another is to give privileged status, among those persons eligible for membership, to those who trace descent in the male line. (Keesing 1976:260)

During the Early Colonial period, the Mexica seem to have done both. There was an emphasis, in genealogical reckoning, on affiliation with the father's kin or through paternal ties, but ties to or through the mother were also used. So, for example, when the husband and father of several Indian women died during or shortly after the conquest, the women went to other houses, in the *barrio* of Atescapan, which were *"el patrimonio e herencia de sus madres"* (the patrimony and inheritance of their mothers; AGN-T 20-1-2: fol. 131r). But marriage may also have been important in narrowing down the cognatic descent lines in which an individual would have claimed primary rights. When a couple married, residence could have determined the primary descent line affiliation(s) of their children. Marriage, then, might have been an important point of interconnection between kinship structure and household organization.

Finally, another structural feature of *tlacamecayotl* may have been that these lines served as the basis for shallow cognatic corporate descent groups. These were groups, three to four generations in depth, that shared legal responsibility for each others' actions, controlled household membership and inheritance rights and claims, and organized certain economic activities (perhaps craft production). Toribio Motolinía, Sahagún, Bartolomé de Las Casas, and the Anonymous Conqueror all mention the joint culpability of kin, extending perhaps to the "fourth generation" for certain criminal acts or in slavery (Motolinía 1971:369; Sahagún 1953:23–24; Las Casas 1958:2:262; Conquistador Anónimo 1941:33).

While *tlacamecayotl* may have functioned as a central descent concept and unit, there were other kinship concepts as well. One of these, *teixhuihuan*, was, as stated earlier, a descendant- rather than ancestor-focused concept, literally meaning 'someone's grand-children'. This unit was apparently not based on lines but on groups of people, including at least the children and grandchildren of an individual. The Spanish translations of the Nahuatl terms for grandchildren often referred to a wider group of kin than simply grandchildren. In one document, the phrase *yn inpilhuan yn [te]ixhuihua* was translated as *todos sus descendientes* (all their descendants; AGN-HJ 298, no. 4:fols. 4r, 13v). The term could not have meant grandchildren here, since it referred to a couple with no living grandchildren or children mentioned. Rather, the phrase was used to express the idea that when these people completed buying the property, their descendants would have the right to inherit it. Another example is an order of sale in which the phrase *teixhuiuh tepiltzin*, translated as *un deudo descendiente* (a descendant relative) in the Spanish, referred to a woman's brother's daughter and not to a grandchild (AGN-T 42-5:fols. 8r–13v). Perhaps the best way to conceptualize the term *teixhuihuan* is through a less literal translation, 'all one's potential descendants'.

Perhaps an individual's children and grandchildren formed a model of what would be thought of as kin, but with a descent implication. This concept appears to be defined more inclusively than *tlacamecayotl*, not in terms of a line tracing upward from an individual to a specific ancestor, but down and outward so that we have a descent-oriented but kindred-like unit.

In addition to *tlacamecayotl* and *teixhuihuan*, there were other terms for kin such as *ioaniolque*, which Dibble and Anderson often translate as 'relatives'. The term *vayulcayotl* is translated as 'consanguineal relationship' by Alonso de Molina (1970:154v). These related terms seem to have referred to kin in general, or the widest group of kin, however bounded culturally, that an individual recognized without reference to a descent line or a concept focused on either an ancestor or a descendant.

One conclusion that emerges from the Early Colonial material analyzed thus far is that, even in the face of the great, disruptive changes that we know occurred (such as demographic disruption, forced labor, forced changes in religious practice and belief, and forced changes in political and economic administration accompanying the conquest), the Mexica were able to maintain certain precolonial patterns of kinship and social organization, obviously different from Spanish patterns of kinship and social organization.[12] Such patterns were also maintained, to a certain extent, in household organization.

ETHNOHISTORICAL EVIDENCE ON
HOUSEHOLD ORGANIZATION

The same archival data cited above make it possible to reconstruct aspects of household membership and to examine questions of size, composition, and residential history of Indian households in the Early Colonial period. There are data on eighty-eight households in thirty-four separate residential sites in Tenochtitlan. While a number of households were made up of single persons or consanguineal families, a surprising number of households were large and complex. Residential patterns, in general, seem to have been part of the fluid, multiplex kinship system already described.

Household data were tabulated according to the following categories: (1) single person households; (2) consanguineal households, which included *a* parent and child or children, or groups of coresident unmarried siblings; (3) nuclear family households, including married couples with or without children; and (4) complex family households. The latter are defined as households in which at least the remnants of more than one nuclear family lived. These household members were almost always kin, and they were usually arranged laterally, that is, around a group of siblings, though the sibling tie may have been one or two generations above the surviving unit, and/or generationally, where adults from two (or more) nuclear families were coresident and the tie was between a

111

TABLE 7-1. Household Types (N = 88)

Types of Households	Number	Percentage
Single person	11	12.5
Consanguineal	15	17.0
Parent and child(ren)	10	
Siblings	5	
Nuclear families	21	23.9
Married couples	10	
Parents and child(ren)	11	
Complex families	41	46.6
Lateral	16	
Generational	13	
Combination	6	
Other	6	

NOTE: Ten of these households include renters, but two factors make it difficult to comprehend the situation of renters. First, in several cases, the exact numbers of renters are not given. And second, because the internal economies of households—and the economic relationships of renters to households—are not understood as yet, the interaction between renters and other household members is unclear. Of the ten renting situations, only four renters are counted in the figures in Table 7-1. Three were renters who were kin or affines of those from whom they rented. And one renter came to own a site after it was partitioned among kin in a suit (AGN-T 49-3) and is counted as a single person household. Most renters were unattached males; some were Spanish, some were Indian, and one was mulatto.

parent and a child. Of another complex family type, we have two examples, both Prehispanic households described in the suits. In both, a husband, wife, and child(ren) co-resided with a "slave woman" and her children, probably by the husband. Such polygynous arrangements would not have been uncommon before the conquest, though they are impossible to investigate in detail due to the suppression of polygyny after the conquest by the Catholic Church.

Table 7-1 gives the number and percentage of household types. Although reliable figures for mean family size are unobtainable for the eighty-eight households, certain *trends* in household size are observable. The range of sizes were the following: consanguineal family households from two to four, nuclear families from two to five, and complex families from two to eight. It is important to remember that some of these are definitely under-

TABLE 7-2. Consanguineal Households: Parent and Child(ren) (N = 10)

| | Daughters | | Sons | | |
	One	Two	One	Two	Mixed
Male	X X	X	X	X	X[a]
Female		X	X X X		

[a]Three children (two sons, one daughter).

counted, but it is difficult to determine by what quantities. Large households were described for several sites, but exact numbers were not reported. The apparent small number of children in the three household types may also be significant in considering Early Colonial Indian demographic patterns.

Analysis of the composition of the other household types reveals the kinship relationships of people living together. Tables 7-2 and

112

TABLE 7-3. Consanguineal Households: Siblings (N = 5)

	Two	Three	Four or More
Sisters	X X		
Brothers			
Mixed	X+[a]		X[b] X[c]

[a] More than two siblings, but total number and their sex(es) unspecified.

[b] Three brothers and one sister.

[c] Several brothers and one or more sisters.

TABLE 7-4. Nuclear Family Households with Children (N = 11)

	Daughters			Sons		
	One	Two	Three	One	Mixed	
Spouses	X X X	X X X+[a]	X	X X	X[b] X[c]	

[a] Two named; document suggests more without identifying by name or sex.

[b] One son and one daughter.

[c] Two sons and one daughter.

7-3 show the composition of consanguineal family households. These were quite small and appear to have resulted from the breakdown, during and after the conquest, of more complex family units, due, primarily, to demographic upheaval.

Table 7-4 illustrates the composition of the eleven nuclear family households with children. This family type, too, seems to have developed as a result of conquest-related historical processes. These families had a tendency to become complex later in their developmental cycles, generally through the marriage of a child, with the child's spouse taking up residence with the family.

There were also forty-one complex family households where the relevant kin tie was generational, through parents, and/or lateral, through siblings. Ties through either relationship could be activated at various points in the life cycle. For example, on one site a woman came to live with her mother's brother after her mother died. The composition of these households is detailed in Table 7-5.

The Tierras documents (AGN-T) show clearly that households grew and sites were partitioned at times, and this partitioning helped create a situation where close kin lived near each other. Marriage and death were two points in the life cycle where partition took place; walls would be built or common property split in such a way that social realignment was made clear (see AGN-T 20-1-2; 37-2 for examples). Likewise, certain types of conflict may also have led to household partition during the Early Colonial period. The patterns of suits among coresident litigants raises the possibility that two or three generations below the founder, often when there was no surviving male head of household, friction would arise that might lead to litigation and/or household partition (Calnek n.d.:7; Kellogg 1980:Ch. 4). For example, in a 1583 lawsuit (AGN-T 48-4), two brothers, Luis Epcoatl and Bernardino Alonso, were left land by their sister where they built a house compound. Bernardino's wife and two children resided there after he died, as did a granddaughter of Luis Epcoatl. Bernardino Alonso's wife and children tried to remove Ana María Tepi (Luis' granddaughter) from the site by suing her, and when Ana won the right to remain it is likely that the site was partitioned in some manner (Fig. 7-3).

Such partitions might give rise to a situation where close kin lived either on the same site or near each other. Before the conquest, the *solar* (house site) of Constanza García was described as populated by her *parientes y amigos* (relatives and friends; AGN-T 22-2-1:fol. 170v). The houses of Magdalena Tiacapan, in the *estancia* of Tulpetlac, also contained some of her kin (AGN-T 17-2-4). Juan Tehuitzil's father-in-law was said to live on a site in front of the site of Juan and his wife (AGN-T 35-1). Don Gerónimo Velázquez' site was bordered on one side by the houses of his aunt, Ysabel Xoco (AGN-T 24-3).

TABLE 7-5. Complex Family Households (N = 41)

P–C Based (N =13)	M–D	M–S	F–D	F–S	P's[a]–D	P's–S
	5	1	0	0	2	5

Sb Based (N = 16)	B	Z	Mixed
	6	8	11

P–C and Sb[b] (N = 6)	M–D	M–2	M–Mixed	F–D	F–S	F–Mixed
	2	0	0	1	0	0
	P's–D	P's–S	P's–Mixed			
	1	1	2			

Others[c] (N = 6)			

[a] Parents (i.e., a married couple).

[b] One of these families represents an example of an elite household which was large partly due to its greater command of economic resources. This was the household of Don Hernando de Tapia whose house site was a *tecpan*, or palace, though it no longer functioned as such by the time of the suit (Edward Calnek, personal communication). It was built by communal labor, served some communal functions, and was also the residence of Don Hernando, son of one of the early indigenous governors of the city. In fact, the building was erected for de Tapia's father, Motelchiutzin, in the late 1520's. While the residential history, as described in the suit by the leaders of San Pablo Tozanitlan and others to remove de Tapia's heirs from the site, is not as detailed as a demographer might like, we do learn that Don Hernando and some of his siblings lived there, and at the time of the suit his widow and other inheritors were resident. This group would have included Don Hernando's two daughters and their husbands, as well as some of his siblings, their spouses, and children.

[c] These six complex family households were made up of people whose relationships are more difficult to describe. Two of them were the Preconquest polygynous households mentioned earlier. Another four were likely to have been coresident kin, though the exact nature of the ties is not elaborated.

Statements from other ethnohistorical sources support the picture drawn here of households which were often large and complex, arranged around sibling or generational ties, and with a developmental cycle in which site partition led to groups of relatives living near each other in *barrios*. Carrasco, for example, has cited Las Casas on the question of household size. Las Casas mentioned households including "three, four, and even up to ten able-bodied men" (1909:131; cited by Carrasco 1964:211). Carrasco also mentions Francisco López de Gómara's description of inheritance, in which he said that the eldest son inherited and managed all property, keeping with him and supporting the siblings, nephews, and nieces, leading to large households (1943:2:222–223, 246; cited by Carrasco 1964:209). According to the *Códice Kingsborough*, written by the inhabitants of Tepetlaostoc, near Acolhuacan, to protest their *encomenderos*, the twenty *principales* of the pueblo "had each one of them for himself seventy-five houses of renters that in each one had three or four adult men who gave or offered tribute each one according to his ability" (*Códice Kingsborough* 1912:13; my translation). Tequixixtlan, near Acolman (between Texcoco and Teotihuacan), was reported to have had large households, ". . . in

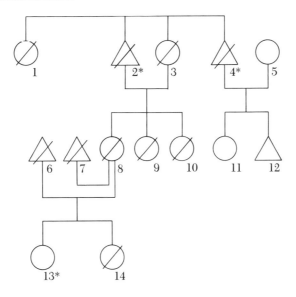

1. Ana Mocel
2. Luis Epcoatl
3. Ysabel Juana (Ana Tiacapan)
4. Bernardino Alonso
5. María Mocel
6. Miguel Quicen
7. Mateo
8. Juana Francisca
9. Marta
10. Magdalena
11. María Tiacapan
12. Juan Baltasar
13. Ana María Tepi
14. María Tlaco (d. ca. 1582)

FIGURE 7-3. Genealogy, AGN-T 48-4 (1583). Asterisks indicate people mentioned in the text; others are individuals cited in genealogical information in the suit.

each house . . . six or seven married Indians, not counting the unmarrieds" (Paso y Troncoso 1905–1906:6:211; my translation).

Woodrow Borah and Sherburne F. Cook's work on demographic patterns in central Mexico also supports the idea of large households. In their monograph on the population of central Mexico in 1548, based on the *Suma de Visitas*, they state that for the area of Mexico-Hidalgo the mean number of married men per house was 2.16 (Borah and Cook 1960:101). In a later discussion in the first volume of *Essays in Population History*, they report that many units in the 1540's included more than one married male (Cook and Borah 1971:125).

Carrasco's work on Tepoztlan and Molotla in the present-day state of Morelos (1964;

1976c) is the most important for comparison because it is not merely descriptive and permits a comparative analysis of household size and composition. He used census materials based on a house-by-house survey, dating from approximately 1540. His sources are obviously quite different from the case material used here. Not only are kinship connections described in more detail, but also the material dates from a single time period, somewhat earlier than the documents used here. In addition neither document refers to an urban settlement, and both settlements discussed by Carrasco are adjacent to, but outside, the Valley of Mexico. Nonetheless, the figures arrived at by the means described in this chapter are supported by Carrasco's data (Table 7-6).

TABLE 7-6 Comparison of Household Types (Percentages)

	Tepoztlan	Molotla	Tenochtitlan-Tlatelolco
Consanguineal	2.5	1.6	17.0
Nuclear families	54.0	36.7	23.9
Joint or complex families	43.0	61.7	46.6

Carrasco's use of the term "joint families" is somewhat different from my use of the term "complex" in this analysis. He says, "Joint families are those including more than one married man, each with his wife" (1967c: 47), whereas I have focused in this chapter on the structure of the ties generating particular units. Nonetheless, the structure of the units Carrasco calls "joint" is revealing. In both Tepoztlan and Molotla, both parental and male sibling ties were utilized. Ties through females were also activated—daughters, sisters, wife's brother, wife's sister, and wife's father—though not as often in Tepoztlan as in Tenochtitlan or Molotla. The structure of Tepoztlan's units may be indicative of a cognatic or patrilineal kinship system. But we have evidence of a household structure that was part of a cognatic system in Tenochtitlan.[13]

Both Edward E. Calnek (n.d.) and I (Kellogg 1980) have explored the interrelationship of household organization and kinship structure. For Tenochtitlan, it was the household, more than any other unit, where kinship, economic, and demographic factors intersected. All these factors influenced the organization of the units into which people were born and in which they lived, married, probably worked, and died. And it is important to remember that these households tended to be large, multifamily units. One of the frustrating aspects of any attempt to analyze Tenochtitlan's household organization as the point in urban social structure where kinship, economics, and demography coincide is that there are many aspects of household organization that are not amenable to description or analysis because of lack of data. One of these aspects is patterns of household headship: Was this position held by one male, as early census data (1530's and 1540's) from Tepoztlan, Molotla, and Tepetlaoztoc imply, or was headship shared by a married couple, with husbands and wives having different and complementary rights and duties, as much Latin American ethnography suggests? What were the patterns of succession to headship? Another is the economic organization of households: What was the occupational structure of the city's inhabitants? How was work organized? What was the relationship between the organization of production and consumption? How was household organization influenced by patterns of production and consumption?

Nevertheless, certain aspects of household organization and their interrelationship with kinship structure are discernible. They include household demography, marriage, and inheritance practices. Household demography was subject to many influences: the biological factors relating to birth rate, life span, and mortality; the household developmental cycle; size limitations on urban house sites which allowed two to six nuclear families (and not many more) to reside together (Calnek 1972:111); and the genealogical and generational structure of *tlacamecayotl*. That the relationship between kinship and household demography was a close one is demonstrated by the observation that there were no property suits

in which household members were more distantly related than as third cousins. There are instances in which second or third cousins evidently could not function harmoniously as a domestic unit, in which case the solution was to subdivide by constructing an internal wall, so that what had been a single household and residential compound became two. This means that viable households could be organized only within the limits defined by the concept of *tlacamecayotl*. Their perpetuation became "difficult" when the boundaries of this unit were approached. The alternatives, when these limits were reached, were either subdivision, or relocation by one segment of the original group. (Calnek n.d.: 7)

Thus, one important factor structuring the *size* of households, in both the Prehispanic and Early Colonial eras, would have been the unit called here *tlacamecayotl*.

Like household demography, marriage was a point in urban social structure where household organization and kinship structure came together. Calnek has hypothesized that, in Prehispanic society, marriage was used as a means of regulating the numbers of household personnel in a system which needed to "stabilize and perpetuate household units consisting of persons related no more distantly than as third cousins, and which rarely included either more or less than three or four elementary families" (n.d.: 10). Most evidence suggests that females tended to marry out (Kellogg 1980: 161–165),[14] though males would have this option if there was no space available for them in their natal households. The slim Prehispanic evidence available in the documentation used here supports a pattern of virilocal marriage. Of seven such marriages, six were virilocal and one was uxorilocal. But the situation was quite different in the Early Colonial era. The number of uxorilocal (approximately forty) and virilocal marriages (approximately thirty-eight) was nearly equal, with a few neolocal marriages (approximately seven). One possible explanation is that household viability (Stenning 1958) was a particular problem in the Early Colonial period. When complex

family units arranged around parent-child, or parent-child and sibling, ties were examined, it was found that uxorilocal marriages tended to correlate with mother-daughter ties. This pattern suggests that these households were particularly subject to problems of viability, because in none of these cases were coresident sons mentioned.

Inheritance of residence sites also demonstrates the intersection and interconnection of household organization and kinship patterns. Rights to residential sites were rarely inherited by only one person; instead, siblings, cousins, and sometimes other relatives were given such rights to share. Of twenty-seven residence sites mentioned in the extant sixteenth-century wills of Tenochtitlan known to me, twenty-two were designated to be passed on to more than one person. This partible inheritance pattern correlates with the multifamily, complex household structure described above. It is consistent with a cognatic kinship structure, a parent leaving his or her residence sites to sons and daughters when both are living, though a pattern of preference for daughters and granddaughters by women seems to nest within the overall cognatic pattern. Such a preferential pattern may indicate some of the demographic disruption of the Early Colonial period, when females outlived males. (See Kellogg 1980: Ch. 3 for further discussion of patterns of inheritance.)

Patterns of both demographic and social response to the conquest and colonial administration can be seen in the above discussion of Mexica kinship structure and household organization. Some of the responses are particularly clear in the case of household organization, where the presence of single person and consanguineal households seems to indicate social disruption. But the prevalence of complex units probably should not be viewed as a response to disruption. These households were not made up of agglomerations of kin or friends who lived together because they had nowhere else to go. Abandonment and reallocation of sites were spoken of much

117

more often in the archival documentation than people moving in with each other.

Even the increasing number of sales of Indian residential sites in the Early Colonial period did not destroy complex households. While some sites were bought by consanguineals or married couples, others were bought by complex families. In one case, a married couple, their son, and his wife bought a site (AGN-T 22-1-5), and in another two sisters and their husbands bought a site together (AGN-T 29-5). Other complex families bought sites as well, although the relationships within them were not always elaborated.

Archival data also indicate that many residential sites reverted to complex family households after the conquest. There are diachronic data for twenty-three sites, sixteen of which had complex family households at some point. Eleven of these sixteen sites were continuously populated or resettled by a complex family unit when the history begins, then tended (seven of eleven) to revert to such units later. Thus, we can conclude that the maintenance of such a household structure where possible, as well as the kinship units already described, signifies that the disruption and transformation wrought by Spanish conquest and colonial administration did not lead to a complete breakdown in Mexica society and culture. As late as the 1590's the Mexica were still using indigenous concepts to describe their households and kin units.

How closely, and in what manner, the Mexica tied together concepts of kinship, descent, and household organization remains unknown. But one of Sahagún's informants suggested that these aspects of Aztec social organization were linked in native thought. The informant described the food distribution at a feast, saying

. . . yn apeoa çan, yn ioaniolque, in vel icalloc, in centlaca, cemeoa, in vel icujtlaxcolloc, yn vel imecaioc . . .

. . . only the relatives, the people of the household—his family, they of the same par-

entage, of the same womb, those of the same clan . . . (Sahagún 1950 : 23)

shared the food. While *imecaioc* might be better translated as 'cognatic descent group' rather than 'clan', the linking of concepts of family and kinship is clear.

CONCLUSIONS

This chapter has argued that archival sources provide anthropologists with information about how the Mexica themselves conceived of their kinship system and household organization, data that challenge certain conventional anthropological views. Contrary to the opinions of early scholars of Aztec society, archival and other sources suggest that the *calpulli* was not central to Mexica kinship. These sources demonstrate the basically cognatic structure of the Mexica kinship system; the centrality of two important kinship units, *tlacamecayotl* and *teixhuihuan*; the importance of large, multifamily household residential units; and interrelationships between kinship structure and household organization exemplified by demographic patterns, marriage, and inheritance practices.

Tenochtitlan's sixteenth-century inhabitants found themselves enmeshed in processes of sociocultural change that were based upon interactions between the old and the new. In kinship structure and household organization, indigenous cultural and social forms were used to generate a colonial social structure, but one vastly changed by the many other influences to which the society was subject. By simply describing particular aspects of Mexica social organization in the Early Colonial period, it is possible to observe and identify some of these influences. But it is also clear that, even in highly urbanized Tenochtitlan/Mexico City, the Indian community in the sixteenth century was as much a product of the indigenous sociocultural system as it was a product of conquest and colonial administration.

118

ACKNOWLEDGMENTS

There are several people and institutions who offered aid in research and writing. Steven Mintz, Edward Calnek, Ross Hassig, and René Millon gave generously of their time and expertise. The late Thelma Sullivan and James Lockhart offered advice on the Nahuatl translations, but I bear full responsibility for their content. The financial contributions of the Henry L. and Grace Doherty Charitable Foundation, the University of Rochester, and the National Endowment for the Humanities (Summer Seminar Program for College Teachers) are also gratefully acknowledged. No research could have been done without the generosity of the AGN and its wise and helpful staff. This chapter is dedicated to the memory of Thelma Sullivan.

NOTES

1. Legal documents may appear to be a narrow base for broad interpretation, but they are one of the very few sixteenth-century archival sources available and the one such source relevant to the issues addressed here. Fifty-five cases were selected from Tierras (AGN-T). These were property suits that had been tried before the royal *audiencia*. They were selected on the basis of three criteria: (1) Only documents concerning natives of Tenochtitlan or Tlatelolco were included. Data from surrounding cities that today are part of Mexico City, or other more rural areas of the Valley, were excluded so that controlled geographic comparison might be possible. (2) The suits were to date from the sixteenth century, and the dates of litigation or supporting documents range from 1557 to 1606. (3) One side in the suit had to be composed of Indians. In addition to the cases from Tierras, other documents were used: one suit concerning sales of two house sites in Tlatelolco from the *ramo* Hospital de Jesús (AGN-HJ); two suits from Vínculos y Mayorazgos (AGN-VM) involving land claimed by a son and wife of Moctezuma; and one suit from the Bibliothèque Nationale de Paris (BNP), on microfilm. It too had been tried before the royal *audiencia*.

Class is another important issue to be raised in exploring the nature of the documents, since it did, to a certain extent, influence whether a case might be heard in the royal *audiencia* (thus leaving us with a written record). Virtually all the cases involving land were litigated by nobles, as were slightly over half the cases involving house property. The other cases were litigated by people who were not nobles. Many of these involved merchants or craftsmen.

Note that the term "Mexica" is used to refer to the inhabitants of Tenochtitlan and Tlatelolco and "Aztec" to the totality of culturally related, Nahuatl-speaking peoples of the Valley of Mexico and its immediate environs.

2. Jerome A. Offner (1983), summarizing more extensive evidence, makes a similar point, that the *calpulli* was not a descent- or kinship-connected concept.

3. The literature on the structure and functioning of bilateral, ambilateral, and/or cognatic systems is so complex as to be almost impenetrable. Because this is not the place for an extended discussion of the proper term for such units (but see Murdock 1960; Davenport 1959; Firth 1963; and Fortes 1969), I will simply say that I prefer the term "cognatic" because it parallels the terms "agnatic" and "enatic" and best expresses the essential feature of non-unilineal descent systems. This feature is that for certain purposes of genealogical reckoning men and women are treated as structurally equivalent and can be used as genealogical points for the creation or structuring of descent-based groupings.

4. This does not mean men and women are "equal" in the sense of status. It simply means that for the establishment of rights and claims or one's place in a line of descendants, men and women are considered equivalent.

5. This bias consists of male children tending to activate their claims to land more often than female children.

6. Don Hernando de Tapia's will (AGN-T 37-2) is especially explicit on this point, but

other Early Colonial Tenochtitlan wills support this picture.

7. There are a number of reasons why the Mexica documents might not indicate a higher proportion of residence rights inherited from females (as the proportion indicated could signify a patrilineal system like the Nuer in which significant numbers of people lived with matrilineally related kin). One is that perhaps joint male-female headship prevailed within the household, while male headship dominated interactions between the household and other, outside, social units. Second, if only males were household heads, then headship itself may be intruding upon recognition or memory of the origin of household property or residence rights (Barbara Rivero, personal communication). Offner mentions examples of widowed and even married women who were household heads in Tepetlaoztoc (1983:214, 217). The issue of household headship is raised again in the final section of this chapter.

8. It was suggested to me that the use of ropes to link people, as a symbol of genealogy, is found elsewhere in Prehispanic Mesoamerica (Clara Millon, personal communication). For example, see Miller (1974). Margaret Mead also has discussed the use of the term "rope" as a genealogical construct in a completely different ethnographic context (1963:176–179).

9. Offner has argued that the unit designated *tlacamecayotl* most closely resembles a kindred (1983:197–213), rejecting the emphasis placed on lineality by Calnek (1974b: 195–200) and myself. Offner argues that because many of the kinship terms were polysemous they automatically designate collaterals also. This clearly is the case, yet documentary evidence indicates that collaterals were often marked in special ways, particularly by the use of the term *huecapan*, '*lejano/a*' in Spanish, 'distant, far' in English. Carrasco (1966b) has analyzed the meaning and use of the term *huecapan*, as Offner notes (p. 181). More evidence on the structure of *tlacamecayotl* would be welcome in

order to decide whether its structure most resembles a cognatic descent group, as argued here, or a kindred, as argued by Offner.

10. My discussion here draws heavily on Calnek (1974b:198–199).

11. Carrasco (1966b:151, 156) cites two other instances of uses of the term *tlacamecayotl*: Fray Juan Bautista's *Advertencias para los confesores de los naturales* (1600: 1:fol. 81r), to which *tlacamecayotica* was translated as '*parientes*'; and the 1548 *Doctrina cristiana*, in which *tlacamecayutl* was translated as '*la linea de generación*' ('relatives; line of succession'). Carrasco (1976a: 21) also discusses the term, defining it similarly to my definition. But he adds, "It must not be thought nevertheless that *tlacamecayotl* refers exclusively to relatives who are members of a *teccalli*; rather it is used for whichever individual with whom there is a common ancestor, that is to say, kinship in general" (ibid.; my translation). There are also instances of the term's use in genealogical documents from other areas of central Mexico.

12. My assertion that the Spanish and Aztec kinship systems are fundamentally different is based, first of all, on my discussion of Aztec kinship concepts. But see also Lavrin and Couturier (1979) for a discussion of other aspects of Spanish kinship and family that would support my point.

13. There is a lot of evidence accumulating which suggests marked regional variation in household size and structure. Offner has analyzed household data from the *Codex Vergara* from Tepetlaoztoc and has shown that there were 6.0 persons and 1.3 married couples per household on average (1983: 214). These figures compare closely with Carrasco's Tepoztlan data. But in both Tepoztlan and Tepetlaoztoc Prehispanic households may have been smaller than in Tenochtitlan. Offner cites several factors which may have influenced household size and structure: class (with households of elites tending to be large; Offner himself rejects this as a factor though the Tenochtitlan evidence supports it

strongly); land scarcity and other economic factors; and ethnic variation (ibid. : 218 221).

14. Since this chapter was written, several important new studies of related topics have been published. These include works by S. L. Cline (1981); Hicks (1982); Carrasco (1984); and Offner (1983; 1984).

8. Socioeconomic Dimensions of Urban-Rural Relations in the Colonial Period Basin of Mexico

᠊᠊᠊᠊᠊᠊᠊᠊᠊᠊᠊᠊᠊᠊᠊᠊᠊᠊᠊᠊᠊᠊᠊᠊᠊᠊᠊᠊᠊᠊᠊᠊᠊᠊᠊

THOMAS H. CHARLTON

AT THE TIME of the Spanish conquest, the Basin of Mexico had attained "the densest population, the largest and most highly differentiated urban centers, and the most complex political and economic organization in the history of Mesoamerican civilization" (Sanders, Parsons, and Santley 1979:1–2). The urban and rural components of Aztec civilization were integrated within a system which had resolved problems of resource procurement and allocation. During the first century after the conquest, modification and reorganization of the Aztec system, in response to major demographic changes, produced a new and dynamic integration of the urban and rural areas of the Basin. This integration rested in part on a Spanish-dominated market system and in part on the hacienda system. Indians and Spaniards were brought into a stable, symbiotic relationship. The result was a flexible and responsive system of urban-rural integration that persisted for three centuries.

THE PREHISPANIC LATE HORIZON (A.D. 1350–1520)

The population of the Basin was distributed through a series of communities differing in size, social organization, and political and economic complexity. Settlements ranged from isolated households and hamlets, through local urban centers (provincial centers), to the Triple Alliance capitals of Texcoco, Tacuba, and Tenochtitlan (supraregional centers) (Sanders, Parsons, and Santley 1979:159). The smaller Late Horizon

FIGURE 8-1. Central Mexico, showing the Basin of Mexico and places mentioned in the text. (Base map derived from sheets E-14 N-II Mexico City and F-14 S-V Pachuca, Geographic Branch, Military Intelligence Division, G-2 General Staff, U.S. Army, 1933.)

1. Mexico City–Tenochtitlan
2. Ozumbilla
3. San Juan Teotihuacan
4. Otumba
5. Apan
6. Pachuca
7. Metztitlan
8. Hacienda Hueyapan
9. Hacienda Santa Lucia (San Xavier)
10. Hacienda Santa Lucia (Tepeatzingo)
11. Hacienda Salinas
12. Eastern Teotihuacan Valley
13. Villa de Tacuba area, Middle and Late Colonial periods (after Pérez-Rocha 1982:66, map 4.)

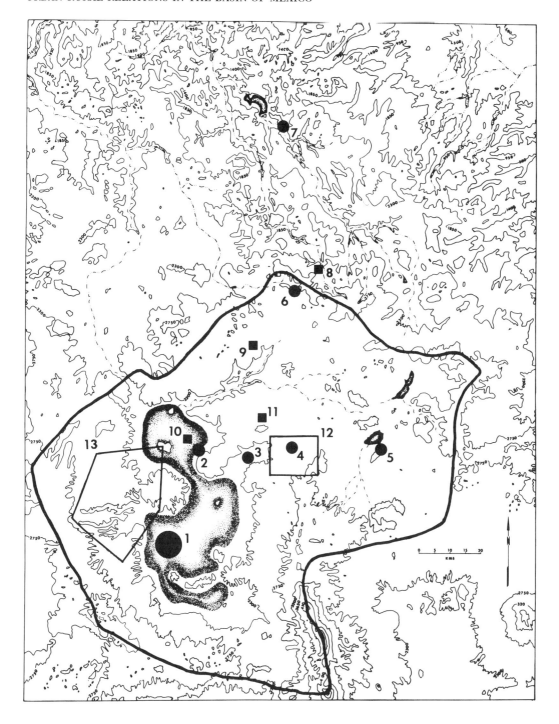

urban centers (provincial centers) were incorporated within the political spheres of the Triple Alliance centers (Bray 1972:162–170; Brumfiel 1976; 1980; Michael E. Smith 1978; 1979a). The rural sites were dependencies of the urban centers and supported them. In the primate city settlement systems of the Middle Horizon (Teotihuacan) and the Colonial period (Mexico City), a single urban center dominated the region at the expense of lesser centers. Although still dominated by a major large center (Tenochtitlan), urbanization in the Late Horizon involved an approximate "log-normal" rank-size distribution of population through the different levels of community size (Blanton 1976:195–201).

Population expansion and an increasing non-agricultural urban population had resulted in the development of a Basin-wide set of mechanisms whereby local raw materials, finished products, and foodstuffs could be produced and distributed. These mechanisms included tribute, interconnected regional markets, state-directed enterprises, and noble estates. They were set within the context of the increasingly centralized political power of the Triple Alliance and may have contributed to, as well as benefited from, such growth. Although there are differences of opinion as to the precise forces involved in the development of the Late Horizon socioeconomic system in the Basin of Mexico, there is general agreement that it was an integrated system (e.g., Brumfiel 1976; 1980; Charlton 1981; Evans 1980; Sanders, Parsons, and Santley 1979; Michael E. Smith 1978; 1979a; 1979b; 1980). Urban and rural settlements were linked within the system through a series of interdependent relationships (Bray 1972:184; Michael E. Smith 1978:100). Such interrelationships had both local and regional dimensions at the conquest (Charlton 1981). Nevertheless, it does appear that the Aztec Basin-wide socioeconomic system was in a state of transition from a "central place system," with a series of hierarchically arranged centers, to a "dendritic central place system" (Appleby 1976; Kelley 1976). There was an increasing tendency for raw materials

and foodstuffs to be directed to Tenochtitlan through a dendritic network, with the intervening units being reduced in function and complexity to mere administrative units (Brumfiel 1976; Sanders, Parsons, and Santley 1979). The Spanish conquest and the developing colonial socioeconomic system continued these tendencies and completed the transition.

THE EARLY COLONIAL PERIOD (1521–1620)

Following the fall of Tenochtitlan in 1521, Cortés and his followers established a centrally located Spanish settlement within the city, assuring the retention of its role as a focal point for the central Mexican socioeconomic system. Mexico City became the preferred or required place of residence for Spanish colonists, their descendants, and their black slaves. Although these norms were not always fully followed (e.g., Davidson 1966:237; Gibson 1954:586; 1964:368–409; Mörner 1970; Palmer 1976:45), the most intensive social, political, and economic activity, along with interaction between Europeans and Indians, was concentrated in this urban setting between 1521 and 1620. Archaeological, as well as historical, data support this view (Charlton 1979; Fournier García 1985; Gussinyer 1969; Lister and Lister 1982). Abundant Spanish architecture and artifacts are found in Mexico City, in contrast with their sporadic presence in rural areas of the Basin during the same period. Substantial remains of religious architecture and cemeteries throughout the region indicate the impact of religion to have been more evenly diffused through both urban and rural areas (Charlton 1979:250–251). Historical descriptions of the variable presence and functioning of Spanish institutions in urban and rural areas during the Early Colonial period are compatible with the archaeological data (e.g., Gibson 1954; 1964; 1966a; 1966b).

Mexico City experienced a dynamic urban growth and elaboration throughout this period (Boyer 1980; Cervantes de Salazar 1953; Florescano 1965:573; Linné 1948) accom-

124

panied by a continuing increase in the European population (Boyer 1977:469; Gibson 1964:377–381). The Indian population declined significantly, contributing to a decline in *total* population from a Preconquest level of 150,000–200,000 (Calnek 1972) to about 70,000 in 1625 (Gerhard 1972b:180–183; Gibson 1964:377–381). Other Indian communities in the Basin underwent massive population declines with no replacement by immigration. Rural Indian population probably stood between 80,000 and 90,000 in 1620 (Gerhard 1972b:52–54, 76–78; Gibson 1964:140–144) and was distributed in small communities throughout the Basin even after the *congregaciones* from 1592 to 1604. The settlement structure shifted from the Aztec approximate "log-normal" rank-size distribution to a pattern in which one community, Mexico City, was much larger than any other Basin community, and should be described as a primate city (Haggett 1966:103).

The development of the settlement system with many low-level centers dominated by Mexico City is associated with the dismantling and leveling of the Preconquest Basin political system. Initially after the conquest, Indian social, political, and religious elites were eliminated, displaced, or reduced in power, within both the regional and the local aspects of the socioeconomic system (Gibson 1964; 1966a). This produced a situation in which Indian control was restricted to *cabecera-sujeto* units which were administrative units mediating between the large Indian population and Spanish institutions. After 1550 the Spaniards appropriated the *caciques'* sources of tribute and labor and further reduced their political powers through the introduction of a Hispanic-based system of elected Indian officials (Gibson 1964:154, 166). Nevertheless, the structure of many weak, low-level centers persisted.

As native population declined, there were correlated changes in the organization of production and distribution required to provision Mexico City. The overall trend was to increase direct Spanish involvement in production and exchange where it affected the

city. During the period, several systems of production operated to supply the city from the rural hinterland. All were based on urban political control over the hinterland, and all were based on Indian labor. Continuing Indian depopulation was a major factor in causing shifts from one system to another (Gibson 1964:246, 272; 1981).

From 1521 to about 1550, Indian labor produced goods and services for the city in three ways: (1) through tribute collected from the *encomienda* system, (2) through *encomienda* labor to produce wheat and livestock on Spanish-owned ranches, and (3) through independent production for commercial market sale to Indians and, to a lesser extent, to Spaniards. The *encomienda* system was a political mechanism involving private jurisdiction over Indian communities. It served "to skim tribute off the top of the conquered economy, while leaving the economic and social organization of the conquered peoples as undisturbed as possible, so that it might produce a maximum of surplus for conqueror and conquered alike at a minimum of cost to the former" (Frank 1979:5). The system operated within the *cacique*-dominated *cabecera-sujeto* units. Tribute exactions, initially in the form of goods and services, and later in money and maize, supported the *encomenderos* in Mexico City. The tribute goods were sold or auctioned to consumers in Mexico City. Within this system, the Indian elite retained some control and enhanced their positions by collecting tribute over and above that requested by the Spaniards (Gibson 1964:184–200; 1966a:67; Liss 1975:97–98).

Commercial Spanish wheat and livestock production on a small scale coexisted with the *encomienda* system of the early sixteenth century. The products were for Spanish tastes, complemented Indian production, and were sold in Mexico City. Lands were held through purchases, *mercedes* (viceregal land grants), and *encomienda* pressure. *Encomienda* labor was used on these privately owned lands. Within the context of small-scale Spanish commercial agriculture, the Indian population learned Hispanic cultivation techniques and the Spaniards acquired organization skills and technical knowledge needed for successful farming in a new environment (Chevalier 1963:62; Gibson 1964: 225, 272–277, 322–326; Florescano 1965: 570–572; Frank 1979:17; Liss 1975:110; Matesanz 1965; Von Wobeser 1983:36–38).

At the same time, some sections of the Aztec market system survived and supplied the Mexico City Indian population with subsistence goods. Given the increased Spanish involvement in, and control over, the Indian markets of the city after 1550, it is probable that some of the goods also supported the conquerors (Gibson 1964:352–359, 394–397).

André Gunder Frank has suggested that the period from 1521 to 1550 was characterized by an attempt to create a dual economy (1979:6–7). However, continuing Indian depopulation prompted a series of changes in the production and distribution systems supplying Mexico City. From 1550 to about 1580, the *encomienda* became less important with the prohibition of labor services in *encomienda* and the expansion of tribute collection by the *corregimiento* (Gibson 1964:200, 225–226; Van Young 1983:22). The power of the *caciques* declined as they were replaced by elected officials (Gibson 1964:154–166). Spanish commerical agricultural production, using the labor *repartimiento*, along with livestock herding, expanded into other areas of the Basin from a distribution previously restricted to the vicinity of Mexico City (Chevalier 1963:83–114; Dusenberry 1963: 174–179; Florescano 1965:583–585; Gibson 1964:277–280). By this time the Spaniards had acquired the skills needed for efficient exploitation of the new environmental zone. Indian depopulation provided both lands and markets for such an expansion.

Tribute, increasingly collected by the Crown rather than the *encomendero*, also continued to supply Mexico City. The trend was a shift from tribute in "multiple commodity payments to stated amounts of money and maize" (Gibson 1964:199). Political mecha-

nisms meant to ensure adequate tribute supplies for the city began to infringe upon the Indian market system after 1550. Attempts were made to regulate commercial production and distribution within the system (Florescano 1965:577–578). This resulted in the expansion of complete Hispanic control over the urban markets and relevant sectors of the Indian rural production and marketing system (Gibson 1964:354–355, 395). Frank has proposed that the dual economy ended at this time and that there was a "progressive incorporation of the entire population and its agricultural pursuits into the mercantile capitalist economy" (1979:28).

These developments indicate an increasingly centralized control of production and distribution of the subsistence goods necessary for Mexico City. They are tied to the demographic and political changes noted previously. Spanish occupation and exploitation of rural areas increased. The economic system operative from 1521 to ca. 1580 produced and distributed goods but did not integrate the Indians into colonial society. The development of the hacienda system and the co-opting of the remaining Indian commercial production provided the institutional framework for that degree of social integration which did occur.

Further population decline between 1580 and 1620 imposed stresses on the *repartimiento* labor system supporting Spanish agriculture, left increasing quantities of Indian lands unused and deteriorating, and reduced Indian production for tribute and commercial sale (Charlton 1972; Charlton and Charlton 1978; Gibson 1964; 1981). These developments, coupled with the continuing growth of Mexico City, meant that supplies for the city were becoming increasingly inadequate. Changes were introduced into both production and distribution systems to alleviate the problem. Indian produce, channeled into the city through the tribute system and the market, declined through these decades. Tribute exactions and marketing operations were increasingly subjected to politically based rules intended to increase production and control

126

distribution in the city (Boyer 1977:470, 476; Florescano 1965.570–575, 603–624; Frank 1979:41; Gibson 1954:598; 1964:204, 326). These controls and the expanding hacienda system resulted in a severe reduction in commercial Indian maize cultivation by 1630. Spanish middlemen began to extend control over Indian production and distribution (Boyer 1977:471; Frank 1979:29; Tutino 1976a:272).

Private service and debt-peonage increasingly replaced labor *repartimiento* as a mechanism to organize and utilize effectively the dwindling labor force in expanding Spanish commercial agricultural production (Gibson 1964:243–256; Frank 1979:66–77; Van Young 1983:22). This was associated with accelerated land acquisition and the consolidation of many small or moderate holdings into a few large estates. The expansion into most of the ecological zones of the Basin was accompanied by a diversification in crop production and the expansion of livestock raising. Within the Basin there was some regional specialization in agriculture and herding (Chevalier 1963:84–114; Dusenberry 1963:174–191; Frank 1979:67–71; Gibson 1964:243–256, 274–292, 329; 1981:19; Konrad 1980:105–106; López Sarrelangue 1975:226; Moreno Toscano 1965:635–639; Pérez-Rocha 1982:128; Tutino 1976a:31; 1976b). The expansion of Spanish commercial agricultural production from 1580 to 1620 coincided with reduced production in other sectors of the economy and an expanding urban market. Areal expansion and crop diversification was based on accumulating experience and knowledge of the Basin. The hacienda system which developed out of this expansion was a Basin-wide, ecologically varied, and diversified production system, making efficient use of the available labor supply. From the point of view of the urban markets, ecological diversification reduced the chance of an overall crop failure. From the point of view of the owners, crop diversification allowed increased flexibility to meet varying environmental and market situations. The system was commercial and functioned to

supply Mexico City directly (Florescano 1980; Frank 1979:57; Gibson 1964; Mörner 1973:191; Pérez-Rocha 1982:128; Van Young 1983:12, 19–20).

By 1620, urban needs were being met by hinterland production through two production systems, both resting upon Indian labor. Grain (particularly wheat), meat (and other livestock products), and *pulque* were produced by hacienda-organized Indian labor on Spanish-owned lands. The hacienda was a rural-based, urban-oriented economic system of production (Aguirre 1982:32). Grain (particularly maize), vegetables, fruits, fowls, and combustibles were produced by Indian-organized labor on Indian-held lands for commercial sale. This system of production was increasingly integrated into urban markets by Spanish middlemen. The key figures in the urban-rural economic integration of the Basin were the members of the developing Indian colonial elite (Tutino 1976a:390). The structure of economic integration subsequently provided a framework for developing social integration in the Basin.

THE MIDDLE COLONIAL PERIOD
(1621–1720)

The non-Indian population continued to increase and diversify during the Middle Colonial period despite the interruption of severe flooding (Boyer 1977:456, 469–470; Davidson 1966:237; Israel 1975). The Indian population stabilized, with some evidence for a slight decline during the period. Estimated total urban population stood at about 85,000 in 1720 (Gibson 1964:377–381; Gerhard 1972b:181–183). The city retained its demographic dominance of the Basin. Economic, political, social, and cultural centralization continued in the urban setting.

The Indian population in the rural Basin continued to decline, reaching a nadir of about 70,000 in 1650. It gradually increased to perhaps 75,000 in 1692 and 90,000–100,000 in 1720 (Gibson 1964:140–144; Gerhard 1972b). Data from ongoing studies of Otumba parish baptismal and marriage records indicate a depressed population from 1630 to 1680, a gradual rise to 1700, and a rapid increase after 1700. This population was found in small *pueblos* and *barrios*, *ranchos*, and haciendas. During the period the *cabecera-sujeto* unit declined in economic and political relevance to the Spaniards (Gibson 1964:55–57). Thus the urban-rural demographic pattern, settlement system, and economic and political framework developed by the early seventeenth century persisted through the Middle Colonial period. Mexico City dominated the Basin.

The success of the hacienda system, developed from 1580 to 1620 as a regional system to supply some of the needs of the city, was confirmed by the early 1630's. Those agricultural estates dependent on *repartimiento* labor during the urban crises of the 1620's and early 1630's failed, while those with hired labor survived (Gibson 1964:248). The formal repudiation of labor *repartimiento* in the early 1630's validated the labor structure of the system. During the Middle Colonial period, land and water acquisition and title consolidation continued. Although the particular sequences and processes varied according to location and time and were dependent upon the fortunes of individual families or corporate groups, the trend through the period was toward the establishment of haciendas and their lands as permanent features of the rural landscape.

Documented descriptions of the growth of the Hacienda Hueyapan in the Regla region north of Pachuca, the Hacienda Salinas near Otumba, and the Hacienda Santa Lucia near Ozumbilla, along with analyses of haciendas and Spanish landholding in the Metztitlan region north of Pachuca and the Villa de Tacuba region west and northwest of Mexico City, indicate that by the end of the period hacienda holdings were extensive and Indian holdings were reduced and hemmed-in (Couturier 1965:47–63; Charlton 1965:87–92; Konrad 1980:46–106; Osborne 1970:79–99; Pérez-Rocha 1982:57–80). Although some regional variation occurred in the extent of hacienda territorial expansion and land con-

solidation during the seventeenth century (Charlton 1985; Osborn 1973; Pérez-Rocha 1982:128; Van Young 1983:20), the gradually increasing Indian population was effectively prevented from reoccupying and using large tracts of lands (Charlton 1965:92; Konrad 1980:163; Tutino 1975:498–501; von Wobeser 1983:52–60, 66–67). Many lands which were not owned by the haciendas were still available to them through the Indian elite as rental properties (Charlton 1985). The success of the hacienda system also rested on diversification. One owner might have haciendas in different areas of the Basin, and individual haciendas might include lands in several different ecological zones (Bellingeri 1980:29–30; Couturier 1965:87; Gibson 1964:290, 329; Konrad 1980:46–105; Tutino 1976a; 1976b).

Economically the hacienda system was an important means of agricultural production for the urban market (Aguirre 1982; Van Young 1983:15). It was a rural-based urban institution into which substantial capital was invested (Van Young 1983:12, 17). Most of these funds must have gone into land, livestock, and crops. Archaeological investigations in the eastern Teotihuacan Valley have located a few structures dating from 1621–1670. There is an increase in identified structures dating after 1670 (Charlton 1983; 1985). All are small with no evidence of grandeur (Charlton 1972). David M. Jones' (1978) archaeological investigations of large extant hacienda structures in the same region determined that none dated earlier than 1700 with most being post-1750. Although sumptuous and grandiose structures may be located under these haciendas, this seems unlikely given the absence of earlier ceramics. There is some evidence that sumptuous structures with large associated residences for workers may be late phenomena throughout the Basin (Konrad 1980:313; Tutino 1976a). Even the apparently large Jesuit hacienda residences of Santa Lucia (Tepeatzingo and San Xavier) were "designed primarily for production rather than residence" (Konrad 1980:312) and were utilitarian. A pattern of small

128

and simple structures correlates well with studies of specific haciendas such as Hueya-pan (Couturier 1965) and Salinas (Charlton 1965) as well as with general descriptions of hacienda development in the seventeenth century (Chevalier 1963; von Wobeser 1983:83).

Such a pattern is also consistent with the demography and the labor systems of the Basin (Konrad 1980:222; Tutino 1976a). In the eastern Teotihuacan Valley the population was depressed between 1630 and 1680, not increasing significantly until after 1700. There was no need for the haciendas to house the few available Indian workers who carried out seasonal labor. Instead, as John M. Tutino's (1976a:314–316) studies of documentary data for the same area during the Late Colonial period suggest, the towns which persisted as separate settlement units were reservoirs of seasonal labor for the haciendas. Herman W. Konrad (1980:322) has similarly described the large Santa Lucia residences as housing only administrators and slaves, with nearby Indian communities being drawn on for non-slave labor. The lack of a large available labor supply would also have been detrimental to the construction of grandiose and sumptuous structures housing the hacienda owners or their administrators. None of the archaeological data suggests large resident populations of workers, Indian or otherwise, in the eastern Teotihuacan Valley between 1621 and 1720 (D. M. Jones 1978:30–37). The occupants were culturally homogeneous, and depending upon the materials encountered, either Spanish or a partially Hispanicized Indian elite (Charlton 1979).

It is probable that Indians became dependent upon hacienda work as lands were lost and access to the remaining Indian-held lands was restricted (Konrad 1980:341–342). The amount of coercion and debt-peonage involved in labor relations remains uncertain (Van Young 1983:23–24). The Indian elite later played a significant role in mediating between the haciendas and their communities, but the development of this role is as yet unclear (Gibson 1975b:305; Konrad 1980:227; Tutino 1976a:313–314, 387). Elite medi-

ation probably developed during the seventeenth century as haciendas and towns became established as landholding entities. The position of the Indian elite would have been pivotal in a situation of labor shortage. It could have enhanced its functions as labor procurer by controlling access to many community lands. Such control would have had the added advantage of providing the elite with profits through land leasing or through the sale of surplus production to Spanish traders. An example of such control is documented for San Juan Teotihuacan (Münch G. 1976; Venegas Ramírez 1969).

The hacienda was one means by which Indians were integrated economically into rural-based, urban-oriented agricultural production. Commercial production and marketing was the other means. Indian commercial agricultural production continued throughout the period, but sale and distribution increasingly fell under the control of Spanish middlemen who marketed the produce in the city. Charles Gibson (1964:360) has described Spanish interference in Indian commerce. If Tutino's (1976a:271–281) analyses apply to the seventeenth century, it is probable that elite Indians were also the "contact persons" mediating between their communities and Spanish traders who sought to purchase surplus production. Studies of Indian commerce in the Middle Colonial period would clarify many of these issues. It is likely that the Indian elite controlled substantial areas of communal lands in the seventeenth century, their estates developing alongside those of the large Spanish landholders (cf. Pérez-Rocha 1982:81–100).

The social and economic integration of the rural Basin is clear in outline if not in detail. Social integration was weak. The haciendas were economic units, not social units. Although J. I. Israel (1975:270–271) has suggested that the large estates functioned as centers of acculturation, the nature of the known Basin haciendas appears to preclude this. The archaeological evidence from this period indicates the persistence of a conservative Indian cultural tradition. Descriptions by Tutino (1976a:390) and Herman W. Konrad (1980) of eighteenth-century situations in which most of the rural population continued to live as Indians under Hispanicized Indian leaders in Indian communities probably apply to the seventeenth century as well. Cultural distinction persisted, social integration was minimal, and economic integration for the majority of the Indians was exploitative.

THE LATE COLONIAL PERIOD (1721–1820)

Despite the recurrence of epidemics, the total population of Mexico City continued to increase during the Late Colonial period, reaching 100,000 by 1750 and 135,000 by 1805 (Gibson 1964:337–381; Tutino 1976a: 120). Both Indian and non-Indian populations increased. Although the city retained its demographic domination of the Basin, the proportion of the total Basin population residing there decreased from 50 percent at the beginning of the period to about 33 percent at the end. Nevertheless, the settlement dominance and economic, political, social, and cultural centralization in the urban center continued (Moreno Toscano 1978; O'Crouley 1972:29–31). The rural Indian population increased from an estimated 90,000–100,000 in 1720 to about 120,000 by 1742 and 275,000 by 1800 (Gibson 1964: 141, 148). Although most of the settlements remained small, there is some evidence of increasing differentiation in size by the end of the period. Throughout the period the *cabecera-sujeto* concept of Indian community organization was gradually replaced by the concept of undifferentiated corporate Indian communities (Gibson 1964:57; Tutino 1976b:182). During this period the urban-rural demographic pattern, settlement system, and economic and political framework, developed by 1620 and consolidated by 1720, persisted with modifications brought about by the growth in rural Indian population.

Although population pressure may be correlated with increasing numbers of suits brought over lands beginning after 1675 and continuing to 1805, the eighteenth-century

expansion of hacienda economy in the Basin did not involve significant usurpation of Indian lands (Charlton 1965; 1985; Couturier 1965; Konrad 1980; Osborn 1970). Exploitation of the expanding urban grain market and increasing specialization in *pulque* production by the northeastern Basin haciendas contributed to this economic expansion (Florescano 1969; Bellingeri 1980:29–31; Gibson 1964:329; Konrad 1980:100–103, 212–214; Tutino 1976a:25, 31). These developments were underwritten by the great increase in the available labor force. After the expulsion of the Jesuits in 1767, there were increased opportunities for investment in hacienda lands serving Mexico City (Konrad 1980:103; Tutino 1976a:24). Despite frequent changes in ownership of secular haciendas (Pérez-Rocha 1982:128; Van Young 1983:31), individual case studies indicate a relative stability in extent of hacienda landholdings. The hacienda system, developed to meet urban needs during a period of labor scarcity, persisted and prospered under conditions of increasingly abundant labor.

The well-documented profits from hacienda operations still do not appear to have been put into large and grandiose structures in the Basin (Konrad 1980:312–313). Archaeological studies of structures and settlement patterns in the eastern Teotihuacan Valley (Charlton 1972; 1975; 1979; 1983; 1985; D. M. Jones 1978; Seifert 1977) indicate that the pattern of small and simple structures, established by 1670, persisted through the Late Colonial period. In the late eighteenth century, after 1750, many of the large extant complex hacienda structures investigated by David M. Jones (1978) in the eastern Teotihuacan Valley and the Apan area were founded. Although these haciendas developed into grandiose and sumptuous structures with quarters for resident workers during the nineteenth century and into the twentieth, it is unlikely that very much of the building elaboration dates from the Late Colonial period. If Enrique Semo is correct (1973:259), the apparent centralization of hacienda activities at a few large structures after

1750 reflects the increasing economic importance and success of the hacienda system. Although such growth was stimulated and made possible in part by the increase in the available Indian labor force, the majority of the labor force continued to reside in the Indian communities (Konrad 1980:323–326; Tutino 1976a:390).

Tutino's (1976a) documentary studies of the 1750–1850 period in the eastern Teotihuacan Valley clearly demonstrate that the housing of large resident worker populations at the haciendas was not a consideration. At Santa Lucia to the west, however, where stability of ownership and extensive landholdings had existed much longer than in other areas of the Basin, a permanent work force numbering up to three hundred people "was housed within the *casco principal* or was confined within the outer wall" (Konrad 1980:322). This does appear to be an exception (Van Young 1983:30–31), and the data tend to support the position taken by David M. Jones (1978) that the development of the extant, large, complex, sumptuous, hacienda structures with provisions for housing a labor force took place after Independence during the nineteenth century. The occupants of all of the Late Colonial period hacienda structures studied archaeologically appear to have been culturally homogeneous with a ceramic and artifact tradition incorporating both Hispanic and Indian elements. Analyses of archaeological data from Indian communities in the eastern Teotihuacan Valley suggest that not all the inhabitants of one community nor all the communities of the region had access to ceramics of Hispanic origin equal to that of the hacienda residents.

Differential distribution of such ceramics would confirm Tutino's (1976a:356; 1976b:182–187) description of Indian corporate communities as possessing marked social, economic, and political hierarchical divisions. The important position of the Indian elite developed through control of Indian lands and labor during the Middle Colonial period. In the Late Colonial period the Indian elite continued to mediate between haciendas and Indians to provide the former with adequate and timely labor forces (Tutino 1976a:343–367; 1976b:191). By maintaining restricted land allocation among residents of Indian communities, the elite assured that the Late Colonial period population increase would result in substantial numbers of landless Indians who needed work on the haciendas for survival (Tutino 1976a:280–288; 1976b:186–187). Growth in the supply of disposable labor enhanced the position of the elite as well as underwriting the growth of the hacienda system. The haciendas had no need to use a formally coercive labor system at this time (Tutino 1976a:314; Van Young 1983:23–24). The hacienda system and the Indian elite evolved under conditions of scarce labor; both prospered when labor became more abundant.

During the Late Colonial period the rural Indian elite continued to prosper through their access to hacienda lands and water, their control and leasing of Indian communal lands, and commercial crop production, and by acting as intermediaries between the community and those Spaniards who sought to purchase surplus production for sale in the urban markets (Konrad 1980:329; Tutino 1976a:271–281). Indian agricultural production continued to be commercially oriented with Spanish dominance of sales and distribution outside the local community. Spanish traders were gaining the profit between production and final sale. Mexico City was ensured an additional source of supply which partially duplicated the products of the hacienda system (Tutino 1976a:120–123). Indian production, geared to the urban market, profited the Indian elite and the Spanish middlemen.

The structure of the social and economic integration of the Basin during the Late Colonial period continued from the previous period. The supply system for Mexico City was based on the hacienda system and the purchase of Indian surplus production at below market prices (Taylor 1979:160–161). Economically, the rural Indians were integrated into the urban-dominated Basin as producers for that center. Coordinating the economic links between Indian producers and the Spaniards in both systems were the Indian elites of the corporate communities. Social integration was minimal through both economic systems. Archaeological and historical data are consistent in suggesting that the rural Basin Indians continued to live with a conservative cultural tradition under Hispanicized Indian leaders in their corporate communities (Charlton 1979; Konrad 1980: 323; Taylor 1979:160–170; Tutino 1976a: 390). Small hacienda structures persisted through the period. After 1750 the precursors of the large, complex, grandiose, and sumptuous nineteenth-century hacienda structures were founded. There is no evidence that any of these structures incorporated large numbers of Indians as residents and functioned as social units until after 1850 (Charlton 1972; 1979; D. M. Jones 1978; Konrad 1980; Seifert 1977; Tutino 1975; 1976a; 1976b). The demographic changes of the Late Colonial period occurred within the persisting structure of urban-rural relations enhancing both the prosperity of the haciendas and the position of the rural Indian elite. It is not until the nineteenth century that demographically induced changes in the structure of urban-rural relations are observed.

The nineteenth-century Basin haciendas, with their sumptuous structures and resident workers were the final expression of a system originally developed under conditions of labor scarcity. Although continued population growth contributed to these developments, its effects were ultimately destructive. Population growth, combined with hacienda acquisition of most remaining Indian lands after 1856, created a large, landless rural population which the hacienda system could not accommodate, thus providing one of the stimuli for the 1910 Revolution.

SUMMARY AND CONCLUSIONS

From 1521 to 1620, population decline contributed to increasing difficulties in supplying Mexico City from the rural Basin and

brought about changes in the regional economic system, in settlement patterns, and in urban-rural relations. Two interdependent, ecologically diversified economic systems were present by 1620, and these persisted throughout the remainder of the Colonial period.

The hacienda system efficiently used nonresident, seasonal Indian labor on Spanish-held lands to produce goods primarily for Mexico City. The haciendas were urban institutions in a rural setting. They integrated the Indians into the system through wage labor. Indian participation was mediated by the developing colonial Indian elite in the corporate communities. The Spanish-dominated market system channeled Indian surplus production to Mexico City. This commercially oriented production became increasingly dominated by non-Indians who paid below market prices at the source and reaped the profits in the urban markets. The Indian elite functioned as intermediaries as well as producers, being sustained by profits from labor brokerage with the haciendas, commercial agricultural production on community lands under their control, the leasing of community lands, and acting as intermediaries with Spanish traders.

Mexico City, as a primate urban center, dominated the rural economy. The haciendas and market systems functioned as a dendritic extraction network in which necessary rural produce was directed to the markets of the urban center. Economic relations within these systems consisted of urban exploitation of rural labor and surplus production. Although some mutual advantages were present, most of the gain went to the *hacendados* and the Spanish traders. The major gain on the Indian side went to the developing elite. When the rural labor force increased after 1680, there were no structural changes within the economic systems. The extra labor was incorporated and used to augment the position and profits of the Indian elite, the Spanish traders, and the haciendas. The economic systems linked the Indian communities with the larger colonial social system but did not lead to full integration. Indian communities persisted as separate, identifiable social units throughout the period. There is neither archaeological nor historical evidence that the hacienda functioned at this time as an acculturative social unit with a large resident worker population.

I have based this outline of the Colonial period social and economic relations between Mexico City and its rural hinterland on archaeological and ethnohistorical data. Future studies in both fields should work within the framework of urban social and economic dominance of the Basin to explore the processes whereby the post-1750 elements of the Colonial period social system evolved. A consideration of the economic and ecological aspects of Indian and hacienda production for the urban markets should clarify the nature of rural social evolution within an urban-dominated colonial society.

ACKNOWLEDGMENTS

William Edwards, in his capacity as research assistant, was instrumental in locating many of the sources used for this paper. Cynthia L. Otis Charlton has provided continuous help in locating references and in preparing the final text and the map. Patricia Fournier G. supplied recent Mexican publications of relevance to the paper. An initial version of this paper was completed in December 1981. In January and February 1983, and March and April 1985, I revised the paper to incorporate the results of ongoing archaeological and documentary studies in the eastern Teotihuacan Valley and to note relevant materials published between 1981 and 1985. Both Ronald Spores and Victoria R. Bricker have provided valuable help in editing this paper.

The writing of this paper was made possible through the assistance of a research grant from the National Endowment for the Humanities and a University of Iowa Faculty Developmental Assignment. I would like to express my appreciation and thanks to these individuals and agencies.

9. One Hundred Years of Servitude: *Tlamemes* in Early New Spain

ROSS HASSIG

SITES AND SETTLEMENT patterns are a major anthropological focus in studies of early civilizations, but it is communications between centers that gives them life. Transportation is the vital link in the spatial organization of areas. Before the Spanish conquest, Mexican civilization lacked wheeled vehicles and draft animals. The flow of goods that linked cities and states was sustained by human porters—a multitude of human beasts of burden conveying all that was essential in Mesoamerican society. Although dealt with only fleetingly and in scattered references in both primary and secondary literature, this portage system shaped inter alia the nature and extent of trade, the complexity of the societies, and the degree of political integration. Although the conquest introduced substantial changes, including draft animals—horses, mules, and oxen—and wagons, these did not eclipse the indigenous system of transportation. Spanish means of transportation supplemented rather than replaced native porters, supplanting them only gradually.

Basic transport in Precolumbian Mesoamerica was by human carriers, or *tlamemes*

(Nahuatl, sg. *tlamemeh* or *tlamamah*, lit., 'he is one who has carried something'; pl. *tlamemehqueh*; called *tamemes* by the Spaniards).[1] They carried goods on their backs in woven cane containers (*petlacalli*) in carrying frames (*cacaztli*) supported by tumplines and covered with hides to protect the contents (Clavijero 1974:239; Sahagún 1957:60).

Who these people were, how they functioned, and how they fared, both before and after the Spanish conquest, are questions virtually ignored in the primary literature. References to *tlamemes* are widespread, but more than cursory treatment is lacking. There is no great chronicler against whom to weigh the scattered comments. Rather, the present treatment of *tlamemes* relies on piecing together information from disparate sources and projecting patterns both forward and backward from the available data, as warranted. Undoubtedly, much of what transpired has escaped recording. Furthermore, much additional information is derived inferentially from prohibitions enacted and complaints received by the viceroy. Consequently, available records reflect considerable strife. While these conditions may be an

134

artifact of the documents preserved, they are nevertheless generally substantiated by the comments of the chroniclers.

TLAMEMES IN THE PRECOLUMBIAN WORLD

Who the *tlamemes* were and how they arose as a group is unclear. But at the time of the Spanish conquest, they formed a separate, apparently hereditary, occupational group (Clavijero 1974:238; Castillo Farreras 1972: 113; Moreno 1931:67–68). Boys were trained to carry burdens, beginning at the age of five (*Códice Mendoza* 1964:122–123). Although hereditary succession was the most common means of *tlameme* recruitment, there were others. For instance, the victorious Aztecs required the people of Tepeaca to augment the *tlamemes* in their city as part of their tribute obligation (Durán 1967:2:158). It has been suggested that this occupation was also voluntarily adopted in the face of extreme poverty, particularly in cities with numerous landless persons (Castillo Farreras 1972: 111–112). Reflecting both the occupation's low status and the increasing demand for portage, entry into the ranks of *tlamemes* appears to have been easy. Egress, however, was difficult, due to a lack of alternatives, since the hereditary nature of other occupations tended to exclude aspirants, and the corporate kin and/or residential nature of commoner land perpetuated the landlessness of the dispossessed.

Regardless of the esteem in which the *tlamemes* themselves were held, the act of carrying in indigenous society was ambiguous. Carrying was frequently used as a metaphor for the burdens of the leaders (Sahagún 1969:258) and of the gods (Sahagún 1953:3) —onerous yet honorable tasks—but actually carrying burdens was less appealing. For instance, tumplines (and other undesirable things) were considered to be gifts of the deity Cihuacoatl (Sahagún 1970:11), and those born in the thirteen-day series beginning with 1 Ocelotl were thought to be doomed to slavery, to the digging stick, and to the tumpline (Sahagún 1957:5). Thus, despite

rhetoric exalting their labor, *tlamemes* occupied the lower rungs of society (Castillo Farreras 1972:113; Moreno 1931:67–68).

In order to understand the role of *tlamemes*, the terms of portage—loads, distances, and pay—must be considered. These dictated what and how goods were transported, but what they were for the Precolumbian period is problematic. The premier statement on the issue is by Bernal Díaz del Castillo (1974:99), who wrote that each *tlameme* carried a load of two *arrobas* for five leagues to the next district before being relieved. This comment has been the subject of much repetition, but despite some credence given these figures and the possibility that they do reflect Precolumbian usage, there are reasons for caution in accepting them at face value. The specificity of the figures suggests a false precision.

The distance of five leagues is ambiguous. If the *legua leal*, or statute league, is intended, five leagues equal thirteen miles (twenty-one kilometers), but if the *legua común*, or common league, is intended, they equal sixteen miles (twenty-six kilometers), a not inconsequential difference (Chardon 1980). But considering the erratic assessment of land distances during the Colonial period (Humboldt 1822:1:xxx), rather than expressing an exact distance, the five-league figure appears to have been a Hispanic convention for a one-day journey under load. Such precise figures are unreflective of Precolumbian practices, where distances were apparently assessed on a per-day basis, taking into consideration variations in terrain, loads, weather, and so forth. Terrain is a factor not only in elevation changes, but also in ground cover (e.g., jungle versus plains) and local topography (e.g., broken land, barrancas, rivers). As for the weather, inclement conditions reduced road serviceability and increased human discomfort. Thus, loads would be lighter or distances shorter when weather or terrain worsened. While extremes are possible, such as carrying very heavy loads or traveling long distances, it is doubtful that they occurred in conjunction.

The weight of *tlameme* burdens is also problematic. There is considerable variation in recorded loads and distances, and the data are scattered and incomplete. But based on logic and fragmentary evidence, it is apparent that distance and load are inversely related. Within a set time span, the heavier the load, the shorter the distance traveled; the longer the distance, the lighter the load. When much larger loads had to be carried, such as persons (Oviedo y Valdés 1979:45), either multiple carriers (Stephens 1969:2:269) or relief carriers were employed. John L. Stephens (1969:1:51) records the use of three reliefs (plus carrier) per person carried, the porters carrying him in relays, while Gonzalo Fernández de Oviedo y Valdés (1979:45) mentions two carriers and two reliefs for a *cacique*. The stated practice of Precolumbian *tlamemes* carrying two *arrobas* (approximately fifty pounds, or twenty-three kilograms) for five leagues per day appears reasonable as a statement of the general terms of portage. But these figures actually reflect Spanish legal limits on *tlameme* labor in effect when Díaz del Castillo wrote. As indicated above, loads, distances, terrain, and climate must all be considered as interrelated variables affecting portage.

The role of *tlamemes* was greatly shaped by the indigenous political system, after which organization they were patterned. At the local level, Indian society was organized by small districts. The native rulers, *tlatoqueh* (called *caciques* by the Spaniards, who imported the word from the West Indies [Gibson 1964:34–36]), resided in capital towns (*cabeceras*). The *cacique* provided *tlamemes* for portage through his district to the next, where they were relieved (Díaz del Castillo 1974:99). Goods passed in relay fashion, with bearers changing in each district. While political districts defined the basic *tlameme* units, precisely how *tlamemes* were organized is not clear, nor is the nature and extent of the *cacique's* control. Although the *cacique* could order *tlamemes* to carry (López de Gómara 1965–1966:2:216), they were apparently free to carry independently

as well. Minimally, the *cacique's* involvement guaranteed the functioning of portage through his district, as one link in an interlocking transportation network.

Tlamemes were professionals and were generally paid for their labor (*Cedulario indiano* 1945–1946:4:309–310 [1549]; Clavijero 1974:238; Sahagún 1959:14), but there were exceptions. Portage of tribute to the *cabecera* was considered part of the tribute—the obligation of the payers—so professional *tlamemes* were either unpaid or unused for this labor. (In the Colonial period, *tlamemes* were paid for carrying tribute, although apparently at a lower wage than for carrying other goods [Scholes and Adams 1938:2:107 (1558)].) *Tlamemes* also had certain obligations to the nobility (*principales*), who had limited rights to their labor. Clearly documented for the Colonial period (FHT 1:87–88 [1576], 1:134 [1576], 2:290–292 [1580]), these rights presumably arose from Preconquest practices, but their extent is unclear. Later sixteenth-century practice (FHT 3:144 [1591]) indicates that *tlameme* journeys were from their home *cabecera* to the *cabecera* of the adjacent district rather than from border to border within their respective districts, allowing a simpler, more centralized organization of *tlamemes* within each district.

The picture that emerges of Precolumbian *tlamemes* is of an expanding, low-status occupational group. The conditions causing people to adopt the occupation of *tlameme*—landlessness and exclusion from hereditary occupations—perpetuated it in hereditary fashion. *Tlamemes* labored as organized, professional carriers with general standards for portage, loads commensurate with distance and road conditions—carrying not only elite goods, such as cacao and gold, but ordinary commodities such as maize and cotton—and with *cabecera*-to-*cabecera* spans establishing distance in the load/distance balance. Loads were adjusted accordingly, extreme weights being avoided in the interest of reaching the next *cabecera* within a day. *Tlameme* organization mirrored local-level political organization and was the vital element linking districts and promoting interregional trade.

TLAMEMES IN THE POSTCOLUMBIAN WORLD

Although the Spanish conquest introduced many changes in Mexico, the practices, patterns, and personnel of the *tlameme* system remained largely intact, and *tlamemes* were employed by Indians and Spaniards alike. However, the labor-intensive *tlamemes* were no match for the efficiency of other transportation systems available to the Spaniards—draft animals and wheeled vehicles. In contrast to the *tlamemes'* 2-*arroba* loads, mules typically carried loads of 10 *arrobas* (250 pounds) (IEPAN 3-670r–v [1528]; AHN 553 [1576]; AA-Co 1-14v–15r [1526]) and operated in strings of pack animals (*recuas*) with one muledriver (*arriero*) for every four or five animals, traversing daily distances roughly equivalent to those of *tlamemes*—about twenty kilometers (P. W. Rees 1971: 214–215). Wagons were similarly efficient. The basic freight wagon (*carreta*) was pulled by two oxen, with a third in reserve, and hauled up to 40 *arrobas* (1,000 pounds), and the large freight wagon (*carro*) was pulled by up to sixteen mules and hauled up to 160 *arrobas* (4,000 pounds) (Ringrose 1970:38). Both of these Spanish transportation systems offered substantial advantages in efficiency over *tlamemes* that should have promoted greater trade, less expensive products, and easier political integration and control. Yet *tlamemes* were not immediately displaced. Rather, their use waned gradually and reluctantly over the following century.

The reasons for the perpetuation of the *tlameme* system of transport are several. First, the indigenous system was in place and functioning. It was available to be used, where *arriero* and *carretero* systems were not. Thus, some of the initial reliance on *tlamemes* can be explained simply in terms of expedience. Second, terrain was a major obstacle. Even had Spanish systems been available, some towns were located where

they could not be served by *arrieros* or *carreteros* at all. Third, despite legal requirements that native laborers be adequately compensated, *tlamemes* could be, and were, paid so little that they were cheaper than other forms of transportation, despite being labor intensive, and this was particularly true where *tlameme* labor was coerced.

Despite these compelling reasons for continued use of *tlamemes*, several offsetting factors contributed to their decline. As originally constituted under Precolumbian conditions, the *tlameme* system could have functioned adequately, but the large populations that met the conquerors were devastated by diseases introduced by the Spaniards. While there is little general agreement on the Preconquest population of central Mexico (roughly the area from the Isthmus of Tehuantepec to the desert north of Mexico City), the following figures may be used, at a minimum, as relational statements. Sherburne F. Cook and Woodrow Borah (1971: 80–82; Borah and Cook 1963) estimate a Preconquest population in excess of 25 million (William T. Sanders' estimate is approximately half that; see Denevan 1976:291), with a decline of 95 percent by the end of the sixteenth century:

1518	25,200,000	1580	1,891,267
1532	16,871,408	1595	1,372,228
1548	6,300,000	1608	1,069,255
1568	2,649,573		

Although the demographic trend was continually downward, epidemic disease caused three precipitous drops, in 1521, 1545–1548, and 1578. By 1620, the native population had reached its nadir of less than a million before stabilizing and then gradually increasing. Consequently, the population that bore the Spanish demand for cheap transportation in the sixteenth century was seriously eroding.

One reason for heavy reliance on *tlamemes* was the lack of viable alternatives. Until midcentury, both livestock numbers and livestock production were low in New Spain (Matesanz 1965:540–543). Due to the great expense of shipping animals from Spain, Crown policy was to encourage livestock production in the New World. However, it was centered in the Indies, and the 1520's saw a struggle between island and mainland producers for the right to breed livestock, the ban affecting the mainland producers being finally lifted in 1525 (Dusenberry 1963: 26–30). Thus, the hindrance caused the Spanish transport systems by the dearth of draft animals encouraged continued use of *tlamemes*.

A further factor hindering use of wagons and mules—and perpetuating the use of *tlamemes*—was the lack of large, passable trade routes. Precolumbian roads were not well developed beyond the confines of major urban centers, particularly beyond the Central Highlands (Castillo Farreras 1969: 183).

The old people also gave the name *coatl* to the road, the main road, etc. Thus they said: "Can it be that it is a little danger, a little serpent of our Lord?" Or they said: "How hast thou come? Can it be that it is the serpent, the road of stumbling?" Thus they named the road "serpent," because it is long and winding. And they called the road *tequatoc*, since there is stumbling, there is the running of thorns into the feet.

(Sahagún 1963: 269)

Not intended for wagons or draft animals, the indigenous roads were rough, hilly, and twisting (ENE 16:16–17 [1531])—factors of little concern for foot traffic.

Animal transport was more dependent on local support than were *tlamemes*, requiring adequate roads, water and feed, and a system of inns en route. Furthermore, barrancas must now be spanned to reduce the danger to draft animals, entailing considerable expense (Ciudad Real 1976:1:24, 84). The effectiveness of Spanish transportation systems was tied directly to the development of suitable roads and support services. The first and most important route in New Spain was between the port of Veracruz and Mexico City. In 1524 or 1525, Cortés ordered the establishment of inns to serve that traffic, but until mid-century there was no fixed route be-

tween the two sites (P. W. Rees 1971: 71–72). Traditional Indian labor drafts were used for road maintenance, but Spaniards were placed in charge at an early date (AC 2:125 [1531]). As establishments such as inns, monasteries, and hospitals were built, they tended to stabilize the routes. The first evidence of governmental road construction dates from 1530, when the *cabildo* of Mexico City referred to a new road to Veracruz that would allow the passage of wagons, although the first wagons were not introduced until 1531. This road departed from the indigenous one due to greater sensitivity of draft animals and wagons to topographical features, and the need for adequate water and pasturage (P. W. Rees 1971: 74–75). In part, the shift was an effort to avoid injury and inconvenience to the Indians who lived along the road and had previously fed and housed traveling Spaniards, however unwillingly (ENE 16:14 [1531]). The indigenous road passed through Indian towns, while the new one avoided them, relying on inns. It was along this latter route that wagons and mule trains passed, only those on horseback taking the old route (Oviedo y Valdés 1979:4:244). By mid-century, major routes linked Mexico City with the Gulf Coast, major centers, and ports to the south. However, Acapulco was still reachable only by mules with small loads in the early seventeenth century (VEA 2: 205–206 [1604]), and travel from the southern ports of Tehuantepec and Huatulco was faster overland 30 leagues to the Coatzalcoalcos River and thence by boat to Veracruz and then overland to Mexico City than directly overland 120 leagues (VEA 1:157 [1566]; Borah 1954:29). Despite repeated royal orders that roads be built and maintained (VEA 1:134 [1550], 164 [1566], 191 [1568], 255 [1585]), many roads remained inadequate (Ciudad Real 1976:1:24; PNE passim).

Early Sixteenth Century

The Spaniards did little about most of the factors affecting *tlameme* use—depopulation, increasing transport demand, rudimentary support systems, and inadequate numbers of draft animals. Indeed, many of these difficulties were not fully recognized by the Spaniards. Even had they been aware of the problems, they would have been able to do little about them. Instead, the Spanish response was to legally mandate restrictions on Indian labor, and it is these records which largely trace the patterns of *tlameme* use. Royal and viceregal laws and policies attempted, repeatedly, to curtail the exploitation of native labor, including *tlamemes*. Spanish regulation of Indian bearers began in the West Indies, before the conquest of Mexico. In 1511, the king prohibited the use of Indians of Hispaniola for carrying burdens, since their numbers were greatly diminished (DIU 1:28 [1511]), and the Indians of San Juan were prohibited from carrying loads greater than twenty-five pounds and carrying them over rough terrain (DIU 1:36–37 [1512]). From the outset, royal policy was concerned with the effects of portage on the natives and sought to place limits on its use. In New Spain, *tlamemes* were employed from the earliest contact. But in 1528, the Ordinances of Toledo forbade forcing Indians to be *tlamemes* (Mendieta 1971:472). Rather than imposing an absolute ban on their use, the Council of the Indies recognized the necessity of using *tlamemes* and outlawed only their use by force. As long as the labor was voluntary and compensated, it remained permissible (*Recopilación de leyes* 1973:6-12-6 [1528, 1549, 1601, 1609]; Simpson 1938:67). The king did, however, ban the use of *tlamemes* to supply the mines (Vasquéz 1940: 143 [1528]). Massive labor drafts did occur during those early years, however, such as Nuño de Guzmán's use of 1,500 *tlamemes* to carry maize from Huejotzingo to Mexico City (Warren 1974:95).

Tlamemes were regarded as necessary and were recognized as a legitimate occupational class whose livelihood depended on this form of labor (Mendieta 1971:472). So, by 1531, the governing *audiencia* established regula-

tions for their use: carrying had to be voluntary, *tlamemes* were to be paid 100 cacaos per day (worth about one *real*—an eighth of a peso—at that time), their loads were to be limited to 2 *arrobas* (although official pronouncements occasionally varied, allowing 3 *arrobas* [AGN-I 4-649-185 (1590)], 1.5 *arrobas* [AGN-M 2-452-182 (1543)], or 2 *arrobas* plus 5 pounds [AGN-M 2-738-321v (1543)]), and they were to go no more than one day's journey from their *pueblos*.[2] Intended was a temporary expedient, the use of *tlamemes* was to be discontinued once pack animals became available (Simpson 1938:67–68). However well intended these reforms were, they did not alleviate the situation. For example, Cortés violated the one-day journey limit by sending *tlamemes* on a round trip from Cuernavaca to Acapulco in 1532 (ENE 2:114), although he did pay them the required 100 cacaos per day. The dilemma faced by the Crown was the excessive hardship portage caused the Indians—heavy loads, long journeys, and harsh treatment—versus the Spanish need for such transport, particularly on the part of merchants, who could not travel as swiftly nor gain access to many places without *tlamemes* (DCLI 1:161–162 [1533]). This impasse was resolved in favor of the Spaniards, and *tlameme* use and abuse continued. This decision was not an unalloyed evil. While it supported Spanish interests, it also allowed the continuation of an established indigenous occupation.

Although *tlamemes* were often used with callous disregard for their well-being, official concern for the portage-related diminution of the indigenous population began in the Indies as early as 1511. It quickly became apparent that *tlamemes* were dying in New Spain as well, but the reasons are not always clear. In some cases, weather was a factor. In 1531, witnesses in litigation between Cortés and Guzmán testified to the deaths of many *tlamemes* en route from Huejotzingo. Two to three thousand maize-laden *tlamemes* were sent to Mexico City despite the winter season. Caught by snow in the pass of Chalco, many died—the accounts vary, ranging from 30 to 113—and more succumbed from fatigue after returning to Huejotzingo (Warren 1974: 95–125 [1532]). Excessive loads were also a common complaint (AGN-I 4-649-185 [1590]), as was the length of many journeys (AGN-I 2-973-224v [1583], 6-1a-656-175v [1593]).

The most crucial variable, however, was change in climatic zones. The shift from *tierra caliente* (land below 1,000 meters) to *tierra fría* (land above 2,000 meters) was devastating (AGN-GP 2-79-39 [1579], 2-920-216 [1580]; Cuevas 1975:161–167 [1550]). The Indians of the *tierra fría* were popularly thought to be much stronger and to work better than those of the *tierra caliente* (DII 6:484–515 [1550]), and the lowlands were regarded as unhealthy (DII 41:149–160 [1537]). However, a simple lowland-to-highland shift was not the sole cause. Deaths occurred during journeys in either direction. The royal officials modified the existing regulations prohibiting *tlameme* travel beyond the confines of their home provinces, and extended the prohibition to journeys between climatic zones within single provinces as well (AGN-GP 2-79-39 [1579]; *Recopilación de leyes* 1973:6-1-13 [1541]). Viceregal regulations on the use of *tlamemes* restricted them primarily to the central plateau area of New Spain.

The organization of *tlamemes* by districts persisted throughout the sixteenth century (AGN-GP 2-79-39 [1579], 4-289-81v [1591]). This was due, in part, to restrictions on *tlameme* journeys between climatic zones, but it was also due to the ease with which the existing organization could be used to recruit and direct *tlamemes*, and to ensure efficient portage by employing a series of fresh carriers.

Official Spanish concern for the *tlamemes* began early and was persistent, albeit often ineffective. When Antonio de Mendoza became the first viceroy of New Spain, the king ordered him to see if the existing regulations provided adequate safeguards and if not,

what additional measures could be taken (VEA 1:29 [1535]). In 1537, the legal limit of one day's journey (five leagues) was reiterated, and the use of *tlamemes* was prohibited in the tropical lands of Veracruz, Soconusco, Tehuantepec, Oaxaca, Huatulco, Colima, Zacatula, and Panuco as well as between climatic zones (DII 41:149–160 [1537]), pointing up the high mortality rates for those so employed. During New Spain's early years, Spanish merchants employed *tlamemes*, arguing to the king that only by so doing could they effectively compete with the Indian merchants (ENE 16:30–34 [1537]).[3] Spanish regulations concerning *tlameme* labor (effective and otherwise) did not apply to the native population. Consequently, a dual system existed in which Spaniards were legally bound to guarantee certain working conditions, but Indians were free to use *tlamemes* without restrictions (presumably in the traditional manner). Indian merchants were thus unfettered by Spanish restrictions on *tlamemes*, which allowed them entrée to areas inaccessible to wagons or mules. Viceroy Mendoza complained to the king about this inequity, stressing the injury to poor Spaniards who could not afford pack animals and were therefore forced to sell their goods to Indian merchants employing *tlamemes*. Also, he said, business trips would be prohibitively expensive if one were forced to hire an *arriero* rather than *tlamemes* (ENE 16:30–34 [1537]). These complaints were apparently effective, as the next year merchants were granted the right to use *tlamemes* to carry cacao to Mexico City (AC 4:134 [1538]), although the age at which Indians could carry as *tlamemes* was regulated (*Recopilación de leyes* 1973:6-12-14 [1538]). The earliest licensed use of *tlamemes* occurred along the major arteries running from Mexico City to Veracruz, Oaxaca, and Acapulco. *Tlamemes* were employed to carry a wide variety of goods, from bulk commodities, such as maize, to cacao (in which there was considerable official interest), imported plants, and bellows and tools for the mines at Culiacan

(Warren 1974:95–99 [1532]; AGN-M 1-131-65r-v [1542], 1-381-176v [1542], 1-430-202v [1542]; AC 4:134 [1538]). The official attitude was that using *tlamemes* was acceptable as long as pack animals were unavailable, due to either scarcity or prohibitive cost. However, attitudes among the Spaniards differed. While the king tried to curtail reliance on *tlamemes*, Spanish colonists favored their extensive use, and the royal officials were placed in the uncomfortable position of mediating conflicting demands, commands, and flagrant violations.

The *New Laws* of 1542–1543 restated the previous general restrictions, that *tlamemes* were limited to areas where pack animals were unavailable, that their burdens were to be moderate, that they were to be paid, and that the work was to be voluntary (*New Laws* 1971:xiii [1542]; Simpson 1938:68). The ban on forced *tlameme* labor was reiterated, including work for clerics (*Recopilación de leyes* 1973:6-12-6 [1528, 1549, 1601, 1609]; *Cedulario indiano* 1945–1946:4:304–306 [1549]). Repeatedly, the lack of roads and animals was held to be sufficient reason to employ voluntary *tlamemes*, but it did not excuse forcing them to carry. It was common, however, for Spanish merchants simply to use *tlamemes* and then to claim that the conditions under which they did so were legal (Puga 1945:200v–201v [1549]). It was the responsibility of the governors and other justices of each jurisdiction and district to oversee the regulations and grant licenses for *tlameme* use where justified, and to establish the number of *tlamemes* needed, the distance they were to go in one day, and their pay (ENE 16:30–34 [1537]). Indians continued to be exempt from these regulations on *tlameme* use, but the newly emerging group of mestizos were not. The *New Laws*, widely disregarded, were suspended in 1544 (Bancroft 1883–1888:10:527, 565).

Whether the threat of the *New Laws* stimulated greater compliance, or greater care was taken to enforce existing regulations to show that new laws were unnecessary, there was an increase in the number of complaints by Indians, denunciations of Spanish abuses, and the issuance of licenses for legitimate Spanish use of *tlamemes*. The licenses granted during the 1540's were, generally, for small parties of *tlamemes*, ranging from fifteen to thirty-five (although one cacao merchant was permitted to bring one thousand *cargas* (*tlameme* loads—fifty pounds each) by *tlameme* to Mexico City (AGN-M 1-131-65 [1542]). There was considerable small-scale and local use of *tlamemes*, for which pay schedules were enacted.[4] But the main routes continued to see most of the *tlameme* flow, despite the prohibition on taking them to the ports of Veracruz or Huatulco (DII 41:149–160 [1537]; AC 4:134 [1538]). Wages were uncertain, although ostensibly based on load and distance or time, and the enforcement of the regulations was uneven and subject to considerable official abuse.

During these early years, some of the demand for *tlamemes* was removed by competing Spanish *arrieros* (a few Indians also became *arrieros* [IEPAN 2-454v–455v (1527)], but they were too few to satisfy the demand [ENE 16:30–34 (1537)]), and their fees were so exorbitant that the Mexico City *cabildo* was forced to set standard rates (AC 2:83–85 [1531]). Wagons too were introduced, although not until 1531 (Kubler 1948:1:162), but, being dependent upon roads, they were primarily used locally to service the mines (ENE 16:30–34 [1537]). Rather than being displaced, *tlamemes* were used in conjunction with both *arrieros* (AGN-M 1-256-121 [1542]; AGN-GP 4-289-81v [1591]; AGN-RCD 3-76-47 [1589]) and *carreteros* (AGN-GP 5-876-184v [1600]; 5-885-185 [1600]; AGN-RCD 3-76-47 [1589]), although often illegally (AGN-M 1-256-121 [1542]).

Middle Sixteenth Century

Between 1550 and 1580, depopulation severely reduced the number of *tlamemes* available, although their decline was partially offset by the greater number of mules and horses available (Matesanz 1965:539–543). At the same time, however, the opening of the northern mines increased the overall demand for transportation. Pursuant to royal order, Luis de Velasco, the second viceroy, implemented the previously suspended *New Laws* (VEA 1:135 [1550]; Bancroft 1883–1888:10:565), but with limited success. In 1568 and 1580, the king again ordered the viceroy to stop *tlameme* portage (VEA 1:191 [1568], 1:232 [1580]). Spanish merchants continued to employ *tlamemes* (Cuevas 1975: 249 [1561]), and the established patterns of use continued, with the commodities carried changing very little (*Cedulario indiano* 1945–1946:310–311 [1552]; Cuevas 1975:183–218 [1554]). Throughout this period, as in the previous one, complaints came to the viceroy of Spanish travelers forcing the Indians in the villages along the roads to be *tlamemes*, often for little or no pay, and for lengthy and arduous journeys (AGN-GP 1-235-47v [1575], 1-732-142 [1576], 1-49-198 [1576]). Even persons legally entitled to limited use of *tlamemes* were guilty of extorting free labor (AGN-GP 2-920-216 [1580]); these included clergymen (ENE 8:116 [1556] and the Spanish officials entrusted with enforcing *tlameme* regulations (AGN-I 2-685-157v [1580], 3-416-96 [1591], 5-6-71 [1590], 6-2a-645-146 [1592]). Though widespread, the mistreatment of *tlamemes* was not universal, and some priests decried it, on moral as well as pragmatic grounds (Motolinía 1973:109). However, as a practical matter, maltreatment was commonplace (Palafox y Mendoza 1893: 54), and the consequences for violating the laws protecting the Indians were minimal. For instance, in 1580, the Indians of Teutitlan complained to the viceroy that Diego Pizarro, a mestizo who resided in the village, forced them to carry as *tlamemes*. Pizarro had previously been banished from the village of Teutila by viceregal order for the same offense, yet further banishment was the only penalty assessed against him (FHT 2:247–248 [1580]). In 1579 the earlier requirements of voluntary, paid portage with moderate

loads where roads and animals did not exist were restated (*Recopilación de leyes* 1973. 6-12-10 [1549, 1579]), reflecting a continuation of the banned practices (ibid.:3-3-63 [1595, 1628]). These impositions were not visited on the Indians solely by Spaniards and mestizos, however. Complaints reached the viceroy both of Indian officials forcing *tlamemes* to work for them (AGN-GP 1-800-148v [1576]) and of their giving *tlamemes* to others (AGN-GP 1-1049-198 [1576]). The use of *tlameme* labor by Indian nobles (FHT 1:87–88 [1576], 1:134 [1576], 2:290–292 [1580]), a right presumably balanced by reciprocal obligations in Preconquest times, was also abused (DII 6:490–491 [1550]). Complaints were raised of *principales* forcing *tlamemes* to work (AGN-I 5-1117-353 [1591]; García and Pereyra 1905–1911:15:122–124 [1558]), although sometimes the nobles joined the commoners' complaints to the viceroy over Spanish abuses (AGN-I 2-685-157v [1580]). The problem, recognized by the viceroy, was one of balancing the nobles' rights and those of the commoners (*macehuales*). If the nobles were allowed to demand too much service, the commoners would suffer, but if the Spaniards unduly restricted the nobles, they would lose their authority over the commoners (VEA 1:42 [1550 or 1551]). The system under which native nobility had freely exercised their rights to *tlameme* labor was breaking down, due to the rise of "nobles" of questionable title, a decline in the commoners' sense of obligation as the nobles provided fewer traditional services, or an attempt by the nobility to increase commoner services, either absolutely or per capita as they attempted to maintain traditional rights in the face of demographic decline (García and Pereyra 1905–1911: 15:122–124 [1558]). In any case, the Spaniards felt that the *caciques* and nobles were exploiting their own people (VEA 1:136 [1550]). While Indian officials remained responsible for *tlamemes*, the extent of their control was diminished. For instance, in 1580 (FHT 2:322–323 [1580]), the priest of Pachuca sought two *tlamemes* from the Indian governor of Tolcayuca to take some clothes to Texcoco. The two *tlamemes*, Juan Yautl and Miguel Huicitl, fled with the goods. Although the governor was manifestly neither implicated in the actions of the *tlamemes* nor able to control their actions, the priest seized him and forced him to pay for the missing goods.

Indian merchants continued to use *tlamemes* (AGN-RCD 3-56-30 [1580]). Reflecting both earlier and later conditions and practices, *tlamemes* consumed tobacco and invoked the gods to protect them from robbers and other dangers during their journeys (AGN-GP 2-616-145v [1580]) and to aid them with their burdens (Ruiz de Alarcón 1984: 73–78). The physical conditions of portage are unrecorded for Precolumbian times, but during the Colonial period, allegations were made (Gage 1958:218–219), or implied in their denial (ENE 16:31 [1537]), that heavy loads bore down on the tumplines of the *tlamemes*, causing bleeding of the foreheads and occupationally induced baldness.

During these decades, there was a great rise in the number of *arrieros*. With the increase in livestock and the demand for *arrieros*, numerous Indians entered that profession. Licenses were required, but do not appear to have been difficult to obtain (AGN-M 6-243 [1563]). By mid-century, however, there still were not enough draft animals or wagons to avoid using *tlamemes* (VEA 1:151 [1555]). This was also the florescent period of wagoneering in Mexico, spurred largely by the discovery of silver in the north. The trip from Mexico City to the mines was entirely on the central plateau, which afforded relatively level and easily crossed terrain (Ringrose 1970:37), and these favorable conditions fostered the development of the large freight *carros* that traveled in convoys through hostile territory. Although draft animals and freight wagons accounted for much of the traffic, *tlamemes* were still employed (Powell 1952:24). The major problem was the extension of the route into unsettled areas. The

mining area stretched into lands inhabited by roving Chichimecs, where there were few or no settled communities, so *tlameme* use meant long-distance treks requiring the supply of food, shelter, and protection in a manner similar to that required for Spanish systems of transport. Consequently, much of the advantage of employing *tlamemes* was lost, and they were not used as extensively on these routes as they were elsewhere in New Spain. There was also an increase in wagon traffic between Veracruz and Mexico City (Hakluyt 1903–1905:9:378–379 [1572]; AGN-O 1-45-41 [1580]), but the use of Indians on this route, even as *carreteros*, was legally restricted to the autumn and winter months (Zavala 1947:235, 248–249 [1580]).

Late Sixteenth and Early Seventeenth Centuries

Following the pestilence of 1578, *tlamemes* continued carrying the same goods (AGN-I 3-560-133v [1591], 4-840-228v [1590], 6-2a-645-146 [1592]; AGN-GP 2-616-145v [1580], 5-876-184v [1600], 5-885-185 [1600]; AA-O 1-156-184 [1613]), but they were used to a much greater extent in carrying local commodities: wood, fodder, charcoal, stone, and clothing (AGN-I 6-2a-645-146 [1592], 6-2a-45-12v [1591]; AGN-RCD 3-31-15 [1587]). Royal orders that the practice be stopped were again issued (VEA 1:255 [1585], 2:133 [1596]) but without significant impact. Spanish travelers continued to force the Indians to carry as *tlamemes* (AGN-I 2-11-2v [1582], 2-62-15 [1582], 2-230-58v [1582], 2-973-224v [1583], 3-112-26v [1590], 4-649-185 [1590], 4-704-198 [1590], 4-859-232v [1590], 5-52*bis*-85 [1590], 5-629-242v [1591], 6-1a-213-55v [1592], 6-1a-1130-310 [1596]; AGN-GP 2-572-136 [1580], 2-743-174v [1580], 2-754-177 [1580], 3-266-188v [1587]), a situation exacerbated by the latest population decline. There was a further surge of complaints to the viceroy of *tlameme* abuse, but they were concentrated in specific areas more than previously. *Pueblos* located on major routes were constantly forced to supply *tlameme* labor for travelers, a fact readily apparent to the Indians. When they moved away from the road, the problem lessened (AGN-I 6-1a-656-175v [1593], 6-1a-1039-281 [1591]), but was not eliminated. Towns at some distance from main routes did not supply *tlamemes* frequently, and when they did, it was usually for local trips. Towns on main routes were compelled to supply *tlamemes* frequently, and they often did so for long distances. The impact of Spanish expansion on *tlamemes* can be seen at Epazoyuca (Epazoyucan, Hidalgo) (Barlow 1949:37). Located on the road to the mines of Pachuca, Epazoyuca claimed to have lacked *tlamemes* before the conquest, but was a *tlameme* town by 1579. During the waning decades of the sixteenth century, the most noticeable pattern in native portage was an increase in the number of non-*tlamemes* forced to carry. Previously, the large numbers of *tlamemes* had been adequate for Spanish needs, but as the population dwindled, increasing complaints to the viceroy indicate a shift to coerced portage by commoners who were not professional *tlamemes*. Although the practice of indiscriminately forcing Indian laborers to act as porters had occurred earlier, the practice now became widespread. The previous reliance on professional *tlamemes* often gave way to simple coercion of available Indians by Spanish travelers. The treatment received by these porters was often abusive and led to personal losses of animals (AGN-I 5-629-242v [1591]; AGN-GP 2-754-177 [1590]), fields, and homes (AGN-I 2-11-2v [1582]).

Many Indians entered or continued in transportation, but often by adopting Spanish roles. As mule trains increased, so too did Indian *arrieros*, although the number of draft animals they could own was restricted (AGN-RCD 3-56-30 [1588]). This period also witnessed the crest of the *carreteros'* development, their numbers waning after 1600 when the flow of silver diminished (Ringrose 1970: 47–48). *Tlamemes* under license were used in conjunction with *arrieros* (AGN-GP 4-

289-81v [1591], 5-876-184v [1600], 5-885-185 [1600]), but they were often in a debt relationship to the *arrieros* (AGN-RCD 3-76-47 [1589]; IE 1299:18-38v-39r [1596], 1590: 28–53r [1598], 1420:23–39v [1598]), and *tlamemes*, with their horses and mules, were forced to carry to the mines (AGN-I 3-560-133v [1591]).

Because the exception under which *tlameme* use had been allowed previously had been abused and had led to great excesses (*Recopilación de leyes* 1973:6-12-9 [1609]), *tlameme* use was virtually banned by 1609. Only limited portage of *corregidor* and ecclesiastical goods was still permitted, although in practice, *tlameme* use continued (AGN-O 1-156-184 [1613]), possibly because enforcement of the restrictions was put in the hands of the priests—the efficacy of which provision the viceroy doubted. In addition, the use of *tlamemes* by Indians remained unregulated (AGN-O 1-158-186 [1613]), and their use by Spaniards remained legal within the confines of cities, provided it was voluntary, paid, and conformed to city laws.

Despite these prohibitions and others reiterating the ban (*Recopilación de leyes* 1973:3-3-63 [1595, 1628], 6-12-6 [1528, 1549, 1601]; Vásquez 1940:283 [1609]), *tlameme* use persisted. It was, of course, illegal (FHT 7:283 [1617]), but widely recognized as occurring (FHT 7:143–144 [1639]), even to the extent that while decrying the use of force, the viceroy continued to demand that the *tlamemes* receive their "usual" pay (FHT 7:315 [1618]). The number of complaints, however, greatly decreased from the high of the sixteenth century. Rather than indicating a discontinuance of the illicit practices, the dearth of complaints reflected the nadir of the indigenous population and the rise of competing forms of transportation—many employing Indians. *Tlamemes* persisted into the late nineteenth and the twentieth centuries as *cargadores*, but in a much reduced capacity. As an organized occupation (except in the loading and unloading of ships), they ceased to be significant in central Mexico, although casual, local portage continued. As a profession, it was gradually peripheralized, being relegated to the jungle areas of Yucatan and Guatemala to the south and to the mountainous regions of the desert north (R. E. W. Adams 1978; Bunzel 1959:30; Flippin 1889: 400–401; Hammond 1978; Morley 1937–1938:2:233–234; Stephens 1963:1:258–259, 328, 340–342; 1969:1:51; 2:269, 274), and to intra-city portage (Calderón de la Barca 1966:328, 504, 547).

LEGACY

Although depopulation, increasing demand, the availability of alternative transportation systems, and governmental regulations all affected *tlameme* use, the relationship between indigenous and Spanish transportation systems was not simply contraction of the former and expansion of the latter. The introduction of Spanish transportation systems did not result in the uniform displacement of *tlamemes*, but yielded varied patterns of use, emphasizing *tlamemes* in certain areas and for certain commodities, and *arrieros* and *carreteros* for others, resulting in overlapping, but separate, transportation niches.

The failure of indigenous roads to meet Spanish needs prompted the development—however incomplete—of a road system adequate for *arrieros* and *carreteros*, and this patterned the use of *tlamemes*, both spatially and temporally. Immediately after the conquest, the route of most concern was Veracruz to Mexico City and then to other cities, and it was along this coast-plateau axis that the Spaniards directed construction. *Arrieros* quickly took over much of the Veracruz–Mexico City transport, supplementing the *tlameme* system which already spanned the same general route. Given *arriero* dependence on roads and inns, their use supplemented *tlamemes* along the developed routes, but in areas with less traffic and poor roads, *tlamemes* continued largely uncontested by animal transport.

Although they did compete with *arrieros*

on long routes (AGN-O 1-45-41 [1580]; AGN-RCD 3-5-4 [1587], 3-22-11 [1587]), *carreteros* usually served in a more restricted sphere. They are mentioned most frequently in the hauling of bulk commodities—such as in the immediate vicinity of Mexico City—and foodstuffs from the nearer sources, e.g., the Valley of Matlatcingo and the Villa of Toluca (AC 8:180:181 [1564]), to which adequate roads had been built (ENE 16:16–17 [1531]) —and particularly in serving the mines (Bakewell 1971:21; Powell 1950:238–240; Ringrose 1970:38–39). Large areas without adequate roads were left to *tlameme* portage (Cuevas 1975:197 [1554]; FHT 5:99–100 [1603]). Putatively, due to rugged terrain, some towns could not be supplied by *arrieros* or *carreteros* at all, as in the case of the Villa of San Ildefonso (San Ildefonso Villa Alta, Oaxaca) (ENE 3:51 [1533]; FHT 5:102–103 [1603]).

Utilization of draft animals and wagons increased in direct proportion to the number of roads built and was further promoted by ordinances restricting *tlameme* use on these routes. The displacement of the indigenous transportation system was most nearly complete along the major arteries, promoted by the demand for greater quantities and an increasing variety of goods, and by the partial *tlameme* vacuum produced by royal edict. In most instances, *tlamemes* competed effectively because of their ability to traverse rugged terrain. But they yielded the easiest, most-traveled, best-maintained, and most profitable routes to Spanish transport encroachment. A major competitive disadvantage of the *tlameme* system was its relative inelasticity. Faced with increased demand, any expansion of *tlameme* services was tied directly to numbers of porters, whereas the *arriero* and *carretero* systems could expand services by increasing capital investment in mules and wagons, rather than increasing the number of men necessary.

While there may have been accepted wage rates for *tlamemes* before the conquest, there was considerable variation in the Hispanic cra. Wages for Indian labor generally rose during the sixteenth century, from .06 *reales* per day in 1524, to 1 *real* in 1590 (Borah and Cook 1958:44), but *tlamemes* were not easily encompassed by such standards, whether customary or legally mandated. Assessing their wages meets with difficulties both in the units of pay and in the labor compensated. Pay rates are somewhat problematic because early *tlameme* wages were calculated in cacao beans (worth 1 *real* per 200 beans between 1544 and 1550 [AC 5:61–63 (1544), 5:289 (1550)]), while later rates were based on Spanish currency.[5] Furthermore, while basic Precolumbian portage was typically a day's journey, and many later rates were so set, fee schedules were often established for specific treks and were primarily concerned with distance (Simpson 1938:70). Initial examination of the data makes clear that there was considerable variation in pay, and further investigation reveals even more pronounced disparities. All too often, Indians were not paid for portage, and when they were, inconsistencies abounded, even when rates were authorized by the viceroy. In addition to differences in the rate of pay, the distances for which *tlamemes* were paid also varied. Some *tlamemes* were compensated for round trips, while others were paid for only one way. Their employers could adhere to officially established daily rates for portage, but pay less by calculating wages only for the distance loads were actually carried, and not for the unladen return. Thus, officially established daily wages offer a façade of standardization belied by practice. Based on records of actual compensation, rather than on official standards, *tlameme* wages did not keep pace with other costs.

Precise wages for *arrieros* and *carreteros* are difficult to calculate, since payment was by load, not by laborer, but they were substantially higher than those for *tlamemes* (AA-Co 1-6r [1525]; AC 2:83–85 [1531]; AGN-RCD 3-16-9 [1587]; IEPAN passim; IE passim; Cuevas 1975:199 [1558]). Occasionally, *tlamemes* also owned horses and both were

employed, the horse costing twice *tlameme* rate (AGN-I 6-1a-1130-310 [1596]).

Throughout the sixteenth century, royal and colonial officials struggled with the problems of *tlameme* use, seeking to find a satisfactory course amid the conflicting needs, demands, abuses, and continuing common practices. From the conquest to 1550, *tlameme* use was variously curtailed and/or outlawed, finally settling into a pattern of regulated loads, distances, and pay, under established conditions—the absences of horses, mules, and roads. *Tlameme* use was regarded as a necessary evil until Spanish transportation systems had been adequately developed. From 1550 to 1580, regulated use of *tlamemes* continued in substantially the same vein. Spanish policy was based on the assumption that *tlameme* use would decline as roads and mules opened larger regions. But the voluntary relinquishment of *tlamemes* by the Spaniards never materialized. After 1580, further restrictions were implemented until the only legal use of *tlamemes* by Spaniards in the early seventeenth century was within cities. However, use of *tlamemes* continued throughout the Colonial period—by Indians, who were never subject to restrictions on their use, and by Spaniards, who violated such restrictions. Though often illegal, *tlamemes* continued to provide valuable service in a restricted sphere, and the decline in reliance on them owed more to drastic population decline than to regulatory restrictions.

The *tlameme* system functioned effectively and well, due in part to topographical factors and in part to the limitations of competing forms of transportation. After Spanish systems expanded, much of the continued *tlameme* transport was coerced, but as it was unpaid, or poorly paid, labor, it remained competitive. But the growing Spanish need for transport could not be met by *tlamemes* in the face of the devastating depopulation.

NOTES

1. While the reason for choosing *tameme* over *tlameme* is uncertain, there are two likely explanations: (1) The Spaniards found the /tl/ phoneme difficult to pronounce and thus altered it, as they did in many Nahuatl words: *ocelotl>ocelote, tomatl>tomate, coyotl>coyote.* (2) Along the Gulf Coast, where Cortés began his inland trek, there were many speakers of Nahuat, a language distinguished from Nahuatl by the use of the /t/ phoneme, instead of /tl/ (Whorf 1937). The /tla/ prefix of Nahuatl would be /ta/ in Nahuat, yielding *tameme.* Thus, the Nahuat version, *tameme*, could have entered Spanish common usage as a consequence of the original invasion route. (There is, however, the further problem of the choice between the nondistinctive variants *mama* and *meme*.)

2. Two exceptions to these general restrictions on Spanish use of human portage are the use of Indians in ports and in mines. Indian laborers were permitted to carry loads to and from ships for short distances until at least the late nineteenth century (Flippin 1889:400). Also, Indian laborers carried metal ores for short distances out of mines, often by vertical ascent. The loads carried were prodigious—up to 350 pounds per bearer—and the practice continued at least until the late nineteenth century (Bakewell 1971:134; Gemelli Careri 1976:93; Flippin 1889:66–67; Humboldt 1822:3:238).

3. Arthur S. Aiton (1967:91, fn 23) questions the date of this document, placing it after 1548, since it mentions the mines of Zacatecas. I concur with his conclusion, but the alteration in dates is not relevant to the point made here.

4. One hundred cacaos/day (ENE 2:116 [1532]); Cholula to Tepeaca, 100 cacaos; Cholula to Mexico City, 200 cacaos (AGN-M 2-109-43v [1543]); Villa Alta to Oaxaca, 600 cacaos (AGN-M 2-452-182 [1543]); Tehuacan to Tultitlan (two days), 160 cacaos; Tehuacan to Tecamachalco (two days), 160 cacaos; Tehuacan to Cuzcatlan (one day), 60 cacaos (AGN-M 2-558-227 [1543]); Amecameca to Los Ranchos, Pue., 80 cacaos; Amecameca to Chimalhuacan, Mex., 40 cacaos; Amecameca to Ecatzingo, Mex., 50 cacaos; Amecameca to Tepopula, 40 cacaos; Amecameca to Tlalmanalco, 40 cacaos (Simpson 1938:70 [1543]).

5. One hundred cacaos/day [.5 *reales*/day] (ENE 2:116 [1532]).

Toluca to Ucareo, 500 cacaos [2.5 *reales*/40 leagues] (AGN-M 1-138-67 [1542]).

Cholula to Tepeaca, 100 cacaos [.5 *reales*] (AGN-M 2-109-43v [1543]).

Villa Alta to Oaxaca, 600 cacaos [3 *reales*] (AGN-M 2-452-182 [1543]).

Tehuacan to Tultitlan (two days), 160 cacaos [1.6 *reales*]; Tehuacan to Tecamachalco (two days), 160 cacaos [1.6 *reales*]; Tehuacan to Cuzcatlan (one day), 60 cacaos [.6 *reales*] (AGN-M 2-558-227 [1543]).

Amecameca to Los Ranchos, Pue., 80 cacaos [.8 *reales*]; Amecameca to Chimalhuacan, Mex., 40 cacaos [.4 *reales*]; Amecameca to Ecatzingo, Mex., 50 cacaos [.5 *reales*]; Amecameca to Tepopula, 40 cacaos [.4 *reales*]; Amecameca to Tlalmanalco, 40 cacaos [.4 *reales*] (Simpson 1938:70 [1543]).

One *real*/8 leagues (AGN-GP 1-141-28 [1575]). One-half *real*/1 league (AGN-I 4-649-185 [1590]).

One *real*/day (AGN-I 4-840-228v [1590]).

Ocumatlan, Gro., to Tecuisiapa (2 leagues), .5 *reales*; Ocumatlan, Gro., to Apongo (6 leagues), 1.5 *reales* (AGN-I 5-52*bis*-85 [1590]).

One *tomin*/day [1 *real*] (AGN-GP 4-289-81v [1591]).

One real/4 leagues (AGN-I 6-1a-1130-310 [1596]).

APPENDIX 9-1. TLAMEME USE

(Recorded instances of *tlameme* use, including citation, date, location of use, and special conditions, such as an order granting licenses or prohibiting their use)

Citation	Date	Location of Use
DIE 4:176 License for *tlamemes*	1527	Mexico City to Acapulco
Chance 1978b:53 License 1529, revoked 1531, reinstated 1532	May 1529	Mexico City and Veracruz to Antequera
Warren 1974:95	1532	Huejotzingo to Mexico City
Simpson 1938:70 License for 25–30 *tlamemes*	18 July 1542	Mexico City to Valley of Oaxaca
Simpson 1938:70	20 Oct. 1542	Coatzacoalcos to Tehuantepec
AGN-M 1-17-10v Coerced by travelers	1542	Huatulco
AGN-M 1-131-65 License of *tlamemes*, 1,000 *cargas* of cacao	1542	To Mexico City
AGN-M 1-138-67	1542	Toluca to Ucareo
AGN-M 1-145-69v License for 15–20 *tlamemes*	1542	Mexico City to port of Huatulco
AGN-M 1-176-83 License	1542	Chiautla to mines of Chiautla and province
AGN-M 1-212-101	1542	Huaquechula
AGN-M 1-234-111v License for 25–30 *tlamemes*	1542	Antequera to province of Tehuantepec
AGN-M 1-256-121 Compelled by travelers and *arrieros*	1542	Zumpango
AGN-M 1-258-122 Prohibition on use of *tlamemes*	1542	Taxquiaca
AGN-M 1-265-125v License	1542	Mexico City to Oaxaca and Huatulco
AGN-M 1-282-131v Prohibition on coercion of *tlamemes*	1542	Huamelula
AGN-M 1-381-176v License for 15 *tlamemes*	1542	Port of Veracruz
AGN-M 1-430-202v Request for *tlameme* license	1542	Port of Huatulco
Simpson 1938:71 Permission by Audiencia to use *tlamemes*	23 Oct. 1543	San Ildefonso (Villa Alta, Oax.) to Antequera and back

Citation	Date	Location of Use
Simpson 1938:70 *tlameme* rate assessment	1543	Amecameca to Los Ranchos, Pue. Amecameca to Chimalhuacan, Mex. Amecameca to Ecatzingo, Mex. Amecameca to Tepopula, Mex. Amecameca to Tlalmanalco, Mex.
AGN-M 2-109-43v Prohibition on coercion of *tlamemes*	1543	Cholula to Tepeaca Cholula to Gu—— Cholula to Mexico City
AGN-M 2-275-105 Prohibition on *tlameme* use	1543	Zacatula
AGN-M 2-452-182 Prohibition on *tlameme* use, including *corregidor*	1543	Province of Zapotecas to city of Oaxaca
AGN-M 2-558-227 Coerced by travelers	1543	Tehuacan to Cuzcatlan to Tultitlan to Tecamachalco
AGN-M 2-738-321v License for 16 *tlamemes*	1543	Antequera to province of Tehuantepec
AGN-HJ 247-119	16 Oct. 1546	Ystacatepeque to Utlatipeque
Simpson 1938:71	25 Nov. 1555	Yurirarupundaro (Michoacan or Guerrero)
FHT 1:8–9 *Tlameme* use forbidden	13 Sept. 1575	Taymeo to mines of Tlalpuxagua
FHT 1:9–10 *Tlamemes* compelled by Spaniards, travelers, *justicias*	13 Sept. 1575	Xalapa, province of Teutila
FHT 1:12–13 *Tlamemes* compelled by travelers, Spaniards, mestizos, mulattos	26 Sept. 1575	Yztapa
FHT 1:19–20 *Tlamemes* compelled	25 Oct. 1575	Tezuatlan in the Misteca
FHT 2:224 Permission for soldiers to use *tlamemes* on way to Acapulco	19 Nov. 1579	Yacapicatlan (*sujeto* of Tistla) on the road to Acapulco
FHT 1:54–55 *Tlamemes* compelled by *teniente*, governor, alcaldes	19 Dec. 1575	Tenanpulco
FHT 1:62–63 *Tlamemes* compelled by travelers	17 Jan. 1576	Coatlan (*sujeto* of Cuernavaca)
FHT 1:81 *Tlamemes* compelled by Spaniards, mestizos, mulattos	3 Mar. 1576	Coroneo (*sujeto* of Acanbaro)
FHT 1:87–88 *Tlamemes* compelled by *principales* and *cacique* for Spaniards	23 Mar. 1576	Zilacayoapa
FHT 1:101–102 *Tlamemes* compelled by miners	8 May 1576	Calmecatitlan to mines of Teutlalco
FHT 1:110–111 *Tlamemes* compelled by *corregidor*	29 May 1576	Ticiuitlan to Puebla

149

Citation	Date	Location of Use
FHT 1:117	5 June 1576	Tanchinoltiquipaque
Tlamemes compelled by governor, *principales* for Spaniards		
FHT 1:124	30 June 1576	Tlacotepec
Prohibition of *tlameme* use by *encomendero*		
FHT 1:127	6 July 1576	Zapotlan, province of Tuspa y Zapotlan
Tlamemes compelled by travelers		
FHT 1:134	27 July 1576	Colipa
Tlamemes compelled by governor, *principales*, alcaldes for *beneficiado* of Mizantla		
FHT 2:190	28 July 1579	Mistepec to Puebla, Antequera, *costa del sur*, and
Tlamemes compelled by *beneficiado* of the *partido*		elsewhere
Caso 1928	1579/1580	Mistepeque, province of Tlaxiaco
Tlameme town		
FHT 2:247–248	11 Feb. 1580	Teutitlan
Tlamemes compelled by resident mestizo		
FHT 2:260–261	26 Feb. 1580	Tagualilpa
Tlamemes compelled by Spaniards and travelers		
FHT 2:269–270	9 Mar. 1580	Tulanzingo to Mexico City
Tlamemes compelled by merchant *teniente*		
FHT 2:289–290	13 May 1580	Atlacomulco to Mexico City and elsewhere
Tlamemes compelled by *justicia* for Spaniards and travelers		
FHT 2:290	16 May 1580	Puebla
Tlamemes compelled by Spaniards		
FHT 2:291	16 May 1580	Yzuco
Tlamemes compelled by *beneficiado*, *principales*, *mandones*		
FHT 2:290–292	17 May 1580	Yzuco to Mexico City and elsewhere
Tlamemes compelled by *beneficiado*, *principales*, *mandones*		
FHT 2:315–316	30 July 1580	Xuluapas, Caqualpa, Cenpalmani, and Cuicalapay to
Tlamemes compelled by *alcalde mayor*, *tenientes*, *beneficiado*		city of Michoacan
FHT 2:322–323	27 Aug. 1580	Tolcayuca
Two *tlamemes* stole goods sent by *beneficiado*		
Barlow 1949:35	1580	Epazoyuca, *partido* of Zempoala
Tlameme town		
AGN-I 2-685-157v	1580	Tacambaro, Michoacan
Tlamemes compelled by *corregidor*		
FHT 2:398	27 Jan. 1581	Mextlalpa to Mexico City and elsewhere
FHT 2:411–412	20 Feb. 1581	*partido* of Motin y Taquili
Viceregal request to *alcalde mayor* re *tlameme* use		

150

Citation	Date	Location of Use
AGN-I 2-11-2v *Tlamemes* compelled by Spaniards	1582	Orizaba, Ver., to other *pueblos*
AGN-I 2-62-15 *Tlamemes* compelled by Spaniards and travelers	1582	Huejotla, Hdgo.
AGN-I 2-230-58v *Tlamemes* compelled by Spaniards	1582	Zapotlan to *pueblos*
AGN-I 2-973-224v *Tlamemes* compelled by Spaniards	1583	Tamazula
FHT 3:42–43 *Tlamemes* compelled by *escribano, teniente,* Spaniards	30 June 1587	Meztitlan, Tenango y Quezala, Atengo
AGN-I 3-192-44v Confirmation of 1588 order not to use *tlamemes*	(1588) 1590	Jalatlaco, Oax.
Simpson 1938:72 *Tlamemes* compelled by *teniente*	14 Sept. 1590	Nopaluca, Pue., to Mexico City and Puebla
AGN-I 3-112-26v *Tlamemes* compelled by travelers	1590	San Juan Teotihuacan
AGN-I 4-649-185 *Tlamemes* compelled by Spanish travelers	1590	Xicatlan, Mich.
AGN-I 4-704-198 *Tlamemes* compelled by travelers	1590	Zoquiango, Pue.
AGN-I 4-840-228v *Tlamemes* compelled by *vicario*	1590	Mizantla, Ver., to Veracruz
AGN-I 4-859-232v *Tlamemes* compelled by many people	1590	Zayanaguilpa, Mex.
AGN-I 5-6-71 *Tlamemes* compelled by *justicias* and others	1590	San Francisco, Colima
AGN-I 5-52*bis*-85 *Tlamemes* compelled by travelers and others	1590	Ocumatlan, Gro., *partido* of Yguala, to Tecuisiapa and Apongo
AGN-GP 4-289-81v License to take 2 *tlamemes* in relays by district	1 Mar. 1591	Mexico City to port of Acapulco
AGN-GP 4-501-142v	13 May 1591	Town of San Ildefonso (Villa Alta) to Mexico City
Simpson 1938:72–73 *Tlamemes* compelled by Spaniards	14 Aug. 1591	Acala y Hueystaca, Gro., to Mexico City
AGN-I 3-416-96 *Tlamemes* compelled by governor, alcalde	1591	Ihuatzio (*barrio* of Patzcuaro, Mich.) to other *pueblos* in region
AGN-I 3-560-133v *Tlamemes* compelled by miners	1591	Nuxtepec, Gro.
AGN-I 5-629-242v *Tlamemes* compelled by travelers	1591	Taximaroa, Mich.

Citation	Date	Location of Use
AGN-I 5-938-310	1591	Tolcayuca, Hdgo., to mines of Pachuca, Mexico City,
Tlamemes compelled by *encomendero*		and elsewhere
AGN-I 5-1117-353	1591	Acapetlahuaca, Pue.
Tlamemes compelled by alcaldes, *alguaciles*, *regidores*, others		
AGN-I 6-2a-45-12v	1591	Tututepec, Oax., to Mexico City
Tlamemes compelled by buyers of *encomendero*'s tribute *mantas*		
AGN-I 6-2a-237-52v	1591	Otumba, Mex.
Tlamemes compelled by *corregidor*		
AGN-I 6-1a-213-55v	1592	Yacapilzotla, Tuxtla
Tlamemes compelled by travelers		
AGN-I 6-2a-645-146	1592	Guatepec to Mexico City
Tlamemes compelled by *alcalde mayor, teniente*		
AGN-I 6-1a-656-175v	1593	Jilotepec, Mex.
Tlamemes compelled by those on the road		
AGN-I 6-1a-1039-281	1595	Cuitlapan y Cacahuamilpa, Tasco, Gro.
Tlamemes compelled on the road		
AGN-I 6-1a-1130-310	1596	Chichinampan (*sujeto* of Acalan, Pue.)
Tlamemes compelled by travelers		

10. Techialoyan Codices: Seventeenth-Century Indian Land Titles in Central Mexico

H. R. HARVEY

ONE RESPONSE of Indian society to protect its territorial base from Spanish encroachment during the Colonial period was the production of "*títulos*," land title documents. At the time of the conquest, Indian communities held their lands by right of possession, but they also kept written documents which described their lands. Alonso de Zorita (1963:110) states that "Pictures on which are shown all of the parcels, and the boundaries, and where and with whose fields the lots meet, and who cultivates what field, and what land each one has . . ." were maintained by Indian towns (Zorita 1963:110). A few examples of these cadastral manuscripts from the Early Colonial period survive.[1] Juan de Torquemada stated in his description of *lienzos* that "on opening one of these rolls, the entire pueblo, its limits and outlines could be seen at a glance" (Torquemada 1943:2:546; trans. Kirchhoff 1954:354). Therefore, precedent existed for land documentation in Preconquest times.

Indian title documents were produced throughout the Colonial period, from the sixteenth century to the nineteenth. Their texts, often in Nahuatl, were sometimes combined with pictorials, which suggests a persistence of native tradition. Land titles were produced in a wide variety of forms, and as James Lockhart (1978) says, "by local figures for a local audience." They exhibit extraordinary differences in the range of skill and knowledge possessed by their respective authors. Some are very crude in appearance, as if made by children. Many contain very conspicuous errors in orthography, etc. However, others are very carefully drafted and impart a strong impression of authenticity.

Although the authorship of title documents varied widely in time and space, certain themes and strategies recur within the group. They are statements of community landholdings that generally describe both jurisdictions and boundaries, but many are also declamatory in tone. They frequently admonish the people to know and observe these boundaries, so that title documents very often give the impression that they were prepared primarily for their holders, the townspeople, rather than for-whom-it-might-concern. It is this admonition that gives them a peculiarly native flavor. Most

153

documents also strongly emphasize that the communities were Christian, having received and accepted the faith. The confirmation of lands and fixing of jurisdictions are frequently attributed to viceregal action at the time when the document either states or implies that it was drafted. The majority of title documents contain early Postconquest dates and a few even assert that they were done prior to the conquest. Perhaps more than any other feature, it was the allegation of early date that often led colonial courts to reject such documents as frauds. For a similar reason, modern scholars have paid little attention to this genre.

Notwithstanding the fact that many title documents contain questionable assertions and were intentionally fabricated to support allegations in pending litigation, some were not. The motivation behind their specific origin is most often obscure, but as a group they represent a remarkably consistent tendency of Indian society to document its territorial claims in a manner and style that is clearly indigenous. Some of the indigenous characteristics we see in such documents may derive from an oral tradition, as Charles Gibson (1975b:321) suggests. After the conquest, adoption of the Latin alphabet enabled oral tradition to become merged with written expression.

One group of title documents which has drawn increasing attention in recent years is the Techialoyan codices. Over forty whole documents and fragments have been identified since the first publication of a Techialoyan codex in 1890 (Quaritch 1890). Some representatives of the group are very handsome documents, drafted on coarse, native *amatl* paper, combining Nahuatl texts with a very distinctive art style. Some because of their degree of deterioration, and most because of their dark, native paper and faded pictorials, give the appearance of being very old documents and have been pursued as collectors' items since the eighteenth century.

With the publication of the *Codex of San Antonio Techialoyan* (modern San Antonio de la Isla, state of Mexico), Federico Gómez

de Orozco (1933) first drew attention to the marked similarity between the codex and five others. Later, Robert H. Barlow (1943) recognized the similar nature of other documents and assigned the name "Techialoyan" to the group. Barlow also proposed a formal system of classification, assigning a letter of the alphabet to each (ibid.:161). Gómez de Orozco (1948:65–67) adopted Barlow's system of classification and added to the list of known documents. Since the number of known documents eventually came to exceed the letters of the alphabet, Donald Robertson (1975) introduced a numerical classification and compiled a catalog of forty-eight items. However, not all items in his catalog are land title documents. The catalog includes a wall mural (no. 745), three panels or maps (nos. 720, 726, 729), and several documents whose present whereabouts are unknown. Eight fragments listed in the catalog are parts of three manuscripts which became separated through the course of time (Robertson 1975:256–257, n.16).

A comparison of the Techialoyan group indicates that their authors followed a standard format for the organization of the information. Each document consists of two parts, a Nahuatl text and a pictorial section, with most drawings accompanied by brief Nahuatl descriptions. The textual section describes town jurisdictions, stresses that the communities had received and accepted the faith, names the patron saint for each locality, and states that their lands were confirmed in a particular year by the viceroy, usually Antonio de Mendoza. The text is signed by local native officials, who often are depicted in the pictorial section. Because of this format it is relatively easy to determine what might be missing from incompletely preserved documents.

Although each document follows a standard format, there are differences among them. There is variation in length, reflecting the range in size and complexity of the jurisdiction, as well as in the number and size of tribute parcels worked by each community. There is also variation in the references each

154

FIGURE 10-1. *Codex of Cuajimalpa*, Techialoyan 703, fol. 5v. Courtesy Archivo General de la Nación, Mexico City.

FIGURE 10-2. *Codex of Tepotzotlan*, Techialoyan 718, fol. 4v. Photo courtesy Bibliothèque Nationale, Paris.

155

makes to local historical events and personages. The similarities in format indicate that these documents were carefully planned as a group, but with sufficient flexibility to accommodate local needs—the number of places to be illustrated, greater or lesser details of local history and the like. They could have been drafted in the local communities, but certainly not by local people, as can be judged by the close similarity of the paintings (Figs. 10-1, 10-2). Rather, they seem to have been prepared by a few skilled artists and scribes who were unlikely to be found in these small Indian communities of the seventeenth century. Probably they were produced in a central "shop" where the information was available to the artists and scribes assigned to the task.[2]

Fernando Horcasitas and Wanda Tommasi de Magrelli's (1975) analysis of the Nahuatl of the *Codex of Tzictepec* supports the thesis that the Techialoyan codices were not a spontaneous creation of local communities. Horcasitas and Tommasi de Magrelli caution against confusing an often atrocious orthography with the ability of the scribe to correctly and simply state the intended message in Nahuatl. They conclude that the Nahuatl style does not reflect any particular local dialect and thus could be understood by a broad range of communities in which some Nahuatl was spoken. This is an important consideration, since Otomí and Matlatzinca were the primary languages of many Techialoyan communities. Only twenty-one verbs are employed in the *Codex of Tzictepec*, and

FIGURE 10-3. *Codex of San Pedro Cuajimalpa*, Techialoyan 703, fol. 2v. Courtesy Archivo General de la Nación, Mexico City.

156

this appears close to the total range used in other Techialoyan codices. Other peculiarities widely shared by the Techialoyan group, such as the recurrent use of certain place names, e.g., Quauhtli ynemian (Place of the Eagle), and the manner in which calendrical dates are expressed (400 + 100 + etc.) is more indicative of shared literary style than actual usage in everyday speech. Thus, there is sufficient evidence to conclude that the Nahuatl style of the Techialoyan codices did not just happen but was intentional.

Not only format and style of linguistic expression serve to distinguish the Techialoyans as a group within the genre of title documents, but also their unusual writing and art styles. The Nahuatl is written in what Robertson (1959:191) has described as "an unusually large, bold, almost childish hand, using unlinked lower case letters." The European art style is no less distinctive (Fig. 10-3). In the Techialoyan drawings, three-dimensionality is conveyed throughout, in human figures, architecture, plants, animals, and landscapes; and both human and animal figures possess a plasticity, a quality of movement, that is thoroughly uncharacteristic of Prehispanic native tradition (Figs. 10-4, 10-5). Robertson (1959:1975) has described this art style in detail. More recently, Joaquín Galarza's (1980) analysis of the *Codex of Cempoala* reveals in great detail the graphic techniques employed by the artist which reflect native conceptualizations.

Whether or not their artistic appeal was a contributing factor, the strong admonitions in

FIGURE 10-4. *Codex of Tepotzotlan*, Techialoyan 718, fol. 8r. Photo courtesy Bibliothèque Nationale, Paris.

FIGURE 10-5. *Codex of Tepotzotlan*, Techialoyan 718, fol. 8v. Photo courtesy Bibliothèque Nationale, Paris.

these documents to guard and protect them often went unheeded. Many passed from the hands of their original owners. Indeed, Robertson (1975) has called the Techialoyans "the most mobile of all colonial ethnohistoric manuscripts." One, the *Codex of San Simón Calpulalpan* (no. 725), was presented by that town to Emperor Maximilian in 1864. Others, such as that of San Antonio Huixquilucan, found their way to the Archivo General de la Nación for translation during the Reform of the 1850's and may never have returned to the towns. Several were collected by Lorenzo Boturini when he was assembling his formidable collection of Mexican indigenous manuscripts: *Ixtapalapa* (no. 706), *Ocelotepec* (no. 708), *Tepotzotlan* (nos. 714, 718, 722), and *Huyxoapan* (nos. 702, 717,

735) (Robertson 1975:264). Boturini's acquisition of several Techialoyans might indicate that these colorful documents were not highly prized by their Indian owners in the 1740's, since they could have been recently painted and known by the Indians to be forgeries. On the other hand, had they been produced seventy-five to one hundred years before, they might have no longer been understood by the Indians, many of whom were not native Nahuatl speakers. Since Boturini is known to have collected old manuscripts, it is reasonable to infer that Techialoyans were vintage documents by his time. The present condition of some that he is thought to have collected suggests that they were not in the best of condition when Boturini acquired them.

158

LANDS

The Techialoyan codices describe town jurisdictions and their locations. They also delineate some of the external boundaries of the jurisdictions, paying special attention to particular ones, perhaps those most often in dispute at the time the documents were drafted. Also, they identify the size of tribute lands within jurisdictions. The latter information is confined usually to the pictorial sections. No effort is made to precisely locate these tribute parcels other than by town or *paraje* name. Such vagueness was perhaps intentional if the significant feature of tribute land was aggregate quantity rather than specific pieces of property, as was characteristic of Preconquest tribute lands.

The size of each tribute parcel is written in Nahuatl, and quantity is expressed in terms of *mecatl*, a Nahuatl term meaning 'measure'. Translation of the Techialoyan *mecatl* is complicated because basic indigenous units of measure varied significantly between communities and regions. For example, in Acolhuacan the standard linear measure of land, the *quahuitl*, equaled three Spanish *varas* (2.5 m). Tenochtitlan's *maitl* was equal to two *varas*, or 1.67 m (Harvey and Williams 1980:500; Calnek 1974a:27). Many localities, particularly in the old Tepanec domain, appear to have had standard linear measures falling between those of Acolhuacan and Tenochtitlan. Furthermore, the term *mecatl* could refer to an areal as well as a linear measure. The standard areal unit of land was a "count," a parcel equivalent to twenty linear units on each side, or four hundred square units. A *mecatl* was an areal fraction equal to one four-hundredth of an areal "count," i.e., a parcel measuring one linear unit by one linear unit, or one square unit. In several codices (for example, *Huixquilucan*, *Ocoyoacac*, *Tzictepec*, *Cempoala*), plots of tribute land are described often as four hundred *mecatl* or multiples of that number, which translate as one or more "counts" of land. The tribute parcels seldom exceed two thousand *mecatl*, i.e., five "counts."

An analysis of the tribute lands in the *Codex of San Antonio Huixquilucan* indicates that these "counts" of land were small parcels (Harvey and Williams n.d.). The Spanish equivalent to twenty linear Indian measures appears to have been fifty *varas*. Faustino Galicia Chimalpopoca commented on the 50-*vara* measure in use in the nineteenth century in the state of Mexico (Gómez de Orozco 1933:327). The 50-*vara* measure was used in the *municipio* of Huixquilucan at the beginning of the eighteenth century and perhaps much earlier. The older fields in the less disturbed zones of the *municipio* appear to have been laid out on the basis of 50-*vara* square units. Thus, at the time these fields were laid out, an Indian "count" equaled 2,500 square *varas* (50 *varas* × 50 *varas*), or less than one-fifth of a hectare (1,764 m^2). Therefore, the individual tribute parcels in Huixquilucan were small, the largest less than one hectare (Table 10-1). The total tribute land in Huixquilucan was 16,780 *mecatl*, slightly more than forty counts, equal to approximately seven hectares.[3] Using the same conversion factor, totals of other Techialoyan localities did not differ appreciably from the amount of lands delineated for tribute in Huixquilucan, for example, Tzictepec, 6.5 hectares; Ocoyoacac, 4.5 hectares.

What factors determined the size of the tribute lands and when were they assigned? A major event which affected Indian settlements in the later sixteenth and early seventeenth centuries was *congregación*. *Congregación* relocated and concentrated the Indian population to facilitate administration. But *congregación* may not have been the occasion for the assignment of the specific tribute lands described in the Techialoyans. In these codices the parcels are described as belonging to the communities; hence they were communally owned tracts worked by tributaries to meet the community's tribute obligations. One method of determining tribute obligation in the later sixteenth and the seventeenth centuries was application of the "ten-*vara* rule," described by Gibson (1964: 203–204): "A rule of 1577, designed to pre-

159

TABLE 10-1. Selected Tribute Parcels from the *Codex of San Antonio Huixquilucan*

Locality	Mecatl	Size of Parcel Counts[a]	Varas[b]	Hectares[c]
San Martin Tecpan	1,200	3	7,500	.53
Santiago Tlapilcayan	2,000	5	12,500	.88
Tepemaxalco	400	1	2,500	.18
San Cristobal Texcalucan	800	2	5,000	.35
San Bartolome Coatepec	600	1.5	3,750	.26
San Francisco Ayotuchco	1,200	3	7,500	.53

[a] A count was equivalent to a parcel measuring 20 × 20 linear units, or 400 units square. A *mecatl* was 1 square unit, or ¹⁄₄₀₀ of a count.

[b] In Spanish measures a count of land in Huixquilucan was equivalent to a parcel 50 *varas* × 50 *varas*, or 2,500 square *varas*.

[c] A Spanish *vara* equaled .84 m; therefore a parcel 50 *varas* × 50 *varas* equaled 42 m × 42 m, or 1,764 m².

vent the abandonment of native agriculture in the crises of further depopulation, required that contributions to the community were to consist not of money but of the produce of maize or wheat plots to be sown by the tributaries. Each full tributary was to cultivate a plot of ten *varas* (about 9 yards). Each male half-tributary was to cultivate a plot five by five varas." Gibson points out that the rule was not invariable, since later notices "indicated ten *brazas* rather than ten varas" (ibid.).

If the tribute lands described in the Techialoyans reflect the ten *vara* rule or some local variant of that rule, they may be converted into a population estimate. Each 400 *mecatl* of land, i.e., each "count" of land, equaled 2,500 square *varas*. If one tributary was to work a plot ten by ten *varas*, 2,500 square *varas* would represent twenty-five tributaries. If one count of land represented twenty-five tributaries, then the total forty counts of tribute land in Huixquilucan suggests a total of one thousand tributaries. Assuming an average family size between four and five, the population of Huixquilucan was four to five thousand, a figure very close to Huixquilucan's population recorded in the first half of the eighteenth century. Other Techialoyan-style documents also seem to il-

lustrate the process involved in the operation of the ten-*vara* rule, for example, *San Pedro Atlapulco* (no. 726) and *San Salvador Tizayuca* (no. 729). These are panels or maps which show produce being carried by individuals coming from various directions to the church, where a table is set up to receive it. The sale of this produce was to provide the income to cover town expenditures.

The information in the Techialoyan texts indicates that *congregación* had already occurred by the time of drafting. If the depicted tribute parcels were established in accordance with the ten-*vara* rule of 1577, these codices could not have been drafted until the very end of the sixteenth century at the earliest.

DATING

Horcasitas commented that "Few groups of documents of the Spanish period have presented problems as complex as the assignment of a date to the Techialoyan codices" (Horcasitas and Tommasi de Magrelli 1975: 247). The dates contained in the Techialoyan documents range from 1504 to 1596. Many attribute their land grants to Viceroy Mendoza and state or imply that the document was drafted as a result of his visit to the commu-

160

nity. However, those codices which refer to Viceroy Mendoza but at the same time bear dates prior to Mendoza's arrival in New Spain in late 1535 are clearly in error. Gómez de Orozco (1948) accepted the possibility of a sixteenth-century provenience for the Techialoyan group, advancing the hypothesis that the artists were a product of the Indian School of Padre Gante. While Barlow dated the *Codex García Granados* as later seventeenth century from identification of some individuals mentioned in it, he did not otherwise question the early dates of the group as a whole (Barlow 1945:468; 1946:434).

It was Robertson who began, as early as 1959, to question the early provenience of the Techialoyan group. In 1960, he stated that although he could not "say when during the periods of Spanish hacienda and *latifundio* growth the Techialoyan group was forged," he could "hypothesize a date after 1640–80 and before c. 1733" (Robertson 1960:123). Robertson subsequently decided that the later period was more consistent with the evidence and estimated that the Techialoyans were made ca. 1700–1743 (Robertson 1975). After publication of his earlier paper, a wall mural was discovered in the Cathedral of Cuernavaca. He felt this to be in the Techialoyan style and has included the mural in his catalog as Techialoyan no. 745 (ibid.). He noted that Augustín de Vetancurt, who described the cathedral in 1697, failed to mention the mural, which must, therefore, have been painted at a later date. Robertson continues to be of the opinion that the art style peculiar to the Techialoyans was of limited duration and that the dating of one painting provides reasonably close dating for the group.

Robertson's argument for an early-eighteenth-century provenience would seem to be supported by the *Codex García Granados*. However, among the Techialoyan codices, the *García Granados* is unusual. In contrast to the land documents, which are in book form, the *García Granados* is a *tira*, measuring 49.5 × 647 cm. Besides the usual Techialoyan colors (reds, blues, greens, and yellows), the *García Granados* contains a substantial amount of gold paint. Finally, it is primarily a genealogy of the Mendoza de Austria family, with a listing of their landholdings. Robertson (1975) has suggested that this document could be the one which Boturini ordered copied from the original which was on the wall of the Azcapotzalco *tecpan* (palace) in his time, ca. 1740. The significance of the *García Granados*, whether copy or original, is that it does indicate that the Techialoyan art style persisted at least until the eighteenth century.

Although the Cuernavaca cathedral wall mural and the *Codex García Granados* may well be early eighteenth century, they differ substantively from the majority of Techialoyans, which are descriptions of town lands. Several details of these land title Techialoyans indicate a seventeenth-century origin. For example, both Mimiapan and Ocelotepec were the subjects of Techialoyan codices. These towns, at one time part of the same jurisdiction, split apart in 1643, each becoming a *cabecera* (Gerhard 1972b:273). Nearby Xonacatlan, another Techialoyan locality, is known to have been a separate jurisdictional entity from Ocelotepec by 1688 (ibid.). If the Techialoyan land documents were produced as a group, the Xonacatlan evidence suggests that they were in existence prior to 1688.

The question of whether the Techialoyans are seventeenth or eighteenth century in provenience is partially resolved by another Techialoyan-style document from the *municipio* of Huixquilucan. It refers to two subject towns in the eastern sector of the *municipio*, San Cristobal Texcalucan and Santa Maria Magdalena Chichicaspa (no. 744). As described in court records, the *San Cristobal Codex* was similar in style and format to the *Codex of San Antonio Huixquilucan* (Harvey 1966). It also attributed its early land confirmation to Viceroy Mendoza and stressed that it had received the faith. Native founders are cited, and two, Chimalpopoca and Totoquihuatzin, appear in both codices. The *San Cristobal* text alleges that one Don Miguel of Tacuba, together with an agent of the king,

161

came to San Cristobal and ordered the title to be written on August 28, 1555. The document further alleges that an account of these proceedings was given to Viceroy Velasco, who gave his approval. With the exception of the date and reference to Viceroy Velasco, the textual portion of the *Codex of San Cristobal* is very similar to the Huixquilucan. The substance of the pictorial section differs, however. Whereas the *Huixquilucan* codex records small tribute parcels of each of its subjects, including two tracts for San Cristobal totaling 2,000 *mecatl*, the *Codex of San Cristobal* lists sixteen *parajes* containing fields ranging in size from 160 to 2,000 *mecatl*. All but two of these tracts are clearly distinct from those listed in the *Huixquilucan*. In total the *San Cristobal* lists 8,960 *mecatl* possessed by La Magdalena and San Cristobal. The *Codex of San Cristobal* claims five times more area than that ascribed to it in the *Huixquilucan*.[4] Thus, there is a conceptual difference between the two codices. The *Huixquilucan* indicates tribute parcels, whereas the *San Cristobal* records town lands.

The question arises as to the relationship between the two pictorial documents. Were they originally prepared at the same time and for the same purpose, or was one modeled on the other? Archival records indicate that the *Codex of San Cristobal* was offered as evidence in land litigation, but the *audiencia* considered it to be a forgery and ordered it burned in 1707. Thus, there was a Techialoyan-type document in existence by the beginning of the eighteenth century. If the *Codex of San Antonio Huixquilucan* was in existence at this time, why was it not used also to support San Cristobal's litigation? Since the *Huixquilucan* identified much less area for San Cristobal and La Magdalena, it would have better suited the Spanish opposition. The circumstances of the case suggest that the *Codex of San Cristobal* was prepared specifically for the litigation. As described in the court record it was Techialoyan in style, but it was shorter than most Techialoyans and focused on the lands of a small

162

subject population rather than on a *cabecera*. Given its similarities in text, format, and style to the *Huixquilucan*, it seems likely that the *Huixquilucan* provided the model from which the *San Cristobal* was drafted. The *Codex of San Antonio Huixquilucan* may not have been a very ancient document at the end of the seventeenth century, but insofar as it was part of what we now call the Techialoyan group and painted on *amatl* paper, it probably was impressive in appearance and carried authority among the Indian population.

PURPOSE

The description of boundaries, jurisdictions, and tribute properties in the Techialoyans suggests that for each community this information was based on a set of facts either acquired through survey (*vista de ojos*), or from official records. Throughout the earlier Colonial period, repeated surveys were made of Indian communities, beginning with the first viceregal governments and continuing through various changes in community land status, such as those affected by *congregación*. These types of occasions requiring surveys seem not to have occurred at the same time among the Techialoyan communities. However, given their great similarities, the production of the Techialoyan codices does seem to reflect a common event, one shared by all the communities which received this specific type of title. The earliest event which may have affected the land status of all the Techialoyan communities simultaneously was the *composición* of 1643. This involved a general review of land titles and a monetary assessment by the Crown in return for the granting of clear title.

Many Techialoyan communities were subject to Tacuba before the conquest and during much of the Colonial period. Tacuba's *composición* of 1643 covered a large area and involved a great number of communities:

Tacuba por si y en nombre y en virtud de el poder que tiene de los demás vecinos y la-

bradores dueños de Haciendas en su Distrito y en el de Tlalnepantla, Azcapozalco, Huisquilucan, S. Miguel Tecpan, S. Pedro Azcapuzaltongo, Tultitlan y demás vicitas de la dicha Provincia . . .

(Testimonio 1864:fol. 19)

The cost of the *composición*, seven thousand pesos, must have placed a heavy burden on the economies of those communities involved. From the viewpoint of the Spanish Crown the *composición* was a device to raise revenue to support its Armada of Barlovento. From the native point of view, it was a mechanism by which defective land titles could be repaired. The land descriptions of the Techialoyans are just the product that might be expected from *composición*. Careful surveys with appropriate notes and the drafting of maps were expensive. General descriptions and the placing of boundary markers agreed upon by the consensus of adjoining communities, however, could have been accomplished with relatively little effort and cost. Unquestionably, each community involved in the *composición* was charged and new taxes to support the Armada were assessed, so that some provision for continuing tax payment would have been a necessary consideration in *composición*. Perhaps this is what was meant when the people of Ocoyoacac acknowledged in their document, "we have set new taxes" (*hemos elaborado [fijado] nuevos impuestos* [Monnich 1974:171]).

Some Techialoyan codices, such as Huixquilucan's and Tzictepec's, were more explicit than others in stressing their relationship with Tacuba.[5] However, the geographic distribution of Techialoyan communities is largely within the old Tepanec domain, and many of these communities are known to have been Tepanec subjects in Prehispanic times (Zantwijk 1969). Apparently exceptions are Calpulalpan (no. 725) and Chalco Atenco (no. 716). But both of these communities could have been linked to Tacuba in the seventeenth century through intermarriage with Tepanec lineages and inheritance of tribute rights. Since Tacuba was responsible

to the Crown for the payment of the cost for *composición*, it seems reasonable to infer that it was the agent involved in the planning, drafting, and distribution of Techialoyan codices. *Cacicazgos* of the seventeenth century were still supported by tribute collected from subject communities. It was in the vested interest of the Indian nobility to protect their tribute domains from encroachment by the Spaniards. Also, and perhaps not unimportant, there was the practical matter of paying for *composición*. In return for their payment, subject communities could be provided with "titles," perhaps Techialoyan codices.

Official documentation of a composition survey does not seem to have survived for any Techialoyan community. This suggests that no official *vista de ojos* by Crown authorities was conducted in these communities at this time. Rather, if any official agreement was reached, it was based on records maintained by the Indian government of Tacuba and details were not recorded. However, the decision to give a title document that might hold no validity in Spanish courts must have rested with the Indian authorities involved. The Techialoyan codices offer a clue as to what Indian authorities hope to achieve. Most Techialoyans place the burden of responsibility on the local community to agree to continue working parcels of defined size and in specific localities to satisfy tribute obligations. Moreover, townspeople are admonished to forever guard and protect the title document. Thus, the Techialoyan codices could be seen as serving a dual purpose. If the definition of a community's territory was confirmed by *composición* and the townspeople paid their tribute obligations by working lands in specified localities, it follows that such lands belonged to the Indian community. Such documents can be seen as protecting both the recipients of a community's tribute and the community itself by defining its landholdings in a form and language which could be understood.

Should the Techialoyan codices be dismissed as forgeries, as some have suggested

163

(e.g., Robertson 1960:122)? Despite the fact that the Techialoyans often state that they were drafted before they actually could have been, the critical question is the intent of the authors, the purpose that they had in mind for making the documents. If the authors' purpose was primarily to provide an accurate record for the community of its boundaries, political jurisdiction, and tribute lands in a form and manner the local community could be expected to understand, the Techialoyan documents can hardly be considered forgeries from the perspective of their Indian authors. To the extent that they drew upon oral tradition to supply historical background, it is easy to account for the vagueness and often garbled nature of what might otherwise be considered historical "fact." The inclusion of such information would certainly have had meaning, at least for the time the documents were drafted, and therefore would have provided some additional basis for local identification with the documents. That some Techialoyan codices were used as evidence in land litigation decades or more than a century after their date of drafting could hardly have been anticipated by their authors.

Based upon present evidence, the Techialoyan codices, rather than forgeries, are better viewed as an organized response on the part of mid-seventeenth-century Indian authorities to record the status of lands of subject communities as these had evolved under Spanish rule and in a manner that could be best understood by local communities. They are useful historical documents for a time period in which documentation for many small communities is scant. Moreover, individually as well as a group, they reflect Indian perspective.

NOTES

1. Humboldt Fragment VIII (Seler 1904); *Codex Vergara*; *Códice de Santa María Asunción*. For a description of these cadastral documents, see Barbara J. Williams (1984).

2. Ulf Bankmann's analysis of handwriting in several codices points to as many as three different scribes for a single document (Bankmann 1974).

3. The total amount of lands in Table I, Harvey 1976, should be read 16,780 rather than 15,880; also, for Atonalecan Zictepatl 300, read: Tetitlan Metlan Atlan 1,200; for Huixquilucan Atlahuytec Coatzalan read: Tepemaxalco; for San Juan Yetepec, read: 1,200 instead of 1,300.

4. Even if three other tracts, (Ahuaquahtla, Quauhtli ynemian, Tomayizquitlan nonacatlan) totaling 2,100 *mecatl* described in the *Codex of San Antonio Huixquilucan*, which might have been located within the territorial jurisdiction of San Cristobal and La Magdalena, are added, the resulting 4,100 *mecatl* are still less than one-half of the 8,960 claimed in the *Codex of San Cristobal*.

5. Following Robertson's numerical classification, the *Codex of San Pedro Tzictepec*, *municipio* of Tenango del Valle, would be item no. 749. Robertson (1975) lists items 739, 740, and 741 as pertaining to a San Pedro Tzictepec, *municipio* of Tenancingo. These were described by Paniagua Jaen in 1943, and photographs were supposedly in the Biblioteca del H. Congreso de la Unión. Neither Robertson nor Galarza was able to locate the photos in the summer of 1966, so that the physical description of all three documents is unknown. Since all three were reported to bear a date of 1562, they are distinct documents from No. 749, described by Horcasitas and Tommasi (1975), whose text contains the dates 1540 and 1543

11. Colonial Ethnohistory of Oaxaca

JOHN K. CHANCE

INTRODUCTION

A DECADE AGO, Howard F. Cline (1972a: 166) designated the territory of Oaxaca as one of six ethnohistorical regions of Middle America—the only region that is largely coterminous with a modern state. Oaxaca's distinctiveness has deep roots in the prehistoric past. As defined for that period by John Paddock and Ignacio Bernal, the region is delimited by the Mixtec- and Popoloca-speaking populations to the west and north and by the Gulf Coast lowlands and Isthmus of Tehuantepec to the east (Paddock 1966:236; Bernal 1962). Events since then have tended to preserve this unity, and for the Colonial period the region and its indigenous inhabitants merit separate treatment. Oaxaca has long been known for its high degree of ethnic and linguistic diversity, though many groups, such as the Triques, Amuzgos, Chatinos, Huaves, and others, have always been fairly restricted in territory and population. Two large linguistic groups have long dominated the region: the Mixtecs, who inhabit the entire western portion of Oaxaca, and the Zapotecs, who are numerically pre-dominant in the east. The mainly Zapotec Valley of Oaxaca, long a major power center in the Southern Highlands, gave rise to the most developed forms of sociopolitical organization in the region. But the Mixteca was not far behind, and is perhaps best known for its striking codices and gold jewelry in Postclassic times. In the fifteenth century, much of Oaxaca became part of the tributary empire of the Aztecs, though their cultural impact was minimal.

In general, Oaxaca represented an "intermediate" level of sociocultural complexity at the time of Spanish contact. Though the Valley of Oaxaca in particular contained a number of populous, highly stratified city-states, they were not as developed or as powerful as many of their contemporaries in the Valleys of Mexico and Puebla-Tlaxcala to the north. Oaxaca's lower degree of political centralization and emphasis on greater community autonomy were to have important repercussions during the Colonial period. Both then and now, Oaxaca's great variety of settlements, cultures, languages, and terrain have made it one of the most complex regions in Middle America.

165

During the last fifteen years numerous Colonial and Contact period studies have appeared which greatly enhance our understanding of the place of Oaxaca in the Spanish colony of New Spain. With the exception of Eva Hunt's (1972) work on the Cuicatecs, most of these studies are concerned with Zapotecs and Mixtecs, and it is on these peoples that this chapter will focus. Prior to the late 1960's, colonial Oaxaca was often regarded as a kind of underdeveloped version of the Valley of Mexico. This implied no particular prejudice, but simply a set of assumptions made in the absence of many concrete studies. Now, happily, all this is changing. Not only is it possible to specify with some precision the distinctiveness of the colonial experience in Oaxaca, but it is also possible to identify variants of this experience within different subregions.

As Cline (1972a: 175) recognized, there is no fully established subregional scheme for Oaxaca. The best to date is represented in Figure 11-1. The nine subregions shown on the map are portrayed as they existed in the sixteenth century, at which time they extended slightly beyond the borders of the present state of Oaxaca. The subregions are based primarily on geographical features, but attempt to delimit as well the broad cultural subunits of the Oaxaca area.

This chapter deals primarily with the Valles Centrales (Valley of Oaxaca), the Mixteca Alta, and the Sierra, for these are the only regions which have been extensively researched for the Colonial period. Hunt's study of the Cuicatecs (1972) supplies some additional information for part of the Norte region. We begin with an overview of levels of social stratification at the time of the conquest, then consider in turn the impact of early stratification at the time of the conquest, then consider in turn the impact of early Spanish institutions, population trends, the economy, community political structure and the position of the native nobility, and finally the special place of the urban Indians in the Spanish city of Antequera (now Oaxaca).[1] Throughout, differences between the

Early and Late Colonial period will constantly be kept in mind, the date 1650 serving as a convenient division. The period 1521–1650 was one of rapid, sometimes violent change for some Indian communities, much of it accompanied by steep rates of population decline. It was during this time that Spanish practices and institutions weighed most heavily on indigenous societies. Several scholars speak of a process of "simplification" of Indian society in the sixteenth century, as many common practices (especially religious ones) were prohibited and even whole social strata (the *mayeques* and slaves) eliminated. It was during this period that the basic accommodations to Spanish colonial society were made, and thereafter the Indians' relationship to the state was largely fixed (Taylor 1979: 170). These phenomena have long been recognized, but we are just beginning to understand the new cultural processes set in motion after 1650 when "Population growth and new markets led to greater peasant activity beyond community boundaries, more pressure on the land, increased circulation of goods, and a more commercial outlook" (Taylor 1979: 20). William B. Taylor sees the period 1650–1800 as one of relative stability in which Indians were free to elaborate on their early adjustments to colonial rule. The simplification of the sixteenth century gave way to new complexities, what Marcello Carmagnani (1980: 1028) calls a process of "restructuring."

Despite the abundant evidence of change, however, a number of core social, political, and economic institutions were remarkably resilient, especially in the Valley of Oaxaca and the Mixteca Alta. These elements of continuity constitute the most distinctive aspects of colonial Oaxaca, at least in comparison to the Central Highlands, and the elucidation of these features will be a principal aim of this chapter.

A Note on Sources

While this chapter is based mainly on secondary works, a few words are in order about

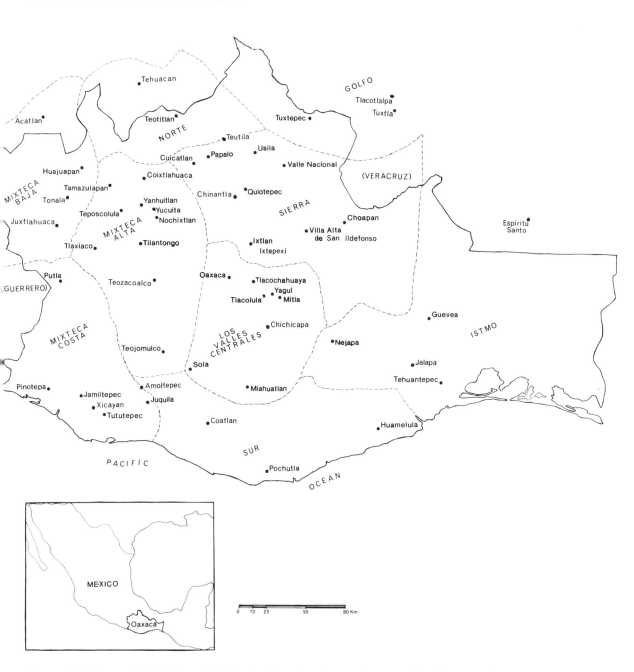

FIGURE 11-1. Oaxaca. Dotted lines indicate the nine subregions as they existed in the sixteenth century. Solid line indicates the present boundaries of the state of Oaxaca. Adapted from an original drawn by Cecil R. Welte.

the various types of primary sources and finding aids available for the ethnohistory of colonial Oaxaca. The famous Mixtec codices comprise most of the documentation in the native tradition, though a variety of pictorial documents exist for many parts of the Oaxaca area and have been surveyed by John B. Glass (1975) and Cecil R. Welte (1981). The ongoing *Catálogo de ilustraciones* published by the Archivo General de la Nación in Mexico City beginning in 1979 will eventually include all pictorials for Oaxaca which exist in that archive. There is also a large corpus of the 1580 *Relaciones geográficas* for Oaxaca, including both texts and maps (H. F. Cline 1972b). Colonial chronicles, on the other hand, are rare. The only ones which deal extensively with Oaxaca are the seventeenth-century works of Fray Francisco de Burgoa (1934a; 1934b). Consequently, most of what we know about colonial Oaxaca comes from primary documentation located in a variety of archives. Brief guides to their contents can be found in works by Taylor (1972) and Chance (1978b). In addition, a number of useful indices for both national and local collections have appeared in recent years (Spores and Saldaña 1973; 1975; 1976; Romero Frizzi 1978; Romero Frizzi and Spores 1976; Chance 1978a; Méndez Martínez 1979). The Cathedral Archive of Oaxaca remains much as it was when described by Woodrow Borah in 1948, but the state capital's civil archives unfortunately now bear little resemblance to the description in his 1951 "Notes."

SOCIAL STRATIFICATION AT SPANISH CONTACT

Before proceeding to the Colonial period proper, it is necessary to review briefly the nature of social stratification and overall sociopolitical development in Oaxaca at the time of Spanish contact. Later I will show that variations in this respect were important determinants of patterns and processes during Colonial times.

Ronald Spores (1965:986) distinguishes five foci of political power for Oaxaca in 1519:

(1) the Aztec capital of Tenochtitlan to which much of Oaxaca paid tribute, (2) Teozapotlan (now Zaachila), the most powerful Zapotec town in the Valley of Oaxaca; (3) Tehuantepec, the seat of Zapotec settlement in the Isthmus; (4) Tututepec, a powerful Mixtec kingdom on the Pacific Coast; and (5) Nahua-speaking Teotitlan del Camino in the northwest. Aside from the Aztec capital, the Valley of Oaxaca is the only focus we can begin to interpret given the available data.[2] However, there are several studies of the Contact period societies of the Mixteca Alta (Spores 1965; 1967; 1974; 1976; Dahlgren de Jordán 1966) and the Cuicatec Cañada (E. Hunt 1972).[3] My own work on the Zapotec Rincon of the Sierra of Villa Alta (Chance 1983) provides yet a fourth area for comparison.[4] These four regions can be placed on an evolutionary scale, in the order mentioned, with regard to complexity of social stratification and centralization of political power.[5]

The Valley of Oaxaca presented by far the most complex ethnic panorama. In addition to the native Zapotecs, the Spaniards encountered a sizable Mixtec population, numbering possibly as many as seventy thousand. They were most influential in the central part of the Valley, with the town of Cuilapan as their chief settlement. Nearby stood the Aztec garrison of Huaxyacac (which later gave Oaxaca its name), on the site of the present city of Oaxaca. Containing a Nahua-speaking population of roughly three to five thousand, its main function was to collect tribute from the Valley Zapotecs and Mixtecs. Oddly enough, barely a trace of Aztec cultural influence has been found, apart from the fact that many Valley *caciques* had become fluent in the Nahuatl language (Chance 1978b:19–20).

Among the Valley Zapotecs no one community was dominant, though Teozapotlan (Zaachila) was clearly the strongest. Warfare was a constant feature of life in the Valley. Political integration above the community level was weak, and unstable federations were formed with one city-state as the head unit and its *cacique* as supreme lord. Political

168

integration was achieved through payment of tribute. The size of the head towns ranged from two to eleven thousand persons, and whole communities from five to thirteen thousand (Whitecotton 1977:138). Each community had a hereditary aristocracy with a ruler or *cacique* heading a separate royal lineage. Succession to this office was by direct lineal descent.

Zapotec society was stratified into four groups: nobles, commoners, serfs, and slaves. Membership in the first three strata was perpetuated by heredity, unwritten sumptuary laws, and probably endogamy. The most clear-cut division was between the nobility and the rest of the populace. The nobles themselves were divided into the two groups, the *caciques* (ruling families) and the *principales* (lesser nobles who served as tribute collectors, administrators, and priests). The ruling families of the various states formed a kind of endogamous stratum, and the *caciques* themselves had virtually absolute power in their communities. They were also large landholders, and the *cacicazgo* estates may have been privately owned. The two largest in the Valley were at Cuilapan and Etla.

The commoners, or *macehuales*, formed the bulk of the population. Most were farmers, but there were many non-agricultural specialists as well, including weavers, dancers, music teachers, curers, witches, diviners, merchants, peddlers, sculptors, painters, interpreters, scribes, and writers. Though details on these people are lacking, Joseph W. Whitecotton (1977:149) feels that some of them worked full time at their trades.

The serfs, or *mayeques*, were permanently bound to the lands of the *caciques* and formed a part of the *cacicazgo* estates. Little is known about them, but they seem to have been few in number. Finally, there were the slaves, who were obtained through warfare and could also be bought and sold in markets. They were employed as servants and also as sacrificial victims.

These were the basic segments that comprised Valley Zapotec society, but there is disagreement over how the stratification sys-

tem should be characterized in formal terms. Spores (1965:969) speaks of a two-class system of nobles and commoners. Whitecotton (1977:142–150), on the other hand, prefers the concept of *estate*—a jurally defined division combining aspects of status, wealth, and hereditary position. He defines three estates of nobles, commoners, and priests, and would place the *mayeques* and slaves outside the system altogether. I agree with Whitecotton that the concept of estate is most appropriate, but am troubled by schemes that leave some groups excluded. I would also favor including the priests with the nobility, since they were drawn mainly from that segment. Thus, the simplest way to characterize Valley Zapotec society would be in terms of two estates: a noble estate composed of *caciques* and *principales*, and a commoner estate subdivided into *macehuales*, *mayeques*, and slaves.

The town-states of the Mixteca Alta were stratified in a very similar fashion. Barbro Dahlgren de Jordán (1966:141–145) characterizes the Mixtec stratification system as composed of two estates, each subdivided in the same fashion as those of the Valley Zapotecs.[6] But there were important differences. There is some doubt whether the Mixtecs were as occupationally specialized as their Zapotec neighbors:

There is no historical, archaeological, or ethnographic evidence to suggest that full time occupational specialization existed in any pre-Hispanic period. Individuals with specialized functions, whether in crafts, services, administration, or ritual, were not free from normal subsistence activity. They were, above all, agriculturalists with identities and behavior determined more by age, sex, and social class than by any special occupational category.

(Spores 1976:213)

Ecological differences were also important. Population pressure was significant in the Mixteca Alta in the Prehispanic period, but was never translated into large urban settlements (such as the Valley Zapotec metropolis of Monte Alban), in part because of the limitations on farming imposed by the mountainous terrain (Spores 1967:182). Approximately 80 percent of the region consists of sharply sloping, rugged territory, and the relatively small proportion of level valley land is no match for the much larger Zapotec Valley of Oaxaca. On the basis of his research in the Mixtec Nochixtlan Valley, Spores (1969; 1972) disputes the inclusion of the Mixteca Alta in Angel Palerm and Eric R. Wolf's (1957) list of five "nuclear areas" of Prehispanic Mesoamerica (the others are the Valleys of Mexico, Oaxaca, Puebla-Tlaxcala, and Guatemala City).

The importance of the area [the Nochixtlan Valley] in Postclassic times is not denied, but it is inappropriate to speak of it as an area of "*massed* economic and demographic power" relative to contemporaneous developments in Puebla, the Valley of Mexico, and in the Valley of Oaxaca. When we compare the level of internal development and probable degree of social, political, and economic influence attained by the other nuclear areas, it must be concluded that the Nochixtlan Valley occupied a decidedly inferior position of power, possibly even during the Postclassic period.

(Spores 1969:568).

Turning now to the small Cuicatec states of the Cañada region, Hunt's thorough study (1972) suggests that they were somewhat less developed than the Mixtec polities, despite the presence of intensive irrigation systems. The general outline of the Cuicatec "incipient state system" conformed in many respects to the highland Mesoamerican model, exhibiting

social classes; occupational groups of a secular character; a permanent, although not elaborate, bureaucracy; a state church with a regularly [*sic*] professionally trained clergy; an organization of ranked army officerships; urbanization; markets functioning outside a redistributing economic net-

work; a territorial arrangement of higher and lower political units, and so on.

(E. Hunt 1972:237)

But there are important qualifications. Hunt points out that Cuicatec communities were not city-states; like their counterparts in the Mixteca Alta, they lacked sufficient size and nucleation to warrant this label. Furthermore, once again evidence for full-time occupational specialization is lacking. Most important, however, were differences in the stratification system. While the familiar two-estate pattern of nobles and commoners was present, there was apparently no *mayeque* group to work the lands of the *caciques* (E. Hunt 1972:203). Furthermore, slaves are mentioned for just one community—Atlatlauca, one of the largest Cuicatec towns (ibid.:205). In the remainder, the commoner estate consisted of a minimally differentiated mass of *macehuales*.

Finally, there is the case of the Rincon Zapotecs in the Sierra of northeast Oaxaca. Unlike the previous three regions, the Rincon offers no level valley lands at all for cultivation. It is one of the most rugged regions of Oaxaca, composed of a series of high mountain chains separated only by deep canyons and narrow ravines. Data on the Contact period Rincon are far from abundant, but a few tentative observations can be made (Chance 1983). I argue that the Rincon and adjacent areas of the northern Sierra approximated the chiefdom, rather than state, level of organization. Compared to those of the previous three regions, settlements in the Rincon were smaller, poorer, only incipiently stratified, and had less specialized economies. The customary Mesoamerican settlement pattern of head town with subject hamlets was less developed in the Rincon than elsewhere. At least in some communities, the priestly and chiefly hierarchies seem to have been one and the same, not separate as was the custom in other parts of Oaxaca. And above all, the stratification system was far less complex. Like the Cuicatec Cañada, the

Zapotec Rincon apparently lacked a *mayeque* stratum, and slavery, if it existed at all, was of very little importance. The Rincon differed, however, in that its *caciques* possessed relatively little land or other forms of wealth to set them off from the commoners. There is no evidence that their standard of living differed significantly from that of the *macehuales*.

While this discussion has been necessarily brief and condensed, the portraits for the Valley of Oaxaca, Mixteca Alta, Cuicatec Cañada, and Zapotec Rincon may be placed on a scale from higher to lower sociopolitical complexity. These differences underlay the regional variants of colonial Indian society that took shape in Oaxaca in the sixteenth century.[7]

THE SPANISH CONQUEST AND EARLY COLONIAL INSTITUTIONS

In comparison to the shock and dislocation that accompanied the Spanish conquest in other parts of New Spain, transition to colonial rule in Oaxaca was relatively smooth and easy. Major Spanish penetration began in 1521, only four months after the surrender of the Aztec capital of Tenochtitlan. Contingents led by Francisco de Orozco and Pedro de Alvarado encountered very little resistance in the Mixteca Alta and in the Valley of Oaxaca. Valley and Isthmus Zapotecs were especially receptive to the conquistadores, since the lord of Tehuantepec had already abdicated his throne and allied himself with Cortés prior to Orozco's arrival. Only among the coastal Mixtecs and in the northern Sierra, among the Mixes, Chinantecs, and Mountain Zapotecs, did the Spanish encounter strong resistance. The conquest of the Sierra region was especially prolonged and extremely brutal. While Spanish control in the Valley and parts of the Mixteca began to be implemented in 1521, the northern Sierra was not pacified until the 1550's (Chance 1978b:30–31; 1983; Olivera and Romero 1973:232–235).

From their base in the newly founded city of Antequera, the conquerors developed a full array of colonial institutions, though their operation came to be strongly influenced by indigenous practices. The region was carved up into political districts—*alcaldías mayores* and *corregimientos*—in the 1520's and 1530's, and Spanish officials were assigned to important Indian head towns to collect royal tribute and otherwise administer the indigenous population.[8] The Church also played an important role from the very beginning, in particular the Dominicans, who lost no time in consolidating their position. By 1570 there were twenty-two Dominican establishments outside of Antequera, scattered over the Mixtec- and Zapotec-speaking regions of the Bishopric of Oaxaca (Chance 1978b:39–45).

By far the most significant of the early Spanish means of exploiting the Indian population was the *encomienda*, a grant of an Indian town or towns to an individual Spaniard with the right to collect tribute. In the early sixteenth century, forced labor was usually demanded as well. The *encomienda* in Oaxaca developed and declined at about the same time and in the same fashion as it did in other parts of New Spain.[9] It reached its peak before the 1550's, and until then Spanish *encomenderos* were largely dependent on their holdings for subsistence. They regularly received such items as clothing (for resale), chickens, turkeys, salt, honey, chile, beans, corn, wheat, wax, and cacao. In addition, there were levies of gold dust and an average of ten to fifteen laborers per day. Under restrictions imposed by the Crown in 1549, however, *encomenderos* were deprived of access to Indian labor, and tribute quotas were fixed by royal officers. In the seventeenth century many *encomiendas* withered away altogether as the Crown gradually succeeded in phasing out the institution (Chance 1978b:48–49).

Mercedes Olivera and Ma. de los Angeles Romero (1973:236–244) have mapped fifty-nine *encomiendas* in the Bishopric of Oaxaca in 1560, and note that all the Indian communities included were also under Dominican tutelage. The most populous portions of Oaxaca were in the hands of *encomenderos*: the Mixteca Alta, Baja, and Costa; the southern Zapotec and Chontal regions, and the Sierra Zapotec region. *Encomiendas* varied in size from one to several towns; one of the largest belonged to Don Luis de Castilla in the Mixteca Costa which included more than eleven *pueblos*, encompassing practically the entire territory of the Prehispanic *señorio* of Tututepec (Olivera and Romero 1973:238). Another exceptional holding, by far the largest of all, belonged to Cortés and his heirs, part of whose Marquesado del Valle lay in the Oaxaca area. In many ways this amounted to one large *encomienda* that included about one-fifth of the Indians of the Valley of Oaxaca (Taylor 1972:17, 31), plus additional territory in the Isthmus of Tehuantepec.[10] Because of the large Marquesado holdings, only four other *encomiendas* survived in the Valley of Oaxaca after 1544 (Chance 1978b:46).

Of all the *encomenderos* in the bishopric, only a third actually resided there (virtually all of them in Antequera); the rest were absentees living primarily in Mexico City and Puebla. *Encomenderos* rarely dealt with their Indians directly, and never resided in Indian communities. Their demands may have placed considerable hardships on the Indians, but they do not seem to have seriously affected indigenous culture (Olivera and Romero 1973:239). *Encomenderos* could not match the cultural impact of the Dominican friars, but the *encomienda* did contribute to the destruction of indigenous political alliances. Frequently even important head towns and their subject hamlets were divided and assigned to different *encomiendas*.

Once Indian labor was removed from the purview of the *encomienda*, an alternative means of coercion was needed. In addition, there were many non-*encomenderos* who sought Indian labor for public works projects, mining, agricultural work, and household chores. The mechanism that emerged to meet these needs was the *repartimiento*, by which workers were drafted from particular

towns for specific purposes. Our information on the *repartimiento* pertains mainly to the Valley of Oaxaca (Taylor 1972:144-147; Chance 1978b:76–80), where the normal period of service was one week, and 4 percent of the tributary males from a given village were expected to work at one time.

Repartimientos furnished most of the agricultural labor on Spanish estates in the Valley in the late sixteenth and early seventeenth centuries. They were also instrumental in the building of churches and monasteries in Antequera, and provided personal service for many Spanish residents of the city. By the end of the sixteenth century, the dwindling Valley Indian population could no longer meet the needs of the urban economy, and in 1609 city *repartimientos* were extended to the Mixteca Alta, the Sierra Zapotec region, the Cuicatec Cañada, and the Chontal region.

Abuses of the system were legion. Indians were rarely paid for their labor and were required to work seven days a week instead of the prescribed six. Because of its rotating nature, the *repartimiento* contributed little to the assimilation or acculturation of the Indian into Spanish society. The documentation suggests, however, that Indian communities suffered greater hardships under *repartimientos* than they did under the *encomienda* system. *Repartimientos* became important during the late sixteenth and early seventeenth centuries at precisely the same time that population losses in many communities were most critical (see below). Taylor has observed that downward adjustments in quotas were often delayed by ten years or more. He summarizes the disruptive effects on Indian life in the Valley:

As population declines made the supply of repartimiento workers inadequate, Spanish landowners forced laborers into longer periods of service with little or no pay. Indians complained in the late sixteenth century that they had no time left to work the lands from which they paid the royal tribute—a fact that the Crown could hardly ignore. Residents of entire towns openly flouted local authorities by refusing to serve in repartimientos, and other individuals avoided service by claiming exemptions as members of the native nobility. (Taylor 1972:146)

Despite its obvious drawbacks, the system persisted in rural parts of the Valley until the last quarter of the eighteenth century and in Antequera until the mid-seventeenth century, when it was replaced by urban Indian wage labor.

All of these mechanisms for harnessing Indian labor on behalf of colonial enterprises had significant consequences, but in my opinion the Spanish institution which had the greatest impact on the indigenous population was the Church, especially the numerous Dominican *doctrinas* established in Indian communities. The friars imposed a distinct brand of forced acculturation that in the end far outlasted the disruptive effects of Spanish labor practices. Unfortunately, missionary tactics and Indian response to them have received little direct study in Oaxaca, and recent scholarship has added little to Robert Ricard's (1966) landmark study for sixteenth-century New Spain. The importance of colonial *cofradías* (religious confraternities) and the Catholic inputs to the Mesoamerican civil-religious hierarchy are well known, but we still lack explicit studies on the origin and function of these important institutions within particular communities and regions.[11]

POPULATION

Population trends in colonial Mexico constitute an important and controversial topic. Reliable census data are generally unavailable before the second half of the eighteenth century, and for earlier periods it is necessary to rely on estimates derived from tribute counts and the like. In this section the principal findings and estimates pertinent to Oaxaca will be reviewed, but space prohibits a lengthy discussion of methods. We will look first at estimates of the population of Oaxaca as a whole, then turn to specific studies of

three regions: the Valley, the Mixteca Alta, and the *alcaldía mayor* of Villa Alta.[12]

We are still very far from a precise estimate of the population of Oaxaca in 1519. Several attempts have been made, but all suffer from a lack of data. Extrapolating Woodrow Borah and Sherburne F. Cook (1963), José Miranda (1967:130) gave an estimate of 3 million. Guido Münch (1978:69) goes even higher and posits 4 million. Spores (1965:964), on the other hand, is more conservative and advances the figure of 1.5 million. None of these estimates is in fact based on direct information, for none exists for the time of Spanish contact. In my opinion, more precise estimates will have to be based in part on Late Postclassic archaeological survey data.

For the sixteenth century, Münch (1978:76) employs Bishop Albuquerque's *Relación* of 1570 to provide an estimate of 500,000 for the Bishopric of Oaxaca in that year. If we accept the lowest of the 1519 estimates, this amounts to a decline of 67 percent; if we accept Münch's own 1519 estimate the decline is 88 percent. In either case the drop is substantial and must be attributed primarily to epidemic disease. Similar trends were present elsewhere in New Spain, however, and in 1570 the Bishopric of Oaxaca contained a quarter of the tributary population of the colony (Münch 1978:77).

Even less information is available for the seventeenth century, though it is well known that the indigenous population reached its nadir sometime between 1620 and 1650. For New Spain as a whole, Cook and Borah (1979:102) calculate that in 1620–1625 the Indian population had fallen to a low of 3 percent of what it had been in 1519. A slow recovery began soon thereafter, and by 1740 the Indian population of Oaxaca had risen to 250,000 (Taylor 1976:63). By 1793, Oaxaca had 411,000 inhabitants, a significant recovery but still far below the Preconquest level (Miranda 1967:135; Taylor 1976:63). Significantly, 88 percent of these people were Indians. The combined Spanish and *casta* (miscegenated) population of the entire Oaxaca territory was still below the 50,000 mark.

TABLE 11-1. Indian Population Estimates for Three Regions of Colonial Oaxaca

Valley of Oaxaca		Mixteca Alta		Alcaldía Mayor of Villa Alta[a]	
1520	350,000	1520	700,000	1520	347,000
1568	150,000	1532	528,000	1532	315,000
1630	45,000	1569	100,000	1568	32,000
1790's	90,000	1590	57,000	1595	21,000
		1670	30,000	1622	21,000
		1742	54,016	1742	49,123
		1803	75,990	1781	47,165
		1826	64,549	1826	48,200

SOURCES: Valley of Oaxaca: Taylor (1972:17, 18, 34); Mixteca Alta: Cook and Borah (1968); Villa Alta: Chance (1980).

[a]The figures for 1520–1622 are estimates derived using the methods of Borah and Cook. For 1568, Cook and Borah (1960) provide data on all but eleven of the eighty-three towns in the district. Estimates for six more were derived by interpolation from the counts in the *Suma de visitas* of ca. 1548 (Borah and Cook 1960). The 1532 estimate is derived by multiplying the 1568 figure by the Cook and Borah (1960:39) Zapotecas ratio of 10.009. Following Borah and Cook (1963:84), I then added 10 percent to arrive at the 1532 figure. The 1520 estimate is derived by adding 10 percent to the 1532 estimate. The 1595 figure is equal to the 1568 figure times the ratio 0.679 derived (by me) for sixteen towns in the district for which counts exist for those years. Data for 1622 come from Cook and Borah (1979). This figure must be regarded as tentative because estimates for twenty-four of the eighty towns had to be interpolated (by me) from data for other years. Sources for the other years in the table are as follows: for 1742, Villa-Señor y Sánchez (1952); for 1781, "Estado o plan de las cuidades, villas, o lugares correspondientes en lo ecclesiástico a la Mitra de Oaxaca que existen situados en el distrito de la administración reunida a Villa Alta" (Colección Castañeda Guzmán, Oaxaca); for 1826, Murguía y Galardi (1827). For 1742, I followed Cook and Borah (1968) and reduced Villa-Señor y Sánchez' number of families for each town by 5 percent and multiplied by 4.9.

Rates of population decline and growth were not uniform in all parts of Oaxaca. Table 11-1 summarizes the results of three regional studies for the Valley of Oaxaca, the Mixteca Alta, and the *alcaldía mayor* of Villa Alta. Significant contrasts are evident, even though all the studies are based to some extent on the same methodology developed by Borah and Cook. In all three regions the decline was steep and probably continuous, with drops of 87 percent (the Valley), 96 percent (the Mixteca Alta), and 94 percent (Villa Alta) from the highest to the lowest points. Recovery began in the mid-seventeenth century.

By the end of the Colonial period all three regions had at least doubled their populations, but were still far below their 1520 levels. Most interesting, however, are the differential rates of decline between 1520 and 1568/1569: 57 percent in the Valley, 86 percent in the Mixteca Alta, and 91 percent in the Villa Alta district. This is the reverse of what one might predict, since the Valley had by far the largest non-Indian population and the isolated *alcaldía mayor* of Villa Alta to the north contained barely any non-Indians at all. The Villa Alta region also reached its nadir—by 1595—sooner than the other areas, which experienced their low points in the seventeenth century. I hasten to add, however, that the sixteenth-century estimates for the Villa Alta district are the most tentative of the three, and further research might well change this picture considerably.

For the Mixteca Alta, Cook and Borah posit a steady rate of depletion of 4.5 percent per year between 1532 and the mid-1570's. Spores has challenged their conclusions on several grounds, however. On the basis of the ecology of the region and his archaeological work in the Nochixtlan Valley, he suggests a 1520 figure of 500,000 for the Mixteca Alta, Baja, and Costa combined (Spores 1967:72). For the Nochixtlan Valley itself, he sees a change from 50,000 in 1520 to 32,000 in 1600, a drop of only 36 percent (Spores 1969:566). He also reminds us that individual communities may differ substantially from regional trends, and cites the important town of Yanhuitlan as a case in point. For this community there is evidence of population decline from 1520 to 1548, then an increase and economic florescence between 1550 and 1570 before another period of decline set in (Spores 1967:75). On the basis of this and other evidence, Spores would support George Kubler's (1942) contention that population decline in the sixteenth century (at least in the Mixteca Alta) was not continuous, but was marked by periodic fall and recovery.

Factors that might have been responsible for such fluctuation are still little understood. Spores (1967:107–108) specifically exempts *congregaciones* (forced concentration of Indian settlements) as a factor, stating that they did not begin in the Mixteca Alta until 1590, and even then were unsuccessful. Recently, however, Peter Gerhard (1977:375–380) has brought to light new data on *congregaciones* in Oaxaca between 1550 and 1564, including Yanhuitlan and several other towns in the Mixteca. Rodolfo Pastor (1981:Ch. 1:32–34) also believes that there were substantial modifications in the settlement pattern of the Mixteca during these years, though he notes that they were limited to towns in the valleys along the Camino Real. Further study might

therefore indicate that movement of population in the mid-sixteenth century was partially responsible for this clouded picture of Mixtec historical demography.

While minimizing its importance in colonial Oaxaca, Miranda (1967:140) attributes what Indian population displacement did occur to "voluntary" abandonment of ancient defended sites after the conquest, as well as to the forced *congregaciones* during the well-known campaign of 1593–1605. There is evidence, however, that many early regroupings in the sixteenth century were not voluntary, but orchestrated by the Dominican friars to facilitate their evangelism. Taylor (1972:26) mentions the cases of Zimatlan and Tlalixtac in the Valley of Oaxaca, and my own study of the documentation for the *alcaldía mayor* of Villa Alta suggests that there the Dominicans were even more influential in resettlement.

Gerhard (1977:375–380) has shown that many first attempts at *congregación* between 1550 and 1564 were indeed successful. He specifically points to five instances for the Valley, seven in the Mixteca Alta, and four in the Mixteca Baja. Even better known are the later *congregaciones* of 1593–1605. Oaxaca was divided into zones, each headed by a special commissioner. Miranda (1967:143–146) discusses eleven cases and concludes that they generally accomplished their mission, notwithstanding a few failures. In the Valley, however, Taylor (1972:27) found that most of the nine *congregaciones* in this period had broken down into their constituent communities by the end of the seventeenth century. In the Mixteca, Spores (1967:107–108) questions whether most scheduled regroupings ever took place at all, since a number of communities apparently won permanent stays of congregation orders.

Where they did occur, the *congregaciones* were at least in part a response to declining population. Both campaigns in the sixteenth century followed epidemics and no doubt contributed even more to the disruption of life in Indian communities. Many towns became extinct altogether. The effect of depopulation on village social structures is still

175

only imperfectly understood, but we do know that it was far from uniform. In the Mixteca Alta, for example, we have the contrasting cases of Yanhuitlan and Santiago Tejupan. We have already seen that the former experienced a period of growth and prosperity in the mid-sixteenth century (Spores 1967: 73–75). Tejupan, on the other hand, according to Borah and Cook (1979:409–431), dropped from a Preconquest population level of about 54,000 to 3,063, in 1569, reaching a nadir of only 565 in the second half of the seventeenth century. The town was moved to a new site sometime between 1564 and 1579, and Borah and Cook point to a great simplification of social structure in the sixteenth century, particularly in religious activities and the *barrio* structure. Judging from the available documentation for the Valley and the *alcaldía mayor* of Villa Alta, the trajectory of demographic change in Tejupan would seem to be more typical of Oaxaca than that of Yanhuitlan, but a final opinion must be reserved until we have more detailed studies of particular communities.

ECONOMY

A distinctive feature of the economy of colonial Oaxaca was the integration of many Indian communities into regional, colony-wide, and even world-wide market systems without any substantial loss of control over the means of production (Taylor 1979:21). The stereotypic view of the colonial Indian laboring on Spanish haciendas and in the mines does not apply to Oaxaca, where landed estates were small and few in number and mining was of minimal importance. Indian villages were able to retain control over much of their land, thereby maintaining a significant degree of economic autonomy. In the regions of Oaxaca with which we are concerned, relatively few communities succumbed to the demands of full-time wage labor or became satellites of Spanish enterprise. For most Indians, subsistence agriculture in one's native community continued as a way of life. Participation in the wider colonial economy was not

unimportant, but it was always conditioned by subsistence and village needs at home.

To be sure, the Spanish conquest introduced a new agricultural technology, draft animals, and new crops. But while oxen and the plow soon replaced the digging stick in many areas, and cultivation of certain indigenous crops (such as maguey and cochineal) increased, there was no real qualitative change in the peasant subsistence economy (Spores 1967:107; Taylor 1974:399). In Taylor's words (1972:4–5), the Indians "usually resisted radical changes in diet, ignoring the abundant meat supply and refusing to produce many European foods."

Agricultural production in colonial Oaxaca was performed mainly by Indians on Indian lands. Even in the Valley of Oaxaca, the region with the highest non-Indian population, Indian communities and individuals controlled roughly two-thirds of the agricultural land in the eighteenth century (Taylor 1974:397). Valley haciendas were small, never producing much surplus for the market, and even Antequera still obtained most of its foodstuffs from Indian villagers in the Late Colonial period (Chance 1978b:149–50).

Indian land tenure in colonial Oaxaca was a complex affair, but certain general trends are clear. In the Valley of Oaxaca and the Mixteca, the Spanish king confirmed *cacicazgo* rights and granted other lands to Indian nobles in the early sixteenth century, long before Spaniards became interested in landholding (Taylor 1972:39–40; Pastor 1981:Ch. 2:38). Colonial *cacicazgos* were privately owned and considered as entailed estates modeled after the Spanish *mayorazgos*. In accordance with Spanish law, succession was most frequently from father to first-born son (Spores 1967:152; Taylor 1972:44). These estates were sometimes of considerable size, especially in the Valley, where they may have been larger in the Early Colonial period than in Prehispanic times (Taylor 1972:43). Many of them survived intact well into the eighteenth century and were an important factor in maintaining the status and wealth of the Zapotec and Mixtec native nobility. I hasten to add, however, that things were different among the Cuicatecs and Rincon Zapotecs, where *cacicazgos* controlled less land and where the concept of private property, at least in the sixteenth century, is in doubt (E. Hunt 1972:225; Chance 1983).

Less is known about the lands of the *principales*, though Taylor (1972:45–47) points out that in the Valley they were not tied to either primogeniture or notions of inalienability. Many estates of *principales* were openly divided at the whim of the noble, a process which helps explain why so many *principales* were downwardly mobile over time (economically, at least), whereas the *caciques* had a much firmer grasp on their sources of wealth.

Besides the *cacicazgo* estates, six types of colonial Indian lands have been distinguished for the Valley of Oaxaca (Taylor 1972:68):

(1) the fundo legal, or townsite, (2) communal lands worked collectively to support religious festivities and to meet other community expenses, (3) communal woods and pasturelands for the private use of all townsmen, (4) communal barrio lands, often divided into plots and worked separately by individuals and families of the neighborhood, (5) communal tracts that were allotted to landless townsmen and "servants" of the community, and (6) privately owned tracts.

While the status of privately owned land in the Cuicatec Cañada and the Rincon remains unclear, all authorities agree that in the Valley and the Mixteca during the Colonial period there was a growing acceptance of private ownership that affected *caciques*, *principales*, and *macehuales* alike (Spores, personal communication; Pastor 1981:Ch. 2:36; Taylor 1972:73).

Detailed studies of particular communities are lacking, but Rodolfo Pastor and his colleagues (1979) have produced an interesting study of eighteenth-century agricultural production in the Bishopric of Oaxaca based on *diezmo* (tithe) statistics. They found that, over time, Indians accounted for progressively less of the *diezmo* revenue and Span-

iards for more, and posit the gradual marginalization of Indian production. They claim that by the end of the eighteenth century, Indians were no longer the key producers in Oaxaca (with the exception of the cochineal crop) and agricultural production for the market was dominated by the Spanish (Pastor et al. 1979:44). This is a very provocative argument, especially given the fact that in 1810, 88 percent of Oaxaca's population was composed of Indians, most of whom were still in possession of their lands. An important task for future research will be to find ways to test this hypothesis with other, more direct forms of evidence.[13]

Indians in the Valley and the Mixteca began to participate in the colonial Spanish economy very early on.[14] By far the most important commodities traded in the market were sheep, silk, and cochineal. In the sixteenth century the Mixteca Alta was the most commercial indigenous region in all of Oaxaca. Beginning soon after the conquest, silkworm-raising had become a flourishing industry by the 1540's, and many *caciques* and Indian communities played an active role. While the *caciques* operated as more or less autonomous entrepreneurs, the *macehuales*, urged on by Dominican missionaries, were more interested in producing silk to pay tribute and finance their community treasuries. By 1580, silk was the chief cash-producing industry in the Valley of Yanhuitlan, and the Mixteca had become the most important silk region in the New World. Soon afterward, however, a decline began in the face of competition from the Far East, and the industry never regained its former prominence (Borah 1943:15, 31, 45–46, 87).

Sheep raising was also important among the Indians of sixteenth-century Oaxaca, and again the Mixteca took the lead.[15] With the exception of a few *caciques* and *principales*, the raising of cattle (*ganado mayor*) was prohibited for Indians, but there was no such restriction on sheep and goats (*ganado menor*). Mixtec sheep flocks grew rapidly between 1551 and 1600, totaling as many as 300,000 head. Licenses were granted to both nobles and commoners, though Miranda was of the opinion that few *macehuales* profited much as individuals. Once again, their efforts were more directed toward meeting community obligations. In any case, the Mixteca Alta was the only region of New Spain where Indians owned more sheep than Spaniards (Miranda 1958:788, 792, 795–796).

Given the above, it is not surprising that the Mixteca earned a reputation for being industrious in commerce. Furthermore, both Spores (1967:75) and Pastor (1981:Ch. 1:29) point to a marked increase in the standard of living in the mid-sixteenth century, when silk, especially, was at its apogee. A famous remark by the Bishop of Oaxaca in 1544 is worth quoting:

. . . the natives are lords of their wealth, and many of them are rich, and all have more than their ancestors ever did . . .

They trade and sell and raise cattle and silk in such abundance that there is a town in the Mixteca where the natives raise two thousand pounds of silk for themselves, and could pay nine hundred pesos of gold dust as tribute. In this way, contrary to what ought to be the state of affairs, the natives are rich and well-treated, and the Spaniards [are] the poorest and most restless people in this out-of-the-way place.

(Quoted by Borah 1943:16)

However prosperous some Indians appeared to be in the sixteenth century, the eighteenth century presents a more complex picture. A significant number of Mixtec and Valley Zapotec ruling families maintained high positions of status and wealth, but the same cannot be said across the board for *principales* and *macehuales*, nor for Indian communities generally. There is little doubt that the landholding community itself gained importance during the Colonial period at the expense of ethnic and regional ties (Taylor 1979:24).[16] Nor can the expanding Indian market activity in the eighteenth century be denied. It is also true, however, that the market system often operated to the Indian peasant's disadvantage, and that pressure on the

178

land had negative consequences in some areas.

Nowhere was this second factor more evident than in the Mixteca, where there was a significant deterioration of the environment during the seventeenth and eighteenth centuries (Pastor 1981:Ch. 1:88). Most serious was the large-scale erosion brought about by overgrazing of sheep and indigenous agricultural practices. These environmental changes, coupled with competition over land and the virtual disappearance of traditional *caciques* after the 1740's (see below) ushered in, for many Mixtec communities, a period of economic decadence which lasted until the end of the century. Ironically, this came at a time when the Bourbon reforms and thriving cochineal trade were revitalizing economic life in the Spanish cities. But Pastor (1981:Ch. 1:96) sees few of these benefits trickling down to rural villages in the Mixteca.

The economic condition of eighteenth-century villages elsewhere in Oaxaca is less clear, for the subject has received little study. Taylor (1972:16) discerns a general economic decline in the Valley of Oaxaca during the first half of the eighteenth century, brought on by a combination of droughts, frosts, wheat blight, and a fatal epidemic among cattle and sheep. The effects, however, were most evident on the Spanish haciendas, and the impact of the depression in Indian communities remains unclear. Generalizing for both Oaxaca and central Mexico in the eighteenth century, Taylor claims that

In neither of our regions was uniform prosperity or pervasive decay of village societies the rule. Some village communities even in the Valley of Mexico, such as Huitzilopochco and Tepetlaostoc, achieved new and remarkably even prosperity for their citizens in the eighteenth century, but even more communities disappeared or underwent divisive internal changes at this time.

(Taylor 1979:24–25)

Clearly, much work remains to be done on the peasant economy of colonial Oaxaca.

Another problematic issue is to what extent Oaxaca's Indians profited economically from the burgeoning trade in cochineal during the eighteenth century. That this trade was truly international in scope and a source of employment and enrichment for many citizens of Antequera is not in doubt (Hamnett 1971a; Chance 1978b). Nor is there any question that the principal cultivators of the tiny bugs were Indians (Dahlgren de Jordán 1963). It is usually assumed that Indians were important traders in this commodity as well. This is the implication of a remark by the Bishop of Oaxaca in 1702 that the Indians knew there was considerable foreign demand for cochineal and that New Spain was the only producer. Further, he pointed to a shortage of corn in the province because the Indians "have left the major part of their fields uncultivated. They are no longer interested in foodstuffs and only look for places where cochineal can be raised. More than two-thirds of the farmers in this province produce it" (quoted by Chance 1979:111). The bishop may have been largely correct, but he left a lot unsaid. Brian Hamnett (1971b:63) has demonstrated that Indians were neglecting their *milpas* not because they were freely trading in cochineal and other goods, but because of the pressure placed on them by the debt-collectors of the Spanish *alcaldes mayores*, who, in collusion with Spanish merchants, monopolized much of the cochineal trade.[17]

The mechanism utilized by these political officials was the infamous *repartimiento de efectos*. This was, in effect, a system of forced production and consumption. *Alcaldes mayores* would forcibly sell commodities to the Indians in their districts at highly inflated prices. Cattle, wheat, tobacco, sugar, cotton, and even corn were often distributed this way (Carmagnani 1978:140). Alternatively, the *repartimiento* (not to be confused with the *corvée* labor system of the same name) often consisted of advances of cash or raw materials, such as cotton, to Indian households which in turn were obligated to use the money to produce cochineal or weave the cotton into mantles. On a specified date, the

alcalde mayor's representative would return to purchase the cochineal or finished textiles at below market prices.[18] While this practice was in evidence in Oaxaca as early as the sixteenth century, it flourished most in the Late Colonial period. Though the *repartimiento de efectos* was technically illegal, all royal efforts to eradicate it failed, and the institution continued to operate until the very end of the Colonial period (Hamnett 1971b:76; Stein 1981).

The importance of this aspect of Spanish colonialism should not be underestimated. In Oaxaca, the *repartimientos de efectos* were a mainstay of the colonial political economy. As Hamnett (1971b:3) has remarked, "the province of Oaxaca was not so much dominated by Creole landowners as by the Alcaldes Mayores and the Spanish Peninsular merchants." This system of forced production and consumption had the effect of benefiting the Spanish colonial economy (and its political officials) while keeping the indigenous communities intact (Carmagnani 1978:143). The forced sale of goods, the textile weaving, and the cultivation of cochineal did not appreciably interfere with traditional subsistence agriculture or the daily round of life in Indian villages as long as the demands of the *alcaldes mayores* were not excessive. This is one of the reasons why much of traditional village culture has persisted in Oaxaca into the twentieth century.

The transition to an overtly capitalist economy in New Spain was well in evidence by the late sixteenth century (Bakewell 1971:226) and became more pronounced with the passage of time. Taylor and I have characterized the emergence of capitalism in Oaxaca in this way:

There was a crucial change in the socio-economic structure of central Mexico [including Oaxaca] in which profits based on forced labor and head taxes (the prerogatives of political command) gradually gave way to a system of commercial capitalism operating through an open marketplace and cash nexus. The first system

179

was based primarily on the exploitation of forced labor and depended on a rigid division between colonizers and colonized in which the "profit motive" was limited to the rulers (mainly political officials and *encomenderos*). Under commercial capitalism, however, profits were based on the exchange of goods and services and were present at various levels of society, not merely among the colonial elite.

(Chance and Taylor 1977:485)

It is obvious that the *repartimiento de efectos* had both capitalist and precapitalist qualities. On the one hand, it often involved forced labor and certainly qualifies as a prerogative of political command. On the other, the *repartimiento* was certainly part of the cash economy, and profits were made at various levels of society (though it is doubtful that they extended down to the level of the average Indian *macehual*). However, if we take a larger view and consider the economic system of New Spain as a whole and the emerging world economic system at that time (Wallerstein 1974), capitalist features are clearly the dominant ones. In the eighteenth century, Oaxaca was integrated into these larger systems in good measure through the textile and cochineal trades. The *repartimiento de efectos* facilitated this integration and kept the Indians in contact with the cash economy, while at the same time reserving the lion's share of profits for the dominant group and maintaining hundreds of peasant villages as semi-autonomous entities in which a number of precapitalist elements survived.

Village Politics and the Position of the Native Nobility

Recent studies have shown that *cacique* families in parts of Oaxaca continued to enjoy substantial wealth and prestige long after their counterparts in central Mexico had gone into decline. Even in mountainous districts like the Zapotec Rincon, where few Prehispanic *cacique* lineages survived the

sixteenth century, overall poverty did not do away with the prestige attached to *cacique* and *principal* status in the Late Colonial period. Far from being reduced to a homogeneous mass of peasants, the Indian population of Oaxaca was characterized by significant forms of inequality until the very end of Spanish rule.

In the early sixteenth century, most of Oaxaca was subjected to the familiar forms of political Hispanicization. But the Spaniards were most concerned with replacing Indian structures above the community level, and in Oaxaca, where these were either tenuous or nonexistent, a substantial proportion of the indigenous sociopolitical organization survived the conquest years (Taylor 1974:406; Carmagnani 1980:1029).

The Spanish system of town government, the *cabildo*, quickly took root in Oaxaca, at least in its outward manifestations. Its composition was subject to much local variation, especially among the lower offices, where indigenous custom prevailed, but the most common form was headed by a *gobernador* (governor) with two *alcaldes* (judges), two *regidores* (councilmen), and a variable number of *alguaciles* or *topiles* (police and messengers) and other community servants (Olivera and Romero 1973:271). All of these were elective offices, but choices had to be approved by Spanish authorities. *Gobernadores* were confirmed by the viceroy. In the sixteenth century, personnel for these offices was drawn primarily from the native nobility, the *caciques* and *principales*, thereby preserving much of the Prehispanic community power structure. Furthermore, at least in the Valley and the Mixteca, it was common for the village *caciques* and *gobernadores* to be the same persons. Until the 1550's, Spaniards often used these terms interchangeably (Spores 1967:111; Taylor 1972:51).

As in many parts of New Spain, Oaxaca's *caciques* were recognized by the Spanish in the early sixteenth century as a practical means of gaining control over the Indian masses. They were granted special privileges and treated as a class apart from the commoners. *Caciques* responded to this favored treatment by eagerly embracing much of Spanish culture, including, as we have seen, forms of economic enterprise. They were among the first to be baptized, spoke Spanish, dressed in European clothing, were often literate, and were quick to grasp the importance of written law. In the Valley of Oaxaca

Caciques considered themselves aristocrats on the Spanish model. In many respects they had more in common with the Spanish society of Antequera than with the people of their own jurisdictions. . . . by 1600 most caciques who could afford it lived permanently in Antequera and only occasionally visited their towns. (Taylor 1972:38)

Despite the growing physical and cultural distance between themselves and their *pueblos*, many *caciques* used their European-style wealth and position as cultural brokers to maintain their political power in their native communities. For the Mixteca, Pastor (1981:Ch. 2:41) makes the important point that some communities *wanted* their *caciques* to remain influential because of the critical role they played in the colonial patron-client system. If their *cacique* prospered, the *macehuales* stood to benefit as well. Even when they fought a *cacique*, they often did it with the help of another or by "creating" a new one.

A notable exception to this persistence of *cacique* wealth, status, and power in the sixteenth century was the Zapotec Rincon. The available data are sparse, but it is clear that the *caciques* of this region did not command the influence of those in the Valley, the Mixteca, or the Cañada. As we have seen, their Preconquest ancestors lacked the power and wealth of the nobility of these other regions. The few Early Colonial *caciques* mentioned in the documentation for the Rincon appear to have had little influence in their villages. They owned little land and in court were

never able to present genealogies to confirm the Preconquest heritage which they claimed. During the sixteenth century, only three viceregal licenses were granted to Rincon *caciques*—all for the use of a mount on horseback. I suspect the reason for such a small number is that the Indians made few requests. Neither Spanish concepts of noble status nor the cash economy had yet made much of an impact in these remote mountain villages, and the *caciques* never developed the independent economic base so crucial to the survival of noble families in other parts of Oaxaca (Chance 1983).

In the Cuicatec Cañada, where the political power of the *caciques* was closely related to their administration of irrigation and the redistribution of land, the nobility remained strong into the early seventeenth century. Up until that time Indian rulers continued to be selected according to native principles of social organization. But between 1590 and 1620, the Spanish reduced the economic value and political prestige of *cacique* positions by "instituting elections, disregarding native preferences, shortening *cacique* title and the tenure of other officeships such as governors to periods such as a year, and suspending the granting of cacicazgo privileges" (E. Hunt 1972:230). Four *caciques* were imprisoned or tried between 1591 and 1618, and Hunt speaks of the "social death" of the Cuicatec aristocracy in the early seventeenth century. By 1700 the basis of its power lay in ruins. After that time the main Cuicatec head towns were gradually taken over by incoming Spanish settlers.

In the Valley of Oaxaca and the Mixteca, however, many *caciques* maintained their position much longer, in some cases until the end of the eighteenth century.[19] As we have seen, Spanish law acted to preserve *cacicazgo* estates (which in these regions, unlike the Cañada, were privately owned) by making them inalienable and standardizing the rules of succession. There was also surprisingly little racial mixing in *cacique* lineages. The few mixed marriages that did occur mostly involved nobles who had moved to Antequera and taken up artisan occupations (Chance 1978b: 136–137, 170; Taylor 1972:39).

The political power of Valley nobles declined in the Late Colonial period as population growth led to more disputes over land ownership, and the growing physical and psychological distance between *caciques* and *macehuales* began to take its toll. The *caciques'* hold on the office of *gobernador* had weakened—only one held the office after 1725—and Taylor (1972:52) maintains that "The caciques contributed to their own political demise by stubbornly maintaining the attitude that any position other than gobernador was beneath their dignity." This political demise did not substantially affect *cacicazgo* wealth, however. Sizable estates persisted, most notably those of Cuilapan and Etla, the largest private holdings of any kind—Indian or Spanish—in the Valley. Even the less well off *caciques* managed to retain a degree of prestige and authority, and sumptuary laws distinguishing nobles from commoners persisted in some Valley communities at the end of the eighteenth century (Taylor 1972:48, 65).

The fate of hereditary *caciques* in the Mixteca followed similar lines, but their ultimate demise as a group came sooner. While a number of the smaller *cacicazgos* had disappeared in the sixteenth century, at least fifty-seven persisted in the seventeenth, and forty-five existed at the beginning of the eighteenth century (Pastor 1981:Ch. 2:37–38). The ancient pattern of linking discrete kingdoms through marriage continued, reaching its peak in 1764, when Don Martín Villagómez and his wife claimed thirty-one titles, "including Acatlan and Petlacingo in southern Puebla, Tonalá and Silacayoapan in the Baja of Oaxaca, Yanhuitlan, Tilantongo, and Teposcolula in the Alta, and Tututepec in the Costa" (Spores 1974:302). But such stunning aggrandizement of a few individuals masked real problems encountered by others, triggered in large part by population growth. Pastor (1981:Ch. 2:41–48) has shown that

the economic conflict of interest between Mixtec *caciques* and their communities finally came to a head in the late seventeenth century, as evidenced by increasing conflict over land. Many *caciques* lost out in their efforts to gain control of community lands and as a result suffered a serious political and economic decline. Pastor goes so far as to speak of a *cacique* crisis between 1710 and 1740, observing that traditional *caciques* practically disappeared altogether in the Late Colonial period. Of the forty-five *cacicazgos* that existed in 1700, only nineteen persisted during the second half of the eighteenth century and a mere eight survived into the nineteenth (ibid.: Ch. 2:41, 88). While some *caciques* continued to enjoy high economic status in the eighteenth century (Romero Frizzi 1975:2), their hold on political power seems to have evaporated.

A distinct trend in the seventeenth and eighteenth centuries was, paradoxically, the multiplication of *caciques* at a time when the number of *cacicazgos* was declining. Dispossessed *caciques* continued to assert their privileges, and it was common for all the sons of a *cacique* to use the title, whether they inherited the *cacicazgo* or not. This led to the proliferation of *cacique* lineages, as in the communities of Teposcolula and Tlaxiaco, for example, each of which had three in the seventeenth century (Pastor 1981:Ch. 2:45). A similar pattern obtained in the Late Colonial Zapotec Rincon, where in some villages the possession of any of five to six surnames conferred *cacique* status (Chance 1983).

The colonial regime also brought about changes in the definition and prerogatives of other indigenous social strata. The institution of Indian slavery had effectively disappeared by the mid-sixteenth century but in parts of the Valley of Oaxaca the stratum of *terrazgueros* persisted well into the eighteenth century. These were tenant farmers on *cacicazgo* lands, most probably descendants of the Prehispanic *mayeques*. The *cacicazgos* of Cuilapan, Oaxaca, and Etla were served by entire *barrios* of *terrazgueros* as late as the mid-eighteenth century, though a spirit of disobedience and rejection of the *caciques'* authority was a frequent problem (Taylor 1972:41–42, 54).

More widespread, and of considerably more import, were the growing tensions between *principales* and *macehuales*. This was, of course, a common phenomenon, but the trend in Oaxaca appears to have differed in some respects from that in central Mexico. With the exception of some land-rich families in the Cuilapan and Etla regions of the Valley, *principales* in colonial Oaxaca did not possess any significant forms of wealth to buttress their claim to noble status. For this they were more dependent on unwritten community sumptuary laws, access to local *cabildo* offices, and exemptions from menial chores occasionally granted by Spanish officials (for examples of the latter see Chance 1983). The main arena for the validation of *principal* status and also for social mobility among the *macehuales* was the *cabildo*, a locus of much conflict and social climbing. Indian commoners gained increasing access to the most coveted *cabildo* posts—*gobernador, alcalde,* and *regidor*—as time wore on. Their aspirations to political power began as early as the second half of the sixteenth century and frequently led to violent conflict with *caciques* and *principales* (Taylor 1972:53). That *macehuales* gained a voice in many town governments is beyond dispute, yet there are no known cases where they managed to unseat the nobles altogether.

Viceregal policy regarding *macehual* participation in government, at least as it was reflected in the Valley of Oaxaca, was more reactive than active. Support for enfranchisement of commoners dates from the early seventeenth century and continued into the early eighteenth century, yet decrees were issued in 1742 and 1768 favoring restriction of voting rights to *principales*. Taylor (1972:50) argues effectively that the extension of voting rights to *macehuales* in several Valley towns reflected compromise solutions to troublesome conflicts rather than any consistent policy of "democratization" of Indian *cabildos*. In any case, it is clear that *principales* domi-

nated the governments of many Valley and Mixteca towns—as electors and as elected officials—at least until the 1770's, often with the help of the *audiencia* (Pastor 1981:Ch. 2:88).

The Rincon Zapotec area provides an interesting example of the complex nature of village politics and prestige in the late eighteenth and early nineteenth centuries (Chance 1983). In this mountainous region, where *cacique, principal,* and *macehual* groups were all equally poor in material resources, serving in the higher municipal offices was virtually the only means of acquiring and maintaining prestige in the eyes of one's fellow villagers. Most Rincon villages allowed *principales* by birth to begin their political careers at the level of *regidor*, whereas *macehual* men had to start on the bottom rung of the ladder in menial positions such as *topil*. However, by climbing up the ladder, many commoners succeeded in being elected to the higher offices, including *gobernador*. Indeed, many villages had no choice, since their small size virtually required all household heads to serve as *regidor* and *alcalde* at some point, frequently more than once.

The main source of conflict in the eighteenth century lay in the fact that there were two ways for Rincon men to become *principales*—by birth, or by holding high office (*regidor* or above). Once a *macehual* had worked his way up into *principal* status, then his sons could justifiably claim exemption from the lower offices (*servicios bajos*) on the grounds of noble birth. Inevitably, this led to a top-heavy prestige hierarchy, and by the late eighteenth century many Rincon communities contained more *principales* than *macehuales*. This left them short of eligible young men to fill the lower posts of *gobaz* (general servant), *topil* (policeman and messenger), and *mayor* (police chief). Desperate for a solution, many *cabildos* tried to alter village custom and force the sons of *principales* into these positions. But the wronged individuals frequently countered with lawsuits designed to maintain their *principal* status and their exemption from *servicios bajos*.

183

These cases were tried by the Spanish *alcaldes mayores* in Villa Alta and almost always ended in favor of the plaintiffs, thereby upholding the hereditary basis of *principal* status. This contradicts the frequently held belief that Spanish colonialism steadily eroded inherited status in Indian communities in favor of status achievement via service in *cabildo* offices. In the Rincon, both ascribed *and* achieved status persisted side by side well into the nineteenth century, spawning interminable conflicts among villagers and swelling the ranks of the *principales* at the expense of the *macehuales*. It appears that support of the principle of inherited noble status by the *alcaldes mayores* was a critical factor in the perpetuation of the system.

In sum, the Oaxaca material on noble status and village politics in the Colonial period shows a selective survival of Prehispanic *cacique* lineages and the maintenance of a large and politically powerful *principal* stratum, despite the fact of penetration by some upwardly mobile *macehuales*. An important factor behind *cacique* survival was political and economic strength at the time of Spanish contact. *Cacique* lineages persisted longest in the Valley of Oaxaca and disappeared soonest in the Rincon. In the Mixteca, a number survived into the eighteenth century, but in the Cuicatec Cañada noble families met their demise roughly a century earlier. In all regions, families bearing the *cacique* title persisted at the end of the Colonial period, but few of them were direct descendants of Preconquest rulers (except in the Valley), and their wealth and political power had been greatly reduced.

The Oaxaca data also indicate the important roles of the colonial economy and the Spanish political system in maintaining the Indian nobility, both the *cacique* and the *principal* segments. Surviving *cacique* families owed their success in no small measure to a favorable legal climate, retention of extensive privately owned landholdings, and their quick integration into the developing capitalist economy in the sixteenth century. Those

that did not or could not make these adaptations soon faded into oblivion, as in the Rincon. The *principal* stratum, in contrast, became heavily dependent on political office-holding for its very existence. In many communities this group underwent significant changes over the years as a rising tide of upwardly mobile *macehuales* sought to enter its ranks. But thanks to the support of the viceroy, *audiencia*, and lower-level Spanish officials, the rank of *principal* itself was never called into question and continued as an important element in the social structure until it was legally abolished after the independence in the nineteenth century.

THE URBAN INDIANS OF ANTEQUERA

No portrait of colonial Oaxaca would be complete without some mention of the large Indian population of the Spanish city of Antequera (Chance 1976). Founded in 1521 on the ruins of Aztec Huaxyacac, Antequera contained only about 2,000 Spanish inhabitants in 1600 and fewer than 5,000 in 1700. It underwent a much faster period of growth in the second half of the eighteenth century, however, as the Bourbon reforms took hold. Commerce and manufacturing increased greatly, the cochineal boom went into full swing, and the urban population reached 18,000 by 1792, including 12,990 non-Indians (Spanish, creoles, mestizos, etc.). As in other highland cities of New Spain, Indians were an indispensable part of Antequera's economic and social fabric. Not only did they build the city, but they also staffed many of the menial but necessary urban occupations.

The history of the Indians in Antequera in broad terms consists of a slow process of ethnic homogenization and proletarianization that lasted 220 years. In the sixteenth century the urban Indian population—numbering about 1,400 in 1565—was remarkably diverse. In addition to many Zapotec and Mixtec migrants from its own hinterland, Antequera contained large numbers of Nahuas from central Mexico who had accompanied the Spanish at the time of the conquest of the Valley. Settled in separate *barrios* in the adjoining Indian settlement of Jalatlaco and other nearby towns, each group of Nahuas maintained a separate identity based on place of origin.[20] They also dominated the urban Indian sector because of their original status as allies of the conquerors and their superior skill as artisans. Nahuatl quickly became the *lingua franca* among the city's Indians, and most Zapotec and Mixtec migrants were obliged to learn it in order to adapt to the urban setting. These migrants were largely confined to the lower-status jobs of manual laborers, petty traders, and household servants, while the skilled Nahuas worked as weavers, tailors, shoemakers, butchers, and bakers. I have argued (Chance 1976) that a distinct urban Indian culture, heavily Nahua in orientation, had emerged by 1580.

By the early seventeenth century, Jalatlaco boasted several new Zapotec and Mixtec *barrios*, though ethnicity based on place of origin had begun to fade. The transformation of an ethnically diverse population into a minimally differentiated urban Indian proletariat was now underway. The period 1630–1750 witnessed continuing in-migration from many towns in the Valley of Oaxaca and the surrounding region. Along with it came a further erosion of ethnic distinctions and a blurring of the division between *principales* and *macehuales*. Antequera's service needs created a demand for Indian skills and labor, though with the exception of a small number of *caciques* and *principales*, Indians still ranked uniformly at the bottom of the city's social hierarchy. The population of Jalatlaco reached a peak of 3,277 in 1729. Nahuatl continued as the primary language there, though most residents were also fluent in Spanish by that time. The ethnic distinction between Nahuas and non-Nahuas was still important, but the various sub-Nahua identities based on ancestral origins were no longer of any consequence. Occupations in Jalatlaco and among Indian residents in the city proper remained much the same as they had been in

the sixteenth century, with the difference that many Indians had now become masons involved in the construction of public and private buildings, replacing in part the earlier system of *repartimiento* labor. Indians also formed an integral part of Antequera's craft guilds, most of them employed as *oficiales* (journeymen) in the shops of non-Indian *maestros*.

Despite the fading of ethnic distinctions within the urban Indian population and the attrition of the earlier Nahua hegemony, Indians as a whole continued to form a tightly knit ethnic group in the city. Of all the socioracial categories in late-seventeenth-century Antequera, the Indians exhibited the highest degree of closure (about 75 percent) in terms of their marriages. The urban *caciques* were a notable exception, however, for by this time they were an extremely heterogeneous group. They had arrived in Antequera from widely scattered areas of Oaxaca, and only a handful of them (those from the Valley, most prominently) occupied positions of power and prestige. Several married Indian commoners, mestizos, or white creoles, and took up artisan trades.

The long process of proletarianization reached its culmination in the second half of the eighteenth century. During this period the rapid development of Antequera was accompanied by growth in its Indian population, which accounted for 5,000, or 28 percent of the total, in 1792. Indian migration to the city vastly increased as the rural population recovered in numbers and the need for labor became more acute in Antequera's textile sweatshops, the construction industry, and a variety of trades and crafts. Significant changes in social differentiation and identification occurred within the Indian sector. By 1777, Nahuatl had virtually ceased to be spoken and the Nahua ethnic identity had largely disappeared. Nor did the status of *principal* hold much meaning now in the urban context. The once populous town of Jalatlaco, which for two centuries had been an important urban labor pool, dwindled to a mere three hundred persons by 1777, as many residents moved to Antequera to work as masons, bakers, artisans, and spinners and weavers in the textile workshops.

Urban Indian occupations and marriage patterns remained largely the same as they had been a century before. Now even greater numbers were concentrated in the more menial, less skilled jobs, the only significant change being a large increase in weavers and cultivators of cochineal. Places of origin of Indian migrants were much the same as before, with over a third coming from Valley towns and large numbers from the Sierra Zapotec region. But now, a much higher percentage of the Indians in Antequera were city-born. With respect to marriage, 64 percent of Indian commoner grooms were still taking Indian wives at the end of the eighteenth century. There was a growing frequency of Indian intermarriage with white creole women, but this was due more to the downward mobility of the creoles than the upward mobility of the Indians. Overall, there was little change in the ethnic boundary between Spaniards and urban Indians, whose position in the city remained essentially unchanged.

The final stage of proletarianization in the late eighteenth century was evidenced by the virtual disappearance of the Nahuatl language, identity, and political hegemony within the urban Indian population; the breakdown of the boundary between nobles and commoners; and the greatly reduced size of the urban *cacique* group. A once highly differentiated population had been transformed into a homogeneous mass of urban workers who identified more with the city than with their rural Zapotec and Mixtec neighbors. Yet this long, slow process did not appreciably alter the boundaries of the urban Indian ethnic category itself, which was effectively maintained by the exclusionist policies of Spanish colonialism. Indians in Antequera found that the only way to escape their inferior status was to cease being Indian. A few managed to do just that, but most did not, and remained in the same servile position until after independence in the nineteenth century, when a number of legal and social barriers were withdrawn.

CONCLUSION

Despite the many changes brought about in Oaxaca by the Spanish conquest and colonization, a major theme of this chapter has been persistence—the continued vitality of a number of social, economic, and political structures long after they had become moribund in other parts of colonial Mexico. In his comparative study of drinking and violent crime in Late Colonial Oaxaca and central Mexico, Taylor (1979:83) noted that the latter region was more deeply affected by Spanish beliefs and behavior patterns; in other words, it was more acculturated.[21] Central Mexican communities tended to be larger, more socially complex, more affected by urban influence (from Mexico City), and more proletarian. They exhibited more uncertainty in village social relations, and the types of conflict they experienced were more unpredictable. Taylor (1979:111) regards them as dependent, lower-class communities, "more affected by outside cultural influences and colonial power, which tended to weaken bonds of community solidarity." On the other hand, in Oaxaca, and especially in the Mixteca Alta, the intracommunity homicide rate was lower, community rituals were stronger, and values and behavior in village life coincided more often.

The political tensions evident in the homicide records of both regions appear to spring from rather different sources: in the Mixteca Alta, macehuales seem to have been fairly sensitive to the legitimacy and responsibilities of village officials; in central Mexico, coercion seems closer to the roots of political authority.

(Taylor 1979:160)

We can add to the list of distinctive traits in colonial Oaxaca the survival of a high degree of community corporateness and control over land; the continuity, in some areas, of native *cacique* lineages and their estates; and the persistence of the *principales* as a significant status and power group at the village level. Even in Antequera, the inexorable process of proletarianization did not significantly affect the outer boundaries of the urban Indian ethnic category, which remained rigid and remarkably intact until the end of the Colonial period.

Such conclusions should come as no surprise, for they confirm what we know about Oaxaca today: it is a poor, underdeveloped region of Mexico deservedly famous for the persistence of its various Indian cultures and languages. What we have learned, however, is that the roots of Oaxaca's distinctiveness stem not only from its recent history and from its Prehispanic past, but also from the peculiar nature of its colonial heritage. Furthermore, we can now begin to understand some of the factors behind the striking regional diversity within Oaxaca itself, though this chapter has admittedly only scratched the surface.

In seeking to account for the maintenance of indigenous patterns in colonial Oaxaca, I agree with Taylor (1979:164) that the "refuge region" hypothesis is inappropriate. Indian culture in Oaxaca did not survive because the region was isolated and economically marginal. It survived because the traditional economy of Oaxacan communities was indispensable to the functioning of the entire colonial society. We can go beyond the recognition of the colony's well-known need for Indian surplus in the form of taxes and services, and the government policies that encouraged strong community identity. In my opinion, it was the special nature of the colonial economy in Oaxaca which lies at the root of much of the cultural continuity discussed in this chapter. Much of the Spanish economic exploitation in Oaxaca can be characterized as a form of "indirect rule." Indians were not forcibly uprooted from their communities and shipped off to mines or haciendas, as they frequently were in other areas. Nor were many tempted to make the trek on their own accord. Instead, they were encouraged to stay put and carry on with the local

traditions *as long as* they also produced silk, cotton textiles, cochineal, and agricultural surpluses for the market and for particular political officials via the *repartimiento de efectos*. The Indians of Oaxaca thus became partially integrated into the expanding world capitalist system in a way which actually reinforced many aspects of their traditional society, polity, and local economy.

This point is illustrated by the Early Colonial experiences in the Valley of Oaxaca and the Mixteca Alta on the one hand, and the Zapotec Rincon on the other. In the former, many *caciques* began to participate in the colonial economy early in the sixteenth century and soon developed an independent economic base that allowed them to perpetuate themselves. In the Rincon, however, the native nobility had neither the means nor the desire for such involvement and soon fell by the wayside. I strongly suspect that marginal regions like the Rincon experienced more far-reaching social change in the sixteenth century than did more developed areas like the Valley and the Mixteca.

Obviously, however, there were limits to this process of economic integration. Mixtec and Valley Zapotec communities noted for their cultural continuity in the Colonial period (such as Yanhuitlan, Teposcolula, and Tlaxiaco in the Mixteca and Cuilapan and Etla in the Valley) were not nearly as integrated into the cash economy as many larger, more proletarian communities in the Valley of Mexico. Oaxacan villages occupied more of an intermediate point on the economic continuum running from a hypothetical complete exclusion from the market (total self-sufficiency) to complete incorporation. Herein may lie the key to many facets of cultural continuity and change in this complex and fascinating region.

ACKNOWLEDGMENTS

I want to thank the following people for kindly providing me with information and copies of published and unpublished manuscripts: Alicia Barabas, Miguel Bartolomé,

187

Lolita Gutiérrez Brockington, Marcello Carmagnani, Pedro Carrasco, Bernardo García Martínez, James Greenberg, Rodolfo Pastor, Ma. de los Angeles Romero, Mary Elizabeth Smith, Ronald Spores, William Taylor, Cecil Welte, and Joseph Whitecotton. My only regret is that I was not able to use all the materials I received. I also thank Ronald Spores for his helpful comments on the initial draft of this chapter.

NOTES

1. The important topics of kinship and family structure have been little studied for colonial Oaxaca, though patterns of marriage and descent among the Mixtec nobility constitute an important exception (see Spores 1967; 1974). Much also remains to be done in the area of religion, especially the work of the Dominican missionaries and the interface between Spanish catholicism and the indigenous religions. Several brief studies of Zapotec religion in the seventeenth century show that much of it persisted remarkably intact (Alcina Franch 1966; 1972; 1979; Berlin 1957; Zilbermann 1966).

2. Nigel Davies (1968:181–213), Mary Elizabeth Smith (1973), and Barbro Dahlgren de Jordán (1966) survey what is known about the Mixtec coastal kingdom of Tututepec. Although this was probably the most powerful political center in all of Oaxaca in 1519, we still know relatively little about it. Even less is known about this region during Colonial times, so I have chosen to exclude it from coverage here.

3. The Cañada lies in the far western portion of the Sierra region and the central part of the Norte region in Figure 11-1.

4. The Rincon is located in the central part of the Sierra region in Figure 11-1.

5. This chapter was written before the appearance of *The Cloud People*, edited by Kent V. Flannery and Joyce Marcus (1983). See "An Introduction to the Late Postclassic" (Marcus and Flannery 1983) for an alternative view which ranks the Mixtecs first.

6. Spores (1976), on the other hand, calls it a three-tiered class system of rulers, nobles, and commoners. He regards the position of the Mixtec *mayeques* as problematic and would exclude them from the system.

7. While it is not possible to deal with kinship systematically in this article, it has generally been regarded as subordinate to community in Oaxaca (though the communal tie may have been less pronounced among the Mixes and Chinantecs). There is no convincing evidence of kin group organization above the level of the extended family. While there was a strong expression of the lineage principle among the nobility, it was lacking among the commoners (Spores 1965:986).

8. For more detailed discussions of Spanish political divisions in sixteenth-century Oaxaca, see Gerhard (1972b) and Olivera and Romero (1973). The latter provide a detailed table of the affiliations of all the indigenous communities of the region.

9. Indian slavery in the technical sense was of little importance in the Valley of Oaxaca, at least, after 1531, and it was outlawed by the Crown in 1543 (Chance 1978b: 50–53). Thereafter, slavery was restricted to blacks and mulattoes, and Indian labor was exploited through the *encomienda* and *repartimiento*.

10. See Bernardo García Martínez (1969) for more information on the Marquesado del Valle. The operation of the Marquesado's livestock haciendas in the Isthmus of Tehuantepec has been clarified by Lolita Gutiérrez Brockington (1982).

11. The work of Rodolfo Pastor (1981:Ch. 5) helps to close this gap. He has unearthed new data on *cofradías* in the eighteenth-century Mixteca Alta which have an important bearing on both the economy and the social structure of the region. See also Chance and Taylor (1985).

12. Gerhard (1972b) also gives summary information on population and settlement patterns in each of Oaxaca's twenty-two colonial districts (*alcaldías mayores*).

13. A significant shortcoming of the *diezmo* figures is that they provide an index only for the production of European crops.

They have little to say about important indigenous crops such as corn, maguey, and cochineal. Pastor et al. (1979) recognize this limitation, but insist that it does not invalidate their conclusions.

14. This generalization does not hold for the Sierra Zapotecs of the *alcaldía mayor* of Villa Alta, where incorporation into the colonial system did not occur until the 1550's (Chance 1983).

15. Romero Frizzi (1979) provides new data on Spanish sheep raising and trade in the Mixteca during the seventeenth century.

16. Carmagnani (1980) hypothesizes a persistence and expansion of indigenous ethnic ties at the supra-community level during the eighteenth century. I find his argument less than convincing, however, for there are few data to support it.

17. Dahlgren de Jordán (1963:29) makes the point that the *alcaldes mayores* absorbed only half the cochineal produced, and that merchants bought up the rest, paying the Indians higher prices. On the basis of Hamnett's (1971a; 1971b) and my own research, however, I am inclined to think that political officials controlled significantly more of the trade, at least in Oaxaca. The involvement of many merchants was indirect, mediated through contracts negotiated with the *al-caldes mayores*. As for the Indians, a significant part of their trading in cochineal was probably carried on among themselves, as they struggled to meet the quotas of their respective *alcaldes mayores*.

18. For more detail on the *repartimiento de efectos*, see Hamnett (1971b). Chance (1983) discusses its operation in Zapotec villages of the *alcaldía mayor* of Villa Alta in the eighteenth century.

19. This generalization does not apply to the Tlacolula arm of the Valley of Oaxaca, where some *caciques* were "virtually indistinguishable from ordinary peasants by the end of the colonial period" (Taylor 1972:64).

20. The places of origin and ethnic identities represented in early Jalatlaco were Tenochtitlan (Mexicanos), Tlatelolco, Colhuacan, Tlaxcala, Huejotzingo, Cholula, and Tepeaca. Other *barrios* ringing the city in the sixteenth century carried the names of Xochimilco, Chiautla, Tula, Tecutlachicpan, Mexicapan, Cuernavaca, Tepoztlan, Acapixtla, Istapalapa, and Tlacopan (Chance 1976:610, 613).

21. Specifically, Taylor deals with forty-five towns in rural districts that were connected with the urban capital of Mexico City. All were located in the Intendancy of Mexico.

REFERENCE ABBREVIATIONS

AA   Archivo Antiguo de Ayuntamiento, Mexico City

  -Co   Compendio

  -O   Ordenanzas

AC   *Actas de Cabildo de la Ciudad de México* (Bejarano 1887–1919)

AGN   Archivo General de la Nación, Mexico City

  -GP   General de Parte

  -HJ   Hospital de Jesús

  -I   Indios

  -M   Mercedes

  -M   Mercedes

  -O   Ordenanzas

  -RCD   Reales Cédulas Duplicadas

  -T   Tierras

  -VM   Vínculus y Mayorozgos

AHN   Archivo Histórico de Notarías, Mexico City

BNP   Bibliothèque Nationale de Paris

DCLI   *Disposiciones complementarias de las leyes de Indias*

DIE   *Colección de documentos inéditos para la historia de España* (Fernández de Navarrete et al. 1842–1895)

DII   *Colección de documentos . . . América y Oceanía*

DIU   *Colección de documentos . . . Ultramar*

ENE   *Epistolario de Nueva España* (Paso y Troncoso 1939–1942)

FHT   *Fuentes para la historia del trabajo en Nueva España* (Zavala and Castelo 1939–1946)

IE   *Indice y extractos de los protocolos de la Notaría de Cholula* (C. Reyes García 1973)

IEPAN   *Indice y extractos de los protocolos del Archivo de Notarías de México, D.F.* (Millares Carlo and Mantecón 1945)

PNE   *Papeles de Nueva España* (Paso y Troncoso 1905–1936)

VEA   *Los virreyes españoles en América durante el gobierno de la Casa de Austria* (Hanke and Rodríguez 1976–1978)

BIBLIOGRAPHY

ADAMS, RICHARD E. W.
1978   Routes of Communication in Meso-
       america: The Northern Guatemalan
       Highlands and the Peten. In *Meso-
       american Communication Routes and
       Cultural Contacts*, edited by Thomas A.
       Lee, Jr., and Carlos Navarrete. Papers of
       the New World Archaeological Founda-
       tion, no. 40:27–35. Provo, Utah.

ADAMS, ROBERT McC.
1966   *The Evolution of Urban Society: Early
       Mesopotamia and Prehispanic Mexico.*
       Chicago: Aldine.

AGUIRRE, CARLOS
1982   La constitución de lo urbano: Ciudad y
       campo en la Nueva España. *Historias*
       1:30–40.

AITON, ARTHUR SCOTT
1967   *Antonio de Mendoza, First Viceroy of
       New Spain.* New York: Russell & Russell.
       (Reprint of 1927 ed., Durham: Duke
       University Press.)

ALCINA FRANCH, JOSÉ
1966   Calendarios zapatecos prehispánicos
       según documentos de los siglos XVI y
       XVII. *Estudios de Cultura Nahuatl*
       6:119–133.
1972   Los dioses del panteón zapateco. *Anales
       de Antropología* 9:9–43. Mexico City.

1979   Calendario y religión entre los zapotecos
       serranos durante el siglo XVII. In *Meso-
       américa: Homenaje al Doctor Paul
       Kirchhoff*, coordinated by Barbro Dahl-
       gren, pp. 212–224. Mexico City: Insti-
       tuto Nacional de Antropología e
       Historia.

ALTMAN, IDA, AND JAMES LOCKHART
1976   (eds.) *Provinces of Early Mexico: Vari-
       ants of Spanish American Regional Evo-
       lution.* UCLA Latin American Center
       Publications, vol. 36. Los Angeles.

ALVA IXTLILXOCHITL, FERNANDO DE
1975–1977   *Obras históricas.* 2 vols. 3d ed.
       Edited by Edmundo O'Gorman. Serie
       de Historiadores y Cronistas de Indias,
       no. 4. Mexico City: Universidad Na-
       cional Autónoma de México.

ALVARADO TEZOZOMOC, HERNANDO
1949   *Crónica mexicayotl.* Translated by
       Adrian León. Instituto de Historia, 1st
       ser., no. 10. Mexico City: Universidad
       Nacional Autónoma de México and In-
       stituto Nacional de Antropología e Histo-
       ria. (Reprinted, 1975.)
1975   *Crónica mexicana.* Mexico City: Edi-
       torial Porrua.

ANALES
Cuauhtitlan
1938 *Die Geschichte der Königreiche von Colhuacan und Mexico.* Translated by Walter Lehmann. Quellenwerke zur alten Geschichte Amerikas, no. 1. Stuttgart and Berlin: W. Kohlhammer. (Reprinted, 1974.)
Tlatelolco
1948 *Anales de Tlatelolco: Unos annales históricos de la nación mexicana y Códice de Tlatelolco.* Edited by Heinrich Berlin. Fuentes para la Historia de México, no. 2. Mexico City: Porrua.

ANDERSON, ARTHUR J. O., FRANCES BERDAN, AND JAMES LOCKHART
1976 (trans. and eds.) *Beyond the Codices: The Nahua View of Colonial Mexico.* Berkeley and Los Angeles: University of California Press.

ANDREWS, ANTHONY P.
1981 Historical Archaeology in Yucatan: A Preliminary Framework. *Historical Archaeology* 15:1–18.
1983 *Ancient Maya Salt Production and Trade.* Tucson: University of Arizona Press.

ANDREWS, J. RICHARD
1975 *Introduction to Classical Nahuatl.* Austin: University of Texas Press.

ANGUIANO, MARINA, AND MATILDE CHAPA
1976 Estratificación social en Tlaxcala durante el siglo XVI. In *Estratificación social en la Mesoamérica prehispánica,* by Pedro Carrasco, Johanna Broda, et al., pp. 118–156. Mexico City: Instituto Nacional de Antropología e Historia.

APPLEBY, GORDON
1976 Export Monoculture and Regional Social Structure in Puno, Peru. In *Regional Analysis,* edited by Carol A. Smith, 2:291–307. New York: Academic Press.

ARA, DOMINGO DE
1571 Bocabulario en lengua tzeldal. MS in Bancroft Library, University of California at Berkeley; copies in Ayer Collection, Newberry Library, and Tulane University Latin American Library.

ARCHIVO GENERAL DE LA NACIÓN, MÉXICO
1979 *Catálogo de ilustraciones.* 9 vols. Mexico City.

ARÓSTEGUI, CARLOS B.
1977 Marriage, Alliance, and Succession in Pre-Columbian Mixtec Society. Paper presented at the 42nd annual meeting of the Society for American Archaeology, New Orleans. MS, Dumbarton Oaks, Pre-Columbian Section, Washington, D.C.

AULIE, H. WILBUR, AND EVELYN W. DE AULIE
1978 *Diccionario ch'ol-español, español-ch'ol.* Serie de Vocabularios y Diccionarios Indígenas Mariano Silva y Aceves, no. 21. Mexico City: Instituto Lingüístico de Verano.

BAKEWELL, PETER J.
1971 *Silver Mining and Society in Colonial Mexico: Zacatecas, 1546–1700.* Cambridge Latin American Studies, no. 15. Cambridge: University Press.

BANCROFT, HUBERT HOWE
1883–1888 *History of Mexico.* Vols. 9–14 of *The Works of Hubert Howe Bancroft.* San Francisco: A. L. Bancroft (vols. 9–11) and The History Company (vols. 12–14). (Reprinted, 1967, by Arno Press.)
1886–1887 *History of Central America.* Vols. 6–8 of *The Works of Hubert Howe Bancroft.* San Francisco: The History Company. (Reprinted, 1967, by Arno Press.)

BANDELIER, ADOLPH F.
1877 On the Art of War and Mode of Warfare of the Ancient Mexicans. In *The Tenth Annual Report of the Trustees of the Peabody Museum of American Archaeology and Ethnology* 2(1):95–161. Cambridge, Mass.
1878 On the Distribution and Tenure of Lands, and the Customs with Respect to Inheritance, among the Ancient Mexicans. In *The Eleventh Annual Report of the Peabody Museum of Archaeology and Ethnology,* pp. 385–448. Cambridge, Mass.
1879 On the Social Organization and Mode of Government of the Ancient Mexicans. In *The Twelfth Annual Report of the Peabody Museum of Archaeology and Ethnology, Cambridge,* pp. 557–699. Salem, Mass.: Salem Press. (Reprinted, 1880, in Cambridge, Mass.; also, 1975, New York: Cooper Square.)

BANKMANN, ULF

1974 Das Ortsbuch von San Martin Ocoyacac, México. *Indiana* 2.133–165.

BARLOW, R. H.

1943 The Techialoyan Codices: Codex H. *Tlalocan* 1:161–162.

1945 Los caciques precortesianos de Tlatelolco en el *Códice García Granados* (Techialoyan Q). *Memorias de la Academia Mexicana de la Historia* 4:467–482.

1946 El reverso del Códice García Granados. *Memorias de la Academia Mexicana de la Historia* 5:422–438.

1949 Relación de Zempoala y su partido, 1580. *Tlalocan* 3:29–41.

BATRES JAUREGUI, ANTONIO

1920 *La América Central ante la Historia*, vol. 2, *La época colonial: El reino de Guatemala*. Guatemala City: Sánchez & De Guise.

BAUDOT, GEORGES

1976 *Utopie et histoire au Mexique: Les Premiers Chroniqueurs de la civilisation mexicaine (1520–1569)*. Toulouse: Edouard Privat.

BAUTISTA, JUAN

1600 *Advertencias para los confessores de los naturales*. Mexico City: M. Ocharte.

BAUTISTA PÉREZ, FRANCISCO

1980 *Chetumal*. Chetumal: Fondo de Fomento Editorial del Gobierno del Estado de Quintana Roo.

BEALS, RALPH L.

1967 Acculturation. In *Handbook of Middle American Indians*, vol. 6, edited by Robert Wauchope and Manning Nash, pp. 449–468. Austin: University of Texas Press.

BEETZ, CARL P., AND LINTON SATTERTHWAITE

1981 *The Monuments and Inscriptions of Caracol, Belize*. University Museum Monographs, vol. 45. Philadelphia: University Museum, University of Pennsylvania.

BEJARANO, IGNACIO

1887–1919 (compiler) *Actas de Cabildo de la Ciudad de México*. 54 vols. Mexico City.

BELLINGERI, MARCO

1980 *Las haciendas en México: El caso de Sn. Antonio Tochatlaco*. Colección Científica, Historia Económica, no. 89. Mexico City: Instituto Nacional de Antropología e Historia.

BELTRÁN DE SANTA ROSA, PEDRO

1746 *Arte de el idioma maya reducido a succintas reglas y semilexicon yucateco*. Mexico City: Vda. de J. Bernardo de Hogal.

BERDAN, FRANCES F.

1976 La organización del tributo en el imperio azteca. *Estudios de Cultura Nahuatl* 12:185–195.

1977 Distributive Mechanisms in the Aztec Economy. In *Peasant Livelihood: Studies in Economic Anthropology and Cultural Ecology*, edited by Rhoda Halperin and James Dow, pp. 91–101. New York: St. Martin's Press.

1978a Ports of Trade in Mesoamerica: A Reappraisal. In *Cultural Continuity in Mesoamerica*, edited by David L. Browman, pp. 179–198. The Hague: Mouton.

1978b Tres formas de intercambio en la economía azteca. In *Economía política e ideología en el México prehispánico*, edited by Pedro Carrasco and Johanna Broda, pp. 77–95. Mexico City: Nueva Imagen.

BERLIN, HEINRICH

1957 *Las antiguas creencias en San Miguel Sola, Oaxaca, México*. Hamburg: Museum für Völkerkunde und Vorgeschichte.

1963 The Palenque Triad. *Journal de la Société des Américanistes* 52:91–99.

1968 Estudios epigráficos II. *Antropología e Historia de Guatemala* 20(1):13–24.

1973 Beiträge zum Verständnis der Inschriften von Naranjo. *Bulletin de la Société Suisse des Américanistes* 37:7–14.

1977 *Signos y significados en las inscripciones mayas*. Guatemala City: Instituto Nacional del Patrimonio Cultural de Guatemala.

1980 En torno a un libro. *Anales de la Academia de Geografía e Historia de Guatemala* 53:228–235.

BERNAL, IGNACIO

1962 *Bibliografía de arqueología y etnografía de Mesoamérica y el norte de México*. Memorias del Instituto Nacional de Antropología e Historia, no. 7. Mexico City.

BLANTON, RICHARD E.

1976 The Role of Symbiosis in Adaptation and Sociocultural Change in the Valley of Mexico. In *The Valley of Mexico: Studies in Pre-Hispanic Ecology and Society,* edited by Eric R. Wolf, pp. 181–201. Albuquerque: University of New Mexico Press.

BORAH, WOODROW

1943 *Silk Raising in Colonial Mexico.* Ibero-Americana, no. 20. Berkeley and Los Angeles: University of California Press.

1948 The Cathedral Archive of Oaxaca. *Hispanic American Historical Review* 28: 640–645.

1951 Notes on Civil Archives in the City of Oaxaca. *Hispanic American Historical Review* 31:723–749.

1954 *Early Colonial Trade and Navigation between Mexico and Peru.* Ibero-Americana, no. 38. Berkeley and Los Angeles: University of California Press.

BORAH, WOODROW, AND SHERBURNE F. COOK

1958 *Price Trends of Some Basic Commodities in Central Mexico, 1531–1570.* Ibero-Americana, no. 40. Berkeley and Los Angeles: University of California Press.

1960 *The Population of Central Mexico in 1548: An Analysis of the "Suma de Visitas de Pueblos."* Ibero-Americana, no. 43. Berkeley and Los Angeles: University of California Press.

1963 *The Aboriginal Population of Central Mexico on the Eve of the Spanish Conquest.* Ibero-Americana, no. 45. Berkeley and Los Angeles: University of California Press.

1979 A Case History of the Transition from Precolonial to the Colonial Period in Mexico: Santiago Tejupan. In *Social Fabric and Spatial Structure in Colonial Latin America,* edited by David J. Robinson, pp. 409–432. Syracuse, N.Y.: Syracuse University Department of Geography.

BOYER, RICHARD

1977 Mexico in the Seventeenth Century: Transition of a Colonial Society. *Hispanic American Historical Review* 57:455–478.

1980 La Ciudad de México en 1628: La visión de Juan Gómez de Trasmonte. *Historia Mexicana* 29:447–471.

BRAY, WARWICK

1972 The City State in Central Mexico at the Time of the Spanish Conquest. *Journal of Latin American Studies* 4:161–185.

1978 Civilising the Aztecs. In *The Evolution of Social Systems,* edited by J. Friedman and M. J. Rowlands, pp. 373–398. Pittsburgh: University of Pittsburgh Press.

BRICKER, VICTORIA R.

1981 *The Indian Christ, the Indian King: The Historical Substrate of Maya Myth and Ritual.* Austin: University of Texas Press.

BROCKINGTON, LOLITA GUTIÉRREZ

1982 The Haciendas Marquesanas in Tehuantepec: African, Indian, and European Labor and Race Relations, 1588–1683. Ph.D. Dissertation, Department of History, University of North Carolina. Ann Arbor: University Microfilms (83-08284).

BRUMFIEL, ELIZABETH M. S.

1976 Specialization and Exchange at the Late Postclassic (Aztec) Community of Huexotla, Mexico. Ph.D. dissertation, Department of Anthropology, University of Michigan. Ann Arbor: University Microfilms (77-28066).

1980 Specialization, Market Exchange, and the Aztec State: A View from Huexotla. *Current Anthropology* 21:459–478.

BULLARD, WILLIAM R., JR.

1973 Postclassic Culture in Central Peten and Adjacent British Honduras. In *The Classic Maya Collapse,* edited by T. Patrick Culbert, pp. 221–241. Albuquerque: University of New Mexico Press.

BUNZEL, RUTH

1959 *Chichicastenango.* Seattle: University of Washington Press. (Reprint of *Chichicastenango: A Guatemalan Village,* 1952.)

BURGOA, FRANCISCO DE

1934a *Geográfica descripción.* 2 vols. Publicaciones del Archivo General de la Nación, nos. 25–26. Mexico City: Talleres Gráficos de la Nación.

1934b *Palestra historial.* Publicaciones del Archivo General de la Nación, no. 24. Mexico City: Talleres Gráficos de la Nación.

CACIQUES DE XOCHIMILCO

1870 Carta de los caciques é indios naturales de Suchimilco a Su Magestad . . . 2 de mayo de 1563. In *Colección de documentos . . . América y Oceanía* 13:293–301. Madrid: Imprenta de Frías y Compañía.

CALDERÓN DE LA BARCA, FANNY

1966 *Life in Mexico: The Letters of Fanny Calderón de la Barca* . . . Edited by Howard T. Fisher and Marion H. Fisher. Garden City, N.Y.: Doubleday.

CALNEK, EDWARD E.

1972 Settlement Pattern and Chinampa Agriculture at Tenochtitlan. *American Antiquity* 37:104–115.

1973 The Localization of the Sixteenth Century Map Called the Maguey Plan. *American Antiquity* 38:190–195.

1974a Conjunto urbano y modelo residencial en Tenochtitlan. In *Ensayos sobre el desarrollo urbano de México*, pp. 11–65. SepSetentas 143. Mexico City.

1974b The Sahagún Texts as a Source of Sociological Information. In *Sixteenth-Century Mexico: The Work of Sahagún*, edited by Munro S. Edmonson, pp. 189–204. Albuquerque: University of New Mexico Press.

1975 Organización de los sistemas de abastecimiento urbano de alimentos: El caso de Tenochtitlán. In *Las ciudades de América Latina y sus áreas de influencia a través de la historia*, edited by Jorge E. Hardoy and Richard P. Schaedel, pp. 41–60. Buenos Aires: Ediciones SIAP.

1976 The Internal Structure of Tenochtitlan. In *The Valley of Mexico: Studies in Pre-Hispanic Ecology and Society*, edited by Eric R. Wolf, pp. 287–302. Albuquerque: University of New Mexico Press.

1978 El sistema de mercado en Tenochtitlan. In *Economía política e ideología en el México prehispánico*, edited by Pedro Carrasco and Johanna Broda, pp. 97–114. Mexico City: Nueva Imagen.

n.d. Kinship, Settlement Pattern, and Domestic Crops in Tenochtitlan.

CAMPBELL, LYLE

1977 *Quichean Linguistic Prehistory.* University of California Publications in Linguistics, no. 81. Berkeley and Los Angeles: University of California Press.

CARMACK, ROBERT M.

1972 Ethnohistory: A Review of Its Development, Definitions, Methods, and Aims. *Annual Review of Anthropology* 1: 227–246. Palo Alto: Annual Reviews.

1979 *Historia social de los Quichés.* Seminario de Integración Social Guatemalteca, no. 38. Guatemala City: Ministerio de Educación.

1981 *The Quiche Mayas of Utatlán: The Evolution of a Highland Guatemala Kingdom.* Norman: University of Oklahoma Press.

1982 Social and Demographic Patterns in an Eighteenth-Century Census from Tecpanaco, Guatemala. In *The Historical Demography of Highland Guatemala*, edited by Robert M. Carmack, John Early, and Christopher Lutz, pp. 137–150. Institute for Mesoamerican Studies, State University of New York at Albany, Pub. no. 6. Albany.

1983 Peasant Rebels of the Guatemalan Highlands: A Social History of Tecpanaco. MS on file with author, State University of New York, Albany.

CARMACK, ROBERT M., AND JOHN M. WEEKS

1981 The Archaeology and Ethnohistory of Utatlan: A Conjunctive Approach. *American Antiquity* 46:323–341.

CARMAGNANI, MARCELLO

1978 Una forma mercantile coatta: Il "repartimiento" nella regione messicana di Oaxaca nell'ultimo terzo del secolo XVIII. *Wirtschaftskräfte und Wirtschaftswege*, vol. 4, *Übersee und allgemeine Wirtschaftsgeschichte*, pp. 139–145. Stuttgart: Klett Cotta.

1980 La ricostituzione delle nazioni indi: Il governo etnico nell'area de Oaxaca nel'700. *Quaderni Storici* 45:1027–1045.

CARNEGIE INSTITUTION OF WASHINGTON

1930–1950 Reports of the Division of Historical Research. In *Year Books* 29–49. Washington, D.C.

1950–1958 Reports of the Department of Archaeology. In *Year Books* 50–57.

CARRASCO, PEDRO

1961 El barrio y la regulación del matrimonio en un pueblo del Valle de México en el siglo XVI. *Revista Mexicana de Estudios Antropológicos* 17:7–26.

1963 Las tierras de los indios nobles de Tepeaca en el siglo XVI. *Tlalocan* 4: 97–119.

1964 Family Structure of Sixteenth-Century Tepoztlan. In *Process and Pattern in Culture*, edited by Robert A. Manners, pp. 185–210. Chicago: Aldine.

1966a Documentos sobre el rango de tecuhtli entre los nahuas tramontanos. *Tlalocan* 5:133–160.

1966b Sobre algunos términos de parentesco en el náhuatl clásico. *Estudios de Cultura Nahuatl* 6:149–166.

1969 Más documentos sobre Tepeaca. *Tlalocan* 6:1–37.

1970 Carta al Rey sobre la ciudad de Cholula en 1593. *Tlalocan* 6:176–192.

1971a Los barrios antiguos de Cholula. In *Estudios y Documentos de la Región de Puebla-Tlaxcala* 3:9–88. Puebla: Universidad Autónoma de Puebla and Instituto Poblano de Antropología e Historia.

1971b Social Organizaton of Ancient Mexico. In *Handbook of Middle American Indians*, vol. 10, edited by Robert Wauchope, Gordon F. Ekholm, and Ignacio Bernal, pp. 349–375. Austin: University of Texas Press.

1972 La casa y hacienda de un señor tlahuica. *Estudios de Cultura Nahuatl* 10:224–244.

1974 Sucesión y alianzas matrimoniales de la dinastía teotihuacana. *Estudios de Culture Nahuatl* 11:235–241.

1976a Los linajes nobles del México antiguo. In *Estratificación social en la Mesoamérica prehispánica*, by Pedro Carrasco, Johanna Broda, et al., pp. 19–36. Mexico City: Instituto Nacional de Antropología e Historia.

1976b Estratificación social indígena en Morelos durante el siglo XVI. In *Estratificación social en la Mesoamérica prehispánica*, by Pedro Carrasco, Johanna Broda, et al., pp. 102–117. Mexico City: Instituto Nacional de Antropología e Historia.

1976c The Joint Family in Ancient Mexico: The Case of Molotla. In *Essays on Mexican Kinship*, edited by Hugo G. Nutini, Pedro Carrasco, and James M. Taggart, pp. 45–64. Pittsburgh: University of Pittsburgh Press.

1977 Los señores de Xochimilco en 1548. *Tlalocan* 7:229–265.

1978 La economía del México prehispánico. In *Economía política e ideología en el México prehispánico*, edited by Pedro Carrasco and Johanna Broda, pp. 15–76. Mexico City: Nueva Imagen.

1979 The Chiefly Houses (Teccalli) of Ancient Mexico. In *Actes du XLIIᵉ Congrès International des Américanistes* (Paris, 1976) 9B:177–185. Paris.

1984 Royal Marriages in Ancient Mexico. In *Explorations in Ethnohistory: Indians of Central Mexico in the Sixteenth Century*, edited by H. R. Harvey and Hanns J. Prem, pp. 41–81. Albuquerque: University of New Mexico Press.

CARRASCO, PEDRO, AND JOHANNA BRODA
1978 (eds.) *Economía política e ideología en el México prehispánico*. Mexico City: Nueva Imagen.

CARRASCO, PEDRO, JOHANNA BRODA, ET AL.
1976 *Estratificación social en la Mesoamérica prehispánica*. Mexico City: Instituto Nacional de Antropología e Historia.

CARRASCO, PEDRO, AND JESÚS MONJARÁS-RUIZ
1976 *Colección de documentos sobre Coyoacan (Visita del oidor Gómez de Santillán al pueblo de Coyoacan y su sujeto Tacubaya en el año de 1553)*. Colección Científica, Fuentes: Historia Social, no. 39. Mexico City: Instituto Nacional de Antropología e Historia.

1978 *Colección de documentos sobre Coyoacan (Autos referentes al Cacicazgo de Coyoacán que proceden del AGN)*. Colección Científica, Fuentes: Historia Social, no. 65. Mexico City: Instituto Nacional de Antropología e Historia.

CASO, ALFONSO
1928 (ed.) Relación de Mistepeque, by Andrés de Cozar. *Revista Mexicana de Estudios Históricos* 2(6) (appendix):142–146.

1956 Los barrios antiguos de Tenochtitlán y Tlatelolco. *Memorias de la Academia Mexicana de la Historia* 15:7–63.

1963 Land Tenure among the Ancient Mexicans. *American Anthropologist* 65:863–878. (Spanish version, 1959, *Memorias del Colegio Nacional* 4:29–54.)

1971 Calendrical Systems of Central Mexico. In *Handbook of Middle American Indians*, vol. 10, edited by Robert Wauchope, Gordon F. Ekholm, and Ignacio

Bernal, pp. 333–348. Austin: University of Texas Press.

CASTILLO FARRERAS, VÍCTOR M.

1969 Caminos del mundo nahuatl. *Estudios de Cultura Nahuatl* 8:175–187.

1972 *Estructura económica de la sociedad mexica según las fuentes documentales.* Serie de Cultura Nahuatl, Instituto de Investigaciones Superiores, Mono. 13. Mexico City: Universidad Nacional Autónoma de México.

CEDULARIO INDIANO

1945–1946 *Cedulario indiano, recopilado por Diego de Encinas* . . . 4 vols. Madrid: Ediciones Cultura Hispánica. (Facsimile reproduction of 1596 ed.)

CERÓN CARVAJAL, JORGE

1905 Relación de Tepeaca y su partido. In *Papeles de Nueva España*, 2d ser., *Geografía y estadística*, edited by Francisco del Paso y Troncoso, 5:12–45. Madrid: Sucesores de Rivadeneyra.

CERVANTES DE SALAZAR, FRANCISCO

1953 *Life in the Imperial and Loyal City of Mexico in New Spain* . . . Facsimile of 1554 Spanish ed. with translation by Minnie Lee Barrett Shepard. Austin: University of Texas Press.

CHAMBERLAIN, ROBERT S.

1948 *The Conquest and Colonization of Yucatan, 1517–1550.* Carnegie Institution of Washington, Pub. 582. Washington, D.C. (Reprinted, 1966, New York: Octagon Books.)

CHANCE, JOHN K.

1976 The Urban Indian in Colonial Oaxaca. *American Ethnologist* 3:603–632.

1978a *Indice del archivo del Juzgado de Villa Alta, Oaxaca: Epoca colonial.* Vanderbilt University Publications in Anthropology, no. 21. Nashville.

1978b *Race and Class in Colonial Oaxaca.* Stanford: Stanford University Press.

1979 City and Country in Colonial Oaxaca: An Economic View. *Journal of the Steward Anthropological Society* 10:105–114.

1980 The Population of the Alcaldía Mayor of Villa Alta, Oaxaca, 1520–1970. MS, Department of Anthropology, University of Denver.

1983 Social Stratification and the Civil Cargo System among the Rincon Zapotecs of

Oaxaca: The Late Colonial Period. In *Colonial Latin America: Essays in Honor of Charles Gibson*, edited by Richard L. Garner and William B. Taylor, pp. 204–230. Bibliotheca Americana 1(3).

CHANCE, JOHN K., AND WILLIAM B. TAYLOR

1977 Estate and Class in a Colonial City: Oaxaca in 1792. *Comparative Studies in Society and History* 19:454–487.

1985 Cofradías and Cargos: An Historical Perspective on the Mesoamerican Civil-Religious Hierarchy. *American Ethnologist* 12:1–26.

CHAPMAN, ANNE M.

1957 Port of Trade Enclaves in Aztec and Maya Civilizations. In *Trade and Market in the Early Empires*, edited by Karl Polanyi, Conrad M. Arensberg, and Harry W. Pearson, pp. 114–150. Glencoe, Ill.: Free Press.

CHARDON, ROLAND

1980 The Elusive Spanish League: A Problem of Measurement in Sixteenth-Century New Spain. *Hispanic American Historical Review* 60:294–302.

CHARLTON, THOMAS H.

1965 Archaeological Settlement Patterns: An Interpretation. Ph.D. dissertation, Department of Anthropology, Tulane University. Ann Arbor: University Microfilms (66-10754).

1972 *Post-Conquest Developments in the Teotihuacán Valley, Mexico, Part 1, Excavations.* Office of State Archaeologist, Report 5. Iowa City.

1975 Archaeology and History, 1519–1569: The Emerging Picture in the Teotihuacan Valley, Mexico. In *Actas del XLI Congreso Internacional de Americanistas* (Mexico City, 1974) 1:219–229.

1979 An Archaeological Perspective on Culture Contact and Culture Change: The Basin of Mexico, 1521–1821. In *Los procesos de cambio: XV Mesa Redonda* 1:247–254. Mexico City: Sociedad Mexicana de Antropología and Universidad de Guanajuato.

1981 Otumba: Archaeology and Ethnohistory. Paper presented at the 46th annual meeting of the Society for American Archaeology, San Diego.

199

1983 Seventeenth-Century Occupations in the Otumba Area, Mexico. Paper presented at the 6th annual Meeting of Midwest Mesoamericanists, Urbana, Ill.

1985 Haciendas and Ranchos of the Eastern Teotihuacan Valley, 1621–1820: Colonial Reality or Republican Reflection? Paper presented at the 8th Annual Meeting of Midwest Mesoamericanists, Madison, Wisconsin.

CHARLTON, THOMAS H., AND CYNTHIA L. CHARLTON

1978 Osteological Data from a Demographic Disaster: The Basin of Mexico, 1521–1625. Paper presented at the meetings of the Canadian Archaeological Association, Quebec.

CHASE, ARLEN F.

1976 Topoxte and Tayasal: Ethnohistory in Archaeology. *American Antiquity* 41: 154–167.

1979 Regional Development in the Tayasal-Paxcaman Zone, El Peten, Guatemala: A Preliminary Statement. *Cerámica de Cultura Maya et al.* 11:86–119.

1985a Archaeology in the Maya Heartland. *Archaeology* 38(1):32–39.

1985b Postclassic Peten Interaction Spheres: The View from Tayasal. In *The Lowland Maya Postclassic*, edited by Arlen F. Chase and Prudence M. Rice, pp. 184–205. Austin: University of Texas Press.

CHASE, DIANE Z.

1981 The Maya Postclassic at Santa Rita Corozal. *Archaeology* 34:25–33.

1985 Ganned, but Not Forgotten: Late Postclassic Archaeology and Ritual at Santa Rita, Corozal, Belize. In *The Lowland Maya Postclassic*, edited by Arlen F. Chase and Prudence M. Rice, pp. 104–125. Austin: University of Texas Press.

CHEVALIER, FRANÇOIS

1963 *Land and Society in Colonial Mexico: The Great Hacienda*. Translated by Alvin Eustis. Berkeley and Los Angeles: University of California Press.

CHIMALPAHIN QUAUHTLEHUANITZIN, DOMINGO FRANCISCO DE SAN ANTON MUÑON

1889 *Annales de Domingo Francisco de San Anton Muñon Chimalpahin Quauhtlehuanitzin: Sixième et septième relations* (1258–1612). Edited and translated by Rémi Siméon. Bibliothèque Linguistique Américaine, vol. 12. Paris: Maisonneuve et C. Leclerc.

1958 *Das Memorial breve acerca de la fundación de la ciudad de Culhuacan.* Aztec text with German translation by Walter Lehmann and Gerdt Kutscher. Quellenwerke zur alten Geschichte Amerikas, no. 7. Stuttgart: W. Kohlhammer.

1963 *Die Relationen Chimalpahin's zur Geschichte Mexico's*, Part 1, *Die Zeit bis zur Conquista 1521.* Edited by Günter Zimmermann. Abhandlungen aus dem Gebiet der Auslandkunde, Universität Hamburg, vol. 68; ser. B, vol. 38. Hamburg: Cram, Degruyter.

1965 *Relaciones originales de Chalco Amaquemecan.* Translated by Silvia Rendón. Biblioteca Americana, Serie de Literatura Indígena. Mexico City: Fondo de Cultura Económica.

CHINCHILLA AGUILAR, ERNESTO

1975 *Blasones y heredades: Historia de Centroamérica II.* Seminario de Integración Social Guatemalteca, Pub. no. 35. Guatemala City: Ministerio de Educación.

CIUDAD REAL, ANTONIO DE

1976 *Tratado curioso y docto de las grandezas de la Nueva España . . .* 2 vols. 2d ed. Edited by Josefina García Quintana and Víctor M. Castillo Farreras. Mexico City: Universidad Nacional Autónoma de México.

CLAVIJERO, FRANCISCO JAVIER

1974 *Historia antigua de México.* 4th ed. Edited by R. P. Mariano Cuevas. Mexico City: Porrua.

CLINE, HOWARD F.

1972a Ethnohistorical Regions of Middle America. In *Handbook of Middle American Indians*, vol. 12, edited by Robert Wauchope and Howard F. Cline, pp. 166–182. Austin: University of Texas Press.

1072b A Census of the *Relaciones Geográficas* of New Spain, 1579–1612. In *Handbook of Middle American Indians*, vol. 12, edited by Robert Wauchope and Howard F. Cline, pp. 324–369. Austin: University of Texas Press.

1972c The Oztoticpac Lands Map of Texcoco, 1540. In *A la Carte: Selected Papers on Maps and Atlases*, edited by Walter W. Rostow, pp. 5–33. Washington, D.C.: Library of Congress.

CLINE, SUE LOUISE

1981 Culhuacan, 1572–1599: An Investigation through Mexican Indian Testaments. Ph.D. dissertation, Department of History, University of California, Los Angeles. Ann Arbor: University Microfilms (81-20933).

1984 Land Tenure and Land Inheritance in Late Sixteenth-Century Culhuacan. In *Explorations in Ethnohistory: Indians of Central Mexico in the Sixteenth Century*, edited by H. R. Harvey and Hanns J. Prem, pp. 277–309. Albuquerque: University of New Mexico Press.

CODICES

Kingsborough

1912 *Códice Kingsborough: Memorial de los indios de Tepetlaoztoc al monarca español contra los encomenderos del pueblo . . .* Edited by Francisco del Paso y Troncoso. Madrid: Hauser y Menet.

Mendoza

1964 In *Antigüedades de México, basadas en la recopilación de Lord Kingsborough*, 1:1–149. Mexico City: Secretaría de Hacienda y Crédito Público.

Santa María Asunción

16th century MS 1497bis, Biblioteca Nacional de México. 80 fols.

Vergara

16th century MSS Mex. 37–39, Bibliothèque Nationale de Paris. 55 fols.

Xolotl

1951 *Códice Xolotl.* Edited by Charles E. Dibble. Instituto de Historia, 1st ser., no. 22. Mexico City: Universidad Nacional Autónoma de México.

COE, MICHAEL D.

1973 *The Maya Scribe and His World.* New York: Grolier Club.

COGGINS, CLEMENCY C.

1975 Painting and Drawing Styles at Tikal: An Historical and Iconographic Reconstruction. Ph.D. dissertation, Department of Fine Arts, Harvard University. Ann Arbor: University Microfilms (76-03783).

COLECCIÓN DE DOCUMENTOS . . . AMÉRICA Y OCEANÍA

1864–1884 *Colección de documentos inéditos relativos al descubrimiento, conquista y organización de las antiguas posesiones españolas de América y Oceanía . . .* 42 vols. Madrid: Imprenta de Frías y Compañía.

COLECCIÓN DE DOCUMENTOS . . . ULTRAMAR

1885–1932 *Colección de documentos inéditos relativos al descubrimiento, conquista y organización de las antiguas posesiones españolas de Ultramar.* 25 vols. Madrid: Real Academia de la Historia.

COLLIER, JANE F.

1969 Changing Kinship Terminology in a Tzotzil Maya Community. MS, Harvard Chiapas Project, Peabody Museum, Harvard University.

COLLINS, ANNE C.

1977 The *Maestros Cantores* in Yucatán. In *Anthropology and History in Yucatan*, edited by Grant D. Jones, pp. 233–247. Austin: University of Texas Press.

CONQUISTADOR ANÓNIMO

1941 *Relación de algunas cosas de la Nueva España y de la gran civdad de Temestitán, México, escrita por un compañero de Hernán Cortés.* Mexico City: Editorial América.

CONTRERAS R., J. DANIEL

1951 Una rebelión indígena en el partido de Totonicapán en 1820: El indio y la independencia. Tesis, Departamento de Historia y Geografía, Universidad de San Carlos. Guatemala City.

COOK, SHERBURNE F., AND WOODROW BORAH

1960 *The Indian Population of Central Mexico, 1531–1610.* Ibero-Americana, no. 44. Berkeley and Los Angeles: University of California Press.

1968 *The Population of the Mixteca Alta, 1520–1960.* Ibero-Americana, no. 50. Berkeley and Los Angeles: University of California Press.

1971 *Essays in Population History*, vol. 1, *Mexico and the Caribbean.* Berkeley and Los Angeles: University of California Press.

1974 *Essays in Population History*, vol. 2, *Mexico and the Caribbean.* Berkeley and

Los Angeles: University of California Press.

1979 *Essays in Population History*, vol. 3, *Mexico and California*. Berkeley and Los Angeles: University of California Press.

CORONA SÁNCHEZ, EDUARDO
1976 La estratificación social en el Acolhuacan. In *Estratificación social en la Mesoamérica prehispánica*, by Pedro Carrasco, Johanna Broda, et al., pp. 88–101. Mexico City: Instituto Nacional de Antropología e Historia.

CORTÉS, HERNÁN
1963 *Cartas y documentos*. Mexico City: Porrua.
1976 *Cartas de relación*. 9th ed. Mexico City: Porrua.

CORTÉS, MARTÍN
1865 Carta de D. Martín Cortés, segundo Marqués del Valle, al rey D. Felipe II . . . In *Colección de documentos . . . América y Oceanía* 4:440–462. Madrid: Imprenta de Frías y Compañía.

COUTURIER, EDITH BOORSTEIN
1965 Hacienda of Hueyapan: The History of a Mexican Social and Economic Institution, 1550–1940. Ph.D. dissertation, Department of History, Columbia University. Ann Arbor: University Microfilms (65-10203).

COWGILL, GEORGE L.
1963 Postclassic Period Culture in the Vicinity of Flores, Peten, Guatemala. Ph.D. dissertation, Department of Anthropology, Harvard University.

CUEVAS, MARIANO
1975 (ed.) *Documentos inéditos del siglo XVI para la historia de México* . . . 2d ed. Mexico City: Porrua. (Reprint of 1914 ed.)

CULBERT, T. PATRICK
1973 Introduction: A Prologue to Classic Maya Culture and the Problem of Its Collapse. In *The Classic Maya Collapse*, edited by T. Patrick Culbert, pp. 3–19. Albuquerque: University of New Mexico Press.

DAHLGREN DE JORDÁN, BARBRO
1963 (compiler) *La grana cochinilla*. Mexico City: J. Porrua.

1966 *La Mixteca: Su cultura e historia prehispánicas*. Mexico City. Universidad Nacional Autónoma de México. (Reprint of 1954 ed.)

DAVENPORT, WILLIAM
1959 Nonunilinear Descent and Descent Groups. *American Anthropologist* 61: 557–572.

DAVIDSON, DAVID M.
1966 Negro Slave Control and Resistance in Colonial Mexico, 1519–1650. *Hispanic American Historical Review* 46:235–253.

DAVIES, NIGEL
1968 *Los señoríos independientes del imperio azteca*. Serie Historia, no. 19. Mexico City: Instituto Nacional de Antropología e Historia.

DENEVAN, WILLIAM M.
1976 (ed.) *The Native Population of the Americas in 1492*. Madison: University of Wisconsin Press.

DE VOS, JAN
1980 *La paz de Dios y del rey: La conquista de la selva lacandona, 1525–1821*. Colección Ceiba, vol. 10. Chiapas: Fonapas and Gobierno del Estado de Chiapas.

DÍAZ DEL CASTILLO, BERNAL
1974 *Historia verdadera de la conquista de la Nueva España*. 10th ed. Mexico City: Porrua.

DISPOSICIONES COMPLEMENTARIAS
1930 *Disposiciones complementarias de las leyes de Indias*. 3 vols. Madrid: Imprenta Sáez Hermanos.

DOCTRINA CRISTIANA
1944 *Doctrina cristiana en lengua española y mexicana por los religiosos de la Orden de Santo Domingo*. Madrid: Ediciones Cultura Hispánica. (Facsimile copy of 1548 ed.)

DUMOND, D. E.
1977 Independent Maya of the Late Nineteenth Century: Chiefdoms and Power Politics. In *Anthropology and History in Yucatan*, edited by Grant D. Jones, pp. 103–138. Austin: University of Texas Press.

DURÁN, DIEGO
1967 *Historia de las Indias de Nueva España e islas de la Tierra Firma*. 2 vols. Edited

by Angel M. Garibay K. Mexico City: Porrua.

DURAND-FOREST, JACQUELINE DE

1981 L'Histoire de la Vallée de Mexique selon Chimalpahin Quauhtlehuanitzin (du XIᵉ au XVIᵉ siècle). Doctoral dissertation, University of Paris.

DUSENBERRY, WILLIAM H.

1963 *The Mexican Mesta: The Administration of Ranching in Colonial Mexico.* Urbana: University of Illinois Press.

DYCKERHOFF, URSULA, AND HANNS J. PREM

1976 La estratificación social en Huexotzinco. In *Estratificación social en la Meso-américa prehispánica,* by Pedro Carrasco, Johanna Broda, et al., pp. 157–180. Mexico City: Instituto Nacional de Antropología e Historia.

1978 Der vorspanische Landbesitz in Zentralmexiko. *Zeitschrift für Ethnologie* 103: 186–238.

EDMONSON, MUNRO S.

1974 (ed.) *Sixteenth-Century Mexico: The Work of Sahagún.* Albuquerque: University of New Mexico Press.

EGGAN, FRED

1934 The Maya Kinship System and Cross-Cousin Marriage. *American Anthropologist* 36: 188–202.

ESCALONA RAMOS, ALBERTO

1943 Algunas construcciones de tipo colonial de Quintana Roo. *Anales del Instituto de Investigaciones Estéticas* 10: 17–40. Mexico City.

1946 Algunas ruinas prehispánicas en Quintana Roo. *Boletín de la Sociedad Mexicana de Geografía y Estadística,* 2ª época 61: 513–628.

EVANS, SUSAN T.

1980 Spatial Analysis of Basin of Mexico Settlement: Problems with the Use of the Central Place Model. *American Antiquity* 45: 866–875.

FARRISS, NANCY M.

1978 Nucleation versus Dispersal: The Dynamics of Population Movement in Colonial Yucatan. *Hispanic American Historical Review* 58: 178–216.

1980 Propiedades territoriales en Yucatán en la época colonial. *Historia Mexicana* 30: 153–208.

1984 *Maya Society under Colonial Rule: The Collective Enterprise of Survival.* Princeton: Princeton University Press.

FELDMAN, LAWRENCE H.

1971 A Tumpline Economy: Production and Distribution Systems of Early Central-East Guatemala. Ph.D. dissertation, Department of Anthropology, Pennsylvania State University. Ann Arbor: University Microfilms (72-09457).

1975 *Riverine Maya: The Torquegua and Other Chols of the Lower Motagua Valley.* University of Missouri, Columbia, Museum Brief No. 15.

1978 Los choles entre los kekchis. *Anales de la Sociedad de Geografía e Historia de Guatemala* 51: 79–112.

1981 Belize and Its Neighbors: Spanish Colonial Records of the Audiencia of Guatemala; A Preliminary Report. MS, Museum of Anthropology, University of Missouri, Columbia.

FERNÁNDEZ DE NAVARRETE, MARTÍN, ET AL.

1842–1895 (eds.) *Colección de documentos inéditos para la historia de España.* 112 vols. Madrid: Imprenta de la Viuda de Calero.

FIRTH, RAYMOND W.

1963 Bilateral Descent Groups: An Operational Viewpoint. In *Studies in Kinship and Marriage,* edited by I. Schapera, pp. 22–37. Royal Anthropological Institute Occasional Paper No. 16. London.

FLANNERY, KENT V., AND JOYCE MARCUS

1983 An Editorial Opinion on the Mixtec Impact. In *The Cloud People,* edited by Kent V. Flannery and Joyce Marcus, pp. 277–279. New York: Academic Press.

FLIPPIN, J. R.

1889 *Sketches from the Mountains of Mexico.* Cincinnati: Standard Publishing Co.

FLORESCANO, ENRIQUE

1965 El abasto y la legislación de grano en el siglo XVI. *Historia Mexicana* 14: 567–630.

1969 *Precios del maíz y crisis agrícolas en México (1708–1810).* Centro de Estudios Históricos, n.s., no. 4. Mexico City: Colegio de México.

1980 Formación y articulación económica de la hacienda en Nueva España. Unpublished MS, quoted by Aguirre (1982:32).

FÖRSTEMANN, ERNST

1906   *Commentary on the Maya Manuscript in the Royal Public Library of Dresden.* Translated by Selma Wesselhoeft and A. M. Parker. Papers of the Peabody Museum of American Archaeology and Ethnology, Harvard University, vol. 4, no. 2.

FORTES, MEYER

1969   *Kinship and the Social Order: The Legacy of Lewis Henry Morgan.* Chicago: Aldine.

FOURNIER GARCÍA, PATRICIA

1985   Evidencias arqueológicas de la importación de cerámica en México con base en los materiales del Ex-Convento de San Jerónimo. B.A. thesis, Escuela Nacional de Antropología e Historia, Mexico City.

FOX, JAMES A.

1978   Proto-Mayan Accent, Morpheme Structure Conditions, and Velar Innovations. Ph.D. dissertation, Department of Linguistics, University of Chicago.

In press   Kinship Terminology and Social Process: Two Mayan Etymologies. *International Journal of American Linguistics.*

n.d.   Comparative Mayan Kinship Terminology. In preparation.

FOX, JAMES A., AND JOHN S. JUSTESON

1979   Hieroglyphic Evidence for the Language of the Classic Maya. Paper presented at the International Conference on Phoneticism in Mayan Hieroglyphic Writing, State University of New York at Albany.

1985   Polyvalence in Mayan Hieroglyphic Writing. In *Phoneticism in Mayan Hieroglyphic Writing*, edited by Lyle R. Campbell and John S. Justeson, pp. 17–76. Albany: Institute for Mesoamerican Studies, pub. no. 9.

FRANK, ANDRÉ GUNDER

1979   *Mexican Agriculture, 1521–1630: Transformation of the Mode of Production.* Cambridge and Paris: Cambridge University Press and Editions de la Maison des Sciences de l'Homme.

FREIDEL, DAVID A.

1979   Culture Areas and Interaction Spheres: Contrasting Approaches to the Emergence of Civilization in the Maya Lowlands. *American Antiquity* 44:36–54.

GAGE, THOMAS

1958   *Travels in the New World.* Edited by J. Eric S. Thompson. Norman: University of Oklahoma Press.

GALARZA, JOAQUÍN

1980   *Codex de Zempoala: Techialoyan E 705, manuscrit pictographique de Zempoala, Hidalgo, Mexique.* Etudes Mesoaméricaines, vol. 7. Mexico City: Mission Archéologique et Ethnologique Française au Mexique.

GARCÍA, GENARO, AND CARLOS PEREYRA

1905–1911   (eds.) *Documentos inéditos ó muy raros para la historia de México.* 36 vols. Mexico City: Vda. de C. Bouret.

GARCÍA AÑOVEROS, JESÚS M.

1980   Situación social de la Diócesis de Guatemala al finales del siglo XVIII. Tesis, Universidad de San Carlos. Guatemala City.

GARCÍA BERNAL, MANUELA CRISTINA

1972a   *La sociedad de Yucatan, 1700–1750.* Publicaciones de la Escuela de Estudios Hispano-Americanos de Sevilla, no. 207: Seville.

1972b   La visita de Fray Luis de Cifuentes, obispo de Yucatan. *Anuario de Estudios Americanos* 29:229–260. Seville.

1978   *Población y encomienda en Yucatán bajo los austrias.* Publicaciones de la Escuela de Estudios Hispano-Americanos de Sevilla, no. 252. Seville.

GARCÍA MARTÍNEZ, BERNARDO

1969   *El Marquesado del Valle: Tres siglos de régimen señorial en Nueva España.* Mexico City: Colegio de México.

GATES, WILLIAM E.

1935   *Arte y diccionario en lengua choltí: A Manuscript Copied from the Libro Grande of Fr. Pedro* [sic] *Morán of About 1625.* Maya Society Pub. No. 9. Baltimore.

GEMELLI CARERI, GIOVANNI FRANCESCO

1976   *Viaje a la Nueva España.* Edited and translated by Francisca Perujo. Mexico City: Universidad Nacional Autónoma de México.

GERHARD, PETER

1972a   Colonial New Spain, 1519–1786: Historical Notes on the Evolution of Minor Political Jurisdictions. In *Handbook of Middle American Indians*, vol. 12, edited by Robert Wauchope and Howard F. Cline, pp. 63–137. Austin: University of Texas Press.

1972b   *A Guide to the Historical Geography of New Spain*. Cambridge Latin American Studies, no. 14. Cambridge: University Press.

1977   Congregaciones de indios en la Nueva España antes de 1570. *Historia Mexicana* 26:347–395.

1979   *The Southeast Frontier of New Spain*. Princeton: Princeton University Press.

GIBSON, CHARLES

1954   The Transformation of the Indian Community in New Spain, 1500–1810. *Journal of World History* 2:581–607.

1964   *The Aztecs under Spanish Rule: A History of the Indians of the Valley of Mexico, 1519–1810*. Stanford: Stanford University Press.

1966a   *Spain in America*. New York: Harper and Row.

1966b   Spanish-Indian Institutions and Colonial Urbanism in New Spain. In *XXXVII Congreso Internacional de Americanistas: Actas y Memorias* (Buenos Aires, 1966) 1:225–239.

1975a   A Survey of Middle American Prose Manuscripts in the Native Historical Tradition. In *Handbook of Middle American Indians*, vol. 15, edited by Robert Wauchope and Howard F. Cline, pp. 311–321. Austin: University of Texas Press.

1975b   Writings on Colonial Mexico. *Hispanic American Historical Review* 55:287–323.

1981   Heritage of Conquest: New Spain/Mexico. In *Latin America Today: Heritage of Conquest*, edited by Dan C. Hazen, Thomas H. Holloway, and David M. Jones, pp. 8–27. Ithaca: Latin American Studies Program and New York State Latin Americanists.

GLASS, JOHN B.

1975   A Survey of Native Middle American Pictorial Manuscripts. In *Handbook of Middle American Indians*, vol. 14, edited by Robert Wauchope and Howard F. Cline, pp. 3–80. Austin: University of Texas Press.

GÓMEZ DE OROZCO, FEDERICO

1933   El *Códice de San Antonio Techialoyan*: Estudio histórico-paleográfico. *Anales del Museo Nacional de Arqueología, Historia y Etnografía*, 4ª epoca, 8:311–332. Mexico City.

1948   La pintura indoeuropea de los Códices Techialoyan. *Anales del Instituto de Investigaciones Estéticas* 16:57–67. Mexico City.

GOSNER, KEVIN

1979   Uman Parish: Open, Corporate Communities in Eighteenth-Century Yucatan. Paper presented at the 75th annual meeting of the Association of American Geographers, Philadelphia.

GRAHAM, ELIZABETH, GRANT D. JONES, AND ROBERT R. KAUTZ

1985   Archaeology and Ethnohistory on a Spanish Colonial Frontier: An Interim Report on the Macal-Tipu Project in Eastern Belize. In *The Lowland Maya Postclassic*, edited by Arlen F. Chase and Prudence M. Rice, pp. 206–214. Austin: University of Texas Press.

GRAHAM, IAN

1967   *Archaeological Explorations in El Peten, Guatemala*. Middle American Research Institute, Tulane University, Pub. 33. New Orleans.

GUITERAS HOLMES, CALIXTA

1947   Clanes y sistema de parentesco de Cancuc (México). *Acta Americana* 5:1–17.

GUSSINYER, J.

1969   El salvamento arqueológico en las excavaciones del "Metro" en la Ciudad de México. *Boletín Bibliográfico de Antropología Americana* 32:89–96.

HAGGETT, PETER

1966   *Locational Analysis in Human Geography*. New York: St. Martin's Press.

HAKLUYT, RICHARD

1903–1905   *The Principal Navigations, Voyages, Traffiques, and Discoveries of the English Nation* . . . 12 vols. New York: Macmillan.

HAMMOND, NORMAN

1978   Cacao and Cobaneros: An Overland Trade Route between the Maya Highlands and Lowlands. In *Mesoamerican Communication Routes and Cultural Contacts*, edited by Thomas A. Lee, Jr., and Carlos Navarrete. Papers of the New World Archaeological Foundation, no. 40:19–25. Provo, Utah.

n.d. The Sun Is Hid: Classic Depictions of a Maya Myth. In *Fourth Palenque Round Table*, edited by Elizabeth P. Benson and Merle Greene Robertson. Forthcoming.

HAMNETT, BRIAN R.

1971a Dye Production, Food Supply, and the Laboring Population of Oaxaca, 1750–1820. *Hispanic American Historical Review* 51:51–78.

1971b *Politics and Trade in Southern Mexico, 1750–1821.* London: Cambridge University Press.

HANKE, LEWIS, AND CELSO RODRÍGUEZ

1976–1978 *Los virreyes españoles en América durante el gobierno de la Casa de Austria: Mexico.* 5 vols. Biblioteca de Autores Españoles, vols. 273–277. Madrid: Ediciones Atlas.

HARSANYI, JOHN C.

1960 Explanation and Comparative Dynamics in Social Science. *Behavioral Science* 5:136–145.

HARVEY, H. R.

1966 The *Codex of San Cristobal and Santa Maria*: A False Techialoyan. *Tlalocan* 5:119–124.

1976 The Techialoyan Land Titles of Huixquilucan. Paper read at the 42nd International Congress of Americanists, Paris. (Published in *Actes du XLII*ᵉ *Congrès International des Américanistes* 7 [1979]: 113–124.)

1984 Aspects of Land Tenure in Ancient Mexico. In *Explorations in Ethnohistory: Indians of Central Mexico in the Sixteenth Century*, edited by H. R. Harvey and Hanns J. Prem, pp. 83–102. Albuquerque: University of New Mexico Press.

In press *El Códice de Huixquilucan*. In *Biblioteca Enciclopédica del Estado de México*.

HARVEY, H. R., AND BARBARA J. WILLIAMS

1980 Aztec Arithmetic: Positional Notation and Area Calculation. *Science* 210: 499–505.

n.d. El Códice Hemenway: Títulos de tierra de San Antonio Huixquilucan.

HASSIG, ROSS

1982a Periodic Markets in Precolumbian Mexico. *American Antiquity* 47:346–355.

1982b Tenochtitlan: The Economic and Political Reorganization of an Urban System. *Comparative Urban Research* 9(1): 39–49.

HAVILAND, WILLIAM A.

1977 Dynastic Genealogies from Tikal, Guatemala: Implications for Descent and Political Organization. *American Antiquity* 42:61–67.

HELLMUTH, NICHOLAS M.

1970 *A Bibliography of the 16th–20th Century Maya of the Southern Lowlands: Chol, Chol Lacandon, Yucatec Lacandon, Quejache, Itza, and Mopan, 1524–1969.* Occasional Publications in Anthropology, Archaeology Series, no. 2. Greeley: Museum of Anthropology, University of Northern Colorado.

1971 Some Notes on the Ytza, Quejache, Verapaz Chol and Toquegua Maya: A Progress Report on Ethnohistory Research Conducted in Seville, Spain, June–August 1971. MS, Foundation for Latin American Research, Guatemala City.

1972 Progreso y notas sobre la investigación etnohistórica de las tierras bajas mayas de los siglos XVI a XIX. *América Indígena* 32:179–244.

1977 Cholti-Lacandon (Chiapas) and Petén-Ytzá Agriculture, Settlement Pattern and Population. In *Social Process in Maya Prehistory: Studies in Honour of Sir Eric Thompson*, edited by Norman Hammond, pp. 421–448. New York: Academic Press.

n.d. An Ethnohistorical Study of the Southern Maya Lowlands in the 16th and 17th Centuries: A Research Design Outline. MS, Foundation for Latin American Research, Guatemala City.

HICKS, FREDERIC

1976 *Mayeque* y *capuleque* en el sistema de clases del México antiguo. In *Estratificación social en la Mesoamérica prehispánica*, by Pedro Carrasco, Johanna Broda, et al., pp. 67–77. México City: Instituto Nacional de Antropología e Historia.

1978 Los calpixque de Nezahualcóyotl. *Estudios de Cultura Nahuatl* 13:129–152.

1982 Tetzcoco in the Early Sixteenth Century: The State, the City, and the *Calpolli*. *American Ethnologist* 9:230–249.

1984 Rotational Labor and Urban Development in Prehispanic Tetzcoco. In *Explorations in Ethnohistory: Indians in Central Mexico in the Sixteenth Century*, edited by H. R. Harvey and Hanns J. Prem, pp. 147–174. Albuquerque: University of New Mexico Press.

HISTORIA TOLTECA-CHICHIMECA

1976 *Historia toltecan-chichimeca*. Edited and translated by Paul Kirchhoff, Lina Odena Güemes, and Luis Reyes García. Mexico City: Instituto Nacional de Antropología e Historia.

HOPKINS, NICHOLAS A.

1982 A Comparison of Tulija Chol and Chalchihuitan Tzeltal Kinship Terminologies. Paper presented at the Sixth Taller Maya, San Cristobal de las Casas, Chiapas.

HORCASITAS, FERNANDO, AND WANDA TOMMASI DE MAGRELLI

1975 El Códice de Tzictepec: Una nueva fuente pictórica indígena. *Anales de Antropología del Instituto de Investigaciones Antropológicas* 12:243–272. Mexico City: Universidad Nacional Autónoma de México.

HOTCHKIN, MICHAEL G.

1978 The Itza of Peten: Tayasal as Understood through Archaeology and Ethnohistory. MS, Department of Anthropology, State University of New York at Albany.

HUMBOLDT, ALEXANDER VON

1822 *Political Essay on the Kingdom of New Spain*. 4 vols. Translated by John Black. London: Longon, Longman, Hurst, Rees, Orme, and Brown.

HUNT, EVA

1972 Irrigation and the Socio-Political Organization of Cuicatec Cacicazgos. In *The Prehistory of the Tehuacan Valley*, vol. 4, *Chronology and Irrigation*, edited by Frederick Johnson, pp. 162–259. General Editor: Richard S. MacNeish. Austin: University of Texas Press.

HUNT, MARTA ESPEJO-PONCE

1974 Colonial Yucatan: Town and Region in the Seventeenth Century. Ph.D. dissertation, Department of History, University of California, Los Angeles. Ann Arbor: University Microfilms (75-02230).

1976 The Processes of the Development of Yucatan, 1600–1700. In *Provinces of Early Mexico: Variants of Spanish American Regional Evolution*, edited by Ida Altman and James Lockhart, pp. 33–62. UCLA Latin American Center Publications, vol. 36. Los Angeles.

ISRAEL, J. I.

1975 *Race, Class and Politics in Colonial Mexico, 1610–1670*. London: Oxford University Press.

JÄCKLEIN, KLAUS

1978 *Los popolocas de Tepexi (Puebla): Un estudio etnohistórico*. Das Mexiko-Projekt der Deutschen Forschungsgemeinschaft, no. 15. Wiesbaden: Steiner.

JONES, DAVID M.

1978 Nineteenth Century *Haciendas* and *Ranchos* of Otumba and Apan, Basin of Mexico. Ph.D. dissertation, Institute of Archaeology, University of London.

JONES, GRANT D.

1977 Levels of Settlement Alliance among the San Pedro Maya of Western Belize and Eastern Petén, 1857–1936. In *Anthropology and History in Yucatán*, edited by Grant D. Jones, pp. 139–189. Austin: University of Texas Press.

1979 Southern Lowland Maya Political Organization: A Model of Change from Protohistoric through Colonial Times. In *Actes du XLIIe Congrès International des Américanistes* (Paris, 1976) 8:83–94.

1982 Agriculture and Trade in the Colonial Period Southern Maya Lowlands. In *Maya Subsistence: Studies in Memory of Dennis E. Puleston*, edited by Kent V. Flannery, pp. 275–293. New York: Academic Press.

1983 The Last Maya Frontiers of Colonial Yucatan. In *Spaniards and Indians in Southeastern Mesoamerica: Essays on the History of Ethnic Relations*, edited by Murdo J. MacLeod and Robert Wasserstrom, pp. 64–91. Lincoln: University of Nebraska Press.

1984a Maya-Spanish Relations in Sixteenth Century Belize. *BELCAST Journal of Belizean Affairs* 1(1):28–40.

1984b Rediscovering the Fugitive: Some Documentary Perspectives on Maya Archaeology. Paper presented at the Seminar on Symbol and Text: Archaeology in Lettered and Unlettered Societies, Colgate University, Hamilton, New York.

JONES, GRANT D., AND ROBERT R. KAUTZ

1981a Archaeology and Ethnohistory on a Spanish Colonial Frontier: The Macal-Tipu Project in Western Belize. Paper presented at the 17th Mesa Redonda de la Sociedad Mexicana de Antropología, San Cristobal de las Casas, Chiapas. MS, Department of Anthropology, Hamilton College.

1981b Native Elites on the Colonial Frontiers of Yucatan: A Model for Continuing Research. Paper presented at the 80th annual meeting of the American Anthropological Association, Los Angeles. MS, Department of Anthropology, Hamilton College.

JONES, GRANT D., DON S. RICE, AND PRUDENCE M. RICE

1981 The Location of Tayasal: A Reconsideration in Light of Peten Maya Ethnohistory and Archaeology. *American Antiquity* 46:530–547.

JOSSERAND, J. KATHRYN, LINDA SCHELE, AND NICHOLAS A. HOPKINS

n.d. Auxiliary Verb + *ti* Constructions in the Classic Maya Inscriptions. In *Fourth Palenque Round Table*, edited by Elizabeth P. Benson and Merle Greene Robertson. Forthcoming.

JUSTESON, JOHN S.

1982 The Evolution of Phoneticism in Mayan Hieroglyphic Writing. MS, Pre-Columbian Section, Dumbarton Oaks, Washington, D.C.

JUSTESON, JOHN S., AND LYLE CAMPBELL

1981 The Linguistic Background of Mayan Hieroglyphic Writing: Arguments against a "Highland" Mayan Role. MS in authors' possession.

JUSTESON, JOHN S., WILLIAM M. NORMAN, LYLE R. CAMPBELL, AND TERRENCE KAUFMAN

1984 *The Foreign Impact on Lowland Mayan Language and Script*. Middle American Research Institute, Tulane University, Pub. 53. New Orleans.

KARTTUNEN, FRANCES

1983 *An Analytical Dictionary of Nahuatl*. Austin: University of Texas Press.

KATZ, FRIEDRICH

1966 *Situación social y económica de los aztecas durante los siglos XV y XVI*. Translated by María Luisa Rodríguez Sala and Elsa Bühler. Serie de Cultura Náhuatl, Mono. 8. Mexico City: Universidad Nacional Autónoma de México. (German ed., 1956.)

KAUFMAN, TERRENCE S.

1972 *El proto-tzeltal-tzotzil: Fonología comparada y diccionario reconstruido*. Centro de Estudios Mayas, Cuaderno 5. Mexico City: Universidad Nacional Autónoma de México.

KEESING, ROGER M.

1976 *Cultural Anthropology: A Contemporary Perspective*. New York: Holt, Rinehart, and Winston.

KELLEY, KLARA BONSACK

1976 Dendritic Central-Place Systems and the Regional Organization of Navajo Trading Posts. In *Regional Analysis*, edited by Carol A. Smith, 1:219–254. New York: Academic Press.

KELLOGG, SUSAN M.

1980 Social Organization in Early Colonial Tenochtitlan-Tlatelolco: An Ethnohistorical Study. Ph.D. dissertation, Department of Anthropology, University of Rochester. Ann Arbor: University Microfilms (80-14332).

KING, ARDEN R.

1974 *Coban and the Verapaz: History and Cultural Process in Northern Guatemala*. Middle American Research Institute, Tulane University, Pub. 37. New Orleans.

KIRCHHOFF, PAUL

1954–1955 Land Tenure in Ancient Mexico: A Preliminary Sketch. *Revista Mexicana de Estudios Antropológicos* 14:351–361.

1959 The Principles of Clanship in Human Society. In *Readings in Anthropology*, edited by Morton H. Fried, 2:259–270. New York: Thomas Y. Crowell.

KONRAD, HERMAN W.

1980 *A Jesuit Hacienda in Colonial Mexico: Santa Lucía, 1576–1767*. Stanford: Stanford University Press.

KUBLER, GEORGE

1942 Population Movements in Mexico, 1520–1600. *Hispanic American Historic Review* 22:606–643.

1948 *Mexican Architecture of the Sixteenth Century*. New Haven: Yale University Press.

KURTZ, DONALD V.
1974 Peripheral and Transitional Markets: The Aztec Case. *American Ethnologist* 1: 685–705.

LADD, DORIS M.
1976 *The Mexican Nobility at Independence, 1780–1826*. Latin American Monographs, no. 40. Austin: University of Texas Press.

LaFARGE, OLIVER
1940 Maya Ethnology: The Sequence of Cultures. In *The Maya and Their Neighbors*, pp. 281–291. New York: D. Appleton-Century. (Reprinted, 1962, Salt Lake City: University of Utah Press.)

LAMBERT, BERND
1977 Bilaterality in the Andes. In *Andean Kinship and Marriage*, edited by Ralph Bolton and Enrique Mayer. Special Publications of the American Anthropological Association, no. 7:1–27. Washington, D.C.

LAS CASAS, BARTOLOMÉ DE
1909 *Apologética historia de las Indias*. Edited by M. Serrano y Sanz. Nueva Biblioteca de Autores Españoles, no. 13. Madrid: Bailly, Bailliére é Hijos.
1958 *Apologética historia*. Vols. 3–4 of *Obras escogidas de Fray Bartolomé de las Casas*. Biblioteca de Autores Españoles, vols. 105–106. Madrid: Ediciones Atlas.

LAUER, W.
1979 Puebla-Tlaxcala: A German-Mexican Research Project. *Geo-Journal* 3:97–105.

LAUGHLIN, ROBERT M.
1975 *The Great Tzotzil Dictionary of San Lorenzo Zinacantán*. Smithsonian Contributions to Anthropology, no. 19. Washington, D.C.
1980 The Great Tzotzil Dictionary of Santo Domingo Zinacantan. MS, Department of Anthropology, Smithsonian Institution.

LAUNEY, MICHEL
1979 *Introduction à la langue et à la littérature azteques*. Paris: L'Harmattan.

LAVRIN, ASUNCIÓN, AND EDITH COUTURIER
1979 Dowries and Wills: A View of Women's Socioeconomic Role in Colonial Guadalajara and Puebla, 1640–1790. *Hispanic American Historical Review* 59: 280–304.

LINNÉ, SIGVALD
1948 *El Valle y la Ciudad de México en 1550* . . . Statens Etnografiska Museum, n.s., Pub. no. 9. Stockholm.

LISS, PEGGY K.
1975 *Mexico under Spain, 1521–1556: Society and the Origins of Nationality*. Chicago: University of Chicago Press.

LISTER, FLORENCE C., AND ROBERT H. LISTER
1982 *Sixteenth Century Maiolica Pottery in the Valley of Mexico*. Anthropological Papers of the University of Arizona, no. 39. Tucson: University of Arizona Press.

LOCKHART, JAMES
1978 Views of Corporate Self and History in Some Valley of Mexico Towns, Late Seventeenth and Eighteenth Centuries. Paper read at Stanford Conference on Native American and Indianist Policy.

LÓPEZ AUSTIN, ALFREDO
1974 Organización política en el altiplano central de México durante el postclásico. *Historia Mexicana* 23:515–550.

LÓPEZ DE COGOLLUDO, DIEGO
1688 *Historia de Yucathan*. 1st ed. Madrid.

LÓPEZ DE GÓMARA, FRANCISCO
1943 *Historia de la conquista de México*. 2 vols. Mexico City: Editorial Pedro Robredo.
1965–1966 *Historia general de las Indias*. 2 vols. 2d ed. Barcelona: Iberia.

LÓPEZ SARRELANGUE, DELFINA E.
1975 La Hacienda de San Jose de Coapa. In *Haciendas, latifundios y plantaciones en América Latina*, coordinated by Enrique Florescano, pp. 223–241. Mexico City: Siglo Veintiuno.

LOUNSBURY, FLOYD G.
1980 Some Problems in the Interpretation of the Mythological Portion of the Hieroglyphic Text of the Temple of the Cross at Palenque. In *Third Palenque Round Table, 1978, Part 2*, edited by Merle Greene Robertson, pp. 99–115. Austin: University of Texas Press.

LOVELL, W. GEORGE
1980 Land and Settlement in the Cuchumatan Highlands (1500–1821): A Study in the Historical Geography of Northwestern Guatemala. Ph.D. dissertation, Department of Geography, University of Alberta.

1982   Collapse and Recovery: A Demographic Profile of the Cuchumatan Highlands of Guatemala (1520–1821). In *The Historical Demography of Highland Guatemala*, edited by Robert M. Carmack, John Early, and Christopher Lutz, pp. 103–120. Institute for Mesoamerican Studies, State University of New York at Albany, Pub. no. 6.

LUTZ, CHRISTOPHER H.
1976   Santiago de Guatemala, 1541–1773: The Sociodemographic History of a Spanish-American Colonial City. Ph.D. dissertation, Department of History, University of Wisconsin, Madison. Ann Arbor: University Microfilms (76-18894).
1982   Population History of the Parish of San Miguel Dueñas, Guatemala, 1530–1770. In *The Historical Demography of Highland Guatemala*, edited by Robert M. Carmack, John Early, and Christopher Lutz, pp. 121–135. Institute for Mesoamerican Studies, State University of New York at Albany, Pub. no. 6.

MACLEOD, MURDO J.
1973   *Spanish Central America: A Socioeconomic History, 1520–1720*. Berkeley and Los Angeles: University of California Press.
1980   Ethnic Relations and Indian Society in the Province of Guatemala, c. 1625–1800. Paper presented at the Conference on Spanish-Indian Contact in Southern Mesoamerica, Cambridge, Mass.

MADIGAN, DOUGLAS G.
1976   Santiago Atitlan, Guatemala: A Socioeconomic and Demographic History. Ph.D. dissertation, Department of History, University of Pittsburgh. Ann Arbor: University Microfilms (76-25934).

MARCUS, JOYCE
1976   *Emblem and State in the Classic Maya Lowlands: An Epigraphic Approach to Territorial Organization*. Washington, D.C.: Dumbarton Oaks.

MARCUS, JOYCE, AND KENT V. FLANNERY
1983   An Introduction to the Late Postclassic. In *The Cloud People*, edited by Kent V. Flannery and Joyce Marcus, pp. 217–226. New York: Academic Press.

MARTÍNEZ HERNÁNDEZ, JUAN
1929   (ed.) *Diccionario de Motul, maya-español, atribuido a fray Antonio de Ciudad Real, y Arte de lengua maya por fray Juan Coronel*. Merida: Compañía Tipográfica Yucateca.

MARTÍNEZ PELÁEZ, SEVERO
1970   *La patria del criollo: Ensayo de interpretación de la realidad colonial guatemalteca*. Colección "Realidad Nuestra," no. 1. Guatemala City: Editorial Universitaria.
1973   Los motines de indios en el período colonial guatemalteco. Paper presented at the Primer Congreso Centroamericano de Historia Demográfica, Económica y Social. San José, Costa Rica.

MATESANZ, JOSÉ
1965   Introducción de la ganadería en Nueva España, 1521–1535. *Historia Mexicana* 14:533–566.

MATHEWS, PETER L.
1975   The Identification of Themes in the Sculpture of Naranjo, Department of Peten, Guatemala. MS, Pre-Columbian Section, Dumbarton Oaks, Washington, D.C.
1980   Notes on the Dynastic Sequence of Bonampak, Part 1. In *Third Palenque Round Table, 1978: Part 2*, edited by Merle Greene Robertson, pp. 60–73. Austin: University of Texas Press.
In press   Glyphic Substitutions, 2: The Affix Cluster. In *Phoneticism in Mayan Hieroglyphic Writing*, edited by Lyle R. Campbell and John S. Justeson. Albany: Institute for Mesoamerican Studies.

MATRÍCULA DE HUEXOTZINCO
1974   *Matrícula de Huexotzinco: Ms. Mex. 387 der Bibliothèque Nationale Paris . . .* Edited by Hanns J. Prem. Graz: Akademische Druck- und Verlaganstalt.

MEAD, MARGARET
1963   *Sex and Temperament in Three Primitive Societies*. New York: William Morrow.

MÉNDEZ MARTÍNEZ, ENRIQUE
1979   (compiler) *Indice de documentos relativos a los pueblos del Estado de Puebla*. Colección Científica, Fuentes: Etnohistoria, no. 70. Mexico City: Instituto Nacional de Antropología e Historia.

MENDIETA, GERÓNIMO DE
1971   *Historia eclesiástica indiana: Obra escrita a fines del siglo XVI*. Mexico City: Porrua. (Facsimile copy of 1870 ed.)

MILLA, JOSÉ
1937   *Historia de la América Central . . .* 2
       vols. 2d ed. Guatemala City: Tipografía
       Nacional.

MILLARES CARLO, A., AND J. I. MANTECÓN
1945   *Indice y extractos de los protocolos del
       Archivo de Notarías de México, D.F.,*
       vol. 1, *1525–1528.* Mexico City: Colegio
       de México.

MILLER, ARTHUR G.
1974   The Iconography of the Painting in the
       Temple of the Diving God, Tulum, Quin-
       tana Roo, Mexico: The Twisted Cords. In
       *Mesoamerican Archaeology: New Ap-
       proaches,* edited by Norman Hammond,
       pp. 167–186. Austin: University of Texas
       Press.

MIRANDA, JOSÉ
1958   Orígenes de la ganadería indígena en la
       Mixteca. In *Miscelanea Paul Rivet, oc-
       togenario dicata* 2:787–796. Instituto
       de Historia, 1st ser., no. 50. Mexico
       City: Universidad Nacional Autónoma de
       México.
1967   Evolución cuantitativa y desplazamien-
       tos de la población indígena de Oaxaca
       en la época colonial. *Estudios de Histo-
       ria Novohispana* 2:129–147. Mexico
       City: Universidad Nacional Autónoma de
       México.

MOLINA, ALONSO DE
1970   *Vocabulario en lengua castellana y mexi-
       cana y mexicana y castellana.* Mexico
       City: Porrua. (Reprint of 1880 ed.)

MOLINA SOLÍS, JUAN FRANCISCO
1904–1913   *Historia de Yucatan durante la
       dominación española.* 3 vols. Merida:
       Imprenta de la Lotería del Estado.

MOLLOY, JOHN P., AND WILLIAM L. RATHJE
1974   Sexploitation among the Late Classic
       Maya. In *Mesoamerican Archaeology:
       New Approaches,* edited by Norman
       Hammond, pp. 431–444. Austin: Uni-
       versity of Texas Press.

MONNICH, ANNELIESE
1974   El altepeamatl de Ocoyacac, México:
       Texto náhuatl y traducción española. *In-
       diana* 2:167–182.

MONZÓN, ARTURO
1949   *El calpulli en la organización social de
       los Tenochca.* Instituto de Historia, 1st
       ser., no. 14. Mexico City: Universidad
       Nacional Autónoma de México.

MORENO, MANUEL M.
1931   *La organización política y social de los
       aztecas.* Mexico City: Universidad Na-
       cional Autónoma de México. (Reprinted,
       1971, Instituto Nacional de Antropología
       e Historia.)

MORENO TOSCANO, ALEJANDRA
1965   Tres problemas en la geografía del maíz,
       1600–1624. *Historia Mexicana* 14:
       631–655.
1978   (coord.) *Ciudad de México: Ensayo de
       construcción de una historia.* Colección
       Científica, Historia, no. 61. Mexico City:
       Instituto Nacional de Antropología e
       Historia.

MORGAN, LEWIS HENRY
1877   *Ancient Society . . .* New York: H. Holt.

MORLEY, SYLVANUS GRISWOLD
1937–1938   *The Inscriptions of Peten.* 5 vols.
       Carnegie Institution of Washington,
       Pub. 437. Washington, D.C.

MÖRNER, MAGNUS
1964   La política de segregación y el mestizaje
       en la Audiencia de Guatemala. *Revista
       de Indias* 24:137–151.
1970   *La Corona española y los foráneos en los
       pueblos de indios de América.* Instituto
       de Estudios Ibero-Americanos, Serie A,
       Mono. no. 1. Stockholm: Almqvist &
       Wiksell.
1973   The Spanish American Hacienda: A Sur-
       vey of Recent Research and Debate.
       Hispanic American Historical Review
       53:183–216.

MOTOLINÍA, TORIBIO (TORIBIO DE BENAVENTE)
1971   *Memoriales; o, Libro de las cosas de la
       Nueva España y de los naturales de ella.*
       2d ed. Edited by Edmundo O'Gorman.
       Serie de Historiadores y Cronistas de In-
       dias, no. 2. Mexico City: Universidad
       Nacional Autónoma de México.
1973   *Historia de los indios de la Nueva Es-
       paña . . .* 2d ed. Edited by Edmundo
       O'Gorman. Mexico City: Porrua. (Re-
       print of 1969 ed.)

MÜNCH G., GUIDO
1976   *El cacicazgo de San Juan Teotihuacán
       durante la colonia (1521–1821).* Colec-
       ción Científica, Historia, no. 32. Mexico
       City: Instituto Nacional de Antropología
       e Historia.

1978   La población del Obispado de Oaxaca en 1570. *Anales de Antropología* 15:67–81. Mexico City.

MUÑOZ CAMARGO, DIEGO

1585   Descripción de la ciudad y provincia de Tlaxcala de la Nueva España y Indias del Mar Oceano para el buen gobierno y ennoblecimiento dellas, mandada hazer por el S.C.R.M. el rey don Phelipe nro. señor. MS, Hunter 242, University of Glasgow Library.

1892   *Historia de Tlaxcala.* Edited by Alfredo Chavero. Mexico City: Secretaría de Fomento.

1981   *Descripción de la ciudad y provincia de Tlaxcala de las Indias y del Mar Océano para el buen gobierno y ennoblecimiento dellas.* Edited by René Acuña. Mexico City: Instituto de Investigaciones Filológicas, Universidad Nacional Autónoma de México. (Facsimile copy of 1585 MS.)

MURDOCK, GEORGE P.

1949   *Social Structure.* New York: Macmillan.

1960   Cognatic Forms of Social Organization. In *Social Structure in Southeast Asia*, edited by George P. Murdock, pp. 1–14. Viking Fund Publications in Anthropology, no. 29. New York: Wenner-Gren Foundation for Anthropological Research.

MURGUÍA Y GALARDI, JOSÉ MARÍA

1827   Extracto general que abraza la estadística toda en su 1ª y 2ª parte del Estado de Guaxaca, y ha reunido de orden del supremo gobierno el intendente de provincia enclase de los cesantes José Ma. Murguía y Galardi. MS, Latin American Collection, University of Texas Library, Austin.

NATIONS, JAMES D.

1979   Population Ecology of the Lacandon Maya. Ph.D. dissertation, Department of Anthropology, Southern Methodist University. Ann Arbor: University Microfilms (79-20363).

NEW LAWS

1971   *New Laws of the Indies for the Good Treatment and Preservation of the Indians Promulgated by the Emperor Charles the Fifth, 1542–1543.* Translated by Henry Stevens. New York: AMS Press. (Reprint of 1893 ed.)

NICHOLSON, H. B.

1963   The Concept of History in Pre-Hispanic Mesoamerica. In *VI Congrès International des Sciences Anthropologiques et Ethnologiques* (Paris, 1960) 2:445.

1975   Middle American Ethnohistory: An Overview. In *Handbook of Middle American Indians*, vol. 15, edited by Robert Wauchope and Howard F. Cline, pp. 487–505. Austin: University of Texas Press.

NUEVOS DOCUMENTOS . . . CORTÉS

1946   *Nuevos documentos relativos a los bienes de Hernán Cortés, 1547–1947.* Mexico City: Imprenta Universitaria.

NUTINI, HUGO G.

1976   Introduction: The Nature and Treatment of Kinship in Mesoamerica. In *Essays on Mexican Kinship*, edited by Hugo Nutini, Pedro Carrasco, and James M. Taggart, pp. 3–27. Pittsburgh: University of Pittsburgh Press.

O'CROULEY, PEDRO ALONSO

1972   *A Description of the Kingdom of New Spain . . . 1774.* Translated and edited by Seán Galvin. San Francisco: John Howell Books.

OFFNER, JEROME A.

1979   A Reassessment of the Extent and Structuring of the Empire of Techotlalatzin, Fourteenth Century Ruler of Texcoco. *Ethnohistory* 26:231–241.

1983   *Law and Politics in Aztec Texcoco.* Cambridge Latin American Studies Series, no. 44. Cambridge.

1984   Household Organization in the Texcocan Heartland: The Evidence in the Codex Vergara. In *Explorations in Ethnohistory: Indians of Central Mexico in the Sixteenth Century*, edited by H. R. Harvey and Hanns J. Prem, pp. 127–146. Albuquerque: University of New Mexico Press.

OLIVERA, MERCEDES

1978   *Pillis y macehuales: Las formaciones sociales y los modos de producción de Tecali del siglo XII al XVI.* Ediciones de la Casa Chata, no. 6. Mexico City: Instituto Nacional de Antropología e Historia.

OLIVERA, MERCEDES, AND CAYETANO REYES GARCÍA

1969   Los choloques y los cholultecas: Apuntes sobre las relaciones étnicas en Cholula hasta el siglo XVI. *Anales del Instituto Nacional de Antropología e Historia*, época 7, 1:247–274.

OLIVERA, MERCEDES, AND MA. DE LOS ANGELES ROMERO

1973   La estructura política de Oaxaca en el siglo XVI. *Revista Mexicana de Sociología* 35:227–287.

ORELLANA, SANDRA L.

1975   La introducción del sistema de cofradía en la región del lago Atitlán en los altos de Guatemala. *América Indígena* 35: 845–856.

1976   Ethnic Identity and the Tzutujil Maya: A Socio-political Analysis, 1250–1815. Ph.D. dissertation, Department of Anthropology, University of California, Los Angeles. Ann Arbor: University Microfilms (76-20208).

OSBORN, WAYNE SMITH

1970   A Community Study of Metztitlan, New Spain, 1520–1810. Ph.D. dissertation, Department of History, University of Iowa. Ann Arbor: University Microfilms (70-15631).

1973   Indian Land Retention in Colonial Metztitlán. *Hispanic American Historical Review* 53:217–238.

OVIEDA Y VALDÉS, GONZALO FERNÁNDEZ DE

1979   *Sumario de la natural historia de las Indias.* Edited by José Miranda. Mexico City: Fondo de Cultura Económica. (Reprint of 1950 ed.)

PADDOCK, JOHN

1966   Oaxaca in Ancient Mesoamerica. In *Ancient Oaxaca: Discoveries in Mexican Archeology and History*, edited by John Paddock, pp. 83–242. Stanford: Stanford University Press.

PAHL, GARY W.

1976   A Successor-Relationship Complex and Associated Signs. In *The Art, Iconography & Dynastic History of Palenque: Part III*, edited by Merle Greene Robertson, pp. 35–44. Pebble Beach, Calif.: Robert Louis Stevenson School.

PALAFOX Y MENDOZA, JUAN DE

1893   *Virtudes del Indio.* Madrid: Imprenta de T. Minuesa.

PALERM, ANGEL, AND ERIC R. WOLF

1957   Ecological Potential and Cultural Development in Mesoamerica. *Pan-American Union Social Science Monographs* 3: 1–37. Washington, D.C.

PALMER, COLIN A.

1976   *Slaves of the White God: Blacks in Mexico.* Cambridge: Harvard University Press.

PANIAGUA JAEN, SALVADOR

1943   Codices Matlatzincas. *Boletín de la Biblioteca del H. Congreso de la Unión* 1(1):22–26.

PARSONS, JEFFREY R.

1976   The Role of Chinampa Agriculture in the Food Supply of Aztec Tenochtitlan. In *Cultural Change and Continuity: Essays in Honor of James Bennett Griffin*, edited by Charles E. Cleland, pp. 233–257. New York: Academic Press.

PASO Y TRONCOSO, FRANCISCO DEL

1905–1936   (ed.) *Papeles de Nueva España*

1905–1906   2d ser., *Geografía y estadística*, vols. 1, 3–7. Madrid: Sucesores de Rivadeneyra.

1914–1936   3d ser., *Historia*. 3 vols. Madrid: Hauser y Menet.

1939–1942   (ed.) *Epistolario de Nueva España, 1505–1818.* 16 vols. Mexico City: Porrua.

PASTOR, RODOLFO

1981   Sociedad y economía en la Mixteca, 1748–1810. Ph.D. dissertation, Departmento de Historia, Colegio de México. Mexico City.

PASTOR, RODOLFO, LIEF ADLESON, ERIKA BERRA, FLOR HURTADO, JOSEFINA MACGREGOR, GUILLERMO ZERMEÑO, AND ELÍAS TRABULSE (coordinator)

1979   *Fluctuaciones económicas en Oaxaca durante el siglo XVIII.* Mexico City: Colegio de México.

PATCH, ROBERT W.

1976   La formación de estancias y haciendas en Yucatán durante la colonia. *Boletín de la Escuela de Ciencias Antropológicas de la Universidad de Yucatan* 19:21–61. Merida.

1979   A Colonial Regime: Maya and Spaniard
       in Yucatan. Ph.D. dissertation, Depart-
       ment of History, Princeton University.
       Ann Arbor: University Microfilms (79-
       28484).

PENDERGAST, DAVID M.
1975   The Church in the Jungle: The ROM's
       First Season at Lamanai. *Rotunda*
       8(2):32–40. Toronto.
1977   Royal Ontario Museum Excavation:
       Finds at Lamanai, Belize. *Archaeology*
       30:129–131.
1981   Lamanai, Belize: Summary of Excava-
       tion Results, 1974–1980. *Journal of
       Field Archaeology* 8:29–53.
1985   Lamanai, Belize: An Updated View. In
       The Lowland Maya Postclassic, edited
       by Arlen F. Chase and Prudence M.
       Rice, pp. 91–103. Austin: University of
       Texas Press.

PÉREZ-ROCHA, EMMA
1978   *Servicio personal y tributo en Coyoacan,
       1551–1553.* Cuadernos de la Casa Chata,
       no. 8. Mexico City: Instituto Nacional de
       Antropología e Historia.
1982   *La tierra y el hombre en la villa de Ta-
       cuba durante la época colonial.* Colec-
       ción Científica, no. 115. Mexico City:
       Instituto Nacional de Antropología e
       Historia.

PERIANO, ROGER D.
1961   Descent, Descent Line and Descent
       Group in Cognatic Social Systems. In
       *Symposium: Patterns of Land Utilization
       and Other Papers: Proceedings of the
       Annual Spring Meeting of the American
       Ethnological Society*, edited by Viola E.
       Garfield, pp. 93–113. Seattle: Univer-
       sity of Washington Press.

POMAR, JUAN BAUTISTA
1941   Relación de Texcoco. In *Nueva colección
       de documentos para la historia de Mé-
       xico*, edited by Joaquín García Icazbal-
       ceta, 3:1–64. Mexico City: Salvador
       Chávez Hayhoe.

POWELL, PHILLIP WAYNE
1950   The Forty-Niners of Sixteenth-Century
       Mexico. *Pacific Historical Review* 19:
       235–249.
1952   *Soldiers, Indians & Silver: The North-
       ward Advance of New Spain, 1550–
       1600.* Berkeley and Los Angeles: Univer-

sity of California Press.

PREM, HANNS J.
1978   *Milpa y hacienda: Tenencia de la tierra
       indígena y española en la cuenca del Alto
       Atoyac, Puebla, Mexico (1520–1650).*
       Das Mexiko-Projekt der deutschen
       Forschungsgemeinschaft, no. 13. Wies-
       baden: Franz Steiner.

PRICE, BARBARA J.
1974   The Burden of the *Cargo*: Ethnographi-
       cal Models and Archaeological Infer-
       ence. In *Mesoamerican Archaeology:
       New Approaches*, edited by Norman
       Hammond, pp. 445–465. Austin: Uni-
       versity of Texas Press.

PROSKOURIAKOFF, TATIANA
1960   Historical Implications of a Pattern of
       Dates at Piedras Negras, Guatemala.
       American Antiquity 25:454–475.
1961   Portraits of Women in Maya Art. In *Es-
       says in Pre-Columbian Art and Archae-
       ology*, by Samuel K. Lothrop et al.,
       pp. 81–99. Cambridge: Harvard Univer-
       sity Press.
1973   The *Hand-grasping-fish* and Associated
       Glyphs on Classic Maya Monuments. In
       Mesoamerican Writing Systems, edited
       by Elizabeth P. Benson, pp. 165–178.
       Washington, D.C.: Dumbarton Oaks.

PUGA, VASCO DE
1945   *Provisiones, cédulas, instrucciones para
       el gobierno de la Nueva España.* Madrid:
       Ediciones Cultura Hispánica. (Facsimile
       copy of 1563 ed.)

QUARITCH, BERNARD
1890   (ed.) *Mexican Picture-Chronicle of Cem-
       poallan and Other States of the Empire
       of Aculhuacan.* London: Bernard Qua-
       ritch.

RADIN, PAUL
1926   *The Sources and Authenticity of the His-
       tory of the Ancient Mexicans.* University
       of California Publications in American
       Archaeology and Ethnology, vol. 17, no.
       1. Berkeley: University of California
       Press.

RAMOS, REBECA, LUDKA DE GORTARI KRAUSS,
AND JUAN PÉREZ ZAVALLOS
1981   *Xochimilco en el siglo XVI.* Cuadernos
       de la Casa Chata, no. 40. Mexico City:
       Instituto Nacional de Antropología e
       Historia.

RATHJE, WILLIAM L.
1971 The Origin and Development of Lowland Classic Maya Civilization. *American Antiquity* 36:275–285.

RECINOS, ADRIAN
1957 (trans.) *Crónicas indígenas de Guatemala.* Guatemala City: Editorial Universitaria.

RECOPILACIÓN DE LEYES
1973 *Recopilación de leyes de los reynos de las Indias.* 4 vols. Madrid: Ediciones Cultura Hispánica.

REED, NELSON
1964 *The Caste War of Yucatan.* Stanford: Stanford University Press.

REES, MICHAEL J.
1977 Mathematical Models of Lacandon Kinship. Ph.D. dissertation, Department of Anthropology, Tulane University. Ann Arbor: University Microfilms (78-07664).

REES, PETER WILLIAM
1971 Route Inertia and Route Competition: An Historical Geography of Transportation between Mexico City and Veracruz. Ph.D. dissertation, Department of Geography, University of California at Berkeley.

REYES GARCÍA, CAYETANO
1973 *Indice y extractos de los protocolos de la Notaría de Cholula (1590–1600).* Colección Científica, Catálogos y Bibliografías, no. 8. Mexico City: Instituto Nacional de Antropología e Historia.

REYES GARCÍA, LUIS
1975 El término calpulli en los documentos del centro de México. Paper presented at the Seminario de Verano sobre Organización Social del México Antiguo, Centro de Investigaciones Superiores del Instituto Nacional de Antropología e Historia, Mexico City.
1977a *Cuauhtinchan del siglo XII al XVI: Formación social y desarrollo histórico de un señorío prehispánico.* Das Mexico-Projekt der deutschen Forschungsgemeinschaft, no. 10. Wiesbaden: Franz Steiner.
1977b Genealogía de doña Francisca de Guzmán, Xochimilco, 1610. *Tlalocan* 7: 31–35.
1978 *Documentos sobre tierras y señoríos en Cuauhtinchan.* Colección Científica,

Fuentes: Historia Social, no. 57. Mexico City: Instituto Nacional de Antropología e Historia.
1979 La utopia en las interpretaciones sociológicas de la sociedad prehispánica. Paper presented at the 43rd International Congress of Americanists, Vancouver.

RICARD, ROBERT
1966 *The Spiritual Conquest of Mexico: An Essay on the Apostolate and the Evangelizing Methods of the Mendicant Orders in New Spain, 1523–1572.* Translated by Leslie Byrd Simpson. Berkeley and Los Angeles: University of California Press.

RICE, DON S., AND PRUDENCE M. RICE
1980 Muralla de Leon: A Lowland Maya Fortification. MS, Department of Anthropology, University of Chicago.
1984 Collapse to Contact: Postclassic Archaeology of the Peten Maya. *Archaeology* 37(2):46–51.

RICE, PRUDENCE M.
1979a Ceramic and Nonceramic Artifacts of Lakes Yaxha-Sacnab, El Peten, Guatemala: Part 1, The Ceramics, Section B, Postclassic Pottery from Topoxte. *Cerámica de Cultura Maya* 11:1–85.
1979b The Postclassic Pottery of Macanche, El Peten, Guatemala. MS, Department of Anthropology, University of Florida.

RICE, PRUDENCE M., AND DON S. RICE
1985 Topoxte, Macanche, and the Central Peten Postclassic. In *The Lowland Maya Postclassic,* edited by Arlen F. Chase and Prudence M. Rice, pp. 166–183. Austin: University of Texas Press.

RINGROSE, DAVID R.
1970 Carting in the Hispanic World: An Example of Divergent Development. *Hispanic American Historical Review* 50: 30–51.

ROBERTSON, DONALD
1959 *Mexican Manuscript Painting of the Early Colonial Period: The Metropolitan Schools.* New Haven: Yale University Press.
1960 The Techialoyan Codex of Tepotztlán: Codex X (Rylands Mexican Ms. 1). *Bulletin of the John Rylands Library* 43(1): 109–130.

1975   Techialoyan Manuscripts and Paintings, with a Catalog. In *Handbook of Middle American Indians*, vol. 14, edited by Robert Wauchope and Howard F. Cline, pp. 253–280. Austin: University of Texas Press.

ROBINSON, DAVID J.
1979   Indian Migration in Eighteenth-Century Yucatan. Paper presented at the 43rd International Congress of Americanists, Vancouver.

ROBINSON, DAVID J., AND CAROLYN G. MC-GOVERN
1979   Population Change in the Yucatan, 1700–1820: Uman Parish in Its Regional Context. Paper presented at the 75th annual meeting of the Association of American Geographers, Philadelphia.

RODRÍGUEZ BECERRA, SALVADOR
1977   *Encomienda y conquista: Los inicios de la colonización en Guatemala.* Publicaciones del Seminario de Antropología Americana, no. 14. Seville: Universidad de Sevilla.

ROJAS, GABRIEL DE
1927   Descripción de Cholula. *Revista Mexicana de Estudios Históricos* 1(6):158–170.

ROJAS RABIELA, TERESA
1979   La organización del trabajo para las obras públicas: El coatequitl y las cuadrillas de trabajadores. In *El trabajo y los trabajadores en la historia de México*, compiled by Elsa Cecilia Frost, Michael C. Meyer, and Josefina Zoraida Vázquez, pp. 41–66. Mexico City and Tucson: Colegio de México and University of Arizona Press.

ROMERO FRIZZI, MARÍA DE LOS ANGELES
1975   *Los conflictos por la tierra en San Martín Huamelulpan, Mixteca Alta, Oaxaca.* Oaxaca: Centro Regional de Oaxaca, Instituto Nacional de Antropología e Historia.
1978   *Indice del microfilm del Centro Regional de Oaxaca; Serie Teposcolula, 1975* Estudios de Antropología e Historia, vol. 8. Oaxaca: Centro Regional de Oaxaca, Instituto Nacional de Antropología e Historia.
1979   Los intereses españoles en la Mixteca—siglo XVII. *Historia Mexicana* 29:241–251.

ROMERO FRIZZI, MARÍA DE LOS ANGELES, AND RONALD M. SPORES
1976   (compilers) *Indice del Archivo del Juzgado de Teposcolula, Oaxaca: Epoca colonial.* Cuadernos de los Centros, Centro Regional de Oaxaca, no. 32. Mexico City: Instituto Nacional de Antropología e Historia.

ROUNDS, J.
1979   Lineage, Class and Power in the Aztec State. *American Ethnologist* 6:73–86.

ROYS, RALPH L.
1933   *The Book of Chilam Balam of Chumayel.* Carnegie Institution of Washington, Pub. 438. Washington, D.C.
1939   *The Titles of Ebtun.* Carnegie Institution of Washington, Pub. 505. Washington, D.C.
1940   *Personal Names of the Maya of Yucatan.* Carnegie Institution of Washington, Pub. 523, Contribution 31. Washington, D.C.
1943   *The Indian Background of Colonial Yucatan.* Carnegie Institution of Washington, Pub. 548. Washington, D.C.
1952   *Conquest Sites and the Subsequent Destruction of Maya Architecture in the Interior of Northern Yucatan.* Carnegie Institution of Washington, Pub. 596, Contribution 54. Washington, D.C.
1957   *The Political Geography of the Yucatan Maya.* Carnegie Institution of Washington, Pub. 613. Washington, D.C.
1965   (trans. and ed.) *Ritual of the Bacabs.* Norman: University of Oklahoma Press.

RUIZ DE ALARCÓN, HERNANDO
1984   *Treatise on the Heathen Superstitions That Today Live among the Indians Native to This New Spain, 1629.* Translated and edited by J. Richard Andrews and Ross Hassig. Norman: University of Oklahoma Press.

SAHAGÚN, BERNARDINO DE
1905–1907   *Historia general de las cosas de Nueva España.* 4 vols. Edited by Francisco del Paso y Troncoso. Madrid: Hauser y Menet.
1950–   *Florentine Codex: General History of the Things of New Spain.* Translated by Arthur J. O. Anderson and Charles E. Dibble. Sante Fe: School of American Research and University of Utah Press.

1950 Book 1: *The Gods*. (Rev. ed., 1970.)

1953 Book 7: *The Sun, Moon, and Stars, and the Binding of the Years*. (Reprinted, 1977.)

1954 Book 8: *Kings and Lords*. (Reprinted, 1979.)

1957 Books 4–5: *The Soothsayers* and *The Omens*. (Reprinted, 1979.)

1959 Book 9: *The Merchants*. (Reprinted, 1976.)

1961 Book 10: *The People*. (Reprinted, 1974.)

1963 Book 11: *Earthly Things*. (Reprinted, 1975.)

1969 Book 6: *Rhetoric and Moral Philosophy*. (Reprinted, 1976.)

1970 Book 1, rev. ed.

SAINT-LU, ANDRÉ

1968 *La Vera Paz, esprit évangélique et colonisation*. Thèses, Mémoires et Travaux, no. 10. Paris: Centre de Recherches Hispaniques, Institut d'Etudes Hispaniques.

SÁNCHIZ OCHOA, PILAR

1976 *Los hidalgos de Guatemala: Realidad y apariencia en un sistema de valores*. Publicaciones del Seminario de Antropología Americana, no. 13. Seville: Universidad de Sevilla.

SANDERS, WILLIAM T., JEFFREY R. PARSONS, AND ROBERT S. SANTLEY

1979 *The Basin of Mexico: Ecological Processes in the Evolution of a Civilization*. New York: Academic Press.

SANDERS, WILLIAM T., AND BARBARA J. PRICE

1968 *Mesoamerica: The Evolution of a Civilization*. New York: Random House.

SCHELE, LINDA D.

1979 Genealogical Documentation on the Tri-figure Panels at Palenque. In *Tercera Mesa Redonda de Palenque: Vol. IV*, edited by Merle Greene Robertson and Donnan Call Jeffers, pp. 41–70. Monterey, Calif.: Pre-Columbian Art Research, Herald Printers.

1982 *Maya Glyphs: The Verbs*. Austin: University of Texas Press.

1984 Human Sacrifice among the Classic Maya. In *Ritual Human Sacrifice in Mesoamerica*, edited by Elizabeth H. Boone. Washington, D.C.: Dumbarton Oaks.

SCHELE, LINDA D., AND PETER L. MATHEWS

1979 *The Bodega of Palenque, Chiapas, Mexico*. Washington, D.C.: Dumbarton Oaks.

SCHELE, LINDA D., PETER L. MATHEWS, AND FLOYD G. LOUNSBURY

1977 Parentage and Spouse Expressions from Classic Maya Inscriptions. MS, Pre-Columbian Section, Dumbarton Oaks.

SCHOLES, FRANCE V., AND ELEANOR B. ADAMS

1938 (eds.) *Don Diego Quijada, alcalde mayor de Yucatán, 1561–1565*. 2 vols. Mexico City: Porrua.

1958 (eds.) *Sobre el modo de tributar los indios de Nueva España a Su Majestad, 1561–1564*. Vol. 5 of *Documentos para la historia del México colonial*. Mexico City: Porrua.

SCHOLES, FRANCE V., CARLOS R. MENÉNDEZ, J. IGNACIO RUBIO MAÑÉ, AND ELEANOR B. ADAMS

1938 (eds.) *La iglesia en Yucatán, 1560–1610*. Vol. 2 of *Documentos para la historia de Yucatán*. Merida: Compañía Tipográfica Yucateca.

SCHOLES, FRANCE V., AND RALPH L. ROYS

1948 *The Maya Chontal Indians of Acalan-Tixchel: A Contribution to the History and Ethnography of the Yucatan Peninsula*. Carnegie Institution of Washington, Pub. 560. Washington, D.C. (2d ed., 1968, Norman: University of Oklahoma Press.)

SCHUMANN G., OTTO

1971 *Descripción estructural del maya itzá del Petén, Guatemala, C.A.* Centro de Estudios Mayas, Cuaderno 6. Mexico City: Universidad Nacional Autónoma de México.

1978 Chortí Phonology and Vocabulary. MS, Pre-Columbian Section, Dumbarton Oaks.

SEIFERT, DONNA J.

1977 Archaeological Majolicas of the Rural Teotihuacan Valley, Mexico. Ph.D. dissertation, Department of Anthropology, University of Iowa. Ann Arbor: University Microfilms (77-21169).

SELER, EDUARD

1904 Mexican Picture Writings of Alexander von Humboldt. *Smithsonian Institution, Bureau of American Ethnology, Bulletin* 28:127–229. Washington, D.C.

SEMO, ENRIQUE

1973 *Historia del capitalismo en México: Los origenes, 1521–1763.* Mexico City: Ediciones Era.

SHERMAN, WILLIAM L.

1979 *Forced Native Labor in Sixteenth-Century Central America.* Lincoln: University of Nebraska Press.

1980 Guatemala, 1470–1620. Paper presented at the Conference on Spanish-Indian Contact in Southern Mesoamerica, Cambridge, Mass.

SIMONS, BENTE BITTMAN

1964 Documents Pertaining to the Area of Cholula (1543–1791). *Tlalocan* 4:289–310.

1970 The City of Cholula and Its Ancient Barrios. In *Verhandlungen des XXXVIII. Internationalen Amerikanistenkongresses* (Stuttgart-Munich, 1968) 2:139–150. Munich: Klaus Renner.

SIMPSON, LESLEY BYRD

1938 *Studies in the Administration of the Indians of New Spain: 3, The Repartimiento System of Native Labor in New Spain and Guatemala.* Ibero-Americana, no. 13. Berkeley: University of California Press.

SMITH, CAROL A.

1972 The Domestic Marketing System in Western Guatemala: An Economic, Locational, and Cultural Analysis. Ph.D. dissertation, Department of Anthropology, Stanford University. Ann Arbor: University Microfilms (72-30705).

SMITH, MARY ELIZABETH

1973 *Picture Writing from Ancient Southern Mexico: Mixtec Place Signs and Maps.* Norman: University of Oklahoma Press.

SMITH, MICHAEL E.

1978 The Aztec Marketing System in the Valley of Mexico: A Regional Perspective. M.A. thesis, Department of Anthropology, University of Illinois, Urbana.

1979a The Aztec Marketing System and Settlement Pattern in the Valley of Mexico: A Central Place Analysis. *American Antiquity* 44:110–125.

1979b Economic Development and the Expansion of the Aztec Empire: A Systems Model. Paper presented at the 78th annual meeting of the American Anthropological Association, Cincinnati.

1980 The Role of the Marketing System in Aztec Society and Economy: Reply to

Evans. *American Antiquity* 45:876–883.

SMITH-STARK, THOMAS C.

1981 A Commentary on the Dynastic History of the City of the Crossed Bands. MS, Middle American Research Institute, Tulane University, New Orleans.

SOLANO, FRANCISCO DE

1974 *Los mayas del siglo XVIII: Pervivencia y transformación de la sociedad indígena guatemalteca durante la administración borbónica.* Madrid: Ediciones Cultura Hispánica.

SOUSTELLE, JACQUES

1961 *Daily Life of the Aztecs, on the Eve of the Spanish Conquest.* Translated by Patrick O'Brian. Stanford: Stanford University Press.

SPALDING, KAREN

1970 Social Climbers: Changing Patterns of Mobility among the Indians of Colonial Peru. *Hispanic American Historical Review* 50:645–664.

SPORES, RONALD M.

1965 The Zapotec and Mixtec at Spanish Contact. In *Handbook of Middle American Indians*, vol. 3, edited by Robert Wauchope and Gordon R. Willey, pp. 962–987. Austin: University of Texas Press.

1967 *The Mixtec Kings and Their People.* Norman: University of Oklahoma Press.

1969 Settlement, Farming Technology, and Environment in the Nochixtlan Valley. *Science* 166:557–569.

1972 *An Archaeological Settlement Survey of the Nochixtlan Valley, Oaxaca.* Vanderbilt University Publications in Anthropology, no. 1. Nashville.

1974 Marital Alliance in the Political Integration of Mixtec Kingdoms. *American Anthropologist* 76:297–311.

1976 La estratificación social en la antigua sociedad mixteca. In *Estratificación social en la Mesoamérica prehispánica*, by Pedro Carrasco, Johanna Broda, et al., pp. 207–220. Mexico City: Instituto Nacional de Antropología e Historia.

SPORES, RONALD M., AND MIGUEL SALDAÑA

1973 *Documentos para la etnohistoria del Estado de Oaxaca: Indice del Ramo de Mercedes del Archivo General de la Nación, México.* Vanderbilt University

Publications in Anthropology, no. 5. Nashville.

1975 *Documentos para la etnohistoria del Estado de Oaxaca: Indice del Ramo de Indios del Archivo General de la Nación, México.* Vanderbilt University Publications in Anthropology, no. 13. Nashville.

1976 *Documentos para la etnohistoria del Estado de Oaxaca: Indice del Ramo de Tributos del Archivo General de la Nación, México.* Vanderbilt University Publications in Anthropology, no. 17. Nashville.

STEIN, STANLEY J.
1981 Bureaucracy and Business in the Spanish Empire, 1759–1804: Failure of a Bourbon Reform in Mexico and Peru. *Hispanic American Historical Review* 61: 2–28.

STENNING, DERRICK J.
1958 Household Viability among the Pastoral Fulani. In *The Developmental Cycle in Domestic Groups*, edited by Jack Goody, pp. 92–119. Cambridge: University Press.

STEPHENS, JOHN L.
1963 *Incidents of Travel in Yucatan.* 2 vols. New York: Dover. (Reprint of 1843 ed., New York: Harper and Brothers.)

1969 *Incidents of Travel in Central America, Chiapas and Yucatan.* 2 vols. New York: Dover. (Reprint of 1841 ed., New York: Harper and Brothers.)

STONE, ANDREA, DORIE REENTS, AND ROBERT COFFMAN
n.d. Genealogical Documentation of the Middle Classic Dynasty of Caracol, El Cayo, Belize. In *Fourth Palenque Round Table*, edited by Elizabeth P. Benson and Merle Greene Robertson. Forthcoming.

SULLIVAN, THELMA D.
1976 *Compendio de la gramática náhuatl.* Serie de Cultura Náhuatl, Mono. 18. Mexico City: Universidad Nacional Autónoma de México.

TAYLOR, WILLIAM B.
1972 *Landlord and Peasant in Colonial Oaxaca.* Stanford: Stanford University Press.

1974 Landed Society in New Spain: A View from the South. *Hispanic American Historical Review* 54: 387–413.

1976 Town and Country in the Valley of Oaxaca, 1750–1812. In *Provinces of Early Mexico: Variants of Spanish American Regional Evolution*, edited by Ida Altman and James Lockhart, pp. 63–95. UCLA Latin American Center Publications, vol. 36. Los Angeles.

1979 *Drinking, Homicide & Rebellion in Colonial Mexican Villages.* Stanford: Stanford University Press.

TESTIMONIO
1864 Testimonio de composición de tierras y aguas del partido de Tlalnepantla sacado a pedimento de algunos vecinos y del comisario del pueblo de San Antonio Huisquilucan de esta jurisdicción. Años de 1864. MS, Archivo Municipal, Huixquilucan, State of Mexico.

THOMPSON, J. ERIC S.
1938 Sixteenth and Seventeenth Century Reports on the Chol Mayas. *American Anthropologist* 40: 584–604.

1950 *Maya Hieroglyphic Writing: An Introduction.* Carnegie Institution of Washington, Pub. 589. Washington, D.C. (2d ed., 1960, Norman: University of Oklahoma Press.)

1951 The Itza of Tayasal, Peten. In *Homenaje al Doctor Alfonso Caso*, pp. 389–400. Mexico City: Imprenta Nuevo Mundo.

1962 *A Catalog of Maya Hieroglyphs.* Norman: University of Oklahoma Press.

1970 *Maya History and Religion.* Norman: University of Oklahoma Press.

1974 *The Maya of Belize: Historical Chapters since Columbus.* Belize City: Benex Press.

1977 A Proposal for Constituting a Maya Subgroup, Cultural and Linguistic, in the Petén and Adjacent Regions. In *Anthropology and History in Yucatan*, edited by Grant D. Jones, pp. 3–42. Austin: University of Texas Press.

THOMPSON, PHILIP C.
1978 Tekanto in the Eighteenth Century. Ph.D. dissertation, Department of Anthropology, Tulane University. Ann Arbor: University Microfilms (79-10255).

1982 Dynastic Marriage and Succession at Tikal. *Estudios de Cultura Maya* 14: 261–287.

TORQUEMADA, JUAN DE

1943 *Monarquía indiana*. 3 vols. Mexico City: Salvador Chávez Hayhoe. (Reprint of 2d ed., Madrid, 1723.)

1975 *Monarquía indiana*. 3 vols. Mexico City: Porrúa. (Facsimile copy of 1723 ed.) Also, Serie de Historiadores y Cronistas de Indias, no. 5. 4 vols. Mexico City: Universidad Nacional Autónoma de México.

TOZZER, ALFRED M.

1941 (ed.) *Landa's Relacion de las cosas de Yucatan: A Translation*. Papers of the Peabody Museum, vol. 18. Cambridge, Mass. (Reprinted, 1966, New York: Kraus.)

TOZZER, ALFRED M., AND GLOVER M. ALLEN

1910 *Animal Figures in the Maya Codices*. Papers of the Peabody Museum, vol. 4, no. 3. Cambridge, Mass.

TUTINO, JOHN M.

1975 Hacienda Social Relations in Mexico: The Chalco Region in the Era of Independence. *Hispanic American Historical Review* 55:496–528.

1976a Creole Mexico: Spanish Elites, Haciendas, and Indian Towns, 1750–1810. Ph.D. dissertation, Department of History, University of Texas. Ann Arbor: University Microfilms (77-03989).

1976b Provincial Spaniards, Indian Towns, and Haciendas: Interrelated Sectors of Agrarian Society in the Valleys of Mexico and Toluca, 1750–1810. In *Provinces of Early Mexico: Variants of Spanish American Regional Evolution*, edited by Ida Altman and James Lockhart, pp. 176–194. UCLA Latin American Center Publications, vol. 36. Los Angeles.

ULRICH, MATTHEW, AND ROSEMARY DE ULRICH

1976 *Diccionario bilingüe: Maya mopán y español, español y maya mopán*. Guatemala City: Instituto Lingüístico de Verano.

VAILLANT, GEORGE

1944 *Aztecs of Mexico*. New York: Doubleday.

1966 *Aztecs of Mexico*. Baltimore: Penguin Books.

VAN YOUNG, ERIC

1983 Mexican Rural History since Chevalier: The Historiography of the Colonial Hacienda. *Latin American Research Review* 18(3):5–61.

VÁSQUEZ, GENARO V.

1940 *Doctrinas y realidades en la legislación para los indios*. Mexico City: Departamento de Asuntos Indígenas.

VEBLEN, THOMAS T.

1975 The Ecological, Cultural, and Historical Bases of Forest Preservation in Totonicapan, Guatemala. Ph.D. Dissertation, Department of Geography, University of California, Berkeley. Ann Arbor: University Microfilms (75-10111).

1977 Native Population Decline in Totonicapan, Guatemala. *Annals of the Association of American Geographers* 67:484–499.

VENEGAS RAMÍREZ, CARMEN

1969 La tenencia de la tierra en San Juan Teotihuacán y su distribución (época colonial). *Anales del Instituto Nacional de Antropología e Historia* 7a(11):323–332. Mexico City.

VILLA ROJAS, ALFONSO

1962 Los quehaches: Tribu olvidada del antiguo Yucatan. *Revista Mexicana de Estudios Antropológicos* 18:97–116.

VILLACORTA C., JOSÉ ANTONIO

1938 *Prehistoria e historia antigua de Guatemala*. Guatemala City: Tipografía Nacional.

VILLA-SEÑOR Y SÁNCHEZ, JOSÉ ANTONIO DE

1952 *Theatro americano* . . . 2 vols. Mexico City: Editora Nacional. (Facsimile copy of 1746–1748 ed.)

VON WOBESER, GISELA

1983 *La formación de la hacienda en la época colonial: El uso de la tierra y el agua*. Mexico City: Universidad Nacional Autónoma de México.

WALLERSTEIN, IMMANUEL M.

1974 *The Modern World-System: Capitalist Agriculture and the Origens of the European World-Economy in the Sixteenth Century*. New York: Academic Press.

WARKENTIN, VIOLA, AND RUBY SCOTT

1980 *Gramática ch'ol*. Serie Gramática de Lenguas Indígenas de México, no. 3. Mexico City: Instituto Lingüístico de Verano.

WARMAN, ARTURO

1976 *. . . y venimos a contradecir: Los campesinos de Morelos y el estado nacional*. Mexico City: Instituto Nacional de Antropología e Historia. (1980, *We Come to*

Object, translated by Stephen K. Ault. Baltimore: Johns Hopkins University Press.)

WARREN, J. BENEDICT
1974 Transcriptions and Translations of Selected Documents. In *The Harkness Collection in the Library of Congress: Manuscripts Concerning Mexico: A Guide*, pp. 31–301. Washington, D.C.: U.S. Government Printing Office.

WELTE, CECIL R.
1981 Check List of Pre-Conquest and Early Colonial Pictorial Manuscripts by Nine Regions of the Oaxaca Area. MS, Oficina de Estudios de Humanidad del Valle de Oaxaca. Oaxaca.

WHITE, LESLIE A.
1940 (ed.) *Pioneers in American Anthropology: The Bandelier-Morgan Letters, 1873–1883*. 2 vols. Albuquerque: University of New Mexico Press.

WHITECOTTON, JOSEPH W.
1977 *The Zapotecs: Princes, Priests, and Peasants*. Norman: University of Oklahoma Press.

WHORF, BENJAMIN L.
1937 The Origin of Aztec *TL*. *American Anthropologist* 39:265–274.

WILLIAMS, BARBARA J.
1984 Mexican Pictorial Cadastral Registers: An Analysis of the Códice de Santa Maria Asunción and the Codex Vergara. In *Explorations in Ethnohistory: Indians of Central Mexico in the Sixteenth Century*, edited by H. R. Harvey and Hanns J. Prem, pp. 103–125. Albuquerque: University of New Mexico Press.

WISDOM, CHARLES
1940 *The Chorti Indians of Guatemala*. Chicago: University of Chicago Press.

WOLF, ERIC R.
1957 Closed Corporate Peasant Communities in Mesoamerica and Central Java. *Southwestern Journal of Anthropology* 13: 1–18.

1959 *Sons of the Shaking Earth*. Chicago: University of Chicago Press.

WOODWARD, RALPH LEE, JR.
1976 *Central America: A Nation Divided*. New York: Oxford University Press.

ZANTWIJK, RANDOLPH A. M. VAN
1969 La estructura gubernamental del Estado do Tlacupan (1430–1520). *Estudios de Cultura Nahuatl* 8:123–155.

ZAVALA, SILVIO
1947 (ed.) *Ordenanzas del trabajo, siglos XVI y XVII*. Instituto de Historia, Universidad Nacional Autónoma de México, 1st ser., no. 5. Mexico City: Editorial Elede.

1967 *Contribución a la historia de las instituciones coloniales en Guatemala*. 4th ed. Estudios Universitarios, vol. 5. Guatemala City: Universidad de San Carlos de Guatemala.

ZAVALA, SILVIO, AND MARÍA CASTELO
1939–1946 *Fuentes para la historia del trabajo en Nueva España*. 8 vols. Mexico City: Fondo de Cultura Económica. (Reprinted, 1980.)

ZILBERMANN, MARÍA CRISTINA
1966 Idolatrías de Oaxaca en el siglo XVIII. In *XXXVI Congreso Internacional de Americanistas: Actas y Memorias* (Seville, 1964) 2:111–123. Seville.

ZIMMERMANN, GÜNTER
1960 *Das Geschichtswerk des Domingo de Muñon Chimalpahin Quauhtlehuanitzin*. Beiträge zur mittelamerikanischen Völkerkunde, no. 5. Hamburg: Museum für Völkerkunde und Vorgeschichte.

ZORITA, ALONSO DE
1941 Breve y sumaria relación de los señores y maneras y diferencias que había de ellos en la Nueva España . . . In *Nueva colección de documentos para la historia de México*, edited by Joaquín García Icazbalceta, 3:67–205. Mexico City: Salvador Chávez Hayhoe.

1963 *Life and Labor in Ancient Mexico: The Brief and Summary Relation of the Lords of New Spain*. Translated by Benjamin Keen. New Brunswick: Rutgers University Press.

INDEX

Acalan, 26, 27, 75, 80–81

Acapulco: early routes to, 138; *tlameme* traffic to, 140, 148, 149

Acculturation: of Guatemalan colonial Indians, 65–66; strategic, 101

Acolhuahcan (Acolhuacan), 44, 45, 159

Adams, Robert McC., 103

Agriculture

—colonial: effect of ecology on, 170; expansion of commercial, 92, 127; population dispersal due to shifting, 96; Spanish domination of, 125–126, 177

—Indian: environmental effects on, 178; new Spanish technology in, 176; in Oaxaca, 176; and tenant farming, 182; and tribute land, 160

Aguateca, 26

Aiton, Arthur S., 147

Albuquerque, Bishop, 173

Allen, Glover M., 32

Alliance: dynastic, 7–34; Itza, 82, 84; and joint rule, 43

Alta Verapaz, 82

Alva Ixtlilxóchitl, Fernando de, 49

Alvarado, Pedro de, 57, 171

Amaquemehcan (Amecameca), 43, 149

Amuzgos, 165

Anderson, Arthur, 36

Andrews, J. Richard, 54

Anguiano, Marina, 36

Antequera: colonial trade at, 179; development of colonial institutions at, 171; economy of, 184–186; food supply for, 176; Indian labor in, 173; Indian nobles in, 181; as residence for *encomenderos,* 172; as Spanish city, 166; *tlameme* use in, 148–150

Apan, 43, 44, 130

Apiculture, Precolumbian, 90

Archaeology: historical, 72, 85; and ethnohistory, 72–75, 78, 88–90; in Teotihuacan Valley, 130

Archival sources: on Central Mexico, 35–37; on kinship and household organization, 118; legal documents as, 119; on Oaxaca, 168

Archivo General de la Nación, 158

Aróstegui, Carlos B., 26–27

Arrieros, 136, 141–146

Artisans. *See* Crafts

Atitlan, 56, 63–65, 69, 70

Azcapotzalco, 41, 43, 44

Aztecs: *calpulli* among, 5; ethnohistorical research on, 4, 35; kinship and social organization of, 103, 104–110; market of, 50; Oaxaca as tributary of, 165, 168; socioeconomic system of, 124; succession patterns of, 27; urban-rural integration of, 122–133

Bacalar, 83, 85

Ballcourts, 51–52

Bankmann, Ulf, 164

Barlovento, Armada of, 163

Barlow, Robert H., 154, 161

Batabs, 27–28, 97, 99–100

Beals, Ralph L., 56, 57, 62, 67, 68, 69

Belize: as archaeological zone, 73; colonial ethnohistory of, 82; Maya legend in, 27; study of, 85; Yucatec language in, 76

Belize Missions subregion, 83, 84, 86

Belize River, 75

Berdan, Frances, 36

223

Berlin, Heinrich, 12, 15, 16, 18, 33
Bernal, Ignacio, 165
Bonampak, 26
Borah, Woodrow, 86, 93, 115, 137, 168, 173–176
Boturini, Lorenzo, 158
Bourbon reforms, 100, 184
Brockington, Lolita Gutiérrez, 188
Brumfiel, Elizabeth M., 52
Bullard, William R., Jr., 79
Burgoa, Francisco de, 168

Cabeceras, 54, 136; in Basin of Mexico, 125; decline
  of concept of, 128, 130; in Tlaxcallan, 41, 43; in Yuca-
  tan, 97
Cabildos, 97, 99, 180, 183, 184
Cacicazgos: in colonial Oaxaca, 176–177; supported by
  tribute, 163; in Yucatan, 99. *See also Caciques*
Caciques: in Basin of Mexico, 125; Colonial Yucatec,
  26, 97, 98; decline of, 178, 182; in Guatemala, 65, 67,
  70; as landlord class, 60, 61; in Oaxaca, 169, 170, 171,
  177, 180–182, 184, 185, 186; and *tlamemes*, 136
Cadastral manuscripts, 153
Cadiz, Constitution of, 100
Caja de comunidad, 58
Cakchiquel, 65
Calakmul, 73
Calnek, Edward E., 36, 52, 107, 116, 117, 120
Calpolli. See Calpulli
Calpulalpan, 163
Calpulli (*calpolli*): in colonial Tenochtitlan, 103–104,
  118, 119; interpretation of, 5; prehispanic, 46–49;
  in Valley of Puebla, 36
Cañada region, 168, 170, 172, 181, 184
Candelaria River, 75
Can Ek (Itza rulers), 82
Capitalism
—mercantile: development of, 126; effect of, on Indian
  culture, 58–59; in Guatemala, 58, 61, 62, 64, 66, 67;
  Indian integration into, 187. *See also* Crafts; Trade
—transition to commercial, 179–180. *See also* Labor,
  Indian; Proletarianization
Cargo system, 100
Carmack, Robert M., 78
Carmagnani, Marcello, 166, 189
Carnegie Institution research program, 72, 80, 88
Carrasco, Pedro, 35–54 passim, 103, 104, 109, 115–
  116, 120
Carreteros, 136, 145–146
Caso, Alfonso, 48, 54
Caste, 58, 61, 66. *See also* Social stratification
Caste War, 73, 86
Castilla, Don Luis de, 172
Castillo Farreras, Víctor, 48
Cattle: restriction on Indian raising of, 177
Cehach, 8, 76
Central Lakes region, 82
Central Zone, 73

Centro de Investigaciones y Estudios Superiores in
  Antropología Social, 36–37
Chalchihuitan, 10
Chalco, 36, 41–43
Chalco Atenco, 163
Chamelecon River, 75
Chan Maya, 73–74, 76
Chapa, Matilde, 36
Chase, Arlen F., 79
Chatinos, 165
Chetumal: boundaries of, 83; Classic characteristics
  of, 76–77; ethnic and economic relations of, 76; and
  Putun, 75; at Santa Rita, 79–80; Spanish conquest
  of, 83
Chetumel Bay, 73
Chevalier-Skolnikoff, Suzanne, 32
Chiantla, 62
Chiapas: ethnolinguistic boundaries in, 94
Chichen Itza, 74, 75
Chichimec, 43, 143
Childbirth: Mexica view of, 105
Children: Mexica views of, 105; as *tlamemes*, 135, 140
Chimalpahin: *Third Relation* of, 36
Chinantecs, 171
Chol(an): kinship terms, 8–14 passim, 31, 32; language,
  74; and Mayan writing, 8; relation of, to Chan Maya,
  76; similarity of, to Yucatecan, 9, 13; Spanish con-
  quest of, 68; survival of, 74
Chol Lacandon, 81, 85
Cholollan (Cholula): alliance and joint rule in, 43, 44,
  45; political power of, 36; *tlameme* use in, 149;
  teteuctin in, 41
Chontal: Acalan, 26, 80–81; cross-cousin marriage
  among, 11; *encomiendos* among, 172; kinship terms,
  11, 14; relation of, to Chan Maya, 76; *repartimientos*
  among, 172; succession patterns among, 27, 28
Chontal Putun, 74
Chorti kinship terms, 13, 14, 31, 32
Christianity: emphasized in native title deeds, 154. *See
  also* Churches; Clergy; Missionaries
Churches: construction and administration of, 90
Cities: as destructive of Indian culture, 66, 70; economic revitalization of, 178; household size in, 116;
  Indian homogenization in, 184–186; migration to
  Mayan, 95; in Oaxaca, 166; prehispanic Mexican, 46;
  rural-urban integration of Aztec, 122–123
Class: formation of, through Indian-mestizo merger, 66;
  importance of, in legal documents, 119. *See also* Social stratification
Classic period: alliance/succession system in, 7–34;
  changes in kinship terms during, 11; connection of,
  to Colonial period, 74–78; cross-cousin marriage during, 11, 12; writing during, 8
Clergy: enforcement of *tlameme* restrictions by, 144;
  and labor extortion, 142; social status of, 169, 170.
  See also Missionaries
Cline, Howard F., 165, 166

Cline, Sue Louise, 50

Cochincal: production, 187; trade, 178

Cofradías, 173; and colonial native isolation, 58; native elite control of, 101; rites of, as Catholic indoctrination, 57; in Yucatan, 93, 99

Coggins, Clemency C., 30

Colhuacan, 36

Colima, 140

Comalcalco, 30

Commercialization: and loss of native culture, 70

Commoners, Indian: in Central Mexico, 38, 45–48, 49, 50; in Oaxaca, 169, 170, 177, 178, 180, 182, 183–184, 186; in Yucatan, 97, 99

Composición, 162–163

Congregación: in Central Mexico, 159–160, 162; in Guatemala, 62; in Oaxaca, 175; in Yucatan, 47, 93, 97

Conquest, Spanish: Indian resistance to, 69 (*see also* Rebellion, Indian); and introduction of new technology, 176; as liberation, 56–57, 59; and native culture shock, 57, 59, 61–62; political and economic results of, 53; of Tenochtitlan, 124

Cook, Sherburne F., 86, 93, 115, 137, 173–176

Copan, 73, 75

Cortés, Hernán: alliance of, with Zapotecs, 171; *encomiendos* of, 172; litigation of, against Guzmán, 139–140; in Peten, 73, 78, 82; at Tenochtitlan, 124; violation of *tlameme* regulations by, 139

Couturier, Edith, 120

Cowgill, George L., 78–79

Coyoacan (Coyohuacan), 36

Crafts: colonial development of, 67; and guilds, 185; introduction of Spanish, 68; and loss of native culture, 70; and racial mixing, 182; in Tenochtitlan, 52–53

Creoles: Guatemalan Indian conflict with, 58; Indian competition with, 63; Indian intermarriage with, 186; as landlord class, 60

Cuajimalpa, Codex of, 155, 156

Cuauhtinchan, 36, 44

Cuchumatan, 61–63, 69, 70

Cuernavaca, 149, 161

Cuicatecs, 166, 168, 170–171, 172, 181, 184

Cuilapan, 168, 169, 182, 187

Culbert, T. Patrick, 73

Culiacan, 140

Culture, Indian: effect of hacienda and plantation on, 58–59; impact of Dominicans on, 172; impact of *encomiendas* on, 172; isolation of, 62; Spanish influence on, 58; strength of, in Oaxaca, 186

Culture, *ladino*, 66

Dahlgren de Jordán, Barbro, 169, 188, 189

Dance-dramas, 57

Davies, Nigel, 188

Dávila, Alonso, 83

Debt-peonage, 129. *See also* Agriculture: Indian

Demography: of Basin of Mexico, 127–128; of Colonial period, 57, 132; of Cuchumatanes, 62; of Guatemala, 57, 59, 66–67; of Maya Lowlands, 75, 86; of Oaxaca, 166, 169, 173–176; of Tenochtitlan, 117; of Yucatan, 92–93. *See also* Disease; Population decline; Population growth

Dependency theory, 101

Descent: cognatic, 105, 106, 119; matrifilial, 106; matrilineal, 7–8, 28, 30; patrifilial, 105; patrilineal, 28. *See also* Kinship; Lineage

Deutsche Forschungsgemeinschaft, Pueblo-Tlaxcala Project of, 37

De Vos, Jan, 81, 85

Díaz del Castillo, Bernal, 135, 136

Diet, Indian, 176

Disease, 130; in colonial Yucatan, 93; effect of, on social structure, 175–176; and Indian accommodation, 57; plague, 62; and population decline, 57, 67, 69, 75, 137, 173

Dispersal. *See* Migration

Documents: ethnohistorical use of, 5, 72–73, 75, 77, 80–81

Dominicans: *encomiendas* of, 171–172; and forced acculturation, 172; and *congregación*, 175; in Mesoamerica, 57, 62; pacification of Verapaz by, 68; role of, in administration of Oaxaca, 171; silk production urged by, 177

Dowry, land as, 48

Dresden Codex, 12

Drift. *See* Migration

Dulce, Rio, 75

Durand-Forest, Jacqueline de, 36

Dyckerhoff, Ursula, 48

Dzuluinizob province, 83

Ecatepec, 43, 44

Ecology: of Oaxaca, 169–170; and regional integration, 94

Economy. *See also* Crafts; Labor, Indian; Markets; Production; Trade; Transportation

—colonial: British logging in, 73; commercialization in, 70; Mexico City dual, 126; of Oaxaca, 166, 176–180, 187; sale of residence sites in, 118; as support of ethnolinguistic boundaries, 94; in Yucatan, 91

—Indian: capitalization of, 68, 70; centralization of, 68–69; in Oaxaca, 168; resistance to change of peasant, 176; sheep raising in, 177–178; silk production in, 177

Eggan, Fred, 8

El Cayo, 19–25, 29

Elites. *See* Nobles, Indian

El Porvenir, 29

El Retiro, 29

El Tortuguero, 29

Encomiendas: in Basin of Mexico, 125–126; cacao production of, 64; in Guatemala, 62; in Oaxaca, 171–172; organization of, 81; services of, 64; urban provisioning of, 125; in Yucatan, 91

Epazoyuca, 144
Epidemics. *See* Disease
Ethnic groups: intermarriage among, 57, 181–182, 186; Mayan, 76. *See also* Creoles; Mestizos
Ethnicity: changes in, 186, 187; distinguished from political economy, 76; of migrants to Antequera, 184–186; and territorial boundaries, 67
Ethnography: historical, 55; use of analogy from, 77–78
Ethnohistory: and archaeology, 78; methodology of, 4; objectives of, 78, 88; use of, 55, 176. *See also* Archival sources; Sources, documentary
Etla, 169, 182, 187

Family organization, 111–118
Famines: in colonial Yucatan, 93
Farriss, Nancy M., 86
Feldman, Lawrence H., 68, 82, 85
Flannery, Kent V., 188
Florentine Codex, 105, 107
Franciscans, 63, 83
Frank, André Gunder, 126
Frizzi, Romero, 189

Galarza, Joaquín, 157
Galicia Chimalpopoca, Faustino, 159
García Añoveras, Jesús M., 56
García Bernal, Manuela Cristina, 93
García Grandados, Codex, 161
García Martínez, Bernardo, 36, 188
Gerhard, Peter, 85, 175, 188
Gibson, Charles, 88, 129, 154
Glass, John B., 168
Gómez de Orozco, Federico, 154, 161
Gosner, Kevin, 95
Guatemala, colonial: *cargadores* in, 145; ethnolinguistic boundaries in, 94; Indian ethnohistory of, 55–70; studies of, 56
Guilds, craft: Indian participation in, 185
Guzmán, Niño de, 139–140

Hacienda Hueyapan, 128, 129
Haciendas: architecture of, 128–129, 130–131, 132; as capital-extensive institutions, 63; development of, 127, 130–131, 132; as different from plantations, 58–59; effect of, on Indian culture, 58–59, 70; in Guatemala, 60; and Indian integration, 126, 129; Indian labor on, 64, 66, 67; and Maya community, 96; in Oaxaca, 176; to supply cities, 128; in Yucatan, 91–92, 101
Hacienda Salinas, 129
Hacienda Santa Lucia, 128–129
Hammond, Norman, 27
Hamnett, Brian, 179, 189
Harsanyi, John C., 78
Haviland, William A., 30
Hellmuth, Nicholas M., 77
Herrera y Tordesillas, Antonio de, 10

Hieroglyphic sources, 7–8, spellings of kin terms, 12–19, 30–34
Hispaniola: *tlameme* regulation in, 139
Historiography: of colonial Indian culture, 55
Hondo River, 73
Honduras, 75
Horcasitas, Fernando, 156, 160
Hotchkin, Michael G., 79
Household: developmental cycle of, 113–114, 116–117; organization of Indian, 111–118; patterns and matrifiliality, 106
Huatulco, 138, 140, 141, 148
Huaves, 165
Huaxyacac, 168, 184
Huehuetenango, 62–63, 70
Huexotzinco (Huejotzingo): archival data on, 36; multiple rule at, 42; noble houses in, 39, 41; *tlameme* use in, 139–140, 148
Huixquilucan, 159, 160, 163
Hunt, Eva, 166, 170, 180
Hunt, Marta Espejo-Ponce, 95–96

Ilocab, 67
Imecaioc, 118
Indians, colonial: acculturation of, 57, 69; in Antequera, 166, 184–186; class stratification of, 57, 60–61; and creoles, 63; cultural isolation of, 57–58; 64, 69; land ownership of, 67; and mestizos, 66; as proletarians, 58; as seen from Spanish perspective, 90; segregation of, 65; as Spanish labor source, 57; and Spanish state, 166; uprisings of, 57; urban homogenization of, 184–186
Indian society, "simplification" of, 166
Indies, Council of the, 139
Inheritance: and descent lines, 110; and household organization, 116; and household size, 114; among Mexica, 105–106; of residential sites, 117
Integration: economic, 176; political, 168; social, 130
Ioaniolque, 111
Israel, J. I., 129
Itza: decline in power of, 78; kinship terms of, 11; Maya, 82; migrations of, 79; related to Mopan Maya, 76; Spanish conquest of, 73, 83; Spanish impact on, in Peten, 90
Itztapalapan, 43, 44
Iximche, 65
Izabal, 82

Jäcklein, Klaus, 36
Jalatlaco, 185–186
Jesuits: expulsion of, 130; hacienda of, 128–129
Jones, David M., 128, 130, 131
Jones, Grant D., 90
Jonuta, 29

Karttunen, Frances, 54
Katz, Friedrich, 48
Keesing, Roger M., 105

Kekchi: colonial experience of, 82; language of, 32; religious conversion of, 68

Kin, joint legal culpability of, 110

King, Arden R., 68

Kingsborough, Códice, 114

Kin site, 22–23

Kinship: in prehispanic Mexico, 38; and social organization in Tenochtitlan, 103–121; study of, 94. *See also* Descent; Lineage

Kinship terms: Aztec, 104; Classic Maya, 7–26, 30–34; Mexica, 107

Kirchhoff, Paul, 36

Konrad, Herman W., 129, 130

Kubler, George, 175

Labor, Indian: agricultural, 172, 176; in Antequera, 184–186; in building churches and monasteries, 172; and class divisions, 64; and cochineal production, 186; coercion of, 92, 139, 144, 171; and craft guilds, 185; as debt peonage, 62, 127; domestic, 48, 92, 127, 172; on *encomiendas*, 172; ethnicity and types of, 185; exploitation of, 172–173; in Guatemala, 58; on haciendas, 128–129, 131; importation of, 65; and Indian culture, 64; in mines, 147; native elite control of, 101; in ports, 147; proletarianization of, 184–186, 187; recruitment of, 58; and *repartimiento*, 172; Spanish legal restrictions on, 136, 139; Spanish use of, 66; to supply cities, 125; wages for, 146. *See also* Crafts; Economy; Production; *Tlamemes*

Lacandon: cross-cousin marriage among, 11, 12; kinship terms of, 9, 11; origins of, 81–82; related to Yucatec Maya, 76; Spanish conquest of, 60; study of, 81

La Farge, Oliver, 56

Lamanai, 80, 84

La Mar, 29

Lambert, Bernd, 105

Land: communal, 129, 171; dispute over, 63, 178, 182; Indian control of, 65, 176, 186; Indian leasing of, 128, 129, 131; male bias in inheritance of, 105; measurements of, 159; prehispanic alienability of, 49–50; Spanish consolidation of, 128; Spanish grants of, to Indian nobility, 176; types of colonial Indian, 177. *See also* Land ownership; Land tenure

Landa, Diego de, 9, 10, 77

Land ownership: colonial Indian, 128, 135, 176–177; colonial Mexican documents on, 50; in colonial Yucatan, 92; disputes over, 130; female, 105–106; and Indian autonomy, 176; lack of, and *tlamemes*, 135, 136; in Oaxaca, 169; preconquest documents of, 153; in prehispanic Central Mexico, 50; Spanish, 125, 127; titles of, 153–164. *See also* Land; Land tenure

Land tenure: and Indian rebellion, 70; Nahuatl terms related to, 48; in Oaxaca, 176–177; in prehispanic Central Mexico, 38, 48–50; types of, 177. *See also* Land; Land ownership

Land titles, Indian. *See* Techialoyan codices

Las Casas, Bartolomé de, 68, 110, 114

Las Montañas, missions of, 81

Laurin, Asunción, 120

Law, colonial: discrimination against Indians in, 66; evidence in land litigation under, 162, 164; regulating *tlamemes*, 141, 142; Mexica, 105–106

Lineage: *batab*, 99–100; commoner Indian, 45–46; and eligibility for colonial office, 99; noble Indian, 38–45, 169. *See also* Descent; Kinship

Lockhart, James, 36, 153

López Austin, Alfredo, 48

Lounsbury, Floyd G., 7, 12, 16, 26

Lovell, W. George, 56, 61, 62

Lutz, Christopher H., 56, 65

Macanche, 79

Macehuales (macehualtin). *See* Commoners, Indian

MacLeod, Murdo, 56, 57, 58, 59, 60, 62, 63, 69

Madigan, Douglas C., 56, 63, 70

Madrid Codex, 14

Maestro cantor, 99–100

Mamean kinship terms, 9

Mams, 59

Manche Chol, 68, 75, 82

Marcus, Joyce, 34, 188

Market economy, 91; and disappearance of native nobility, 98; Indian integration into, 176

Markets: expansion of urban, 127, 130, 131; frequency of, 52; and population expansion, 124; production for, 125; and redistribution, 50; for slaves, 169; Spanish control over urban, 126; and tribute, 52

—Indian: of Aztec empire, 50–53; at Chiantla, 62; Colonial Aztec, 126; during Colonial period, 68; expansion of, 178; as "peripheral," 52; in prehispanic Central Mexico, 50; socioeconomic consequences of, 166; to support cities, 126; transformation of, 68, 126; in Yucatan, 91

Marquesado del Valle, 172

Marriage: brother-sister, 27; and cognatic descent, 110; colonial evidence of alliance in, 26; cousin, 8, 10, 11, 12, 28; and household organization, 116, 117; and matrilineality, 28; and patrilineality, 28; and residence patterns, 117; urban Indian patterns of, 186

Martínez, Hildeberto, 36

Martínez Peláez, Severo, 56, 58, 59, 60, 61, 66, 67, 69, 70

Mathews, Peter L., 7, 12, 16, 26, 32, 33

Matlatcingo, Valley of, 145

Matrilineality, 7, 26–30

Maximilian, Emperor, 158

Maya: alliance/succession system of, Classic, 7–34; analogical use of colonial studies of, 74; cargo system of, 100; Chan, 73–74; cultural relations among Classic, Postclassic, and Colonial, 3, 4–5; frontier impact on, 90; institutional centralization of, 78; Lake Peten, 78–79; loosening social ties among, Colonial, 94–95; migration among, Colonial, 94–96; writing system of, 3, 8; Yucatec, 73, 89–91. *See also* Guatemala; Maya Lowlands; Maya texts; Yucatan

Maya Lowlands, archaeological zones in, 73; colonial

ethnohistory of, 71–87; ethnic groups of, 76; languages of, 76, map of, 72, research traditions for study of colonial, 74–78

Maya texts: Cauac day sign in, 16–19; gender patterns in, 12; generational patterns in, 12; hieroglyphic spellings of kinship terms in, 12; and loan translation, 14; logograms in, 14; and relexification, 13–14; semantic and phonological shifts in, 12; similarity of rulers' names in, 25–26; status of women in, 26; Turtleshell compound in, 16, 18, 19; and Yaxchilan Lintels, 16

mayeques, 166, 168, 169, 170, 171, 182, 188

Mendoza, Antonio de: complaints about *tlameme* restrictions by, 140; land grants of, 154, 160–161

Mendoza de Austria family, 161

Mercedarians, 62

Merida, colonial migration to, 95–96

Mestizos: class stratification of, 60–61; as militia, 66; relations of, with Indians, 58, 66, 70; social origins of, 90; and *tlameme* use, 141

Metztitlan region, 128

Mexica: resistance of, to Spanish influence, 47, 111, 118; social organization of colonial, 103–118. *See also* Tenochtitlan

Mexico, Basin of: colonial urban-rural relations in, 5, 122–133; map of, 123; response to social change in, 103. *See also* Mexico, Central; Mexico, Valley of; Mexico City; Tenochtitlan

Mexico, Central, 5–6; demography of, 137; domination of Mesoamerican historiography by, 91; Indian land titles in, 153–164; joint rule in, 43, 44; loss of power of native rulers in, 97; maps of, 37, 123; prehispanic society of, 35–54; recent research on, 36–38. *See also* Mexico, Basin of; Mexico, Valley of; Mexico City; Tenochtitlan

Mexico, Valley of, 4; city-states in, 165; land tenure in, 49; noble houses in, 38; political power in prehispanic, 35; subjection of commoners in, 46–47. *See also* Mexico, Basin of; Mexico, Central; Mexico City; Tenochtitlan

Mexico City: agricultural supply of, 124–127, 131, 132–133; demography of, 130; effect of, on Central Mexican communities, 186; first road to, 138, 145; markets in, 52; as primate center, 125, 132; Spanish colonists' preference for, 124; *tlameme* traffic to, 140, 143, 148–152; urban growth of, 124–126. *See also* Tenochtitlan

Mexicon newsletter, 38

Migration: to Antequera, 184–185, 186; effects of, on social organization, 95; and low-status urban jobs, 185; prevalence of, in colonial Yucatan, 94–96; reasons for colonial Mayan, 95; as response to Spanish domination, 81, 83; role of family ties in, 95

Mimiapan, 161

Mines: ban on *tlamemes* in, 139; Indian labor in, 66; lack of, in Yucatan, 91–92; silver, 62, 143; transportation to, 141, 142, 145

Miraflores, 29

Miranda, José, 173, 175

Missionaries, 51; among Cuchumatanes, 62; cultural indoctrination by, 57; evangelization of, 90; interference in local affairs by, 65; native language use by, 57; and syncretism, 60, 67. *See also* Dominicans; Franciscans; Jesuits

Missions: of Las Montañas, 81; used for conquest, 83; *visita*, 80, 83

Mixes, 171

Mixteca: codices and gold jewelry of, 165; reputation for industriousness of, 178; settlement patterns of, 175; soil erosion in, 178

Mixteca Alta, 166, 168; as commercial region, 177; *congregaciones* in, 175; *encomiendos* in, 172; homicide rate in, 168; population trends in, 174–176; *repartimientos* in, 172; sheep raising in, 178; social stratification in, 169; Spanish conquest of, 171; strength of rituals in, 186

Mixteca Baja, 172

Mixteca Costa, 172

Mixtec codices, 168

Mixtecs: marriage alliance among, 26–27; marriage posture of, 12; in Oaxaca, 165, 166, 168; resistance of, to Spanish conquest, 171

Molina, Alonso de, 111

Molloy, John P., 29

Molotla, 115–116

Monjarás-Ruiz, Jesús, 36

Monte Alban, 169–170

Mopan: colonial experience of, 82; descended from Chan Maya, 76; kinship terms, 8, 11; Maya, 75–76; Spanish conquest of, 68

Morelos, Valley of, 38

Mörner, Magnus, 56

Moteuczomah II, 44

Motolinía, Toribio, 110

Münch, Guido, 173

Muñoz Camargo, Diego, 36

Naco, 75

Nahua: influence on Maya succession, 28; language, 168

Nahuas: in Antequera, 184–185

Nahuatl: decline of, 185, 186; importance of documents in, 38; in Oaxaca, 168; style of Techialoyan codices, 156–157; terms for land tenure, 48–50; urban spread of, 185

Naranjo: alliance of, with Yaxha and Tikal, 30; representations of rulers' wives at, 12; rulers at, 18, 26

New Spain: economy of, 180; place of Oaxaca in, 166

Nezahualcoyotl, 41, 48, 49

Nezahualpilli, 41, 49

Nicholson, Henry B., 55

Nito, 75

Nobles, Indian: in Central Mexico, 38–45; disappearance of, 96–101, 125; economic bases of power of, 181; hispanicization of, 181; integration of, 29; as labor procurers, 129, 131; lack of kin ties with commoners of, 46; as mediators, 129, 131, 132; in Oaxaca, 166, 180–184, 187; Spanish control of, 100; Spanish recognition of, 180–181; Spanish reduction of power of, 181; use of *tlamemes* by, 142

Nochixtlan Valley, 170

Nohha, 82

Nutini, Hugo G., 104

Oaxaca, Aztec cultural impact on, 165; cultural continuity in, 166, 186–187; distinctiveness of, 165, 186, 187; economy of, 166, 176–180, 187; impact of Spanish institutions on, 166, 171–173, 187; map of, 107; Mixtecs in, 168; political structure of, 165, 166, 168–169, 171, 180–184; population trends in, 166, 169, 173–176; social stratification in, 97, 165, 166, 168–171, 178, 180–185, 186, 187; scholarship on, 165–166; sources for, 6, 166–168; Spanish conquest of, 171; *tlameme* use in, 140, 148, 149; transition to capitalism in, 179–180; urban Indians in, 166, 184–186; use of Indian labor in, 172–173. *See also* Antequera

Oaxaca, Valley of: economic integration of, 187; city-states in, 165; noble families in, 184; population trends in, 174–176; sociopolitical organization of, 165; Spanish conquest of, 171; *tlameme* use in, 148

Occupations: hereditary nature of, 135; specialization in, 169

Ocelotepec, 161

Ocotelolco, 41, 43

Ocoyoacac, 159

Odena Güemes, Lina, 36

Offner, Jerome A., 119, 120

Olivera, Mercedes, 36, 171, 188

"Omaha" system, 10, 33

Oral tradition: evidence of, in land titles, 154

Orellana, Sandra L., 56, 63, 64

Orozco, Francisco de, 171

Pacheco, Melchor, 80, 83

Paddock, John, 165

Palenque: as center of polity, 29; rulers at, 16, 18, 21–22, 25

Panchoy Valley, 65

Panuco, 140

Pasion River, 75; archaeological zone, 73

Pastor, Rodolfo, 177, 178, 188, 189

Patrilineality: Classic Maya, 18–19, 23, 28–29; in colonial Mesoamerica, 60

Patronage system, Spanish, 66

Paxbolon, Don Pablo, 98

Paxbolon-Maldonado papers, 26, 81

Peasants: Indians as, 60, 62, 64, 67, 70; under colonial organization, 57

Pendergast, David M., 84

Peninsulares, 58

Peonage debt, 62, 63

Pérez-Rocha, Emma, 36

Peru, colonial, 97

Peten, 73; colonial ethnohistory of, 82; economic alliances in, 82–83; ethnic and economic relations of, 76; Maya, 76; research on, 77, 85; Spanish failure to conquer, 82; static population in, 79; Yucatec language in, 76

Peten Itza, Lake, 73, 76

Piedras Negras: alliance and succession at, 15–25, 30; as center of polity, 29; family relationships at, 8; representations of rulers' wives at, 12; rulers at, 7

Pipiltin, 38, 39

Plague, 63, 143

Plantations: different from hacienda, 58–59

Pochtecah, 50

Pokomchi, 68

Political organization: joint and centralized rule, 45; of Oaxaca, 166, 168–172, 180–184; prehispanic, 36

Polygyny, 41, 112

Pomona, 29

Popol Vuh, 67

Population decline: in Central Mexico, 137; of colonial Indians, 69, 125, 127–128, 130; due to disease, 65; due to miscegenation, 65; due to Spanish colonization, 81; economic consequences of, 125, 126, 172; effect of stress on, 93; effect of, on village social structures, 175–176; and forced labor, 143; in Guatemala, 63; in Oaxaca, 173–176; and *tlameme* decline, 137, 138, 141; and traditional rights of noble Indians, 142. *See also* Demography; Disease

Population growth: and decline of elite power, 182; in Oaxaca, 173–176; in prehispanic Mixteca Alta, 169; and proletarianization, 185; socioeconomic consequences of, 124, 166. *See also* Demography

Population movements. *See* Migration

Postclassic period, 11, 12, 26; transition to Colonial period from, 71–73, 78–80, 90

Potonchan, 75

Prem, Hanns J., 36, 48

Prestige, hereditary basis of, 184. *See also* Nobles, Indian; Social stratification

Price, Barbara J., 77

Principales, 177

Production
—Indian: of cloth, 84; of cochineal, 179; in Colonial period, 68; and economic integration, 127, 129; importance of, to Spanish, 187; marginalization of, 177; in Oaxaca, 176; postconquest changes in, 126–127; specialization of, by community, 68; Spanish influence on agricultural, 131, 132; of textiles, 179; types of urban, 185, 186; for urban markets, 131–132. *See also* Crafts; *Repartimiento*; *Tlamemes*
—Spanish: diversification of agricultural, 127; and livestock in New Spain, 137

Proletarianization: of Indian culture, 66; of Indian labor, 187

Property, private, concept of, 177. *See also* Land ownership

Proskouriakoff, Tatiana, 7, 12, 15, 16

Prospero, 82

Proto-classic period, 11

Proto-Yucatecan, 11
Puebla, 4; *calpulli* in, 104; city-states in, 165; colonial power in, 35; *tlameme* use in, 149, 150, 151
Puebla, Valley of, 36, 38, 47, 49
Pueblo: and social integration, 94; at Tecpanaco, 60
Putun, 75, 76

Quiche: ethnicity and territorial boundaries of, 67; haciendas at, 70; persistence of prehispanic patterns at, 69; Spanish conquest of, 59–61, 63, 69
Quichean languages, 32; kinship terms in, 9
Quirigua, 73

Race. *See* Ethnic groups; Ethnicity
Rathje, William L., 29
Rebellion, Indian, 66, 83; at Atitlan, 65; class origins of, 61; dynamics of, 70; in Guatemala, 59; of Itza, 83–84; at Tecpanaco, 60; and threat to cultural integrity, 61
Rees, Michael J., 8
Religion, Indian: anti-Christian cults in, 83; prehispanic, 38; revitalization of Itza, 84; Spanish prohibition of, 166; transformation of, 67
Repartimiento: in Basin of Mexico, 126–127, 128; in Guatemala, 58, 64; in Oaxaca, 172–173, 179–180, 185, 187; in Yucatan, 91, 92, 93
Repúblicas de indios, abolition of, 100
Republics, Spanish attempts to establish Guatemalan, 65
Resistance, indigenous, to colonial expansion, 83–85. *See also* Rebellion, Indian
Reyes García, Cayetana, 36
Reyes García, Luis, 36, 47, 104
Ricard, Robert, 173
Rice, Don S., 79
Rice, Prudence M., 79
Rincon Zapotecs, 170–171, 183–184
Roads, development of, 138, 145
Robertson, Donald, 154, 157, 158, 161, 164
Robinson, David J., 95
Rodríguez Becerra, Salvador, 56
Romero, Ma. de los Angeles, 171, 188
Roys, Ralph L., 26, 80–81, 89–90, 98, 101
Rule, indirect Spanish, 57, 69; of Atitlan, 63–64; at Quiche, 67; at Tecpanaco, 59
Rule, joint, 42–45
Rulers, Indian: Classic Mayan, 7–34 passim; prehispanic Mexican, 41–42; subjected by Spanish, 53; succession of, 7
Ruwet, Wayne, 53

Sac Bahlan (Sac Balam), 81
Sahagún, Bernardino de, 49, 50, 107, 110, 118
Saint-Lu, André, 68
Salama, 68
Salamanca de Bacalar, 85
Salpeten, Lake, 79
San Antonio Huixquilucan, Codex of, 158, 161–162
San Cristobal Codex, 161–162

San Ildefonso, 145, 148, 151
San Juan, 139
San Pedro Atlapulco (document), 160
San Salvador Tizayuca (document), 160
San Simón Calpulalpan, Codex of, 158
Santa Rita, 79–80
Santiago Atitlan. *See* Atitlan
Santiago de Guatemala, 56, 65–66, 69, 70
Santiago Tejupan, 176
Schele, Linda D., 7, 12, 16, 26
Scholes, France V., 80–81, 90
Semo, Enrique, 130–131
Serfs. *See Mayeques*
Sheep raising, 176–177
Sherman, William, 56
Sierra region, 171, 172
Silk production, 177, 178, 187
Silver mining, 143, 144
Simons, Bente, 36
Slavery: of blacks, 124; in Central America, 56; disappearance of, 182; on haciendas, 129; in Oaxaca, 169, 188; and polygyny, 112; prehispanic, 47–48; among Rincon Zapotec, 171; in Santiago de Guatemala, 65; Spanish elimination of, 166; in Verapaz, 68; in Zapotec society, 169
Smith, Carol A., 70
Smith, Mary Elizabeth, 188
Social stratification: change in colonial Indian, 70; in colonial America, 57; within colonial caste structure, 58; and conflict, 183–184; in Cuicatec states, 168, 170–171; in Guatemala, 64; among Indians, 60, 62, 64, 131; of Mixteca Alta, 168; in Oaxaca, 165, 166, 168–171, 178, 180, 185, 186; persistence of native, 60; prehispanic, 38; among Rincon Zapotecs, 170–171; and social mobility, 183; and sumptuary laws, 182; in Tenochtitlan, 103–104, 168; and *tlamemes*, 135; in Yucatan, 98. *See also* Class; Nobles, Indian
Society, Indian, colonial restructuring of, 166
Soconusco, 140
Solano, Francisco de, 55, 56, 57, 58, 67, 69, 70
Sources, documentary: for Central Mexico, 36–38; for colonial Guatemalan ethnohistory, 56; on differences between Classic and colonial Maya, 27–28; forms of, 5, 7; hieroglyphic, 7–8; pictographic, 7; Techialoyan Codices as, 5–6. *See also* Archival sources
Spores, Ronald, 168, 170, 173, 175, 178, 188
State. *See* Political organization
Stephens, John L., 136
Succession: Classic Maya, 7–34; on colonial *cacicazgos*, 176; and colonial political office, 90; in Oaxaca, 169; Postclassic Maya, 7, 26–28; standardized by Spanish law, 181
Surveys, colonial, of Indian communities, 162
Syncretism: religious, 57, 60; Spanish-native, 64

Tabasco, 75
Tacuba, 122, 162–163. *See also* Tlacopan
Tacuba, Don Miguel of, 161–162

Tamalcab, 80

Tamub, 07

Taxes, acculturative pressure of, 58

Tayasal, 75, 78, 79, 80

Taylor, William B., 166, 168, 172, 175, 176, 177, 178, 179, 183, 186, 187, 189

Techialoyan, 162, 163

Techialoyan codices, 153–164; controversy about, 5; as forgeries, 163–164

Tecpanaco (pseudonym), 56, 59–61, 69–70

Tecuanipa, 43

Tehuantepec: alliance of, with Spanish, 171; early routes to, 138; power of, 168; *tlameme* prohibition in, 140; *tlameme* use in, 148, 149

Teixhuihuan, 110–111, 118

Tekanto, 97

Tenochtitlan, 4, 5, 35–54 passim; archival data on, 36; *calpulli* in, 104; centralized multiple rule in, 43, 44; in colonial period, 5; dynastic succession in, 27; ethnohistorical emphasis on, 35; expansion of, 52; kinship and social organization in, 103–121; land control in, 41, 159; markets in, 52; Oaxaca tribute to, 168; political power of, 35, 44; social stratification in, 41, 168; surrender of, 171; as urban center, 122, 124. *See also* Mexico City

Teotihuacan, 36, 124

Teotihuacan Valley, 128–131 passim

Teotitlan del Camino, 168

Teozapotlan, 168

Tepanec, 43, 159

Tepeaca, 135, 149. *See also* Tepeyacac

Tepeticpac, 43

Tepetlaoztoc (Tepetlaostoc), 36, 114

Tepeyacac, 36, 42, 45. *See also* Tepeaca

Teposcolula, 187

Tepotzotlan, Codex of, 155, 156, 158

Tepoztlan, 115–116

Tequixixtlan, 114–115

Terminal Classic period, 11

Terminos, Laguna de, 73

Terrazgueros, 182

Teteuctin, in Central Mexico, 38–41; in Valley of Puebla, 36

Tetzcoco (Texcoco): archival data on, 36; centralized multiple rule in, 43, 44; land alienation in, 49; land reclamation in, 41; land tenure in 41, 48; markets in, 52; social stratification in, 38, 41; as urban center, 122

Teuctli. See *Teteuctin*

Teutitlan, 142

Texcoco. See Tetzcoco

Textiles, production of, 179

Thompson, J. Eric S., 30, 32, 73, 74–77, 86

Thompson, Philip C., 8–9, 27, 30, 33, 97

Tikal, 18, 26; alliance of, with Naranjo, 30; in Central Zone, 34; marriage pattern of, 29

Tipu, 75, 80, 83, 84

Tixchel, 75

Tizatlan, 43

Tlacamecayotl, 40, 116, 117, 118, 120; meanings of, 106–111

Tlacopan, 41. *See also* Tacuba

Tlahtoani (pl. *tlahtoqueh*), 39–54, 136. *See also* Caciques

Tlalixtac, 175

Tlaltecahuaqueh, 47

Tlamemes, 134, 147; decline of, 145; effect of Spanish expansion on, 137, 138–139, 141, 144–145; Precolumbian, 134–137; recorded instances of, 148–152; recruitment of, 135; regulation of, 139–145, 146; status of, 135, 136; wages of, 136, 146; work load of, 135–136

Tlameme system, 5; inelasticity of, 145; perpetuation of, 137

Tlatelolco, 4; conquest of, 44; joint rule in, 43; as market of Mexico, 50. *See also* Tenochtitlan

Tlaxcala, 4; *calpulli* in, 104; city-states in, 165. *See also* Tlaxcallan

Tlaxcallan: archival data on, 36; markets in, 51, 52; multiple rule in, 42, 43; noble houses in, 38, 39, 41

Tlaxiaco, 187

Tlaxilacalli, 104

Tobacco, consumption of, by *tlamemes*, 143

Toledo, Ordinances of, 139

Toluca, 145, 148

Tommasi de Magrelli, Wanda, 156

Topoxte, 79

Toquegua, 82

Torquemada, Juan de, 49, 153

Totonicapan, 59, 66–67, 70

Tozzer, Alfred M., 32

Trade: in cochineal, 178, 179; colonial development of, 67; effect of transportation on, 134, 137; Indian long-distance, 68; Mayan agricultural export, 84; networks of, 81–82; prehispanic, 38, 50; routes of, 82–83; Spanish interference in, 129

Transportation: draft animals and wagons as, 137, 138–139, 141–142, 143, 145; modes of, 134–147; and political integration, 134; and trade, 134, 136–137, 140

Tribute, 39; avoidance of, 64, 65, 66; lands, 159–160; liability of nobles for, 101; and markets, 52; as means of political integration, 168–169; in Oaxaca, 168, 171; paid to *cacicazgos*, 163; to pay *composición*, 163; prehispanic, 38, 46–47, 50; to provision cities, 125; and rebellion, 61; redistribution of, 50; as result of population expansion, 124; silk production to pay, 177; *tlameme* work as, 135, 136; transportation of, 136; types of, 171; among Yucatan Maya, 91, 92, 93. *See also* Tribute system

Tribute system: changes in, 126; and disappearance of native nobility, 98; Indian control of, 125; regulation of, 171. *See also* Tribute

Triple Alliance, 41, 54; capitals of, 122–123; joint rule of, 43–44; socioeconomic system of, 124

Triques, 165

Tulija, 10

Tutino, John M., 129, 130, 131

Tututepec, 168
Tzeltal(an). kinship terms, 10, 13, 31, 32; and Mayan
    writing, 8
Tzictepec, 159, 163
Tzictepec, Code of, 156
Tzotzil, 13, 31, 77
Tzul, Atanasio, 60
Tzutiyil Indians, 63, 64

Uaymil, 76–77
Ulrich, Matthew and Rosemary, 8
Urbanization, 185–186. *See also* Cities
Usumacinta River, 75, 81; archaeological zone, 73
Utatlan, 59, 78

Vayulcayotl, meaning of, 111
Veblen, Thomas T., 66–67
Velasco, Luis de, 142, 162
Veracruz: first road to, 138, 145; *tlameme* prohibition in,
    140; *tlameme* traffic to, 140, 141, 143, 148
Verapaz, 68, 70, 85
Vetancurt, Augustín de, 161
Villa Alta: *congregaciones* in, 175; demography of,
    174–176; *tlameme* use in, 148, 151; Zapotec Rincon
    in, 168
Villa de Tacuba region, 128
Villagómez, Don Martin, 182
Villa Real, 80

War: as parallel to death in childbirth, 105; prehispanic,
    38; in Oaxaca, 168
Weeks, John M., 78
Welte, Cecil R., 168
West Indies, Spanish regulation of native labor in, 139
Whitecotton, Joseph W., 169
Wisdom, Charles, 13

Wolf, Eric R., 94, 103
Women: political power of Maya, 30; status of noble
    Maya, 26; in Tenochtitlan, 105–106, 117, 119, 120

Xaltocan, 44
Xillotepec, 43, 44
Xiu family, 98
Xochimilco, 49; archival data on, 36; joint rule in, 44;
    political power of, 36; subjugation of, to Triple Al-
    liance, 41
Xonacatlan, 161

Yanhuitlan, 175, 176, 187
Yaxchilan, 32; as center of polity, 29; rulers at, 16, 25,
    26
Yaxha, 26, 30
Yucatan: *cargadores* in, 145; colonial economy and so-
    ciety of, 90–94; ethnohistoric tradition in, 88–90;
    fate of native nobility in, 96–101; geography of, 91;
    map of, 89; migration in, 94–96
Yucatec: colonial *caciques*, 26; cross-cousin marriage,
    12; succession, 7, 26, 27, 28
Yucatec(an), 10; colonial spread of, 90; kinship terms,
    8–14 passim, 31, 32; and migration, 83; similarity
    of, to Cholan, 13
Yucatec Maya, 91

Zaachila. *See* Teozapotlan
Zacatula, 140, 149
Zaculeu, 59
Zapotecs: alliance of, with Spanish, 171; in Antequera,
    184–185; *encomiendos* among, 172; in Oaxaca, 165,
    166; Pinion, 168, 181, 182, 187; Valley, 168–169
Zavala, Silvio, 56
Zimatlan, 175
Zorita, Alonso de, 36, 47, 153